MW01451976

# A LIFETIME GUIDE TO
# Practical Pet Care

## BETTER HEALTH AND HAPPIER HOMES FOR DOGS AND CATS

### Jeff Nichol, D.V.M.

PRENTICE HALL

Library of Congress Cataloging-in-Publication Data

Nichol, Jeff.
    A lifetime guide to practical pet care : better health and happier homes for dogs and cats / by Jeff Nichol.
       p.   cm.
    ISBN 0-13-033844-3 (PPC) — ISBN 0-13-043069-2 (C)
    1. Dogs.  2. Cats.  3. Dogs—Diseases.  4. Cats—Diseases.  5. Dogs—Health. 6. Cats—Health.  I. Title.

SF427 .N533  2001
636.7'0887—dc21
                                                                                                  2001021971

Acquisitions Editor: *Edward Claflin*
Production Editor: *Jacqueline Roulette*
Formatting: *Robyn Beckerman*
Interior Design: *Dimitra Coroneos*

©2001 by Prentice Hall

*All rights reserved. No part of this book may be reproduced in any form or by any means, without permission in writing from the publisher.*

*Printed in the United States of America*

10  9  8  7  6  5  4  3  2  1           10  9  8  7  6  5  4  3  2  1

ISBN 0-13-043069-2 (C)         ISBN 0-13-033844-3 (PPC)

Portions of this book appear in *Is My Dog OK?* and *Is My Cat OK?*, ©Prentice Hall

This book is a reference work based on research by the author. Any techniques and suggestions are to be used at the reader's sole discretion. The opinions expressed herein are not necessarily those of or endorsed by the publisher. The directions stated in this book are in no way to be considered as a substitute with a duly licensed veterinarian.

---

**ATTENTION: CORPORATIONS AND SCHOOLS**

Prentice Hall books are available at quantity discounts with bulk purchase for educational, business, or sales promotional use. For information, please write to: Prentice Hall Special Sales, 240 Frisch Court, Paramus, New Jersey 07652. Please supply: title of book, ISBN, quantity, how the book will be used, date needed.

---

**PRENTICE HALL**
Paramus, NJ 07652

http://www.phdirect.com

*To my caring and supportive wife Carolyn, who, like our children and me, loves our pets like children.*

# Contents

*A Warm Heart for a Cold Nose*   xi

## PART 1
## COMING ON BOARD

1 *Why Have a Pet in the First Place?* . . . . . . . . . . . . . . . . . . . . . 3

2 *Choosing the Right Pet* . . . . . . . . . . . . . . . . . . . . . . . . . . . . . 5

3 *Choosing the Greatest Puppy for Your Life* . . . . . . . . . . . . . . 7

    The Right Age Puppy—It's Important!   7
    Matters of Breed   8
    Other Realities of Dog Breeds   9
    Temperament Testing   10
    Get Set   12
    Arriving on the Scene   12
    Individual Testing   13
    Happy Ending   16

4 *Choosing the Greatest Kitten for Your Life* . . . . . . . . . . . . . 17

    What Is a Cat?   17
    Kitten Socialization Facts   18
    Temperament Testing   19
    Picking and Choosing   20
    Play   21
    Breed Variations   22
    Nothing But the Best   22

**5** Dr. Nichol's Cardinal Rules of Dog Care . . . . . . . . . . . . . . . . 23

**6** Dr. Nichol's Cardinal Rules of Cat Care . . . . . . . . . . . . . . . 32

# PART 2
## ALL YOUR DOG QUESTIONS ANSWERED

Barking   45
Basics   49
Biting and Fighting   60
Breeding and Reproductive Organs   78
Cancers, Lumps, and Masses   89
Destructive Behaviors   99
Dog–Human Diseases   106
Ears   109
Eyes   111
Fearful Behavior   113
Feeding and Nutrition   119
Grooming   135
Heart and Breathing   136
Joints and Bones   144
Mouth Problems   163
New Pets in the Home; Loss of Pets and Pet Owners   173
Odd Noises and Interesting Habits   179
Outdoor Living and Related Problems   189
Poisoning   195
Seizures and Staggering   199
Skin Problems   203
Stomach and Intestinal Problems   222
Symptoms of Sickness   233
Training   241

Urinary Problems    246
Urination and Defecation Behaviors    248
Vaccinations    260

# PART 3
# ALL YOUR CAT QUESTIONS ANSWERED

Basics    265
Biting and Fighting    270
Breeding and Reproductive Organs    276
Cancers, Lumps, and Masses    280
Cat–Human Diseases    287
Destructive Behaviors    289
Ears    293
Eyes    298
Feeding and Nutrition    302
Grooming and Skin Care    307
Heart and Breathing    309
Intestinal and Stomach Problems    311
Joints and Bones    322
Mouth Problems    324
New Pets in the Home; Cats Who Leave Home    326
Odd Noises and Interesting Habits    333
Poisoning    345
Safety Tips    349
Seizures    351
Skin Problems    353
Symptoms of Sickness    358
Traveling Cats    370
Urinary Disease    372
Urination and Defecation Behaviors    377
Vaccinations    385

## Part 4

## Medical Care: The Best Pet Hospital and First Aid at Home

*How to Choose the Right Veterinarian* .................. 391

*Emergency Home Care: Recognize the
Signs—Do the Right Thing First* ..................... 396

*Index*     449

*About the Author*     465

# Acknowledgments

This book has been a true labor of joy because of the emotion and importance that we invest in the pets who share our homes. While I have learned much about medical and behavioral needs through my formal education and professional experience, I did not reach this place alone. I have learned much from the many people and pets I encountered along the way. I have thought often about these individuals, but this is my chance to celebrate some of them. Without a team of coaches, mentors, and my own successes and failures, I would never have developed the skills to help pets and educate their loving families.

Putting all this knowledge on paper was one thing; making it readable and easy to use was quite another. Writing a weekly newspaper column and then a book has caused me to hone my writing skills, but without the help of a handful of knowledgeable and helpful folks, something of lesser value would have resulted.

In 1958 my father and I took my first dog, Scott, to an excellent veterinarian, who inspires me even still, Dr. Lyle Tuck. It was Dr. Tuck's knowledge and generous manner, and my father Ira's encouragement, that at age 8, kicked my career into motion. A high school job as kennel boy in the employ of Dr. Howard Nurse, and the early mentoring of Dr. Bill Mullin, during my time as a Boy Scout, showed me what fine humans veterinarians can be. Entering veterinary school in 1970 and graduating in 1974 would have been impossible without the drive of assistant dean Dr. John Newman. Without the late "Black John," I would not be a member of the profession that he so fiercely shepherded.

My days as a D.V.M. began in 1975 at the St. Francis Animal Clinic in Albuquerque, NM. Drs. Richard Heise and Dennis Elliott were my first teachers in general practice. Both of these stalwarts of the healing art of companion pets remain in practice to this day. Other doctors who have practiced under the same roof and whose daily consultation has helped me avoid mistakes and teach me good medicine and compassion are Dr. Lloyd Beal of Sacramento, CA, Dr. Virginia Vader of Nashville, TN, Dr. Sue Tornquist of Corvallis, WA, Dr. Sue Chellstorp of St. Louis, MO, and Drs. Christine Appel and Cheri Potter, who share with me now the daily ups and downs of making better the lives of canine, feline, and human animals.

Those are the people whose knowledge of veterinary medicine has made a major difference. I must also say thanks to the thousands of people who have entrusted me with the lives of their beloved pets. Without that faith, I would not have done much good. But there have been a few nonhumans who have been the closest to me. These boys and girls have been my family and have stood by me through the good times and bad. They are Scott (my childhood Brittany Spaniel), Billy Bones (my beagle and first obedience dog), Bob (15 pounds of high energy, short-legged independent spirit), Frieda (the German Shepherd, who taught me patience), Juan Gomez, UD (the Airedale who, aside from being my best friend and a nationally ranked obedience competition dog, taught me fatherhood), Chase (Old English Sheepdog, the sweetest child to ever wear a dog suit), and finally the great American family dog Peter Rabbit (the Border Collie of the Nichol family who is right now teaching the next generation that being kind is better than being a barbarian).

My lifetime of cats has been no less critical to my well being and love of life. They are Polly (white-as-the-snow Persian, highly dignified), Bernard (silver Persian donated to me by a loving owner who could not afford his surgery), Arizona (the gentle orange tabby girl who died tragically beneath the wheel of a speeding car), Curious George (the Nichol boy's most special gray tabby), Pecos (the most gentle orange boy cat), and Raoul de Las Orcas (the orange tabby who is still showing no signs of aging at 15). Without this family of God's purest of spirits, my life would have been of lesser value.

My gratitude also goes to those who have helped make writing a skill for me. My first and greatest teacher of the English language is my mother, Joan Nichol. She is the best mom ever to grace the planet and surely the finest grammarian alive today. What has culminated in this book began, and continues, as a weekly question/answer column for the *Albuquerque Journal*. My editors at the *Journal* who have helped my work make sense are Karen Moses (who gave me a chance to contribute in the first place), Ellen Marks, and Barb Chavez. But the first person who recognized that I had something to share in book form was Matthew Hoffman. Matthew, thanks for helping me believe I could do it.

Last, and for Prentice-Hall, the publisher of the book open in front of you now, I give my thanks first to Ed Claflin whose generous wisdom and patience with a first-time author helped me stay on track and get the job done. And without the help of Jackie Roulette, this book would not be of a quality fit to read.

# A Warm Heart for a Cold Nose

When I hear the words "pet care" it sounds too much like work—and more work is something you probably don't need.

Everybody works—and most of us work way too much. Having a dog or cat in your life shouldn't add to your workload. In fact, just the opposite. For most of us, a pet is a safe and reliable presence, a special bit of insurance against the many hard times of human life. That smiling, often goofy presence is also a way to remember that maybe we're not really here just to learn hard lessons.

One mighty important reason to live on this planet is to have a great time. Pets are here not only to remind us of that, but to be our partners in having fun.

So this won't be a book about pet care that's a lot of work. Let's make it fun and easy to allow our dogs and cats to be our partners in anything we want. They will never ask, "Are you sure you want to do that?" or "Is that the best you can do?" or "I bust my tail all day and this is the thanks I get?"

You might hear this kind of thing from other quarters in your life, but dogs and cats are a higher life form than that. Your pets do not want to be a burden to you. They just want to be there.

So here is what I'm going to do for you: I'll make it easy for you and your pets to live together for as long as possible. Dog or cat, they're man's and woman's best friend. Yes, there's some care involved—but not work. You should all have a good time.

A special note before we get going: I use the personal pronouns *him* and *her* instead of *it* when referring to pets. My past newspaper editors have often edited my columns to reflect the Queen's English. They have changed *him* and *her* to *thats* and *its*. But you and I know better. We know that our pets are real individuals. They are not objects; they can't be put on a shelf when we're done playing with them. Dogs and cats have lives just like the rest of us; they are neither toys nor trophies. So I call them *him* or *her*, not *it*.

Interestingly, our Western cultures and legal systems see pets, and all nonhuman animals, as possessions—mere chattel. You've already learned that if you've ever endured the modern American horror of divorce. Back in 1988 I paid my dues to that truly life-changing cataclysmic rite of passage with the demise of my first marriage. Having finally realized that there was no way to pursue a healthy life and remain married, I was astounded to learn that pets, in the eyes of the law, have the same status as houseplants.

At that time, I had three beloved pets—Juan Gomez, an Airedale terrier, and two orange tabby cats, Raoul and Pecos. According to the court, my former spouse and I were supposed to divide our pets like so many sets of dishes. They very well could have been a garage-sale find. I was utterly amazed that they weren't automatically going to stay alternately with each of their parents. How could it not be so? We each loved those three intensely. What a rude surprise to learn that Juan, Pecos, and Raoul were but additional items on the list of property to be divided.

The situation was solved by my former wife offering me all three pets in exchange for some additional cash and the return of my wedding ring. It was her final act of love for me. I jumped at the offer, coughing up both the money and the ring, and those three boys guided me into the next chapter of my life. I will remain forever indebted to my first wife. Without my dog and two cats, I could not have endured the greatest loss I have ever felt. They were, and will always be, this man's best friend. Whatever the legal system says, they are not, and will never be, potted plants.

Pets are as real as any person. Each of them has a spirit. Most of those spirits are more pure and uncluttered than ours. We have them in our lives to help us learn the real meaning of being. They are God's creatures.

Jeff Nichol, D.V.M.

# PART 1
# Coming on Board

# CHAPTER 1

# Why Have a Pet in the First Place?

If you're interested enough in pets to read this book, you already have some idea of why you would invite a member of the animal kingdom (that includes you and me, by the way) to share your home. We know that pets provide companionship and an outlet for our own nurturing instincts; and those are good reasons. But why share your home with an animal of a different species?

There are many reasons why people have pets. Like most close personal relationships, the owner–pet relationship is kind of, well, private. So you don't need to tell me. But if you're thinking of adding a pet to your home, I recommend that you actually write down on paper why you want to do something that weird.

Weird? Sure. Just think of any time you've been so confounded by a pet's completely alien behavior that you came to your wits' end over it. Consider that each of us has lived at least part of our lives with other people. If another person is sick, you can probably relate on some level; you might have some sense of what's going on, what to do. But a different species has some very different maladies. What does it mean if your dog stops dead in her tracks, lowers her head, and suddenly snorts like a pig for several seconds? Nothing you do makes her stop. Seizure? Heart attack? And just as you are ready to throw her to the floor and start thumping on her chest (you know, like they do on "ER"), she stops the pig thing and goes on as though nothing happened. (*Answer:* postnasal drip. Give Benedryl and it will stop. Or give nothing; it doesn't really matter.)

If a space alien came to your home or mine and saw us with our pets, as different in appearance as they are, wouldn't they find it odd? How many nonhuman animals keep a different species as such close friends or family members in their lives? Certainly there are other species with symbiotic or parasitic relationships, but these all have truly practical functions that enhance the survival of one creature or both. We pet lovers share our lives with our pets for very different reasons.

The veterinary profession has recognized three types of pet owners. In the first group are those who describe their pets as children. The second group is comprised of folks who consider themselves "practical pet owners." They set limits on what they'll invest. And in the third category are people who regard pets as "just animals."

If you're reading this book, you're probably the first type of pet owner. Certainly, that describes my family and me. Our household has a number of children; some just bear more of a physical resemblance to their parents than others.

By now I've been a practicing veterinarian for one half of my 50 years, and I've dealt with lots of pet owners. Some of them carry secrets pretty well. Others don't. I was a very small veterinarian indeed when I got over believing that I could judge a pet owner's true motives.

The truth is, I don't have to play psychologist. My job is to help you find the right pet and make that friendship last a long time. Whatever reason you have for wanting to get involved in that relationship is strictly your own, but it helps to get started right. Accidental pairings work out about as often as winning at roulette. I believe in attraction at first sight, but not long-term, healthy relationships at first sight. So whatever your motives for pet ownership, the guidelines I offer for pet selection will be helpful.

But what about fate, you ask? If you take a gander at a litter of puppies or kittens, doesn't the right one just run right up to you and steal your heart? Ever get married like that? Ever even take a job that way? Are you crazy? Please say no.

If you want a pet and you want to get the right one, where do you start? Find yourself a veterinarian you can trust (you know, start a relationship). Ask for some advice on where to find a potentially healthy pet in your locale. Any D.V.M. (doctor of veterinary medicine) who's been at this for very long will ask you a few useful questions, then steer you in a good direction.

This pending human–pet relationship could last for a big part of your life. Take it slow and do a bit of research, so you can make as many correct choices as possible. Much of life is a crapshoot. We'll try to minimize the gamble where your new pet is concerned. Turn the page and I'll tell you more about choosing the best pet you have ever known.

# CHAPTER 2

# Choosing the Right Pet

By now you know that life is complex and often difficult. Much of our existence is left to chance, or at least to events we could never have imagined. But in those areas of life where making informed choices is possible, you might as well exercise that choice. One of those areas is choosing a pet.

You can't choose your relatives, but you really can choose a family member if he or she comes disguised as a dog or cat. To be effective at this, however, you must be willing to accept some imperfections and risk.

There is no such thing as a perfect pet. The only *perfect* pets I know are cute and cuddly—but they're also stuffed. A couple dozen of them litter the bedroom shared by my two young sons.

Besides, you don't really want a perfect pet. If you're planning for a cat because cats require less work than dogs, are more "feminine," are less likely to wreck your stuff, then what you really want is a stuffed cat (see above). If you want a dog because a dog can be trained to come when called, will protect you, will greet you at the door, and will be your best friend at *all* times, I suggest you rent a Disney movie. True, these lofty wishes may be realized when you get your new pet, but they are much too specific. Remember that this whole business entails an element of risk.

So let's start the process of matching you with a pet who works well in your life, although not perfectly. Why not perfectly? Well, there are two reasons. First, there are no perfect pets just as there are no perfect spouses. Second, if you had a perfect pet, there would be no way of learning from that pet.

Pets can be many things—companions, entertainers, poopers, scratchers, and yappers; but they are, most of all, our friends and teachers. If it is true (as I believe it is) that we have all been put in this life for growth of the spirit, you can bet that if you find the right nonhuman companion, he or she will be your partner in that endeavor.

So let's begin with a sense of optimism. With good planning, you'll be able to choose a sporty new dog or cat who will enhance your life.

First, let's narrow down the field of applicants.

# CHAPTER 3

# Choosing the Greatest Puppy for Your Life

I know this is a rather lofty title, but, heck, I really love dogs. And I've made two great choices in my career as a dog owner, if I do say so myself.

The first great dog of my life was Juan Gomez (named for the outstanding veterinary radiologist). At the time I found Juan, I was childless. I handpicked him for personal companionship, for backpacking in the wilderness, and for obedience competition. He carried off the first two like no other dog on the planet. On the last score, my boy was a nationally ranked, high-scoring obedience competitor. Made his daddy real proud. So, yes, the first choice worked.

The dog currently in my family's life is an absolutely wonderful Border Collie named Peter Rabbit. But the only thing perfect about this dog is that he is perfectly goofy.

For a family that includes two barbarians, aged 7 and 8 as of this writing, Peter Rabbit is just the right dog. He does do bad things, of course, so he fits right in. And I knew he would, because I carefully selected him using the techniques I'm about to share with you.

## THE RIGHT AGE PUPPY—IT'S IMPORTANT!

A lot is known about the socialization process in dogs. We know that puppies need to be with their mothers and littermates until they reach the age of 5 to 7 weeks. This early development time is critically important, because they need to learn to relate in healthy ways to other dogs. If puppies are separated from their little families of origin too early, they tend to be afraid or aggressive around other dogs, and perhaps a bit too attached to their humans.

It's also necessary for the kids (that is, the puppies) to leave home at a healthy time. If they stay with Mom past 12 weeks of age, they tend to get stuck in the dog-pack mentality. That too-tightly-knit pack then develops a culture that excludes humans. Such a pup, growing up in your home, probably won't work well with people. He or she may always prefer dog company to human company.

All things considered, then, the best age for puppy adoption is about 7 to 12 weeks.

## Matters of Breed

Many people seem to think that choosing a dog by breed is like choosing a brand of car or stereo. It ain't so. Dogs do not roll off an assembly line. You can select a purebred dog for color, haircoat, and size. But I have never known a dog who was traded in for a different model because of an imperfect paint job.

When dogs do flunk out of the lives of their well-meaning owners, the reason is nearly always a problem of temperament. In other words, it's who they are. There is much variation in temperament within the same breed. In fact, there are huge differences between individuals in the same litter. Those differences underscore the importance of careful selection. Assume nothing.

If you must, first choose the racy appearance of your shiny new dog. Color and size are fairly predictable; little else is. Then close the book on that dog breed. Selecting a breed will not guarantee the temperament. Every dog is an individual, just as people of different races are individuals.

Am I crazy? Don't I know that your favorite breed is courageous and brave and loyal and fun-loving and romantic and kind and thoughtful and sensitive? Of course I know that. The dog books say the same things about every breed. Can every breed be the same? Don't forget who writes those books: breeders of those dogs (you know, the manufacturer).

Having said all of that, it is true that some dog breeds have been developed for specific functions. Examples are hounds, sled dogs, bird dogs, herding dogs, rat-killing terriers, and fighting-and-disemboweling-other-dogs dogs. In some cases this means that a given individual will have an overpowering urge to do that one, breed-specific thing compulsively and incessantly, to the exclusion of all normal and healthy activities. These dogs represent the minority.

In a broad sense (with lots of room for exceptions), I recommend against such single-purpose breeds. In other words, avoid choosing your new companion because his or her breed is so pretty. If you want great looks, choose great art. The same rules don't apply to choosing good companions.

## OTHER REALITIES OF DOG BREEDS

How much do you enjoy pet hair as a fashion accessory? If you are adverse to it, you'll want to consider dog breeds without hair, like the Chinese Crested or the Mexican Hairless. Airedales, Schnauzers, and Poodles are also good candidates, since they have continuous hair growth and don't shed much.

On the other hand, when a cold-weather dog lives in a warm-weather clime, you can count on a lot of shedding. That seems like a common-sense observation. But you'd be amazed at the number of thick-furred arctic dogs who are living as pets in the desert state of New Mexico, where I practice. We see huge numbers of Huskies, Malamutes, and Chow Chows. These pupsters really suffer in the heat. They shed great hunks of hair in their attempts to acclimatize. Please, exercise common sense. Look carefully at your individual or family circumstances and make a logical decision when choosing a dog.

Next, tell me whether you want a small, medium, or large dog, and I'll confide my favorite breeds in each category. Here's the lineup:

### *Small Breeds*

- Yorkshire Terriers
- Lhasa Apsos
- Shih Tzus
- Shetland Sheepdogs (Shelties)
- Miniature Poodles
- Mixed breed

## Medium Breeds

- Border Collies (of course, but not for everyone)
- Australian Shepherds
- Standard Poodles
- Mixed breed

## Large Breeds

- Labrador Retrievers
- Golden Retrievers
- Airedale Terriers
- Mixed breed

Is that all, you ask? Well, there are great individuals in *every* breed. There are also perfectly horrible, unhealthy, biting, pooping, horrific dogs in every breed. It's just that these are the breeds that seem, in my experience, to be least likely to give you serious health issues and poor temperaments.

My very best advice, however, is to do what I do when I plan a new car purchase: Talk to the folks who provide service for the model you are considering. If the car I plan to buy gets a thumbs-down from my mechanic, then I'm not going to buy it, no matter how sexy I'd feel driving it.

Likewise, ask your veterinarian what breeds of dog are good in your locale. Border Collies are strong in Albuquerque, but, for all I know, they may be turkeys in Peoria.

# TEMPERAMENT TESTING

I am about to provide some simple and fun little tests that will help you select a puppy from a litter. But first, I implore you *not* to do a few things.

First, please do not allow the owner of the litter to select your puppy for you. Even if this person knows the purpose and function for your new dog, she will select the dog who works for her. Remember, dogs are neither cars nor appliances. They don't roll off an assembly line. They are real individuals with real emotions. Thus, because the puppies have their own personalities, they will respond differently to different people. A puppy who seems submissive to the owner of the litter may respond to you with dominance, the prospective soul mate. So who should choose your dog? You, of course, even if you have to travel all the way to Poughkeepsie to do it.

Second, when making the trip to select a new puppy, don't bring your kids.

"Oh, but this will be their dog," you say.

No, it won't. Unless your children are nearly adults, this dog will rely on you when your well-meaning, but normal, careless youngsters forget to feed, house, clothe, nurture, and educate "their" dog. This will really be *your* dog, Mom and Dad.

I know this. I am the "owner" of my children's dog. Fortunately, I love Peter Rabbit because he is our great American family dog. I chose him for my family barbarians, and he works out just fine.

I also know that if you bring your children with you to choose your family's great American dog, the kids will be so tightly wound that all the puppies in the litter will feed off this energy and they'll behave with great exuberance, just like your kids. You will learn nothing about the individual personalities of the pups in the litter. You will come home with the fastest tail-wagger—and that's like spinning the roulette wheel.

Third, please don't pick a puppy who is not part of an established "pack." In other words, don't take the last puppy. This poor little guy is sad and lonesome. He or she is without a family and will beg you for a home. You will feel that failing to welcome this waif into the next 15 years of your life will mean that you have turned your back on this baby's last hope.

Still, please don't do it. I respect your feelings of empathy. These feelings are what make pet owners such high-quality people. The problem is that without the established politics that only a dog pack (or litter) can provide, there will be no means for comparison. That solo remaining puppy's exuberance over seeing you is in no way a useful predictor of the future of your relationship together. Let a different dog lover take that puppy.

## GET SET

Start with the phone. When you talk to the owner of the litter, be sure to tell him or her that you'll want to spend some uninterrupted, quiet time *alone* with the litter. Do *not* listen to anything to the contrary. As graciously as possible, tell this nice person to butt out. Also, tell the nervous puppy grandparent that you will need a separate nearby enclosure so that you can segregate the puppies as you test them.

In order to rate the puppies, you will need to label them and make some notes. Before you leave home, grab an assortment of different colored ribbons, a pad, and a pen. You will also need an assistant, perhaps a spouse or friend. (But remember, no children!)

## ARRIVING ON THE SCENE

When you arrive, you will need to remind the litter's owner that you will be spending some time alone with the puppies. Dog breeders love their puppies, but if allowed to hover during your choice of your puppy, he or she will only serve to confuse the process.

When you enter the puppy area, say nothing. Sit on a chair or squat close to the ground. Standing may invoke an immediate dominance–submissive response in the babies.

Instead, watch and wait. This may be the most important part of the whole process. Observe the group dynamic. Is each puppy minding his or her own business, or are they fussing and cavorting with each other? If the puppies look like a bunch of independent spirits, then an individual taken from this bunch may always be the loner type. A highly social group, on the other hand, will contain "people" dogs who want to be part of your social group—your family.

Observe the individuals: If they are busy pushing and shoving (you know, not keeping their hands to themselves), look carefully for the pushiest, bossiest puppy. This is the character who is most often at the top of the puppy pile. He or she is also the one who nips and yaps at the other guys if they step out of line. I suggest you mentally eliminate this one, unless you think you'll enjoy being dominated by a dog. (Incidentally, it doesn't matter whether this pushy pup is male or female. An in-your-face personality can come in either flavor.)

Next, watch for the shy baby. This one steps aside for everyone. He or she may be standing off alone, or may be participating one step behind everyone else. This submissive position is exactly where the puppy who's on the lowest rung wants to be. In dogdom all groups have a top dog and a bottom dog. If you select the bottom dog, you may have a tough time with training. Submissive dogs often wrap themselves around the legs of their owners while walking, roll over and urinate when given an order, and cry every day. Some submissive dogs become so fear-based that they become fear biters. I recommend against choosing the scaredy-cat dogs.

When you're clear about who's on the top and who's on the bottom of the dominance order, quietly remove these two puppies. Now you're ready to test the rest.

# Individual Testing

This is the controversial part. There are behaviorists who believe that any puppy from the "middle" of the dominance order should work out fine. They say that splitting the group further lacks value. Other experts believe an individual puppy has a "general appeal" for an individual person. I am in the latter camp. Dogs have complex personalities just like you and I. If you want a generic pet, get a stuffed animal. If you plan to have a real relationship, you'll want to get serious about choosing the right one.

For the next part of the selection process, bring out some different-colored ribbons you brought and tie a different colored ribbon around each puppy's neck. On separate pages of your writing pad, jot down the ribbon colors as headings.

Labeling the babies is important. Aside from giving you a greater understanding of each puppy's dominance level, the tests that follow will tell you which puppy really wants to be led by you. While you will be this dog's friend, you will also be his or her leader. Your dog will see you as the leader of the pack—or so we hope. Thus, you are using these tests to learn which one of the pups will follow your lead and have a good time doing it.

As you carry out these tests, try to avoid giving verbal praise. If you lavish these wannabes with words of encouragement, you may foster the notion of competition for your favor. Remember, you don't want the most aggressive puppy; you want the right puppy.

Oh, and one more thing. If any of the babies has a urine or stool accident, ignore it. They're only babies, after all.

Do each test with each puppy in the following order. Only when you are finished with each puppy should you pick up the next applicant.

### 1. Socialization

Take a pup out of the holding area and set him or her on the ground. Be sure to squat. If you stand, you are displaying dominance—and some puppies will retreat.

As you're watching the puppy, remain still and silent. Does the puppy come straight to you, or go the other way? If he walks away, does he notice you and come back? Does he make a rude gesture? Rate this pup on a scale of 1 to 5, with 5 indicating the greatest interest in social interaction.

### 2. Calling

Next, set the puppy on the ground 6 to 8 feet away from you. Call the pup in a happy voice. If you get ignored, this probably isn't the puppy you want. (Don't take it personally.) If he comes racing for you with his tail up, make a positive note. If he comes slowly or with his tail down, he could be Mr. or Miss Wrong. Again, use the 1 to 5 rating scale.

Isn't this easy? You can already see that if you want the exuberant puppy versus the more reserved personality, you have some basis for your choice. But there's a second part to this step.

Set the puppy a few feet away from you. Stand up and walk away slowly. Rate the energy level of that pup, based on whether he follows you with glee, follows at a distance, or ignores you. Use the same scale of 1 (least energetic) to 5 (most energetic).

### 3. Restraint

Now that you know who connects most with you, let's advance our knowledge of who wants to call the shots and who is more willing to follow your lead.

Squat down, clasp your fingers under the pup's belly, and lift her off the ground. Say nothing. Suspend the puppy and wait.

Some puppies will struggle right away and may even get aggressive. Others may be content to just lie there for as long as you hold them. The middle guys will hang loose for a while, but will finally start to fidget.

My preference is for the middle pup because she'll to go along but has enough intelligence to get bored at some point. The puppy who's willing to hang there forever is not going to be highly motivated to try new things—like training. But that's just my view—and it's your choice. If you want the low-key, relaxed personality, then this is your baby. On the other hand, if you like a high-energy challenge, take the guy who won't hold still for a minute.

## 4. Dominance

What's called the "inversion test" will tell you volumes about a puppy's dominance.

These youngsters come equipped with the instinctive knowledge of canine communication. By inverting the puppy—that is, rolling him on his back and holding him there—you are sending clear signals that you intend to be the captain of the ship. Will your new dog accede to your authority or tell you to buzz off?

Quietly and silently roll the puppy on his back. Hold the baby in this position with just one hand and wait. If you have a dominant puppy, there won't be much of a wait, as the puppy will start to flail and struggle right away. If the puppy bites and growls, you've learned even more.

If he's willing to lie there until the next millennium, you have a passive fellow who will roll over and play dead for anyone and everyone, including the next burglar. My preference (not necessarily yours) is the puppy who goes along for 20 or 30 seconds, then starts to negotiate.

Whether you want Dirty Harry or a cream puff, I'll respect your choice. This is your pupster. But even if you think you have already chosen your baby, try to remain objective and rate each puppy objectively on that scale of 1 to 5.

## 5. Buy-In

This last test is the easiest. Immediately after the dominance sequence, put the puppy down, quietly stand up, and walk away. Who follows you and with what energy? Rate each puppy on how much she still likes you and how well she enjoyed being tested by you.

## Happy Ending

After you've gone through the routine with each of the puppies, you're probably ready for a break. Leave the testing area and chat with the litter owner. It won't hurt to tell her what a splendid job she has done raising and socializing the babies. She'll beam. These pups are an extension of her inner child.

Then go back over your notes. Eliminate the puppies who just aren't right and retest the others. Take all the time you need.

It's all pretty easy, but it's difficult, too. Administering these tests to *every* puppy in *every* litter you consider can be emotionally taxing. If you didn't love dogs, you'd never bother. And if you're like me, you'll find something engaging and beautiful about each of them. But you're taking only one puppy.

If none of the puppies seems quite right, continue to trust this method. *Do not* take a puppy from any litter until you find the one who is best for you.

While the five-point scoring system is an attempt at objectivity, we all know that every bit of this is highly subjective, as it should be. There isn't much that's cut-and-dried about love.

# CHAPTER 4

# Choosing the Greatest Kitten for Your Life

Can you choose the great feline friend who will be the faithful, excellent companion you have always wanted? I think you can, but there are many "ifs" involved. This is an issue that is both simple and rather complicated all at once.

Why is this important? Because, by far, the leading cause of death in pets in the United States is euthanasia—due to behavior problems. That's far ahead of auto injuries, cancer, kidney failure, you name it. Most of this tragic waste of life is preventable if people really understand what they want in a pet and whether the pet they choose can deliver on it.

Each year, 25 percent of pet cats leave their homes permanently. Only one-third of cats are in the same homes for their entire lives. For the average American home, dogs are much more likely to stay put. Most of this is not because the cats were bad, but because the cat owner's choices were bad.

In my attempts to help you find the cat you want, I will also try to help you avoid the cat who could make your life a living hell (or a living heck, if the cat is only moderately evil). So let's start with expectations.

Dogs are a lot like people. Cats are not. Yes, that is a gross generalization with plenty of exceptions, but for you to adequately understand how to find a good cat, I will explain who and what cats are in general terms.

## WHAT IS A CAT?

While puppies get about half of their temperaments from each parent, kittens genetically inherit the *majority* of their personalities from their dads. Sorry to say, most of these losers are nowhere to be found when the kids need their diapers changed. No kitten support, no college tuition. Mom may be quite friendly—a real charmer. But meeting her doesn't do much good. Even if she's tolerant and kindly, her children could be like their father—lifelong barbarians. Sounds like my family.

But that's only the beginning. The biggest difference between cats and nearly all other mammalian species is that they are fundamentally asocial. In other words, they are natural loners.

But wait, you say. You've known lots of cats who have groomed and cared for each other. There are reasons for this that I will explain later. For now, understand that choosing a kitten is very different from choosing a puppy, or a human friend, or a romantic partner, or a job. These life choices are based on social needs. Cats don't really have social needs in the same way.

So, when you evaluate a litter of kittens, you're learning very different things than you would from a litter of puppies. Cats are not just dogs with short ears. Cats are cats.

But the mere fact that cats are not a highly socialized species does not mean they don't have an important process of socialization. It's just not essential for their survival, the way it is for animals like humans, dogs, or any other species that live in communities (packs, cities, flocks, or herds).

Cats, on the other hand, really don't need it. They can do fine on their own. So if they don't have lots of human handling in ample amounts at the appropriate times in early kitten-hood development, they manage to look after themselves and do fine. But these cats cannot be effectively tamed and kept as acceptable pets. Therefore, you will need to find out whether the litter of kittens you're examining has been socialized for you.

If you arrive at the home of the proud owner of an aesthetically pleasing litter of dynamite kitties and you learn that they have not been properly acclimatized to humans, please feign acute abdominal distress and make a quick exit.

## Kitten Socialization Facts

During the first three weeks of life outside the womb, kittens spend their nonsleeping and noneating time imprinting on their mothers. In other words, they learn how to be cats. But between ages 3 weeks and 9 weeks, their brains allow them to become accustomed to any species that shares their lives—and I do mean *any* species. You can introduce rats, mice, birds, dogs, humans, or other cats with kittens during this time, and these species will be seen as friends throughout the lives of those kittens. But if that window of time is missed, the result will be a cat who responds in a socially inappropriate way to other creatures.

Thus, orphaned kittens will have a hard time with other cats the rest of their lives. Kittens raised by feral mothers simply cannot be tamed into being decent pets if they did not get human contact at the right time. On the other hand, kittens who were exposed to nonfrightened rodents or dogs have no hard feelings at all for these "natural enemies."

There are cats who like people, and others who like to bite and scratch people. If a kitten was handled gently by many different humans as a youngster, he or she is likely to be a relaxed and affectionate pet. Kittens handled roughly are more prone to biting and scratching when they are petted. And, just like children, kittens go through phases with gradual transitions as they mature.

As a general rule, it's best to allow kittens to stay with their mothers and littermates until they're 5 weeks or older. Kittens who are adopted when they're younger than this can become aggressive toward other cats—or may "act out" with self-mutilation.

So, you can determine a lot about a kitten if you just ask the owner a few simple questions, such as:

- When were the kittens born?
- Who handled them and when?
- How much were the kittens handled?
- Have the kittens learned to play roughly or gently?
- What was Dad like? (Aside from being an irresponsible lout, that is.)

If they were given a whole bunch of gentle affection every day, there's a good chance this litter has the kitten you're looking for.

# TEMPERAMENT TESTING

Now let's pick a great kitty.

I love cats. I can tell within a few minutes of evaluating a given litter of kittens if they are a great bunch or if they are just not right. So let's say the answers to the above questions are good ones and you're standing there gazing upon a frolicking, cavorting bunch of cuties. Try not to miss some important signs.

Rule number one: Even if the new kitty is for your children, leave the children at home. They'll be so excited that the kittens won't know what descended on them. You won't learn anything about who these babies are.

Next, ask the cat owner to let you meet the litter alone. (Yes, somehow you need to convince the owner to leave the room!)

Then—sit quietly and observe. This is critical. The babies will tell you nearly everything you need to know if you watch and wait.

If the babies are between 5 and 10 weeks of age, they are in a social period. You'll see the kitten litter politics being played out in front of you, and it won't take long to see who the dominant kitten is. This is the pushy one in charge. You probably don't want this tough guy or gal—it's usually the one who's less affectionate than the others.

Is there a runt? We all feel sorry for this underdog (undercat?). But think twice about the little one. If this baby is seriously intimidated by her brethren, she may be poorly socialized. And please, please remember that you should not feel obligated to adopt the least desirable kitten because maybe no one else will. You're only choosing for yourself; someone else may have completely different preferences and different ideas of what kind of cat they want to live with.

## Picking and Choosing

Have an enclosure nearby for keeping the kittens after you've evaluated each one.

Quietly pick up a kitten and let the baby sit in your hands. Is the baby relaxed or anxious? A restless, uncomfortable kitten probably won't relate well in social situations.

Now put the kitten on the ground and start to walk away. Does the kitten follow? What happens when you stop? Does the kitten stay relaxed and start to explore his or her surroundings? If so, that's a good sign.

Clap your hands. Does the kitten panic and bolt? A jumpy kitten is likely to remain that way—so if you want a relaxed, friendly cat, the panicky kind probably isn't for you.

Sometimes the kitten's posture can tell a lot, too. Watch for a few minutes, and you might see some clues. Here's what they mean:

### Head Up

A kitten who has her head up and her back straight is relaxed. If the tail is straight out, you have a cool cat. You want this.

### STRAIGHT REAR LEGS WITH A HIGH RUMP

These are the signs of a take-charge cat—the kind who will tell you where to go. This could be your new boss. Is this what you want?

### BELLY UP

If the kitten you are observing rolls on her back, you have a kitten who believes he or she may be in a conflict soon. It also usually means that in such a conflict, this cat will fight only if really pushed. He would prefer to run away. This is not a relaxed posture. I would avoid this kitty.

### ARCHED BACK

I don't think you need much help here. This cat is ready to rumble.

### PURRING

This may seem like an obvious sign of affection. But it's a little more than that. There are actually two kinds of purrs, though you'd need to be an expert on cat-speak to tell them apart.

As we all know, many cats and kittens purr when they are content. If you are holding a prospective family member who purrs, it's understandable that you would be favorably inclined. But did you know that many kittens purr in a slightly different way when they are anxious? If being held causes anxiety, you'll want to know it.

So, how can you tell? Believe it or not, a meow is much more reliable than a purr. If the baby meows when you hold him or her, you almost certainly have a relaxed kitten.

## PLAY

This could be among the most useful predictors of social success in a young kitten. While nearly all kittens play, you'll learn a lot if you take note of *who* plays *how*.

Kittens who play roughly, with claws extended, are likely to do the same with you at home. Between ages 5 and 10 weeks, their socialization period, you'll want a pet who acts, well, social. It's become clear to behaviorists that timid kittens in this age group are likely to remain aloof throughout their lives.

To be concise, if the kitten won't play with his family, he won't play with you, either. The bottom line is that if you like the way a kitten interacts with his or her siblings during this phase of development, then that baby may have your name on him.

## Breed Variations

Folks who are big on a particular breed feel strongly. Many purebreed cat fanciers feel such a gut-level commitment to their breed that they find it impossible to allow others to have opinions. I'll provide a few facts.

The cat breeds that have been popular for a long time have, in some cases, been carefully developed to make good social pets. The best example may be the Siamese. This works because there are so many individuals who are not even eighteenth cousins once removed. The gene pool is big. You can mate personalities that you like and not have a case of incest on your hands.

It's a different matter when you're dealing with the less common breeds of cats. In many cases, those rarer breeds come from very small families of cats that were imported into this country—hence, a small gene pool. Interbreeding these closely related individuals has helped to perpetuate a host of physical defects. It has also had the effect of producing more asocial cats.

Thus, I recommend popular breeds, or best of all, the all-American mix. Fortunately, the vast majority of cats for you to have in your life are the latter.

## Nothing But the Best

I hope reading this discourse on the nuts and bolts of kitten behavior has been helpful and not a chore. For many cat lovers, the addition of a new kitty is such an affair of the heart that it seems painful to even introduce things like logic.

All of us feline-friendly folk are fools for a fuzzy face. But despite the urge to open our hearts to every deserving cat, I advocate using our heads, too. Carefully select the greatest companion of your life.

Life is short and friendships are precious. Wonderful cats are that way because they are well matched to their human counterparts. But to build that relationship into everything you want it to be, you must start with a good match.

# CHAPTER 5

# Dr. Nichol's Cardinal Rules of Dog Care

Having said all those things about the fun and joy of sharing your life with a dog, why have a list of rules? Are rules fun? Aren't we all anarchists at heart? I know I am. I'm just like my 8-year-old son (or maybe he's just like me). He wants to know why we can't all just do whatever we want—anytime. He's serious. My response: "Me too. That's what I want."

But I must add to that. I must remind my lawless children that rules can be good because they can preserve the fun. If I just landed here from Neptune, I would want someone to tell me what would happen if I chose to drive on the other side of the road. Frankly, despite my anarchistic proclivities, I always drive on the right because I know I'll have less fun if I don't.

So here are the basic rules for avoiding disaster, and thus maximizing the fun of having your beautiful dog in your life. These are by no means the only rules, but, shucks, they're a pretty good start.

### RULE 1: Make sure your dog always has access to a place to urinate and a way to get there easily.

Urination is basic to life. It's the single most important way our bodies eliminate the waste that results from our minute-to-minute internal functions. If we don't let go of this fluid at regular intervals, some very negative things begin to happen. For starters if your dog is confined to your house or apartment and can't get out to urinate, she just isn't happy.

Here's why: Dogs are den animals. Humans are not. We can punish other humans for their crimes by putting them in a small enclosure called a cell. We humans hate this so much that many of us are motivated not to commit crimes for fear of this consequence. Dogs, on the other hand, have no problem with snug places. Exhaustive studies of the behavior of wolves, as well as of wild and domestic dogs, show them clearly to be den animals. Any time a dog feels a threat, needs to nurse her wounds, or wants a safe place to raise her young, she (or he) seeks the security of the den. Hand-in-glove with this instinct goes the commitment not to soil that den.

What does your dog regard as her den? The whole house.

Remember when you house-trained that puppy? Remember how she went to a part of your home far from her bed to make her indoor messes? As a baby, she was only mature enough to regard her sleeping area as her den. But as she developed into an adult, she learned that her den was really your entire home. She has not needed additional house-training because her (or his) instinct not to soil the den matured right along with the rest of the dog.

So now this poor boy or girl is stuck inside her den, which she is loath to foul. When left alone all day with no way to get outside, she must endure the pain of holding large volumes of urine. Add to that the stagnation of urine in her bladder, and bacteria start to grow. Now we have infection. But it doesn't stop there. Bacterial colonies set the stage for bladder stones and kidney disease.

The simple rule is this: Remember that your dog is a dog. Allow your den creature an escape from her precious den. Install a dog door.

Aren't there dogs who "know better" and urinate inside anyway? Yes, and for those who do we have a behavioral management challenge. If this is your dog, you will find help in the question-and-answer section of this book.

### Rule 2. If your dog's behavior is a problem, don't wait for it to be outgrown. It'll never go away by itself.

In my practice I spend a significant amount of time counseling pet owners on problem behaviors. I have developed this expertise because I love dogs and I love the relationships between dogs and their people. Improving the pets' behavior can be a life-saving endeavor. It's hugely important.

When we discuss major canine health concerns, we think first of the most common causes of death, which vary with age. For example, young dogs are more likely to die from hit-by-car injuries than older dogs. Geriatric pets are more prone to cancer and organ failure. But there is one cause of death far more common than any accident or disease, and that's euthanasia.

Why are so many dogs put to sleep? Because they don't fit. They just don't work out in their homes. So they're taken to animal control centers or humane shelters in the hopes that some other person or family will take this dog under its wing and the problems will vanish. Sometimes it works out. Most often it does not. Five to ten days after these pets are put on display for adoption, the vast majority are still without homes and they are humanely destroyed. This is tragic. It tears our hearts out.

Is it totally avoidable? No, I don't think so. While I have always loved dogs and am an optimist about positive change, I have learned much in my 25 years in the practice of veterinary medicine. One of the lessons I've learned is that we cannot win every fight. But with skill, talent, experience, and sheer dedication, we can make a difference in the lives of many of the caring pet owners who need our help in preserving the bonds with their pets.

The take-home message of Cardinal Rule 2 is: If your dog is acting badly, have the wisdom to recognize the problem early and get help.

I have never seen angst like that experienced by a loving dog owner who waited so long to address a behavioral problem that it just got too late to fix. Doesn't the same go for human problems? How much worse can it get? Keep waiting and you'll see; or act now and face it. Remember that you don't have to try to fix the problem alone. There are knowledgeable resources available to you.

The art and science of canine behavioral medicine is a complex and ever-changing pursuit. If the life of your dog is truly important to you, make the sacrifice of your time and paycheck, and find a doctor with the knowledge and energy to help. Neglected behavior problems never get better. In fact, they become so deeply engrained that they literally lay down nerve pathways in the brain. Behavioral habits become conditioned responses. If you want to preserve the fun of having that dog in your life, get an early grip on that behavior problem before it gets to be "unfunny."

### RULE 3. When a dog coughs every day, it means trouble. Get help.

Breathing is a good thing. I do it continually and so do my pets. Healthy lungs are a blessing that should not be taken lightly.

Coughing, on the other hand, is a disruption of normal airflow. Wheezing, choking, and hacking are bad signs.

If your dog hacks and coughs about once a year, well, okay, we'll live with that. But I'm downright nervous if I hear a cough and I can remember the one before it.

Can we talk about denial? I see so many dog owners who can *hear* their dogs coughing, but who prefer to think it really isn't all that important.

No one really wants to dwell on his or her pet's mortality anyway. You want to keep your pupster forever. If my dog, Peter Rabbit, coughs a time or two, I'll say "Aw, t'weren't nothin'." That's because he's mine. In fact I unconsciously think of Pete as an extension of me. My wife and our two boys do the same thing. We just love this guy. Who in our family wants to think of life without Peter Rabbit?

Fortunately for Pete, anytime he has any symptom, like coughing, one of us has a flash of maturity and wisdom and says something like "Maybe we should check this out." You may think that having a veterinarian in the family would make this easier, but it does not. After a long day of paying close attention to the woes of pets and their families, the last thing I want is to come home to the pets I love the very most and face their mortality. Even I need an occasional reality check.

Listen to that still, small voice in the back of your head when it says, "Hmmm, didn't this guy cough another time in recent memory?" Don't trifle with this symptom. It could be an early sign of heart failure, heartworm disease (even if monthly prevention has been given faithfully), lung tumors, collapsing trachea, or asthma. Get your veterinarian involved early, and keep that dog around for more good times.

### RULE 4. Dogs who have a tendency toward respiratory problems or heart disease are at huge risk in homes with tobacco smoke. Don't smoke.

It seems clear to me that most of us will extend ourselves far more for the betterment of someone else than we will for ourselves. Love knows no bounds when we shower it upon another.

The destructive effects of smoke on our lungs kills far more people than any other drug. Some of those whose health is destroyed are the pets who share air in the homes of loving owners who pollute that air.

Love your dog with intensity by allowing him or her to breathe healthy air. You and your dog can then grow old together.

## RULE 5. Vomiting and/or diarrhea that occurs more than twice in one day may be the start of something important. Get help.

Have you ever known anyone to stay in denial about vomiting and diarrhea? Hard to ignore, aren't they? These are mighty ugly symptoms that can lead to some really messy problems. I've seen dogs so sick that they have failed to eat for a few days. Asking folks if the dog is vomiting or having diarrhea, I hear "No, she can't be doing that, Doc; she hasn't eaten in days." Oh, brother.

When the stomach and intestinal walls become seriously inflamed, they get leaky. Fluids and electrolytes like sodium and potassium flow easily from the bloodstream directly back into the inside of the gut. Once inside the stomach and intestines, these essential components mix with overgrown bacterial populations, and away they go. That poor dog's body loses even more water and essential ions and gets even weaker.

If a dog starts to vomit and have diarrhea, watch that rascal like a hawk. If you see those symptoms again in the same day, go directly to the nearest veterinary hospital.

## RULE 6. A swelling that doesn't resolve on its own in 2 hours needs attention.

There are lots of mishaps in the daily life of a dog that can result in swellings of the skin. Bumps, tussles, and minor insect stings are all pretty common. But if the swelling lasts for more than a couple of hours, your dog may be headed for trouble.

A contaminated puncture wound, allergic reaction, or a growing tumor that just got noticed won't go away by itself. It needs treatment. A wound can abscess, a reaction can go systemic, and fast-growing cancers can kill. Go ahead and watch it for two hours if your dog seems to feel okay otherwise. But don't gamble for much longer than that.

### RULE 7. "Innocent" lumps may not be. See your vet.

What about the lumps and bumps? Some masses are on the surface of the skin while others are beneath the skin. Have you ever felt like just keeping an eye on them? You hope that as long as those bumps don't get any bigger, things will probably be fine. And then, a few weeks later, "Oh, okay, it's a little bigger, but it's growing slowly."

Are these the musings of someone who doesn't want to accept the possibility that a skin mass could be an aggressive malignancy? I will not argue that there is a time to take a wait-and-see approach, but not when your dog is growing new anatomy. If the Maker didn't put it there in the original dog, it is our job to figure out what it is.

Many of these are innocent, benign masses. But in the case of an early malignancy, you may only have a narrow window of time in which to cure your pet, and you must act decisively. Your veterinarian can perform a fine-needle aspirate in the exam room. And that's usually enough to tell if "waiting-and-seeing" is okay.

If the cytology report comes back equivocal, which it sometimes does, I live by the law given to me by my veterinary school surgery instructor, Dr. D. J. Krahwinkel: "When in doubt, cut it out."

### RULE 8. Seizures will not cause a dog to swallow his or her tongue.

If your dog has a seizure, don't lose your head—one of you needs to remain conscious. Observe carefully, but keep your hands away from that mouth.

Observing a thrashing, crashing, and unresponsive pet is surely one of the most unnerving experiences of dog ownership. You are suddenly aware that your dog might . . . who knows? Start by breathing from your tummy. It clears the head and allows you to do the next most important thing: Think.

For starters, your dog will not swallow his tongue, but he is literally out of control. He is unconscious during a true seizure and is likely to start chomping furiously. Your job during a seizure is to observe closely and document what occurs.

For now, wait, watch, and, if you must, boil some water. It's harmless and will keep you occupied until your dog relaxes. All seizuring dogs need medical attention, but if a seizure lasts longer than three minutes, or occurs more than three times in one day, get help fast.

## RULE 9. An active fat dog might just be training you to improve the menu. Don't fall for it.

Is your dog fat? This is a sad problem, but a funny subject.

Talk about denial! Over the years, I've learned to be a bit more sensitive. I used to walk into the exam room and make comments about the Goodyear blimp or references to a baked potato on toothpicks. I was intending to get people's attention—which I succeeded in doing—but instead of turning their attention to improving their dog's health, they just learned to hate my guts. I felt like a skin mass. My clients diagnosed me as malignant and wanted to do surgery on me.

Now I'm better, thank you. For many of us, our dogs are extensions of ourselves, so while folks still hate hearing that their dog is moderately overweight, they regard me as benign and allow me to remain. The point is this: If a licensed doctor of veterinary medicine tells you that the reason your dog can't walk anymore is that her feet can only touch the ground on one side at a time, please try not to shoot the messenger. The doctor is only trying to keep the two of you together in this life for as long as possible. Prescription diets and other methods of weight management are easy for pets to live with.

The truth is that it is *your* fault that your dog is now bigger than your car. You allowed yourself to be dog-trained. Since you used food rewards every time that poor dog begged at the table, you have convinced her beyond any doubt that she was performing quite well. She is now an Olympic-level beggar. You both score a 10.

## RULE 10. Any dog who fails to eat for more than one day may be yelling, "I am sick." Fall for that.

Of all the varied symptoms seen in dogs, failure to eat consistently may be the most common. It could also be the most important. Poor appetite is an important signal of many diseases. It can also be the first sign in a progression of negative events.

Our dogs communicate with us any way they can. Sometimes you could swear they speak something akin to English. But when it comes to telling us they're sick, the messages are simple. If your good eater takes an unexpected break from her favorite pastime, see your veterinarian. Help your dog to get well when she's only a little sick. If you "wait and see," you may have to face your pup when she's big sick.

**RULE 11. Be very careful with a canine vacuum cleaner. Dogs with this bad habit may need a full-time personal surgeon.**

Speaking of dogs who are ruled by their stomachs, I want to discuss junk collectors. Remember the TV show "Sanford and Son"? These guys collected and hoarded everything that wasn't nailed down. Some dogs do that, too. But instead of amassing these treasures in the yard, they pile them up in their gastrointestinal tracts.

Unfortunately, the gut is not meant for nonfood items. If your dog is an incessant eater of all objects great and small, you had better control his environment. If you don't, you will learn the true value of pet health insurance.

**RULE 12. Don't hit a dog. It's not part of his instinctive communication. He doesn't get it. It will either hurt the dog's feelings or "agitate" him. A frightened dog is not man's best friend. An angry dog could very well be your enemy.**

Can you train a dog to be better when she just keeps on doing bad things? If she's really man's best friend, why can't she learn a little faster?

Maybe you have a really smart dog who has learned to "get your goat." Is she really just messing with you? Sometimes, it seems that the harder you try to get that dog to behave, the worse she gets. How much scolding or punishment should it take to make her obey? At some point, you can lose your temper.

Behavior problems are often really hard. A great number of the questions reprinted in this book are pleas from folks who are desperate. They believe that if they can't get a handle on these problems soon, they will have no choice but to part with their dogs. It's a heartbreaker.

I wish I could offer simple solutions. But managing these challenges is complicated because the causes are complicated. There is one basic point that is simple and direct. It is the foundation of managing any canine behavior problem: Dogs are a different species.

That may seem obvious, but most of us bond to our dogs on such a personal and emotional level that we forget the reality of those species differences. I have seen so many well-intentioned dog owners and dog trainers try to force sensible human solutions on dogs that I could just dig up the yard in frustration. If I hear one more person say that they're going to hit their dog, why, I'll just rip up the couch and poop on the rug. Am I making any sense? No? Good. Dogs with behavior problems need *canine*, not human, behavior modification. Different species—different rules.

I will repeat my mantra: We bond so closely with our dogs because we have so many feelings, emotions, and needs in common. But there are other basics of dog behavior that have to do with things like pack dominance order, territorial behavior, competition for resources, and heredity. We human animals don't have that stuff. Dogs are very similar to us *and* they are also very different. Some human rules of communication apply and some don't. Still other signals with very clear meanings to humans have totally different meanings for dogs—with sometimes scary results. So let's try not to foist human concepts on dogs. When we think "discipline," the dog might think "attack."

How can you know what to do? Read the parts of this book that deal with behavior. The problems that arise are fascinating, informative, and, in some ways, unsettling. Have you ever heard of beloved dogs who are the sweetest, most gentle family members, but who pack up with other neighborhood dogs and attack not just livestock but schoolchildren at the bus stop? This stuff really happens. How is this possible? Is this a Jekyll and Hyde routine? No, this is the same dog simply living out different parts of his basic psyche.

Scary? Maybe. But domestic dogs are firmly ensconced in our culture because they bring so many healthy joys to our lives—and we to theirs. When we take "ownership" of a different species, we accept the responsibility to find ways of maintaining harmony. It is my mission in writing this book to teach you enough so that you can share some of the successes of dog ownership with me.

# CHAPTER 6

# Dr. Nichol's Cardinal Rules of Cat Care

Rules for cat care?

You must think I'm joking.

The word "rules" implies structure, and who ever heard of a cat with any regard for structure?

Cats don't care about that stuff. We humans (most of us anyway) believe in some semblance of organization. We may not like all of the laws that govern our lives, but we seem to agree that they're somehow necessary.

But cats . . . well, they are a little different. To them, any rules are for beings from other planets, not for them. In fact they think *people* are from another planet. But, heck, we do have a few good points. So our cats hang out at our house and we think they're cool. So cool, in fact, that people like us can't imagine life without them.

We interact with them, feed and care for them, and generally treat them like our children. Pet people need that. It's mighty healthy too. Folks with pets have been shown to live longer, healthier, better lives.

We recognize the differences between us and our cats and we like it that way. But cats are different not because they're smarter than we are nor that they're smarter than dogs, either. It's because they are a different species of animal than humans. Not only do they have some very different behaviors and methods of communication; they are fundamentally different socially. That's basic.

Humans, like most other mammalian species, are community animals. Most people live in cities, horses in herds, birds in flocks. Cats, by contrast, are loners. Heresy, you say? We all know folks whose group of cats seems to do just fine together. But while they can commune cooperatively, there is an element of stress in a group of cats. It is not their natural state. When a member of a more highly socialized species, like a dog, becomes ill, others in the community come to his or her aid. These critters communicate their need for help. But cats, being natural loners, say nothing. The typical sick or injured cat crawls into a secluded space and does his or her best to get well alone. So if you love your cat, you must learn to observe his or her behavior carefully.

But as much as we understand why we share our lives with cats, we still may have a hard time. What does it mean when a cat vomits often, or frequently urinates in the wrong place? How can you effectively discipline cats—or at least change their behavior?

Some cats are a breeze to live with. Others can make you crazy. My job in presenting the information in this book is to make a lot of this easier. I'll help you sort through the problems and solve a few of them, too.

## The Beginning of Feline Guidance

In addition to fixing a flock of feline physical frailties in a general veterinary practice, I have training and broad experience in the management of their behavioral problems as well. But before we try to correct bad behavior, we must first know and understand what is normal.

What is truly normal for a cat? Is it reasonable to believe that what is normal in a human home is somehow typical in the wild, too?

There are perfectly happy, well-functioning wild cats who belong to the same species as that cuddly kitty who's rubbing your leg right now. How can those two sides of a cat be compatible? On one hand, there's the independence of the hunting feline survivalist; on the other hand, the close companionship of a housecat.

While our cats are a truly adaptable species, they are the same creatures in the wild as they are at home. It isn't that they adapt to fit our lives. Instead, we are seeing different sides of the same coin. Within the confines of our homes, we bring out one side of a cat while life in the wild accentuates a whole different part of the beast.

To manage this complex web of intricate contradictions, I offer you my Cardinal Rules of Cat Ownership. I'm sure they don't cover everything, but I think they hit the high points.

## Dr. Jeff's Cardinal Rules of Cat Ownership

**RULE 1.** A cat who doesn't come when called may just be stuck up. But cats instinctively hide serious illness. So the cat who hides may be gravely ill.

Stuck up? Well, of course your cat is stuck up. All cats are, to some degree.

But a sick cat isn't acting. Don't interpret a cat's behavior using human rules.

**RULE 2.** Any cat who spends too much time in the litter pan needs a doctor fast. His plumbing can kill him.

The inability to pass urine or stool is a miserable state. But it can be a lot more than that. Our cats, being private, don't advertise their constipation or inability to urinate unless they're in real trouble. Constipation is common in older cats. As in humans, it usually develops gradually. It is important and it's treatable, but it's not an emergency. Only cats who are in excruciating pain will cry out. So, again, you must be observant.

If a cat makes frequent visits to the litter pan, you might assume that the problem is constipation; you're job, however, is to assume nothing. Take a close look at what, if anything, your cat leaves behind when he walks away. To know for sure what all the squatting is about, dump the litter and put a piece of clean white paper in the bottom of the pan. Add a small to moderate amount of litter, then check the paper after the next visit. Look for small amounts of blood-tinged fluid on the white paper.

If the problem child is a male cat, have a helper hold the kitty's front end. Reach up to your cat's abdomen from between his rear legs and gently squeeze. If that boy cries, go to the nearest veterinary hospital. That little guy may have a urinary blockage. Kidney shut down could be just around the corner.

Move quickly. If he doesn't get help fast, he may die.

**RULE 3.** Cats who cough or breathe too fast are in trouble now.

Here is another big difference in *Felis silvestris catus* (that's fancy-speak for domestic cat). Most other species cough every now and then.

Even if it's due to a respiratory or heart problem, it may not be an emergency. Coughing, in many creatures, may even resolve on its own.

Not in cats. In another demonstration of their rugged individualism, cats are loath to make an outward show of a disability. If they have any breathing impairment, they simply adjust their lives so that they require less breathing. In other words, they do more sitting still and less running around.

Now, that subtle change in behavior can be tough to observe. Most of the time when I look at my cat, he's just kicking back anyway. If I don't require him to run around, I won't know whether he can. Only when lung disease gets really advanced does a cat's breathing get difficult and rapid, even when he's at rest. A cat with a slow accumulation of lung fluid just doesn't jump around to chase mice and dust bunnies.

If your first clue is your cat's rough breathing while she's sitting still, well, she's already in deep trouble. Make that baby's trip to the doctor stress-free, but get there fast.

---

**RULE 4. Eighty-five percent of all skin lumps and bumps on cats are malignant. Have them removed soon.**

Everybody who wants surgery for their cat, stand up and wave.
Hmm, no takers?
Well, I'm not surprised. I haven't met many people who favor getting their cat cut open. Most of us will postpone, delay, rationalize, or deny that our cat has any problem requiring surgery until a skin mass begins to ooze and stink. We'd rather shrug and say, "Oh, it doesn't seem to be growing—much." Or "He's getting a bit older. It's normal to get lumps and bumps when somebody ages."

Well, don't shrug.

Nowadays we are informed consumers. If we don't feel comfortable with professional advice, we'll get a second opinion. I give second opinions all the time, right after my first opinion and just before my third opinion—all to the same pet owner. Cats who have lumps and bumps of the skin—what are called "skin masses"—are usually terminal if those skin masses are ignored. That's why my first, second, and third opinions are all the same: When in doubt, cut it out.

I've seen the studies, and I've treated cancer in cats since 1974. There are times to be conservative, but not when your cat has skin cancer. Sure, you can hope that it's a benign skin mass, but betting on that is a long shot.

All competent veterinarians remove all feline skin masses with "wide, deep, aggressive excisions." In other words, we take a lot of seemingly normal tissue around the mass and beneath it. We know that if we cut across the advancing microscopic tumor cells, we rile them up—and they're not cute when they're mad. They advance much faster. If your veterinarian advises you to "just keep an eye on your cat's skin tumor to see if it grows," pay your bill and leave.

**RULE 5. Cats who won't eat may be finicky. They may also be sick. Not eating is often the first real sign of serious illness.**

This is a tough call. Even the most devoted and knowledgeable cat owners get fooled. Some are so concerned if their cat fails to eat every time that they have an ever-ready smorgasbord of gastronomic delights waiting constantly in the wings of their kitchens. Let's not get carried away. The central concern is not that a cat will wither away and blow off in a stiff breeze if one meal is missed. The point is, if a consistent eater stops eating consistently, there may be cause for closer observation.

The hard part is that all cats are different. A lot of cats have variable appetites one day to the next normally. So I suggest two approaches.

### NUMBER ONE:

Don't vary your cat's diet. Oh, I know, they like variety just like you and I—and eating is life's greatest pleasure, isn't it? It better not be. You got that cat for fun and mutual enjoyment—you know, a relationship. What kind of relationship do we have if the best part is you training the cat to become a feline garbage disposal and the cat training you to deliver a multitude of diverse menu items at his whim? I think not.

Feed the same high-quality hard, dry diet (moistened with water for indoor males) twice daily in measured amounts. Your job is to protect the health and well being of that trusting friend. Feed no junk. Control that kitty's diet to maintain a healthy weight. (Your veterinarian should advise you on your cat's ideal weight.)

### NUMBER TWO:

If your cat's intake changes, go into vigilance mode. Still normally active? Normal bowel movements and urine output? Drinking a normal amount? Less? More? Showing signs of weakness or lameness? Cries when handled? Call the doctor. Invest in an exam fee and be sure, but please, eat the caviar yourself. It tastes sooo good. I love my cat, but I don't share the champagne either.

---

**RULE 6.** Cats who do bad things, like urinating on your bed, are quite naughty. But you can't train them. You can fix the problem, but you'll have to do all the work.

You have to wonder.

We humans communicate by speaking words; writing notes; sending e-mail, voice mail, hate mail, junk mail, and chain letters. We've used carrier pigeons and smoke signals. But cats do none of that. They do something like peeing on your bed.

Or worse.

I know one cat who somehow crapped under the pillow of his college fraternity owner repeatedly. Maybe the cat disliked Dad's girlfriend. Maybe he wanted to move to another frat house or thought his owner should change his major. Who knows? Annoying, isn't it?

But losing one's patience doesn't help. In most cases, getting rid of your cat won't help either—because you'll miss that cat.

One more thing: The greatest cause of death in cats is neither a disease nor an injury. It's euthanasia—and the most common reason for euthanasia is behavior problems. You may not be the person ordering the death of your cat, but if his behavior is unacceptable and you move him out of your home, his behavior is likely to restart in his next abode. His ultimate destination may be animal control.

The solutions to problems like this are not simple, but they work. Nearly every behavior problem cat can work out. Read the sections of this book on feline behavior problems. I cover all of the common ones. And yes, you will do all the work. I'm sorry. Life isn't fair. You already knew that. Now you know that I know it, too.

---

**RULE 7.** Cats who vomit more than twice in one day need help fast. Cats who vomit now and then need help at the next available appointment.

Puking pussycats. Hey, I never promised you rose gardens in this tome on cat health. It's all here, the good, the bad, and the vomit.

That said, I really hate it when people call or e-mail me and ask why their cat is vomiting. If I were to list every possible cause of vomiting in cats, you'd be holding a much thicker volume in your hands. Nevertheless, I will provide a bit of guidance.

## NUMBER ONE:

A barfing cat with little or no prior history of vomiting may be really sick. Look for other symptoms, including things that may seem unrelated.

Your veterinarian may look like Dr. Dolittle. I'm sure he or she really does talk to the animals. I certainly do. But, sadly, animals don't talk back. That's why veterinarians rely heavily on the close observations of pet owners.

Yes, I'm trying to convince you to pay close attention to the how's and why's of your cat's vomiting. Don't let your cat down. Watch like a hawk and tell us what you saw. Take notes. When it comes to information, more is better.

One more thing: Don't waste a lot of time. Call the doctor's office and head on over. Don't wait for the folks at the front desk to say that the appointment schedule is full. Just go.

## NUMBER TWO:

A lot of cats vomit just now and then—you know, like it's a sport or something. I don't know about you, but I'd rather file my knuckles with a cheese grater than vomit. But cats aren't that averse to the whole process. For some of them, it's, like, "Well, the sun's out and the barometric pressure is 29.4 and rising so I guess I'll just heave right here." No apparent reason.

If it doesn't seem to happen often, you just wipe it up and life goes on. But here's the rub: Over time, it does occur with increasing frequency. And that creates a snowball effect. Each time your cat vomits, stomach acid is forced up into the esophagus. The stomach and small intestine become a little more inflamed. Then the cycle repeats a little faster.

If you can still remember the last time that cat tossed his cookies, it's happening too often. I have a section on it in this very book. Even if all of the other cats do it, that doesn't make it OK. Invest in a thorough diagnostic workup and get it treated. Chronic vomiting never goes away by itself.

You'll find many more insights into this complicated phenomenon in Parts 3 and 4 of this book.

## RULE 8. Cats losing weight are quite sick.

Let's face it: A lot of us have fat cats. So, if they lose weight it's OK, right?

Well, the answer is, it's OK only if that kitty is losing weight because we want him to. Any cat (fat or thin) who starts to lose weight for no clear reason is in trouble. Unexplained weight loss is a problem that many cat owners try to forget or ignore.

In most cats, weight loss is a signal of chronic disease. The list of potential deadly causes is long and frightening. Common causes are kidney failure, malignant cancers, thyroid disease, intestinal disorders, feline AIDS, and leukemia. There are many more.

The moral of the story is that if you even *think* your cat is losing weight, immediately take her to the doctor. Even if you don't think it's serious enough to warrant an exam, ask the staff to weigh her for you. Chronic wasting diseases are often curable, or at least manageable.

If you kill time, you may kill your cat. When we are in denial, we may think we are effectively keeping our fears out of our minds, but our spirits are paying daily. Get your fears confirmed or erased—and trust your veterinarian to get the best possible result.

## RULE 9. Cats don't "look out for themselves" more than dogs. They're just not very social creatures. They communicate less, but need every bit as much care. Always observe your cat closely.

By now I'm sure you realize that cats truly need careful monitoring by a knowledgeable owner to ensure that they don't get old before their time.

Sure, a great many cats have little or no medical history. There's a good reason in most cases: They're mixed breed. Just like human cultures—inbred individuals get weak. We see it in purebred dogs, horses, cattle, and royal families. But, fortunately, there has never been a major demand in our society for purebred cats. Nearly every cat in America is of such mixed parentage that they have "hybrid vigor."

That said, I should add that I've been a busy cat doctor for a long time, and I can tell you that with the way cats tend to hide illness and injury, they *need* us to care. I truly believe that most cats who have been assumed to have simply "run off to live with another family" actually hid out and died.

We need our cats. They need us, too. If you assume that their secretive nature is really a greater state of health, I'll bet you still believe that cats are really just dogs with short ears.

Wrong answer! Cats are cats.

**RULE 10. Never strike a cat or speak harshly. Cats think we belong on a different planet anyway. To be a cat's friend, you must speak softly and carry a big menu.**

Did I mention that cats are different from humans and dogs? Good. They are not socialized the way we are.

If you bawl out your cat very often, he will simply be an independent spirit someplace else.

I'm sure we've all noticed that the female pronoun is more commonly used when speaking of cats. We just assume that the cats are the girls and the dogs are the boys. Again, we are anthropomorphizing. We assign these different species human traits and then expect it to work. It goes along with the idea that the world was created in our image and likeness.

Sorry, not so. We humans are just one of millions of species meant to share this place. I don't mean to imply that we should never treat our pets like people. I think that's where the fun is. My pets have human names (well almost): Raoul is our cat and Peter Rabbit is our dog. They are like two more children in a family that shares everything. But I have taught my human children that they will never get a cat to relax and enjoy a relationship if they rush after him and grab him like a stuffed animal. Instead, they must sit quietly, speak softly, and wait.

**RULE 11. Don't let your cat train you into feeding junk food. He already believes in his superior intelligence. Don't encourage him.**

Remember the different sides of the same feline coin? Our indoor housecats are living out one aspect of their instinctive selves while the outdoor, free-living cats are simply displaying another essential facet of catdom. Whichever part your cat is playing, he or she needs to eat fairly frequently.

But wait, there's a paradox here. Clearly, the game-hunting, outdoor cat is much more active and thus burns many more calories than the house dweller. So why do indoor cats want to eat so much more?

The couch-potato cat isn't spending his time and mental energy sleuthing out his next snack. In fact, most indoor cats are just plain bored. And if you're like many Americans today, boredom can be cured by food. A little bite for me, a little bite for my kitty—you know how it goes. The more you cater to your cat's tastes, the more fussy they become.

So, OK, we accept all that. But is it really important? So what if your cat is pleasingly plump?

Here's the problem: As cats gain weight, many will infiltrate their livers with fat. All seems to go well until they have reason not to eat—any minor stress can do it. But the body needs calories, so it breaks down the fat in liver storage and that cat starts a dangerous slide into potentially fatal liver failure. It's completely unnecessary.

So, save yourself and your kitty the heartache and be structured in some healthy, twice-daily measured feeding. Cure boredom with games and toys. (Elsewhere in this book, you'll find some tips for taking the boredom out of the life of a fat cat.) Just don't allow your cat to gradually convince you that she will wither away quickly without that canned salmon. That salmon is for you, the human, not for your feline friend.

# PART 2

# All Your Dog Questions Answered

# Barking

## When Barking Means Hello
*Correction first, reward later.*

### QUESTION:
I love my indoor dog; she's a great guard dog. The problem is that when I come home from work, she barks and barks and barks. I know she's very happy to see me, but she makes so much noise. What can I do to keep her silent when I come home? I don't want to put one of those antibark collars on her because I want her to bark while I'm away.

### DR. NICHOL:
You have forged a healthy, loving relationship with your dog. She's just so darn happy to see you that she wants to tell you—and the whole world—all about it. But, hey, the barking is also kind of annoying.

Part of the problem is that your girl's enthusiasm has driven a ritual of anxiety that you may be encouraging inadvertently. If you cuddle, hold, or just speak soothingly to her during these wild times, your dog gets the idea that she's being rewarded. Instead, she needs an early correction. The best tool for the job is a Promise head halter, which your dog can wear comfortably while you're gone. Adjusted properly, it will allow her to eat, drink, pant, and even bark normally.

Here's the plan: As soon as she starts barking, grab the lead on her head halter and pull so that her mouth closes. Tell her, "No." Speak quietly but firmly. Wait until she begins to calm down before you say, "Okay." When she's collected herself, reward her with a yummy biscuit. End of lesson. Repeat hundreds of times.

Want a faster solution? You can add a citronella antibark collar. There could be other causes for all the noise. Some dogs may have serious anxiety or a form of obsessive-compulsive disorder (OCD). For these dogs, we also have medications. But whatever you do, correct this problem early and correct it often.

## A Compulsive Barker
*Cintronella could set this Schnauzer on the straight and narrow.*

## QUESTION:

When out in the yard one of my Schnauzers will just bark at nothing and then, when I run out and scold her, she's flat on her back with the "I'm so sorry, Mom" look. I'll put her back in the doghouse, but she doesn't mind it at all. Any suggestions?

## DR. NICHOL:

Dogs are pretty funny, aren't they? They'll do something compulsive, then feel contrite about it. Now, that sounds just like human behavior. The real reason your Schnauzer feels so badly is not because she did something wrong, but because you got upset with her. You're her best friend and she doesn't want you to be angry. Still, all that noise is not acceptable.

Correction must occur at the time of the offense. It must be negative but humane. A new type of antibark collar sprays citronella under a dog's chin at the time of the bark. While it has a faint orange smell to humans, it is apparently obnoxious to dogs. For most barking dogs, it has been quite effective.

# Can You Debark a Dog?

*Excessive barking can destroy neighbor relations. Antibark collars and surgery are viable options.*

## QUESTION:

I've heard of "debarking" a dog, especially one that disrupts the entire neighborhood. Is it really a cruel thing to do, aside from the psychological aspect of taking away the animal's mode of expression?

## DR. NICHOL:

Allowing a dog to bark is a truly cruel way to treat one's neighbors. But surgery is not your only choice. Antibark collars that spray a citronella mist can be an effective and pain-free method to quiet the baying of your hound.

Understand that nothing is guaranteed. Debarking surgery (removal of the vocal cords) can be done through the mouth, but the approach from beneath the larynx (voice box) is far more effective. The result is a dog who continues his attempts to howl, but can't say much (although dogs also communicate through body language that most of us never notice). A sure failure is the yelling-out-the-window method. If anything, it encourages more howling and barking because your dog will succeed in getting your attention. Moreover, your neighbors will then have two howlers, and I don't think we want to debark both of you.

## The Safety of Antibark Collars
*Citronella collars are harmless and effective.*

### QUESTION:
In a recent column, you mentioned an antibark collar. I was told at the pet shop and by a vet that these collars are cruel and burn the neck. I have a "mostly" Spitz who barks too much, and I can't seem to stop her. Would you recommend this collar for her?

### DR. NICHOL:
I'm glad you are concerned about the safety of antibark collars. Punishment (discomfort) has a definite place in dog training, but none of us want to hurt our dogs.

Electric shock collars have been around for a long time. Unless they are used incorrectly, they will not burn a dog's neck. They are effective in most cases. But with the recent development of citronella collars, shock collars have become unnecessary and old-fashioned. These newer collars shoot a fine spray of citronella under the dog's chin when she barks. Nearly every dog will stop barking with these collars because they can't stand the smell. It's negative, but it's harmless as well as effective.

## Car Rides and Barking
*Dramamine should help calm the wild beast.*

### QUESTION:
I'm a faithful reader of your column and have often wondered if you have a solution to a problem that is swiftly driving me crazy. My girlfriend, a black Chow cross, loves to ride in the car, but she can't control herself. It's yap, yap, yap, pant, pant, bark, bark, continuously. We have tried everything imaginable short of Valium but nothing fazes her. She didn't start her riding experience until she was 4 or 5 years old, and she's now 9. Because she has a hip problem, a seat harness is out of the question. I have tried the back seat, front seat, and now the center between the front seats so she can see everything. Do you have any suggestions?

**DR. NICHOL:**

I know exactly what you mean. I had a girlfriend like that once, too. Could not control herself. And they called it puppy love.

So, car riding. You must really love this girl. I'm the same way. We love to have our Border Collie puppy, Peter Rabbit, go everywhere with us. While most dogs just love to ride in the car, there are those who get motion sickness and others who get so darned excited they become overactive.

Here is my advice: Give this pup Dramamine about 30 minutes before leaving. It is not only effective against mild forms of motion sickness, it also has a mild tranquilizing effect. But while it is likely to help your girlfriend with her self-control and possible nausea problems, I recommend against allowing her to drive while under its influence.

# Basics

## Pet Age Compared to Humans

If you're adopting a dog or cat, you may be wondering about life expectancy. After all, teaching new tricks to a human septuagenarian is quite different from dealing with the behavior of an adolescent teen—and the same goes for a pet.

### Question:

Could you please tell me how to figure a dog's age? I know it isn't like everyone says, just seven years for every one of ours.

### Dr. Nichol

Do our pets hang out around the water bowl and debate their humans' ages in pet years? I don't think so. But, heck, it's fun so here's a chart:

| DOG | HUMAN | CAT | HUMAN |
| --- | --- | --- | --- |
| 1 year | 15 years | 1 year | 15 years |
| 2 years | 24 years | 2 years | 24 years |
| 4 years | 32 years | 5 years | 36 years |
| 7 years | 45 years | 7 years | 45 years |
| 10 years | 56 years | 12 years | 64 years |
| 15 years | 76 years | 15 years | 76 years |
| 20 years | 98 years | 18 years | 88 years |
|  |  | 21 years | 100 years |

For small dogs, these charts are a pretty good predictor of life expectancy; but large-breed dogs age much faster. Even so, many pets in their "seventies" can outrun a person of similar age. I say we should all stop counting. Life is short. Let's eat dessert first.

## The Expense of Raising Pets

*There are places to trim costs and do just fine. But cut quality on the wrong priorities and your pets will pay more later.*

## QUESTION:

Should I give vitamins to my pets? I have a whole menagerie. I have two guinea pigs, three cats, two dogs, and some fish. I try to feed good food, but it can get expensive. Is it good to feed food that's just okay and add vitamins? Which vitamins are good?

## DR. NICHOL:

I think I understand where you're coming from. A lot of us animal lovers surround ourselves with a whole family of pets. It's great to never be alone, and your pets are never alone either. I feel the same way. The down side, of course, is that providing good care for that many critters can be costly. What's important is to know where you can economize and where it's actually cheaper in the long term to spend the extra cash.

First, let's look at places to shave expenses. Cat litter is one. Since providing unused fresh litter is a good way of preventing urinary disease in cats, there is no point in paying for a gold-plated latrine. Buy the cheapest litter you can find, use very small amounts, and throw it away after every use. Canned pet food is another needless cost. Seventy-five percent of it is water, and you pay about 20 cents just for the can. As for grooming, you can lose the shampoo in almost all cases, and brush your pets instead. They like it, it's a great way to bond with them, and it's much healthier for their skin than bathing anyway. In fact, a lot of folks clip their own dogs' hair to save expenses, although they might end up looking like Gomer Pyle. As for the guinea pigs, they don't need cedar shavings for bedding. Cedar is nice, but they'll do fine with shredded newspaper as long as you replace it daily.

Now, here is where your pet-care dollars are best spent: good food. When it comes to pet food, you will not get what you don't pay for. Compare ingredients and analysis if you must, but better diets have better digestibility. This means that your pets will absorb the nutrients they need better and stay healthier on better food. Will these diets work even better if you add vitamins? Not really. The real beauty of high-quality food (yes, good food is beautiful) is that it already has every important vitamin and mineral in the proper amount. If you add to a truly complete, balanced diet, you will throw it out of balance and actually diminish the nutritional plane of that pet.

Will adding vitamins help if you feed a mediocre diet? Sure. But you would also have to add everything else this diet lacks or you still won't make a real difference. So use good food in the first place and have peace of mind.

Now the exceptions: Guinea pigs must have vitamin C every day. Use the liquid supplement and add it to their drinking water. Follow the label instructions. Pets recovering from surgery or illness, and pets who are stressed due to a move to a new home, travel, or boarding are also candidates for good-quality supplemental vitamins. Finally, working dogs, especially those who don't work hard consistently but only now and then, benefit from vitamin supplements. This includes hunting dogs, field trial dogs, and dogs who play professional sports like hockey and basketball. Treat these guys like stars. Feed the best food and give a good chewable multivitamin every day. Ask your veterinarian for a recommended brand.

## Belly Buttons

*Everybody has one. Here's how to hunt one down.*

### QUESTION:

Why don't dogs have belly buttons like people?

### DR. NICHOL:

The truth is that they do, but they're just a bit more modest about them. I've examined the tummies of countless dogs, cats, ferrets, rabbits, hamsters, gerbils, rats, mice, and guinea pigs—and everybody has one but they are all strangely unfestooned with rings and studs and starburst tattoos. Each of them is discreetly covered with hair. Nonhuman mammals never seem to display their navels. I just don't get it.

To find your dog's belly button (navel or umbilicus), roll that baby on his or her back under a good light. It's located about one-third the distance between the rib cage and the pelvis. Many dogs have a little cowlick with their belly button in the middle. While none of us need a belly button after we leave the womb, that little scar serves as a reminder of the essential connection we had with our mothers that was the pipeline for nourishment during our first months. I still love my mom.

## Where to Find Good Care for Your Dog When You're Out of Town

*Leave out food and water? Friends who visit your home? Expensive kennels? Here's how to choose.*

## Question:

Soon our children will be back in school and our family has one last vacation planned. We have a cat and a dog, but we don't know where to turn for reliable pet care while we're gone. Please advise us.

## Dr. Nichol:

You show real concern for those other family members—your pets. Here are some bad ideas first. Do not leave a pet home alone (indoors or outdoors). Remember Murphy's Law: Anything that can go wrong, will. The water bowl gets dumped over, the critter gets stranded in the sun, or he or she gets sick and no one is there to care for him or her. Also, do not ask a neighbor child to stop over to feed and water them. True, pets are great for teaching responsibility, but determining when a pet is less than healthy is best left to an adult.

How about a few good ideas? Asking a trusted adult friend to visit two or three times daily is usually fine. Another good option is a home dog-sitting service. Good dog-sitters are bonded and can provide references.

Finally, there are boarding kennels for dogs. Like most things in life, some are better than others. How do you know who's good? Call your veterinarian's office and ask the staff for recommendations on pet-sitters and kennels. They've had experience with the good and the bad.

Lastly, be sure that whoever looks after your beloved pets has the phone number and name of your veterinarian and a number where you can be reached, too. If a problem does develop, we'll want your consent to take care of it right away.

## Boarding Kennels and the Vaccinations They Require

***Protecting your dog is important. But you need to be better informed than the kennels.***

### Question:

I travel for business a fair amount and I live alone except for my dog and cat. I have used two different boarding kennels for my pets. One of the kennels insists that my dog have a Bordatella vaccine, given within the past year. The other kennel wants a vaccine against kennel cough. What's the difference?

## Dr. Nichol:

So many questions, so little time. Okay, let's get down to business.

What's the big deal about dogs and their contagious diseases? The concern is that canine infectious tracheobronchitis, also known as parainfluenza or kennel cough, is highly infectious. This means that the two organisms responsible for this disease can spread through a group of dogs in almost no time. A dog with kennel cough can infect a whole kennel full with just a few coughs. In a few days, every dog in the place can be hacking up a storm. While kennel cough is not a fatal disease, it can make your dog and you miserable for two or three weeks while he hacks and coughs day and night. Sound like fun? Kennel operators don't think so either. No way do they want to be responsible for a mess like that.

Here is how you can protect your pooch. First, I will confuse you. (It's a real talent of mine.) The distemper-parvo combination vaccine that your dog gets every year covers the viral component of the kennel cough problem with a vaccine called parainfluenza. That used to be enough protection. But several years ago, a bacteria that used to infect only pigs made its debut in the canine world. It's called Bordatella bronchiseptica, and the old vaccine isn't effective against it.

Enter the intranasal kennel-cough vaccine. This stuff is actually pretty nifty in that it is not injectable, but is administered instead as a nosedrop. The best part is that the intranasal kennel-cough vaccine provides a reliable immunity within 24 to 48 hours. So, if you forgot to plan far enough ahead of your trip to vaccinate old Bowser, you can get quick results in just a day or two before you take off.

Now the down side. While the insert that comes with the intranasal Bordatella (kennel cough) vaccine claims a full year of immunity, new research indicates that it's reliable for only four to six months. So your best bet is to get your pup vaccinated when you know that he will be kenneled, rather than just doing it at the time of his regular vaccinations. That way he'll have it when he needs it.

# Normal Body Temperature
*101.0°F (+ or – 0.5 degree)*

## Question:
I'm curious as to the normal body temperature for a dog.

## Dr. Nichol

The official answer is 101.0 degrees Fahrenheit, plus or minus 0.5 degree, but anything between 100 and 102 is fine. *Really* excited, but normal, dogs can sport rectal temperatures of 103.5. Forget using ear thermometers, though. They will annoy your dog and the darn things don't even play music.

## Daily Dog Care

*The basics...*

### Question:

What do you have to do to take care of a dog daily?

### Dr. Nichol:

This is a great question.

Food: Give excellent food in two measured feedings each day. Pick up the food bowl when he or she walks away from it. If you have more than one pet, feed them at the same time but in separate places so they can't see each other. This prevents competitive eating which leads to obesity.

Clean the water bowl and refill with fresh water at least twice daily. Pets drink more when the water is fresh. This reduces wear on the kidneys and promotes strong immunity and long life.

Restroom activities: Make it possible for your dog to get outside at least every few hours. If he or she can't urinate often, the risk of bladder and kidney diseases will escalate.

Add a good brisk walk or other regular exercise and life will be darn near perfect—unless your dog is goal-oriented. In that case, I recommend a college savings plan.

## Microchips and Tattoos for Pet Identification

*Each has its place, but microchips are the latest and greatest. They are quick to implant and highly reliable. Worth the modest expense.*

### Question:

Are doctors trained to look for identifying tattoos and microchips? A friend of mine recently lost her Labrador Retriever, a very valuable show dog as well as a beloved pet, when he broke through the gate and took a walk. She hired the services of a search-and-rescue dog, advertised in the local newspapers, put up flyers all over the area, visited the humane society every day, and *faxed* information about the dog and his identifying tattoo to *every* veterinary clinic in the area. When she located this Lab after three and a half weeks, she was told that the dog had been neutered just a few days previous. The vet who did the neutering was told that the dog was a "stray." I hope vets understand that a pet is a very important family member, and that they should assist in attempting to reunite a lost animal with its family, in much the same way we would work to reunite a lost child with his or her parents.

## DR. NICHOL:

Wow. What a harrowing story. Your friend must have been not only worried sick, but also frustrated. Unless her Lab shows in obedience or tracking, being neutered takes him out of the game completely. You are right about the feelings we have for our pets. They are just like our children. Most of us work very hard to get the family back together when this kind of thing happens.

For those who are not knowledgeable about microchips and tattoos, I will provide a bit of education. Both methods of identification are permanent and each has its advantages. A microchip is implanted by a quick injection of an inert glass-encapsulated, encoded device about the size of a grain of rice. It has no power source, but will relay its unique code back to a "scanner" on a digital display. High tech. Microchips have been around for several years now, and they have enormous value *if* the person who finds a pet gets him or her scanned. Since there is no way to know whether a pet has a microchip under the skin, animal shelters are usually given free scanners by the manufacturers so they can scan every pet upon arrival. Pretty slick.

What about tattoos? You don't need fancy electronic gadgets to find them. (Ask anyone born after 1970.) But if you find one, who do you call? Unless your friend's dog had his owner's phone number on his inner thigh, the veterinarian may not have known where to go next.

What's better? I say both are better. If your local animal-control facility (and every veterinary hospital) has each of the different scanners and uses them all on every pet, and looks for tattoos, more lost pets will get home. To make these systems work, we need to raise the level of awareness. Here is what can be done: Call the National Dog Registry at 1-800-637-3647. Tell them you want informational brochures you can distribute to all area veterinary hospitals, shelters, boarding kennels, and grooming shops. Next, have your pets tattooed or implanted with microchips. Finally, register their permanent identification with the National Dog Registry (they do cats, too). If your lost pet's chip or tattoo gets called into these folks, they will provide your name and phone number to the caller. And if you're real lucky, your dog will arrive home still in possession of the family jewels.

## Anesthetic Safety in an Older Dog

*Age is not a disease. Safety is really a function of health. Complete lab work will resolve the safety question.*

### QUESTION:

My beloved Cairn Terrier is 13 years old and his vet has recommended neutering him to prevent testicular cancer and prostate problems. He will also clean the dog's teeth and remove some warts. Because he's the equivalent of 91 human years, of course I'm worried about Excalibur surviving the surgery and wondering how long his possible life span might be after such surgery (or, for that matter, without it).

### DR. NICHOL:

I can understand your concerns about Excalibur's safety. You love this boy. If he only has a little while longer, why would you put him through the stress? As much as I occasionally disagree with my colleagues, your veterinarian is correct in his recommendations.

I'll start by helping you put Excalibur's age in perspective. He is *not* similar in age to a 91-year-old person. With all deference to folks over 90, I'm betting that your boy can outrun, outjump, and outdance any person over 85. The point is that dogs age much differently than we do.

Small-breed dogs like Cairn Terriers develop quickly as youngsters (they're sexually mature at age 6 or 7 months) and age quite slowly during their middle adult years. When they do get older, the aging process begins to accelerate. By contrast, we humans age at pretty much the same rate throughout our lives. The old 7-years-to-1 comparison doesn't hold up for one more important reason: Modern medicine has allowed us to dramatically extend the active and joy-filled lives of dogs like yours. Shucks, I bet Excalibur still works full-time. On weekends, he parties till he pukes. So, let's not put this pup out to pasture.

Why neuter at his age? Your boy's prostate has suffered a continued hormone onslaught all its life. By now he's at risk for swellings, infections, and even cancers of that male gland. In addition, older unneutered male dogs have a high incidence of tumors and hernias of the rear end. Neutering is good prevention; the sooner, the better.

What about anesthetic risk? Make sure Excalibur gets a thorough exam and lab profile first. At our place, we like to get chest X-rays, an ECG, and a Doppler blood pressure along with blood and urine tests. If he checks out fine and his anesthesia is monitored carefully, he should do as well as a puppy. But have his teeth cleaned a few weeks later. If he has a lot of tartar and gum inflammation, you could put him at risk if other procedures are done at the same time.

You've had this boy in your life for quite a while. If your fears stop you from providing Excalibur the routine preventive maintenance he needs, you'll actually shorten his life. Now is your chance to push out his life expectancy another few years. Go for it.

## Double Dewclaws

*Surgical removal is only necessary for field dogs.*

### QUESTION:

We recently adopted a 6-month-old German Shepherd-mix puppy from an animal shelter. He is double dewclawed on his hind legs. Do they need to be removed? One vet said they should be removed; the other said it's optional. I'm planning on walking him every day in fields and on forest trails, also some rugged hiking in New Hampshire. I understand that removing dewclaws is more of a prophylactic measure—"just in case" they get snagged—as well as cosmetic. (Personally, I don't care what his feet look like!) What are the chances of his ripping or snagging his dewclaws, and could I just throw an Ace wrap in my backpack if that happens, and *then* get them removed?

### DR. NICHOL:

Great question. We hear this one often. I will elucidate for those unfamiliar with this part of the canine anatomy.

Dewclaws are the small, useless, finger-like appendages on the inner aspect of the front legs and, on many dogs, the rear legs, too. They have a normally shaped nail like the other toes. In evolutionary terms, dewclaws are considered vestigial. In other words, they have the same anatomic root as our thumbs and big toes. But in dogs, they are only partially developed. Too bad. If dogs had real thumbs and big toes, they could write, play the piano, and kick a football.

What about surgical removal? You can go either way. But if your dog rips a dewclaw in the woods, he'll be hurtin' for certain. Because the dewclaws are attached to the joint, snagging them is a lot like having your thumb ripped away from your hand. You could just wait for it to happen—but if it does, your boy could bleed a bit, develop a nasty infection, and have a lot of pain. Given your hiking plans, I'd say that prevention is best; have them removed. The last point on dewclaws: If they are not removed, they will not wear down by walking and running like the other nails because they don't reach the ground. Thus, dewclaws need frequent trimming while the other nails may not.

## Nail Trimming

*Long toenails make for painful arthritic feet. Black nails are hard to trim safely. Here is the how-to.*

### QUESTION:

I've recently acquired my deceased mother's dog. I'm taking her to the vet soon to have her checked out and to get shots updated. My question deals with her toenails which are so long that they curve and lay to the side. Can I trim them back to the normal length without causing her any harm? I'm really concerned about her.

### DR. NICHOL:

Caring for your mother's dog is a genuine act of love. Your compassion for that little girl surely comes in part from the example set by your mom. She would be proud.

Taking this pup to the doctor is the way to start out on the right paw. A thorough physical exam may uncover a few more things that need routine maintenance. I recommend carefully following advice on dental care, skin problems, or managing any lumps or masses. This way your mom's dog can stay around for a long time.

Those long, curved nails laying on their sides are twisting the joints in this dog's toes when she walks. Arthritis can result. Buy a Resco nail trimmer at the pet supply store. To make sure that you don't trim her nails too short, look carefully at their shape and color in good light; they will be either black or clear. You're in luck if they're clear, like human nails, because you can see the pink tissue inside that carries the blood supply. If you cut into the pink area, you will cause her to bleed and feel pain. You want to trim off the clear part to a point about an eighth of an inch away from the pink area. So that she's relaxed for her pedicure, give her a rawhide or other snack, and she'll be yours forever. And as long as you're giving her a pedicure, make her feel real special and give her a facial and massage, too.

All of that works great IF her nails are clear. But what if they're black? The internal anatomy of her nails is the same either way but until you have experience knowing where the blood supply is you could make the mistake of cutting them too short. For black nails, I advise you to take a lesson from the staff at the veterinary clinic. Don't try this at home; we're professionals.

# Biting and Fighting

## Food Protection

*Even dogs need their space. Don't push it.*

### QUESTION:

We have the most wonderful Akita puppy, and we have spent an enormous amount of time in obedience school, training him to be a sweet, well-behaved dog. But Kotei is overly protective of his food. Though I disagreed with the obedience trainer, I deferred to her experience and began to do "dominance" exercises, for example, removing his food, then returning it. Things have gone from bad to worse, culminating in his attacking me and biting me. He is so mellow and playful 98 percent of the time. Any advice?

### DR. NICHOL:

You are right to be concerned. One of the underpinnings of canine behavior is the "binge and gorge" eating instinct (yes, that's its real name). While all domestic dogs are descendents of wild canids like wolves, the Huskies, Malamutes, and Akitas are mighty close cousins. They never know in the wild when they will bring down game, so when they do have food, they defend it aggressively.

Those "dominance exercises" really have worsened the problem. Kotei has a natural distrust of anyone who is near his food anyway. Now the person he loves the most is messing with his survival (his perception of it, that is). Please don't feel badly. Getting him to mellow out should not be difficult. Because Kotei is still a youngster, he'll adapt quickly.

Simply put, your assignment is to let the poor guy eat in peace. Put Kotei's bowl in a quiet, isolated place in your home, then close the door. When he finishes eating allow plenty of time before picking up the bowl—whether it's empty or not. Never go near his bowl if he can see you. Follow this plan for the rest of his life.

But wait, doesn't this mean your dog is training you? Well, let me say this about that. Pets are in our lives for mutual benefit and enjoyment. Attempts to "control" anybody will only diminish the relationship. Certainly a dog like Kotei should be well-behaved and manageable (great job with the obedience work), but he is his own dog. Moreover, he is a different species; he shares some emotions with you, but there are differences, too. People who insist on challenging their dogs don't have man's best friend. In fact, they may have a time bomb.

## Biting in Puppies
*Play biting or aggression? Make the right call, then handle it.*

### QUESTION:
Is it proper to hit a puppy on his nose to cure him of biting?

### DR. NICHOL:
No, no, a thousand bites, no. So many people do this that it's actually considered basic to puppy training. But it sends the wrong message and it may create problems.

Before I give you a better solution, you must first determine whether your puppy is just playing or biting aggressively. Puppies who play bite (it's a rare puppy who doesn't) simply need to be taught what to bite instead. I recommend carrying a toy in your pocket. Whenever that young hoodlum starts chewing your hand, shoe, furniture, or priceless Persian rug, first get the toy in one hand and then take the wrong thing away with the other hand. As you pull your soggy, slimy hand or shoe away, say "No!" Immediately pop the toy into his or her mouth and lavishly praise this baby genius as though she had thought of the whole thing herself. Repeat hundreds of times.

Ah, but your puppy is snarling and attacking when he bites you, eh? Bad dog. This is the aggressive biter. If you hit this puppy on the nose, he will interpret your discipline as throwing down the gauntlet. Now you and your new best friend have a duel. Only one of you can walk away with honor. Don't get into a power struggle with your puppy. Instead, remind him that you are the lead dog in his pack. When he tries to bite, quickly grab the scruff of his neck and patiently hold him off the floor until he relaxes. When he (or she) concedes the issue, the lesson is over. Repeat hundreds of times.

You can't do that? I understand. But this is important. Puppyhood is the time when healthy limits can be set. Don't miss this window of opportunity to give your new dog a clear and secure picture of the friendship the two of you will share. If you have any doubts, see a veterinarian with training in behavior medicine. Now is the time to set the right course.

## Aggressive Puppies—Arctic Breeds

*Vicious dogs can be recognized as youngsters. Some can be managed, but the challenge may not be for everyone.*

### QUESTION:

I may be having trouble getting along with my new puppy. She's a 12-week-old Malamute named Cody. Sometimes when I tell her to sit or to stop biting my hand, she seems to get angry at me. She raises her lips and snarls. As soon as I stop trying to get my way, she's nice again. Will she outgrow this? I don't want her acting this way when she's a 75-pound adult dog.

### DR. NICHOL:

I am so glad you are asking for help with Cody now. So many people don't recognize behavior problems in their dogs until much later, which makes it much harder or impossible to manage them. I will help you by first explaining why Cody is doing this.

One of the most important things to any dog is to figure out where he or she fits into the dominance order (or pecking order) in her pack. Don't be confused. Even though Cody is an only pet, she still sees you and other humans in your home as members of a pack. All dogs think this way; but the Arctic breeds like Malamutes, Huskies, and Samoyeds are even more inclined to do so because of their close relation to their wild cousins, the wolves. So, why is Cody acting so tough with you? It's because she likes you just fine, as long as you remember your place, which, in her mind, is beneath her in the dominance order. When she snarls at you, she doesn't really plan to hurt you; she is just telling you that you are supposed to be submissive around her. Cody has it backwards, doesn't she?

I will first tell you what *not* to do to manage Cody's behavior. Do not hit and do not yell. To communicate effectively with a dog, you must use a language that she will understand—instinctively. When dogs interact among themselves, they demonstrate dominance by a few different methods. You could grab the skin on either side of her face and glare into her eyes, then shake her a little and give her a firm "No." While this works with some dogs, I advise against it with a Malamute. These dogs tend to be so set in their perception of their place of dominance that this action may inflame her and cause her to be even more aggressive in return. Instead, do as her mother did when Cody was a baby. Pick her up by the scruff of the neck with one hand and let her hang there until she stops yapping and squirming. You must *not* put her back down until she relaxes. Every time Cody acts tough with you, repeat the neck scruff. Don't shake her. Don't say a word. Don't get angry. Just repeat the correction, hundreds of times if you need to.

Will it work? If you are totally consistent, Cody will be a happier girl growing up knowing what her place is in your life. Our dogs should be willing to change to fit into our lives; not the other way around. What if it still doesn't work? The sad truth is that not every puppy can fit into a home environment. If Cody becomes dangerous, she may not belong with you. Whatever you do, don't let your dog beat up on you without getting help—early.

## Aggressive Puppies—Rottweilers

*Hostility is genetically inherited in many individuals of this breed. You can control the dog, but you may be unable to control the behavior.*

### QUESTION:

My husband and I bought a Rottweiler puppy five weeks ago. We named him Malibu; we got him as a protector and companion for our baby daughter. The problem is that now Malibu is 12 weeks old and he is snapping at our little girl. We love them both, but we can't let our baby daughter be at risk. Can we change Malibu's behavior?

### DR. NICHOL:

This is a very difficult problem. I will do my best to help you, but you may also need a professional examination and consultation to manage Malibu. Until the behavior is well controlled, don't assume anything about your daughter's safety in the presence of the puppy.

The first thing that must be determined is whether Malibu is aggressive toward the baby as a result of fear or because of a natural dominance tendency. One simple test is to observe their interaction: If Malibu tries to escape when the baby approaches him, it is likely that his aggression is fear-related. On the other hand, if Malibu approaches the baby aggressively or snaps when she gets near his food or toys, it is likely to be due to an innately dominant personality. The answer to this question will determine the best method of behavior modification for the puppy. It will also help us to know our chances of success.

What can be done? Number one: Protect your child. **Never** leave the puppy and child together unsupervised. When they are together, keep a wire basket-type muzzle on the puppy—or better still, a "head halter." Head halters are an excellent training aid that give you total control of the dog and allow you to make corrections without causing any pain. When the puppy and your little girl are together, praise them both, as long as the puppy appears calm and relaxed. The emphasis is on rewarding Malibu for tolerating the little girl, not on punishing him for intolerance. Again, to carry this off, you may need professional help.

Remember that it may not be possible to safely keep a child and an aggressive dog in the same home. While many Rottweilers are gentle with children, many others are bred for dominant personalities. If Malibu's dominance is inherited, there will be no way for you to "cure" him. It could be best for him to be placed in a new home.

## Biting and Indoor Urination and Defecation

*Even a small dog can control a household. The "pack," including the humans, must have a leader. The human "top dog" must take charge.*

### QUESTION:

Our Yorkie is the dog from hell. She is a control freak. If we don't go to work at the usual time, she starts barking and acting anxious; the same applies to going to bed at the usual time. If we do something out of the ordinary or something she doesn't seem to like, she pees. She defecates in the doorway around 2:30 a.m. She used to sleep with us until she wet the bed and, on one occasion, bit me on the cheek when I turned over. She also seems to be a fear biter and freely nips at strangers if they try to pet her. If I do something she doesn't like, she will bite me. Strangers coming to the house is another occasion for wetting the floor. I no longer want to put up with the smell, nor do I want to be controlled by a dog.

### DR. NICHOL:

Dog from hell? Such strong language. Kidding aside, your Yorkie has a problem with attention-seeking behavior, and she believes she is the dominant dog in the pack. The pack, by the way, includes you and your husband. How's that for hell (or at least heck)? The good news is that I think there's hope.

Start by scheduling specific times for positive interaction twice daily. You'll need at least 15 minutes each time. Play her favorite game. Your dog loves a predictable schedule. The two of you will look forward to these good times. What's important is that you strengthen your bond with this girl with healthy activities, at the same time rewarding only good behavior.

Biting? Not good. This high-strung Yorkie is anxious. She also believes that acting out in any way she wants, including biting, is okay if it means getting your attention. And, like all dogs, she is committed to the concept of the pack hierarchy. She feels she has a right to take over your bed because she came equipped from birth with a dominant personality. You step out of line, you pay the price. You are right: You have been controlled by a dog. Is this fun or what? Your mission, should you decide to accept it, is to take charge of your pack. Enroll in an obedience training class. The "down" command, in particular, will give you a healthy, dominant position. From your dog's point of view, this will put her in an appropriately submissive posture. You won't change who your dog is, but you will change your relationship with her. Your twice-daily one-on-one sessions will include obedience practice. You'll make it fun. You'll also be the boss.

As far as your dog using your house as a canine bathroom, there is little question that in your dog's case, predictable house soiling is just one more attention-seeking behavior. And, because your girl needs to learn she is of lower rank in your pack, she must be permanently banished from your bedroom. Dogs are naturally den-living creatures. Crate her at night and when you have guests. Her anxiety can be partly corrected with the security of having her own "den."

To help make the transition easy, I recommend that your veterinarian dispense the anti-anxiety drug Clomacalm for several weeks. Don't forget—it's for the dog. Be consistent and patient. Now, get in there and be top dog—and have a good time while you're at it.

## Moderate Aggression Toward Strangers

*A protective dog can be carefully trained to learn appropriate behavior, but is only reliable when controlled.*

### QUESTION:

I think we have a big problem. We have a German Shepherd named Harpo who is about 10 months of age. He's great around our kids and our kids' friends. But just let an adult he doesn't know come around, and he'd like to kill. We didn't think much of it until he spied a lady on the sidewalk across the street. Harpo got down low and then charged across the street and bit her on the derriere. She wasn't badly hurt, but what do we do next time? I'm afraid that if this gets worse, we'll have to get rid of Harpo. What can we do?

## Dr. Nichol:

You are right; you do have a big problem. But it's clear that you love Harpo enough to do what it takes to help him change. I will give you the broad outline of the problem, plus an understanding of how to fix it.

Why would such a sweet guy want to hurt someone? First, remember that Harpo was born with his own personality. We can give him consequences for his behavior, but he will always have the same basic tendencies. Dogs by nature are protective of their territory, and they are predators. Young Harpo has these instincts more strongly than most.

Here's the plan: We start by understanding that the road to success will be a long one. For it to work, Harpo must *not* be permitted to slip back into his old behavior—even once. That means you must prevent him from having any opportunity to do anything aggressive. In other words, don't let him near strangers until he's ready. Next, get him a head halter. This gizmo fits on the dog's head. It has a place under the chin for a lightweight leash that you will have Harpo drag around the house for a few days until he forgets it's there. Next, have a friend who Harpo does not know come to your door. Be ready with your hand on the leash. As soon as Harpo even begins to act aggressively, you pull down on the leash, causing Harpo's head to come down and his mouth to close. Have your friend back away immediately so as to reduce Harpo's aggression. As soon as Harpo stops his angry behavior, hand him a treat. Repeat this set up until Harpo behaves better; then have your friend come closer. When Harpo repeats his aggression, you respond again by pulling down on the head halter, then rewarding him with a treat when he relaxes. Gradually you'll train him to think positive thoughts (associated with food) when strangers come by. In addition, you will be teaching him to become less dominant.

What happens when you're not there to correct Harpo? Remember the story about Pavlov's dogs? Pavlov rang a bell just before feeding enough times that the dogs began to salivate whenever they heard the bell—even if there was no food. In other words, Harpo will begin to associate feelings of pleasure with the appearance of strangers if you do the "counterconditioning" gradually—like over several weeks to months. But what if we go "too far"? Will Harpo quit being protective at all? Not to worry. Your dog's protective nature is deeply ingrained. He will always protect his family. What if Harpo doesn't want to change? Well, how many Californians does it take to change a light bulb? It only takes one, but that light bulb really has to want to change.

## Severe Aggression Toward Visitors

*A dog who is dangerous is best confined when guests are expected. For potentially vicious dogs, attempts at behavior modification are pointless.*

### QUESTION:

Our Akita puppy, Kotei, is now 9 months old and 93 pounds, and has decided to become ultraterritorial. No one but myself and my wife are acceptable in the house. When visitors come, he becomes aggressive and goes into his attack mode, growling and trying to get at them to bite them. There must be something we can do to break this destructive habit. Locking him up every time someone comes over seems to me to send the wrong message to the dog, angering him even more. We don't want to lose him.

### DR. NICHOL:

You are smart to take Kotei's aggression seriously. But he didn't "decide" to become territorial. The reality is that, like the cat who compulsively hunts birds, your boy is simply being himself. He believes he owns you, your wife, and your home. No one else belongs there. Not all dogs are this way, but this individual is.

Here is what you can change and what you cannot: You can correct a dog's relationship with you by being his pack leader. But trying to make him less territorial or protective will fail because you will be asking Kotei to be someone he is not. His personality was genetically wired into his hard drive when he was conceived. He is who he is.

But you *can* manage him. Train Kotei to use a crate (an instinctive den). Put him in his crate, away from the public areas of your home, when you expect guests. An outdoor run could work fine, too. Treat him like a dog when you need to. It won't upset him. Despite your desire to make him a person (which he is on many levels), he is also a dog.

## Biting of the Human Family

*Confusion over the dominance order often results in dogs who bite to rule the roost. Take charge the healthy, effective way.*

## QUESTION:

We have an 18-month-old female spayed Beagle. She is a wonderful dog in many ways; however, she growls, snaps, and lately I fear she will actually bite me when she gets a hold of something she isn't supposed to have. When I approach her to get whatever it is out of her mouth, she starts growling, has her jaws shut so tight it's impossible to pry them open, and lately will get very mean and lash out at my hand to bite me. Is this something that can be corrected, or is it hopeless and do we need to find a new home for our dog?

## Dr. Nichol:

It's really unsettling to find yourself afraid of someone you love. You folks consider your dog a member of the family. But she threatens you when you try to take something away from her. Here is the problem: Dogs are very much like us and, at the same time, they are quite different. Unbeknownst to you, this Beagle has determined that you are beneath her in the dominance order.

Nonsense, you say? Again, never assume that dogs are identical to us. All dogs view the other creatures in their group as members of their pack. Because dogs are born with an innate sense of their dominance or submissiveness, they find their place in a pack right from the start. Your Beagle loves you just fine. But since she feels you are beneath her in the hierarchy, you must be put in your place when you get out of line.

Upside down, isn't it? So take charge. Show this goofy dog that she has it all wrong. But be sure to communicate in the language that a dog understands. She will comprehend neither a lecture nor physical punishment. In fact, hitting her will only agitate her and add to the problem. (I shudder to think what she would do to this page if you asked her to read my words of wisdom.) Instead, get a head halter from your veterinarian or pet supply dealer and have her wear it continuously. When she attempts to bite you, simply pull on the lead and the head halter will put her in a submissive posture, reminding her that she takes orders from you and not vice versa. A head halter works because it speaks directly to the submissive side of her personality. No pain is involved. With enough repetition, she should understand the true order of dominance in your pack. If you still have trouble, find a veterinarian with training and experience in dominance aggression. Please don't give up.

# Behavior Changes, Like Biting, in Older Dogs

*Biting may be a serious sign of physical disease or pain. A thorough health evaluation is essential to getting your old friend back again.*

## QUESTION:

I am in a terrible situation and I hope you can help me. My wife and I have an older dog, about 10 years old, who has been considered a member of the family. The problem is that she has started to bite us. We love her and we want her to stop, but the problem is that we are afraid of her now. We are both elderly and we are afraid that if she bites us badly the infection could be very serious. We are thinking of having her put to sleep. This decision is tearing us up. We don't feel we are going to be able to find a home for an older dog, especially one with this problem. Are we making the right decision?

## DR. NICHOL:

You are in an extremely difficult situation. It is very hard to consider euthanasia for a pet. It's bad enough when the pet has a terminal disease. But with a dog whose behavior has become unacceptable, it feels even worse.

First, while changes in a dog's behavior are most often psychological, there are some physical causes that need to be considered. It would be great if our pets could talk; but since the medical history must be gotten from you instead of from your dog, you must be observant. Watch this old girl carefully to see if she walks in circles. Look for a tilt of her head, a tendency to bump into things, or to press her head into the corner of the room. Also watch to see if she acts confused or deaf. Does she act as if she's in pain when she gets up or lies down? Does she cry when moving? Does she shake her head? If any of these symptoms are present, there may be a physical reason for your dog's bad behavior. Can we do anything to help with this kind of problem? Often, we can.

If her biting is caused by pain or aging changes, there are several methods of improving her quality of life. There are medications such as Rimadyl and Anipryl that may help. In addition, there are veterinarians who are knowledgeable in acupuncture and other holistic therapies. So if it's pain we need to manage, you may be able to keep your beautiful old dog.

What if she has a brain tumor? Admittedly, some of these are untreatable, making euthanasia the only option. But with CT scans and MRIs, we can get remarkably good images of the inside of the brain, and, yes, some brain tumors are operable and curable.

Here is what I suggest: Take this cranky old bird to her veterinarian for a thorough physical exam. Tell the doctor if there are "yes" answers to any of the above questions. If she has pain, have her X-rayed and ask for ways to make her comfortable. On the other hand, if she has signs of a brain lesion, get a referral to a veterinary neurologist for diagnosis and treatment.

If she is physically normal, you have a tough decision to make. I have to agree that finding a home for an old dog who bites is next to impossible. Further, you can't put yourself and your wife at risk of serious injury. While there are behavior-modification methods for biting dogs, there is never a guaranteed cure. In your situation, having your dog put to sleep may be the only decent option, even though it is extremely hard to say goodbye to man's best friend.

There are many good reasons to euthanize a pet. I have had to do this more times than I can count, and it is still just as hard as it was the first time. I always find myself searching for an alternative, but it usually comes down to a pet owner making the right decision for their pet and for their family. Because it requires such soul searching, sacrifice, and courage to make the decision to euthanize, it should never be judged by others. In the end, it is part of the responsibility of taking on the care of a pet. If we really love our pets, we must make choices—even hard ones. We must also keep ourselves and other family members safe.

I admire your sensitivity and your fortitude. Do not have your dog put down until you and your wife know deep down that you are at peace with your decision. But when you are ready, move ahead with resolve. This is very hard. You and your beloved old dog are in my prayers.

## Biting Children

***While this is never tolerable, it can be managed. Get serious early, and restructure the family "dog pack."***

### QUESTION:

My husband and I have a Jack Russell Terrier who has been a part of our little family since he was a baby three years ago. He's always been a bit feisty, but we figured that was part of being a terrier. Now we have our first baby. Our dog, Johnny, has been allowed to do anything he wants. He sleeps with us, but sometimes growls when he is disturbed in bed or on the couch. He's even bitten us a few times.

**When he acts tough, we turn him on his back and hold him there until he stops growling. Now that the baby is crawling, she upsets him, too. Yesterday, Johnny bit the baby but not badly. What should we do?**

## DR. NICHOL:

I can tell that you've been doing your best to manage Johnny. By holding him on his back, you have tried to show him that you are the top dogs in his pack. He recognizes this when he finally stops his growling, but he continues to repeat his behavior. Now, of course, your problem has become much more important with the addition of your new human child. Let's try to make some sense of all this.

Being a terrier can be a tough business. These little rascals have been bred to be tenacious and strong-willed, so we can't blame Johnny for being who he is. On the other hand, he must learn proper decorum if he wants to avoid military school. Here's the plan: Manage Johnny as though he were a dog. In other words, we will use communication concepts that he understands instinctively. This will make Johnny be good.

We'll start by reminding Johnny of who the top dogs in the pack really are: *all* humans, even the little ones. Now, I know this goes against the grain of our modern American culture. We enlightened beings treat everyone the same, right? No second-class citizens. Well, I, too, cling firmly to these beliefs, but you and I aren't dogs. (Okay, I am very dog-like, but I can tell that most other people are not.) Johnny, a true dog, knows that finding one's place in the pecking order is of major importance. Your mission, should you choose to accept it, is to teach him that while his dog-like attitudes are fine, he is *not* at the top of the heap. And while it will be time consuming for you to teach him this, you can do it.

You will begin his training (brainwashing?) by banishing Johnny not only from your bed, but from your bedroom as well. Next, you will feed him twice daily in a separate room, picking up his bowl only after he has walked away from it. I also suggest that Johnny have his toys only when he is alone. Are we punishing poor Johnny? Nope. Instead we are showing him that only those above him in the dominance order enjoy fun things when they are with the pack (family). When he is alone, he can do what he wants.

This isn't harsh. It won't stay this way. As Johnny learns his new place in the pack, you will gradually allow him to play with you higher dogs. But when other pack members (people) are present, he will get fed and rewarded last. All human dogs will come first. Johnny will eventually accept his new place, but you must always watch this guy. He will never stop wanting to be top dog. Not only must you frequently reinforce these lessons, you must also carefully watch him around your children. You need to be especially vigilant when your children's friends come to visit.

I know this is a lot to accept. It was pretty simple living with Johnny before the baby. Now things have changed. To succeed you will need an important tool called a head halter. This will help because you can use it to put Johnny's head in a submissive posture when he starts to get aggressive. While all of this is doable, Johnny will never be "cured." He will always be ready to reassume his former dominance, possibly putting innocent children at risk. So in addition to all of the above, I recommend building a run outside so that Johnny can be kept out of trouble when you adults are not available to control this boy.

Because this behavior problem will require lifelong management, I suggest you consider carefully whether you really want to pursue it. If not, you can keep Johnny outside or find him a new home. I know this is hard. It's clear that Johnny is very special to you both.

## A Dog Easily Startled Can Be Dangerous

*Dogs are born with their own unique personalities. Easily frightened dogs may bite. But we can teach new behavior, making them safer to be around.*

### QUESTION:

I have a 2-year-old Great Dane. He's very playful and loving, but he is very much a one-person dog. The problem is that he is very easily spooked. He's real jumpy sometimes when you touch him. He also growls in his sleep and sometimes starts awake barking or angry. He does not like strangers and even barks at people he knows if they look unfamiliar, like if they have on a hat or sunglasses. I have at times wondered if this is just a behavioral problem, or if there may be a medical issue. He does worry me, and I don't take him out in public without a muzzle. Thank you for your help.

### DR. NICHOL:

This is a fairly common problem and it is often found in the Great Dane. Your dog is inherently nervous, but I am confident that his problem can be managed. While his aggressive behavior is not acceptable and can be improved, his jumpy nature will always remain a part of who he is. To be sure that we are applying the correct method of management, we must distinguish between fear or anxiety, and true nastiness. Because you describe your boy as reacting this way only when startled, we will assume his behavior to be motivated by fear.

So, now that we know why he does this, what can be done? I'm glad you asked. Our method of improving your boy's odious behavior is called counterconditioning. Be assured that it will help, but it will also take time and patience. It's simple because we will replace his feelings of fear when startled with a pleasant emotion—eating a snack, and I don't mean someone's hand.

Understand that fear and the pleasure of eating are two feelings that cannot coexist in the dog at the same time. Have some treats in your pocket at all times. Try to anticipate when your dog is likely to act out his nervousness. As soon as you feel he is starting to get anxious, have him sit or lie down, then offer him a treat. Reward his good behavior immediately by speaking soothingly to him. In this way, you will reinforce his new optimism. The trick is to give him the treat early, *before* he behaves aggressively.

Easy? Sure. But you must be consistent for this to work. This means your dog must never get another chance to act out his fear—even when you are not at home. Your mission is to house him in such a way as to prevent all surprises unless you are right next to him with the treats.

## Aggression Between Dogs

*Fighting is seldom truly dangerous, unless the humans get involved. Understand why dogs must do this, and be observant.*

### QUESTION:

We have four dogs, all of whom have been spayed or neutered, and who always got along very well. About a week ago, one dog started to act like she was afraid to go outside with the other dogs. Then, a few days ago, without warning, she was attacked by one of the other dogs, who seemed to be doing his level best to kill her: His jaws were locked onto her neck, she was screaming in absolute terror, and it took three people and a garden hose to pry him loose. We've tried putting them together a couple of times since, but both became rigid and started to tremble and it appeared that the slightest movement would set off another bloody melee. (By the way, the only blood shed in the previous encounter was by me and my wife.) We are afraid that the only way to ensure peace and doggie safety is to put the attacker up for adoption. We would be most grateful for your advice.

## Dr. Nichol:

I know how terrifying this must have been for you. There was no way for you to know whether one of your beloved pets was about to be killed. I would never promise you that it could not happen, but in cases like this injuries are rare. I will explain.

Dogs in a group are, in their minds, living in a pack. As such, they are subject to all of the instincts that any wild dog or wolf has. Essential to their social structure is a dominance hierarchy. Now we enlightened Americans don't condone the idea that some of us are better than others or that the person on the bottom rung of the ladder deserves to be dominated. Our dogs, on the other hand, live with a very different reality. Yes, we love them partly because they are so much like us; but there are differences that we must accept. This means allowing the dominant dogs to dominate and the submissive dogs to submit. Except when two dogs disagree on who should be the leader of the pack, they all find comfort in their positions—including the dogs on the bottom of the heap.

So, what should you do? Accept their dogness. Do not interfere, and do not show favor to a submissive dog in the presence of his or her superior. If you try to level the playing field, you could spark a genuinely bloody melee. Oh, and by the way, keep all of your dogs. They are not trying to hurt your feelings. They're just being who they are: dogs in a pack. But to keep it simple, I will give you a few dos and don'ts.

- Do not feed them together. Two dogs who each want to be dominant are almost guaranteed to fight over food. Feed them at the same time, but in separate locations so they can't see each other.

- Do not become a part of the politics by giving them treats or playing with them when they are together. When they finally work it out some day, you can try playing with the dogs when they are together.

- Do not try to break them up—you are likely to get bitten in the frenzy. If you must stop them, use a hose.

One final word on brawling dogs: If you join the fray, the blood shed will be yours. Except in rare cases, the results are limited to the swapping of slobber.

# Fighting Between Father and Son

*Pack dominance is not set in stone. The political deck can be reshuffled. Here is how to manage it.*

## QUESTION:

I have a problem with my two West Highland White Terriers. They are father and son and have always lived with us. The father is 7 years old and neutered, and the son is 3 years old and unneutered. They got along very well the first two years of the son's life, since the younger dog was submissive to his father. For the last year, we have had to keep them separated because the father tries to attack the son, and the son will not back down. It is difficult to keep them apart and we hate to keep them crated to prevent fighting. Thank you very much for considering our problem.

## DR. NICHOL:

This is an extremely hard situation for you. You love these boys, yet they continue trying to hurt one another. But it will be your love for them that will drive your success in managing their dominance conflicts.

Why are they enemies when once they were such friends? Let's start with the basics. Number one: This has nothing to do with their being father and son. It does have a lot to do with their being males and Westies. That's because, way back when terriers were developed as a breed, their aggression was prized. Terrier breeders selected for it. (A few still do.) On top of that, they are male dogs with dominant personalities. Their interest in establishing leadership of this dog pack is a major priority with these hoodlums. But take heart, I think there is promise.

Your first move is simple: Neuter the younger dog. While any dog can get into dominance aggression, unneutered males have that annoying hormone problem that just adds fuel to the fire. Won't this just increase his risk of getting bullied? No; instead, he is likely to be less interested in standing up to his old man. Since it is clear that the son was born with a less dominant personality, he may simply go along with his dad's dominance gestures, which is the way dominance hierarchies in dog packs are really supposed to function.

What if neutering the younger kid doesn't fix the whole problem? It might not, so be ready for the next step: Watch these guys closely and you will see behaviors of yours that trigger the brawls. My guess is that if you feed or show affection to the son in the presence of the father, the old guy might start to whup on the youngster. Instead, make it a habit never to feed them together. Never show affection to the son in the presence of the father. Do give the dad some love when the kid is around. In other words, reinforce the father's dominance and the son's lower rank. (But when the old grouch is elsewhere, you can treat the kid any way you want.)

Is this fair? Not by human standards. But remember that as much as you have bonded to these boys, they are still dogs with all dog behavior as standard equipment. They thrive on a predictable dominance order. Part of your job will be to play along with it, consistently. One last thing: You are a major player in the dominance hierarchy of this pack. That's because it really isn't a two-dog pack, but a three-dog pack. The lead dog is you. Just don't let all that power go to your head.

## The Worst Horror: The Family Dogs Kill a Family Cat

*"Normal" pack behavior can take over the sweet nature of trusted dogs. Understanding who and what our pets are can help prevent tragedy.*

### QUESTION:

Thank you for writing so compassionately about animals. I am truly hoping that you might have some insight into a problem we are having with our animals. Paul had three cats and each of us has a dog. We had lived together for only four months with the dogs before we introduced the cats onto the scene. Paul's dog had lived with the cats before, so he was somewhat used to them, although there had always been some antagonism. My dog had not been around cats much, and mostly seemed curious around them. Nonetheless, we chose to slowly introduce the animals to each other in the house. We would bring the dogs to the cats' room and have them sit and look at each other, try to talk to them about how they had to try to be friends, and so on. The two dogs had become quite a pair, meanwhile. They did everything together. One night we came home to find that the dogs had literally busted the lock on the bedroom door, burst into the room, and had killed Eno, Paul's pride-and-joy cat. It was really traumatic. We banned the dogs from the house entirely. We have yelled at them and yelled at ourselves for not somehow being wiser in this situation. We just couldn't believe they could do such a thing.

**We don't trust them; don't know if they could do this again; don't know if they know exactly what they did wrong, although we think they know. Do we find the remaining cats new homes? Could we bear to give up the dogs? What can we do?**

## DR. NICHOL:

Wow, this is as tragic as it gets. I have known of similar situations, but this has to be the worst nightmare for any pet owner. We love our pets like children. How could this happen? How could dogs raised in such caring homes be capable of such savagery?

If we can distance ourselves from this horror for a moment, it is possible to understand and even predict this event. Remember what dogs are and what they are not. We raise them and develop their personalities as though they were people, just like us. Their feelings are like ours in so many ways; but there are differences that we must accept. These are instincts that are as fundamental as the parts we love. And among the irrefutable facts of dog life are pack behavior and predation.

This sounds frightening. Hasn't the stuff of *Call of the Wild* been bred out of domestic dogs? Yes, to some degree, in some breeds, but it is alive and well in most. In the case of your dogs, we have a pair who "did everything together" and, I suspect, were led by the dog with a history of antagonism toward cats. Once the hunt started, pack behavior took over. Worse still, they enjoyed hunting in a pack. Given the opportunity, you can bet they will repeat the scenario. They seem guilty about it only because, at the same time, they love you and want to please you. They know you are angry.

Confused? Don't be. We dog lovers have a hard time believing that man's best friend could be so inhuman. Remember, here are differences that must be accepted. Your dogs only did what was natural for them. Your next step is preventing a repetition. Here are the hard facts. Dogs who have tasted the thrill of the chase should never be trusted with cats again—even when they are not with "the pack." As much as they are now incurable cat killers, they are no more likely to harm a human. Be sure that both dogs are neutered and are always kept as solitary pets with no exposure to cats.

I know there is nothing I can say to lessen your pain, but you are in the company of a great number of pet lovers. All of us share your loss. Know that by sharing your story, you have helped others to see the early warning signs. God bless you.

# Breeding and Reproductive Organs

## Testing for Ovulation

*The Target test is less than 100-percent accurate, but it has value for timing a breeding.*

### Question:

Hi, my name is Junice and my question is regarding the use of the Target test in bitches to check when they are ovulating or in season. How does it work? What is the concept behind it?

### Dr. Nichol:

Junice, does your mother know you talk this way? Quick, somebody get me a bar of soap!

Junice, you are an informed bitch owner. (Yes, I said it. For our sensitive readers who are unfamiliar with the real use of the term "bitch," it means nothing other than an unspayed female dog. It is not a verb. It is used most commonly by dog breeders.)

Now that we know what and who we are talking about, let's get down to business. The Target test that Junice is asking about is used in the onsite laboratories of veterinary hospitals to determine the best time to breed a dog. Let's start with a little basic reproductive physiology. The average female dog has a reproductive cycle that is about six months in length. The most important part of the cycle is ovulation, when the eggs are released by the ovaries. It is useful to know when a dog is ovulating because this is the best time for breeding. The Target test can predict this event by measuring the rising blood levels of the hormone progesterone. The test is also useful in letting us know when the mother-to-be is no longer ovulating, thus making it useless to have her bred.

Why is all of this important? Many breeders ship dogs long distances for breeding, or need to time breedings based on show schedules. Or in some cases the bitch won't let the male dog breed her. So if you need to know when the time is right for a quick weekend tryst or simply for successful artificial insemination, you need to have reliable information.

What about accuracy? The Target test uses a method known as ELISA. The test is easy to run and is about 70-percent accurate. And this is fine for natural breedings or artificial insemination if the father-to-be is right there on the scene. That's because fresh dog sperm stay viable for five to six days after breeding, thus giving them plenty of time to find the eggs of their dreams. But what about long-distance parenting using frozen semen? I'm glad you asked. Frozen sperm, once thawed, is good for only up to 12 hours. For that we need accuracy that can only be achieved using the RIA method available at a full-size veterinary lab.

Either way, Junice, breed your bitch two days after the test turns positive. Now, don't we all feel better knowing that we can use that word in polite company?

## Bleeding from the Penis
*Prostate disease and cancer are serious. Get medical attention soon.*

### QUESTION:
I have a dog who is 7 years old and, for a couple of years now, he's been bleeding from his penis. At first it wasn't much, but now it's getting worse. We put gauze on top of his penis and a bandage around his waist, but it still bled, sometimes not much and sometimes more. I don't know what to do anymore. Please help us; we love our dog.

### DR. NICHOL:
This is a very important problem; I'm glad your wrote in. There are many possible causes for this bleeding, including prostate disease and cancers of the penis. But considering how long it's been going on, I would suspect that your dog has a long-standing bladder infection that may also involve bladder stones.

It will be impossible for you to help this dog unless you take him to the doctor. Do your best to prevent him from urinating for a few hours before his appointment so that the doctor can get a sample for urinalysis and culture. X-rays of his abdomen and blood tests will also be important. Allow your dog's doctor to carry out whatever testing is needed. Taking shortcuts to save expense will only prolong your beloved friend's misery; they could even cost him his life. Don't delay.

## Breeding for the Young and Restless

*Everything you ever wanted to know about dog breeding, but were afraid to ask.*

### QUESTION:

My family and I got a 7-month-old Boxer this weekend. And of course, wouldn't you know, she is in heat! My first question is: How long does a heat usually last? Also, we plan to breed her once. Obviously, we should wait for her second heat, or will she still be too immature at that time?

### DR. NICHOL:

Congratulations on your new baby. Boxers are such fun dogs. They always seem happy to see anyone. Here's the skinny on reproduction in the adolescent Boxer: Seven months of age is about average for a female dog of this size to have her first heat, or reproductive, cycle. From the time her vaginal discharge is first noticed until the end of the "heat" period is usually 18 to 21 days. It is as short as 14 days for smaller dog breeds.

Breed now or later? If she is an unwed adolescent, I recommend abstinence, of course. Just say no. But you are right about the second estrus (heat) cycle. With most of these girls cycling approximately every six months, she will be over one year of age at that time and she can be a December bride.

But why in the heck do you want to breed her in the first place? If you've been told that having a litter of puppies is important to the maturity or health of a young bitch (sorry, that's the proper name), you have been misinformed. Not only are there no benefits to your girl from this exercise, allowing her to endure repeated estrus cycles will only serve to increase her risk of breast cancer. In fact, unspayed dogs have triple the risk of women. On the other hand, if you have eight or a dozen friends who won't be able to live another day without one of her puppies, go ahead and breed her. But do have her spayed when her days as a love slave are over.

## Badly Timed Pregnancy: How to Know and What to Do About It

*Pregnancy is difficult to diagnose in the first month but is best left to proceed normally. Here are the alternatives.*

## QUESTION:

My 10-month-old Lab recently finished her first heat. Is there a way to tell whether a dog got her pregnant? I am hoping she is not because I only want purebred Labs. Is there a method to abort dog pregnancies?

## DR. NICHOL:

Can she talk about it? Is she craving pickles or chocolate? Here's the straight story: Pregnancy (gestation) is 62 to 63 days long in dogs. Because of its short duration, there has been no reliable pregnancy test developed for use in dogs. What we can do is feel (palpate) her abdomen. After the 28th day, the fetuses are big enough for us to give an answer. What we cannot know is whether they are purebred Labs until they are born. The greater question is: How important is it to know?

It has been felt by many people that it may be a mistake to allow a dog to have puppies after her first heat (reproductive) cycle. I have to agree that some of these youngsters may lack the maturity to mother their babies. Lord knows, most dogs this age aren't even out of high school yet. But more often than not, they do just fine anyway. The mothering instinct is pretty strong.

What about finding good homes for crossbred puppies? If the puppies are of mixed ethnicity, there will be plenty of deserving homes willing to adopt a multicultural dog. And having a mixed-breed litter now will have no influence on your dog's ability to deliver purebred Labrador Retrievers later. That assumes, of course, that Mr. Right will not be concerned about a woman with a past.

Abortion of the litter? Yes, this is possible, using injections that are given in the veterinary hospital. It would require your dog to stay for a few days. The process is uncomfortable for the dog and may carry some risk. It is not recommended and is generally unnecessary. You can instead choose to let her deliver the babies. As soon as they are 7 to 12 weeks of age, it should be easy to place them with good families. In fact, many people prefer mixed-breed dogs because of their lower tendency toward birth defects.

The last reason to let this young lady go ahead with this possible pregnancy is that it will give both of you a chance to learn the ins and outs of the delivery and neonatal process. To get you and your mother-to-be on the road to a healthy reproductive adventure, be sure to have her examined by her doctor soon. In addition, to a confirmation of the pregnancy, I advise you to ask lots of questions. Within a day or two of delivery, return to your veterinarian's office with the whole family (you can leave Dad, the irresponsible lout, at home) to make sure that Mama and her uterus are fine. At that time, the babies will also be checked for problems. I say let nature take its course, but get good hands-on medical advice while you're at it.

## Spaying

***It prevents more unwanted puppies. It also protects against breast cancer and uterine disease.***

### QUESTION:

I just got a Golden Retriever. She has just gone into heat. What can I do to keep the mess off the carpet and from getting it all over the house? I am struggling with the issue of whether or not to have her neutered. She is an inside dog and will be put outside come spring, due to my asthma and my son's asthma. That leads me to the next question: What can I do about the handfuls of hair that come off her each day? I vacuum, and in no time you can't tell that I did it. Please help!

### DR. NICHOL:

I don't do vacuuming and I don't do windows. I just want to get that straight, in case you're asking for a house call.

The answer to your dog's heat periods is simple. If you know folks who cannot live another day without a puppy from your Golden Retriever, then breed her if you must. On the other hand, if you have no plans to add more dogs to a world with an already tragic oversupply, spaying is the only way to go. The procedure, an ovariohysterectomy, will eliminate her risk of breast cancer and infections of the uterus. Both diseases are far more common in unspayed dogs than in people. Spaying will also allow you to enjoy your beautiful Retriever without those annoying boyfriends of hers with their empty promises of undying love. And she'll be much cleaner.

Regarding dog hair, take this girl to the groomer. Explain that you want her undercoat stripped out. A haircut will reduce the shedding even more. In addition you can ask the groomer to train you on effective brushing and combing to eliminate even more mess. To reduce the airborne dander, apply a product called Allerpet D to her coat. This will reduce the asthma problems.

I hope it's not all too much for you. Dogs can cost a few bucks to maintain and eat up a bit of your time, too. But nowhere else can you get the love and fulfillment that only a dog can give. Golden Retrievers are among God's greatest gifts to pet lovers. Congratulations.

## Can Females Be Overbred?
*Some advice on pacing, and a healthy retirement for Mom.*

### QUESTION:
As a woman and dog owner, I can't comprehend making my Border Collie pregnant over and over again for the money. I feel it's such a betrayal of my gender. Have you come across females who have been constantly overbred? What condition were they in?

### DR. NICHOL:
I understand your concern. There are animal breeders who will turn out litters nonstop without regard for the mother's well-being. It's a mistake. Having said that, if the mother is given a high-quality diet and good care, she is likely to do okay.

So what's best? The conventional wisdom for optimal health and production (if your dog is a puppy factory) is to breed her on two successive heat cycles, followed by a rest of one cycle. Then repeat. Spaying around age 7 usually gives a working mother a decent retirement. Then she can spend her golden years knitting booties and fawning over her grandpuppies.

Do I agree with all this? Hey, I'm a "pets as children" person. I spay and neuter early, read to them at night, send them to school, and give them human names like Raoul and Peter Rabbit.


## A Dog Who Appears to Be Pregnant May Really Be in False Pregnancy
*Hormones can play tricks on the body and on the mind.*

### QUESTION:
My dog Miranda has been out of heat for about ten days. She is only 11 months old and we were very careful about watching her. We never saw any dogs anywhere near our yard while she was in heat. But she is acting a little strange since she began her heat. She is kind of lazy, lying around a lot. Also, her nipples are swollen. Is it possible she could be pregnant? Do we have to go to the vet for some kind of test?

## Dr. Nichol:

You describe a scandalous situation. I'm sure you know that this type of teen pregnancy occurs in the best families but I bet you always thought it could never happen to yours—and she seemed like such a nice girl.

Now that we have dealt with the social stigma, we can discuss what's really going on. Either Miranda is pregnant or she is not. In either case, she could act as if she is. That's because she may be having a false pregnancy, or pseudocyesis, for those of us who insist on sounding intelligent.

Here's what happens: When the ovary releases an ova (egg), a structure forms called a corpus luteum. Its job is to secrete the hormone progesterone. In the event of a fertile breeding, progesterone keeps the environment in the uterus right for carrying the puppies. It also puts into motion the release of other hormones that cause the mammary glands to develop, the body to retain fluid, even behavioral changes like nesting and mothering. Normally, if mating does not occur, the corpus luteum just goes away and nothing changes. If it stays around too long, you have a dog like Miranda who thinks and acts like she's in a family way. She might even start to mother a toy and protect it, fiercely.

While it may sound alarming, this charade will last only several weeks, after which time she will suddenly stop this nonsense. Her hormone levels will become normal again and her body will say "just kidding." How cruel.

Some dog owners want treatment for false pregnancy. We can give hormones to make it stop, but it is likely to reoccur after her next heat cycle anyway. It is harmless and it will resolve by itself. It will have no impact on her fertility. If Miranda is bred, she is likely to deliver a normal litter. But false pregnancy is tough on fathers. It's hard to know whether you need to start that college fund or not.

How can you know for sure? Since pregnancy is short (63 days) in dogs, no test has been developed. If you must know as soon as possible, you can have an ultrasound, or wait until she would be 45 days pregnant and have her X-rayed. Or you can just wait. If your girl starts knitting little booties—well, who needs fancy tests at that point?

While there are hormonal remedies for this condition, none are truly safe. False pregnancies are self-limiting. Girls who go through this often repeat the process after subsequent reproductive cycles, but they are just as likely to conceive a "real" litter of puppies if they are bred by Mr. Right.

## Neutering a Male Dog

*Age doesn't matter much, unless you need a macho man in the yard.*

### Question:

I have a 5-1/2-month-old male puppy. Do you recommend neutering this young? Are there any adverse effects? I have never had a dog this young neutered before, and have heard that the lack of hormones may affect their growth, especially males.

### Dr. Nichol:

You are not alone in your concern. Age at the time of neutering used to be considered an influence on growth, but it is now understood that it doesn't matter at all. Just have it done before your boy develops nasty habits like brawling and chasing floozies. While humane associations usually do it when these guys are still kids (as young as 6 weeks old), you can wait until he becomes a man if you want to.

How do you know when he's a real man? When he hikes his leg to urinate on all things he claims for his own, of course. This may be important to you if you have a nice lawn and prefer not to have him squatting to relieve himself, which will kill spots of grass. If this macho stuff means a lot in your home, allow him to own this bit of machismo for at least a few weeks before neutering. That way he will always strut his stuff—even though he will no longer really have his stuff.

## Neonatal Care for Mom and Puppies

*Feeding, bedding, housing, and vaccinations for the whole family.*

### Question:

Our Black Lab just had eight puppies. She is being a super mom. To me she looks real thin. Is this normal? Also, what kind of diet should she be on? We are putting a heat lamp on them at night. They are inside a calf hut with straw in it. When it comes down to the time that they are 6 weeks old and we want to give them their shots, can you tell us what they need? This is just all new to us. I want to thank you so much for helping us out.

### Dr. Nichol:

Thanks for asking. Your questions help get important information to other folks who need to know about this. There is an important reason why this mamma is thin. It takes an enormous amount of calories to produce milk for eight rapidly growing puppies. So feed a high-quality puppy food like Science Diet; your veterinarian has it. Have it near her at all times. This is not just for energy. Science Diet has the correct ratio of calcium to phosphorus for a milk producer like this mom dog. A calcium deficiency in a nursing dog can result in eclampsia, which causes seizures.

*Housing:* It's fine for them to be outside, but please lose the heat lamp. For normal development and the well-being of this whole family, they need a normal day–night light cycle. If the hut is free of drafts and keeps out the rain, they should do fine. *Bedding*: Straw can cause trouble because it retains bacteria. The puppies and their mother can get infections. Use old sheets or towels that you can launder daily.

*Vaccinations*: Great idea. Have your veterinarian give a distemper–measles plus a separate high-titer parvo at 6 to 8 weeks of age. Booster with a distemper–parvo combination in three weeks, then again three weeks later. *Do not* buy your own vaccine. We see lots of vaccine failures this way. Don't put the babies at risk. Finally, you can bathe the puppies once before finding them homes, but, please, don't throw the babies out with the bath water.

## Vaginitis Is Often Caused by Straw Bedding
*Cloth bedding is easy to launder and is much safer. It's also more comfy.*

### Question:

Our family has an 8-year-old Golden Retriever named Macaroni. She would much rather be outside, even in cold weather. But when we put a rug in her doghouse, she drags it out, so a few weeks ago I put straw in there. Now she has a discharge from her vagina and she is licking that area a lot. Could the straw be causing that?

### Dr. Nichol:

This is a tough problem. We love our pets and we want them to be as comfortable as possible in the cold weather. But there is no question that some bedding can cause trouble.

First, I'll give you the reasons to avoid straw and sawdust for bedding: Both of these can retain dust, so pets exposed to them tend to have respiratory problems. In addition, both straw and sawdust retain bacteria that can cause the vaginitis Macaroni has. They can also be responsible for infections of the breasts (mastitis) in nursing mother dogs, as well as infections of the sheath of the penis in male dogs. Finally, straw is not very absorbent.

Instead, my best advice is to go back to the idea of putting a rug in Macaroni's doghouse. Not only will it absorb moisture, it can be easily laundered. Unfortunately, it doesn't do any good if she keeps dragging it out. I have known other dogs who have done this. Most of them are bored and throw their bedding around for fun. I suggest you give Macaroni some toys. Hard nylon chew toys like Nylabones are great because they are virtually indestructible. She might also enjoy a Nylafloss toy. This is a nylon rope (you can get them in different sizes) that she can fling around like a rug. A Nylafloss rope is also good because it will help keep her teeth and gums healthy; the nylon strands are designed for a dog's mouth. If you really want to give Macaroni an excellent present, consider a mat for her doghouse that is stuffed with cedar chips. It will help her to smell better and it will be harder for her to haul out of the doghouse.

## Vaginal Discharge in an Unspayed Dog Means Serious Trouble

*Major infections of the uterus are common in middle-aged to older female dogs. Get help for these girls fast.*

### QUESTION:

Trouble, our 8-year-old Poodle, has a vaginal discharge. She seems to feel okay but I think she might be a little bit less active for the past three or four weeks. She may be drinking more water than normal, too. When this discharge started, we thought she was just coming into heat again, but this time the stuff around her back end looks more like pus than blood. Is Trouble sick?

### DR. NICHOL:

Yes, she is and you are lucky that Trouble is not in worse shape. It is very likely that she has a disease called pyometra. Her problem is that on one of her previous reproductive cycles (heat period), her open cervix allowed bacteria into the inside of her uterus. The resulting infection caused pus to accumulate, resulting in a huge abscess inside Trouble's uterus. Pyometra requires immediate treatment.

The best cure for pyometra is ovariohysterectomy (spaying). While a uterus with a minor infection might be curable, the damage caused by pyometra is irreversible. Surgical removal of the uterus and the ovaries will not only eliminate a potentially fatal infection from Trouble's body, it will prevent recurrence. The spaying surgery will also reduce her risk of breast cancer and diabetes.

Trouble is lucky because her cervix (the circular muscle at the base of the uterus) is open, which is allowing some of the pus to drain. Her open cervix not only made the problem easy for you to spot, it allowed her to stay fairly stable. Many dogs with pyometra are not so lucky. In these girls, the cervix is closed; it does not permit any pus to drain. With no discharge, the problem is harder to recognize. Worse still, with all of the pus bottled up inside, pyometra advances much faster and causes death much quicker.

The moral of the story is this: Unless a female dog is intended for breeding, have her spayed before she has her first heat cycle (6 months of age or younger). This eliminates the risk.

## Nipples and Newborn Puppies

*Even with more babies than nipples, Mama will teach her children to take turns and share.*

### QUESTION:

I'm 8 years old and I have a dog named Wilma. How many nipples does she have? If she has more puppies than nipples, can the extra puppies still live and grow up?

### DR. NICHOL:

Most dogs have ten nipples—five on each side. Some have as few as eight or nine total. But a healthy mother dog makes lots of milk. If Wilma has more puppies than nipples, the puppies will need to learn to take turns eating. This is a good thing for you to teach them. You sound quite mature. I know you can do a good job.

# Cancers, Lumps, and Masses

## Cancer, the Leading Cause of Death in Older Dogs

*Do we just accept this? There are risks that can be avoided and symptoms that you can recognize. You can improve your dog's chances.*

### Question:

Cancer seems to kill a disproportionate number of dogs. Is it because of carcinogens in their diet, background radiation, excessively chlorinated water, ultraviolet rays, and our attitude? Why are some breeds more susceptible than others? What can be done to prevent cancer in dogs?

### Dr. Nichol:

Cancer is the most common cause of death in older dogs. But while we talk of cancer as a disease, it is actually a very big group of diseases. Each cancer type is a specific disease unto itself, with its own causes, treatments, and preventives.

It appears that we are seeing more cancer in dogs. Part of the reason is that pets, like people, are living longer. Cancer was seldom seen prior to 1900 because the life expectancy for all of us was about one half of what it is today. But I would never suggest that you try to prevent cancer by dying young. Do be aware of the known risk factors: prolonged sun exposure for pets with unpigmented skin, skin exposure to petroleum products, unnecessary vaccinations, and genetics.

Genetics? You bet. There are known heritable factors for many cancers, just as in people. For example, Boxers have long been known to have far more cancer than any other breed. But perhaps the most valuable way to protect your dog is to be observant. Any lump or bump on the skin, in the mouth, under the tail, on the breasts—anywhere—should be examined. Do *not* take the conservative wait-and-see approach. While 85 percent of skin masses in dogs are benign, many malignancies appear round and moveable and innocent in their early stages. Some of the most dangerous and aggressive cancers are in fact curable if completely removed early. While you wait to see if a benign-looking mass is going to grow, you are inviting an early death for your dog.

Pets have many of the same illnesses as people. The big difference is that their lives are compressed into only 13 to 15 years in most cases, so diseases advance quickly in pets. The most effective way to protect your dog from cancer is to have every abnormal sign checked by your veterinarian. That means all symptoms, like drinking too much water, diarrhea, vomiting—anything. Be alert and save your best friend's life.

## Skin Lumps: When Is It Safe to Watch and Wait?

*A quick sample from the inside of the mass can give an early diagnosis without surgery.*

### Question:

We have an 8-year-old Sheepdog and I just found a lump under her skin. Should I be worried, or watch it, or have it removed, or what?

### Dr. Nichol:

A very good question. My answer is not to gamble. To learn more about a lump, you can have it checked using a technique called a fine-needle aspirate. Your veterinarian can do this right in the office. If it's benign, you heave a big sigh of relief. If it's not, it's been caught early. Your Sheepdog could be cured of cancer if you have it surgically removed. Don't gamble with this girl's life. Get an answer ASAP.

## Mast Cell Tumors

*Mast cell tumors can be dangerous. Don't "wait and see." Have them removed.*

### Question:

Our boy is a 10-year-old Rottweiler and German Shepherd cross who had a mast cell tumor removed from his side five months ago. The tumor was caught early and the surgical margins were clear. He is doing great, but we were wondering if there is any routine screening that should be done to detect a recurrence. Also, what are the chances of the tumor coming back?

### Dr. Nichol:

These are mighty important questions. Some mast cell tumors are easily cured by simple surgical removal. But survival rates vary between 13 percent and 77 percent depending on the aggressiveness of the tumor. It's a common cancer representing 20 to 25 percent of skin tumors in dogs and ranking number four in prevalence in cats.

Mast cell tumors can be found anywhere on a dog's body. They often have a history of being "watched carefully" by a cautious pet owner who later finds the mass suddenly growing. The reality is that once they grow noticeably, many have already started to invade the surrounding tissue and spread to other parts of the body. Your concern for your boy's future is well founded because his cancer could still spread. Ask your veterinarian to show you the locations of your dog's "regional" lymph nodes. Learn to palpate for swellings in these areas. In addition, check every area of his skin often for more masses. Finally, bring him in for a physical exam every three to six months. Any suspicious swellings should be aspirated with a syringe and evaluated by a pathologist.

I'm sorry this sounds so ominous. Your boy may well be cured. If he does have a recurrence, the new masses can be removed with follow-up chemotherapy or radiation treatments. Be observant, and take every day of love and companionship as a gift.

## Bleeding, Open Skin Tumors

*A needle aspirate is a quick and simple way of getting more information from suspicious masses. Get a diagnosis early.*

### QUESTION:

We have a dear old Basset Hound (about 10 years). Recently we have noticed lumps under his skin. Now one of them has ruptured and is an open sore. I am assuming these are tumors of some kind. He started with one and now has three. I have heard from friends that if they bleed, they are usually cancerous. I have also heard that when these tumors are removed, there is a good chance of them reoccurring and that removal can be quite expensive. Are they dangerous to humans or other animals? What are a dog's chances once these start occurring? Are most of the tumors that bleed malignant? What is the usual treatment and cost?

### DR. NICHOL:

I am glad you are taking these masses seriously. Cancer is the leading cause of death in dogs the age of your Basset. What you need is a diagnosis so that you can make an informed decision on treatment.

While bleeding is a serious sign, it suggests that the masses could be abscesses instead. A good physical exam by a doctor will determine which problem your dog has. If the initial diagnosis is cancer, have an impression smear or fine-needle aspirate done. These are simple outpatient procedures that will allow a pathologist to give your dog's veterinarian enough information to advise you. The advice could take several forms.

If the masses are benign, and many are, surgical removal may be unnecessary. If they are malignant, the best treatment will depend entirely on the exact cancer type. Some are best treated surgically, while others respond better to chemotherapy, radiation, or combinations of these things. And, yes, it can get costly. But remember that the doctor has a few jobs to do for you. One is to diagnose; another is to provide you clear options. His or her last and most important function is to do as you ask. Your veterinarian works for you.

There is no evidence that cancers in dogs are contagious. The only thing that is contagious is fear. Don't be influenced by stories from your friends. Get help from a pro.

## Tumors Near the Rear End

*Often malignant, rapid tumor growth demands rapid attention.*

### QUESTION:

My 11-year-old Chihuahua has a large lump in the area of her rectum and genitals causing both to extend out. The lump is as big as a golf ball and is firm. Pebbles has not shown any signs of discomfort, but recently has started having trouble walking. What could this lump be caused by?

### DR. NICHOL:

You're making me nervous. Cancer is the leading cause of death in older dogs. By far the most common age group for dogs to get cancer is 8 to 11 years. The clear danger sign for Pebbles is that this mass is growing noticeably.

What else could it be? If Pebbles has not been spayed, she may have a noncancerous problem like vaginal hyperplasia or vaginal prolapse. Either of these would be good news because they can be cured surgically.

Whether Pebbles has cancer or not, she is facing a serious risk. While age 11 is advanced for many large-breed dogs, healthy and well-cared-for Chihuahuas often reach their late teens. By that measure, Pebbles may have a lot of miles left on the clock. I strongly advise you to get her examined. Surgery of some kind will be in the plan. Although her situation is urgent, be sure to have her doctor do a lab profile and chest X-rays prior to surgery to make sure anesthesia is a safe bet. Do whatever it takes to put her right. She has a big problem. You will only have one shot at saving her.

## Fatty Tumors Beneath the Skin

*Lipomas are common in older dogs. They are usually harmless. Be sure they are "just" lipomas.*

### QUESTION:

My female yellow Lab is 9 years old, weighs 81 pounds, and has fatty tumors. What is causing them and can they be removed?

### DR. NICHOL:

Fatty tumors go by the name *lipoma*. They are benign, but they can grow to several pounds beneath the skin and get large enough to get in the way of normal function. They can be surgically removed, but on overweight dogs (like an 81-pound Lab) they will often shrink rather nicely with a return to a normal weight (like 65 pounds).

Be sure they are only lipomas. Have your veterinarian take fine-needle aspirates so a pathologist can assure you that they aren't a dangerous malignancy instead. Then ask your dog's doctor for prescription diet r/d so that your girl can shed those unsightly extra pounds. She'll feel more active and playful, and her old joints will be much less prone to painful arthritis. Wow! Lose weight, feel better, and tumors shrink. Ah, life is good.

## Bone Cancer

*There are treatments for this devastating disease, but it's tough.*

### QUESTION:

Our wonderful 6-year-old Lab has been diagnosed with osteosarcoma on his back leg. We keep getting conflicting reports on the efficacy of taking the leg off, which seems so drastic, and chemotherapy. Is it worth it to the dog to put him through this before it comes back or should the dog be put down? He is a wonderful affectionate dog and I can barely write those words.

### DR. NICHOL:

This has to be the hardest part of loving a pet. Losing this boy will be gut-wrenching, whenever it happens. The honest answer is that his malignant bone cancer is terminal. At the same time, it is also true that treatment can extend his active and enjoyable life one to two years.

If your Lab is like the majority, he is not only lame but in quite a lot of pain. Amputation will eliminate his pain; he should do fine missing one rear leg. If you follow this with chemotherapy (well tolerated in most dogs), you can spend some good time together. But if you really want him back to his old self for that time, he can avoid amputation by having a "limb salvage" procedure. This involves removing the cancerous bone tissue and surgically grafting a length of normal bone. While this surgery will not improve your boy's survival time, he should enjoy a truly normal life.

Is all this worth it to this fellow you love so much? Osteosarcoma is a common malignancy. My experience is that the disease itself is much worse than its treatment. In your heart is the decision as to what is right for the two of you. You'll be in my prayers.

## Cancer of the Spleen in Older Dogs

*A common malignancy in older dogs, it is handled best with surgery followed by chemotherapy. While not a cure, most dogs feel great and live well for nine to twelve months after treatment.*

### QUESTION:

Doctor, I hope you can help me and my Sadie. The worst has happened to us. Last week she was weak one day and didn't want to walk or eat. The vet found her to be anemic and found out she had a cancer on her spleen. They operated and took out her spleen and she has started on chemotherapy. Is there anything else I can do? Even with chemo they say she only has nine to twelve months. I can't believe that's all.

### DR. NICHOL:

I know how frightening this can be. I have shared this emotional roller coaster with countless families. In fact, my own beloved Airedale, Juan, had this cancer. The thought of losing Sadie before her time really shakes you. You will feel better when you know what to expect.

Cancer is truly a major problem. It is the leading cause of death in older dogs. We find ourselves making the best of this bad situation almost every day at our hospital. But it's not all negative. Cancer research in veterinary medicine is moving ahead quickly. The current reality is that only a few types of malignancies are truly curable, but treatment is still very worthwhile for Sadie.

The cancer type most often involved in the spleen of dogs is called hemangiosarcoma. It is malignant and fairly aggressive. It causes tumors that usually get pretty large. They can put enough pressure on other organs to make a dog like Sadie lose her appetite. As a splenic tumor gets bigger, its growth accelerates. Some masses exceed 8 inches in diameter. When they're that size, they get fragile and can split open and bleed into the abdomen. With enough blood loss, a dog like Sadie will start to feel weak due to her anemia.

I don't mean for this to sound hopeless. Treatment usually makes a big difference. Our first move is always to make our patient stable. Cases of active bleeding may require a blood transfusion. Next we X-ray the chest and abdomen to look for possible spread of the cancer to other organs. Ultrasound can be helpful. If the tumor appears confined to the spleen, we remove it. Yes, we can live without a spleen. It has some important functions, but most are also carried out elsewhere in the body.

So why isn't surgical removal of the cancer enough to cure it? Because this malignancy spreads early on a microscopic level. The tumor cells are carried to other parts of the body in the blood and lymph. Without further treatment, Sadie may live only a few more months. But with chemotherapy, she is likely to feel great and enjoy life as though nothing happened. How long? The average with chemotherapy is the nine to twelve months that Sadie's doctor told you. Some, like my dog Juan, get as much as two years. A few get much less. It's definitely a gamble.

The last question everyone asks is whether the treatment is worth it. This has to be your decision. Unlike most people, dogs have very few side effects from chemotherapy. The treatment for hemangiosarcoma is actually one of the safest. What you can do for Sadie at home is to improve the effectiveness of treatment with diet. Preliminary research shows that Omega-3 fatty acids will enhance the benefits of chemotherapy in cancers like this—and it's easy. Start her on a prescription diet called n/d. It will also help fight against the weight loss that can be a part of cancer treatment.

I know how unfair this is. Pets' lives are way too short anyway. Their physical functions run at a faster speed than ours. It's as if our 75- to 80-year life expectancy is compressed into about 13 years for most dogs. In that sense, gaining nine to twelve months is actually pretty good. Do your best to enjoy your life with Sadie. Every day is God's gift.

## Hernias

*Umbilical hernias are common in puppies. Most are insignificant. A few can be dangerous.*

### QUESTION:

We have a 10-week-old white German Shepherd puppy and I just noticed a lump about the size of the tip of a pinky finger on her tummy, below her rib cage. What could it be?

### DR. NICHOL:

You describe an umbilical hernia. This is a birth defect that is usually quite minor. The lump you are noticing is likely to be a small amount of normal fat that has slipped into the location of the umbilicus (belly button). The hernia, an opening in the muscle wall of the abdomen, is the result of an incomplete union of the two halves of the body during fetal development. If the hernia stays very small, it will need no treatment. On the other hand, if it gets bigger as the puppy grows, it may allow a loop of intestine to slip through the opening and become twisted. This would cut off the blood supply to the intestine and would require emergency surgery. Ask your veterinarian to check the hernia at the time of each vaccination booster—about every three weeks. If the hernial opening gets big enough, the doctor will recommend that it be closed surgically. The procedure will require general anesthesia, but is quite safe, and recovery is speedy.

## Another Kind of Hernia

*Inguinal hernias are a form of birth defect in puppies. They need surgical correction, but they do great. If a hernia is neglected, a life may be at risk.*

### QUESTION:

My husband and I have a 5-week-old Yorkie puppy who has a swollen place near his groin that our vet said was a hernia. We hoped we could wait until he was older to get it fixed but now the hernia is getting bigger. Is it risky to wait? Is our baby too young to have it fixed?

### DR. NICHOL:

I share your concern. Who wants surgery—especially on someone that young and tiny? I suspect your baby weighs all of about one and a half pounds. The truth is that allowing a puppy to get bigger is usually best. But in the case of your little guy, waiting may be too risky.

What you are describing is an inguinal hernia. It's seldom a big problem because its cause is nothing more than a slight anatomy problem. Here is how it works: The abdomen is where our intestines, and a lot of other organs, belong. Things are supposed to stay bundled up here. But there is a passageway on each side, near the rear portion of the abdomen (the groin of a person), where arteries and veins go to the back legs. This is called the inguinal canal. Normally the canal is not wide enough for anything else to slip through. But in your baby, the canal is much too wide and this has allowed some of his intestines to slide into the canal. What you are seeing and feeling in Junior's groin are loops of intestine under the skin.

The good news is that he is acting fine, which means he's still okay. If you wait too long to have the hernia repaired, you will notice a sudden onset of pain, loss of appetite, and inactivity. That will occur because enough intestine has found its way through this extra-wide canal and has become strangulated. *Strangulated* is a real medical term that means what it sounds like—the blood supply to this area of intestine has been choked off. This is bad. It would not only require immediate surgery, but would result in the removal of a portion of dead intestine. Not good.

My advice is get it fixed now. If it were still small and staying that way, waiting would be fine. Safety? We do this type of surgery on small fry often. We use small instruments and sutures. On a little tyke like this, we would put in some liquid food by stomach tube under anesthesia and provide extra fluid under the skin. This would prevent low blood-sugar problems. Keeping him warm during the procedure is important, too. But in experienced hands I predict success. Go for it.

## Cancer Surgery of the Mouth and Throat: Here Is How a Pet Can Be Fed

*A tube implanted into the stomach wall makes it simple to feed a recovering dog at home.*

### QUESTION:

My old dog just had surgery of the throat. The surgeon removed a tumor and said that it would take time to heal. So that we could get some food into Sarge, he put in a P.E.G. tube for feeding. Can I feed Sarge at home with this? Will he need this his whole life?

## Dr. Nichol:

I'm glad Sarge's doctor has taken the long view. If Sarge can't eat for a while after surgery, the P.E.G. tube will solve the dilemma.

P.E.G. stands for *percutaneous endoscopic gastrostomy*. In plain English, this is a feeding tube that connects the inside of the stomach to the skin on the outside of Sarge's abdominal wall. While installing a P.E.G. tube requires some sophisticated equipment, they work well and they are tolerated just fine by cats and dogs.

Placing a P.E.G. tube requires general anesthesia and a long snake-like instrument called an endoscope. It takes about 20 minutes to implant the tube, which can then be left in place indefinitely. Even if Sarge never goes back to eating, he can always get the nutrition he needs through his P.E.G. tube at home.

P.E.G. tubes are used more and more because they work in a lot of cases when a pet cannot or will not eat. If a pet is nauseated, for example, and refuses food, the ability to pump soft food directly into the inside of the stomach using a syringe can easily save his life. Feeding Sarge this way is simple to learn and takes only a few minutes at home. When Sarge is well, the tube can be removed at his doctor's office without anesthesia.

P.E.G. tubes do have their limitations. For example, never try to force a T-bone steak through one. And if Sarge loses his voice from the surgery on his throat, I don't think he will ever learn to bark through his P.E.G. tube.

# Destructive Behaviors

## Puppy Chewing: How to Save Your Home

*Destruction and mayhem are a normal way of life for puppies. But you can train that wild child to chew the right toys and leave your stuff alone.*

### Question:

We just got a new Cocker Spaniel puppy who we named Boots because she has white paws. She's 10 weeks old now and we have a new reason for her name—she chews everything—including a brand new boot. She even chews our hands. She won't stop! What can we do?

### Dr. Nichol:

You sound frustrated. I understand how you feel. There seems to be no end in sight to this destructiveness. But there is a way to change Boots's behavior and have fun doing it.

First understand that Boots has a good reason to chew. She has new teeth that will be breaking through her gums soon. Not only that, she has enormous amounts of energy—like a 2-year-old child. So if we simply tell her not to chew your hands or boots, she'll want to be good but will lose her little mind trying to manage all that unspent energy. So, here's the plan. Start by getting six or eight indestructible toys like Nylabones or Gumma Bones. Avoid toys that can be ripped apart like soft rubber or stuffed animals. We do plenty of surgery to remove bits of plastic, rubber, and stuffing from the intestines of puppies. (Remember Murphy's Law: Anything that can go wrong, will.) Next, have everyone in your family keep a toy in their pocket at all times—ready for a chance to train.

Okay, you're sitting there minding your own business when you witness a vicious predatory attack on a hand or other prized object. First, don't scream. Instead, reach into your pocket and grab your toy. Then, with your other hand, take the soggy victimized thing (or hand) out of Boots's mouth; as you do this, you say "Boots, no!" Don't yell "NO"—just put a firm tone on it. Now, here's the important part: After you take away the wrong thing, you immediately pop the toy into Boots's mouth and begin to play with her with the toy. The two of you then have a wonderful time as though the whole thing were her idea. After you share a good time, let her run off with her prize. Then put another toy in your pocket so you're ready for your next opportunity to train.

How many times will you need to do this to get your point across? Hundreds, maybe thousands. But, remember, when you are training, never lose your patience and keep it fun. The fun part is what motivates Boots, who loves you and who thinks that seeing you happy is her greatest joy. Like all good training, your delivery of this performance must be the same every time. When this plan has succeeded, you will find your pride and joy pouncing on her toys when she's ready to eviscerate an imaginary enemy. She'll even bring them to you so that you can share the destruction with her. Isn't this fun?

Lastly, a couple of things *not* to do: Don't give Boots her own old shoe or anything else that resembles what you want her to avoid. If you do, she is guaranteed to confuse good with evil. Also, don't throw away a Nylabone that has lost her interest. The flavor put there by the manufacturer will eventually go away, but you can "recharge" her Nylabones by putting them in some boiling water with a couple of bullion cubes. Happy chewing to both of you!

## Destructiveness When Left Alone

*Frantic with anxiety and fear, some dogs wreck the house in the owner's absence.*

### QUESTION:

At this point I can't take any more of my dog's hyperness and destructiveness. She's in the car now while I'm at work. The only time she's not destroying something is when she's locked in the car. She was so awful last weekend, I tried to return her to the pound. I cried going in because I didn't want to give up and take her; I cried on the way out because I couldn't stand another night with her. She just doesn't seem to be able or want to fit into my household. Last night she destroyed my bathroom carpet and yipped and whined *all* night. This morning she's torn up something in my yard. If I keep her, I'll lose it someday and hurt her. I'm a nervous wreck, worn out from no sleep and I'm angry about needing to play God. This hurts me very much. Do some dogs just need to be put down? Even if they aren't biting people?

## Dr. Nichol:

This is extremely hard. I have known dogs like this. In fact I had a dog myself who seemed beyond the usual methods of managing the separation anxiety that you describe. I remember how conflicted I felt. We love our pets so much and we commit to them in the deepest way. Why can't she just see how much she is loved?

If feelings were logical, every one of us and our pets would be perfectly well-adjusted. But our lives are a challenge for a reason. I believe that, like us, our pets are on a journey. What your poor dog is enduring is even harder on her than it is on you. She is doing badly and she knows it. You have choices to make in this situation, but you need more information.

You describe a hyperactive dog who seems quite anxious even when she's with you. When she is alone, her anxiety escalates to include destructiveness. If we could lower her general anxiety level, we might be able to manage or eliminate the injury to your home. We can give anti-anxiety medications while boarding her at a kennel until she begins to relax. If she seems more functional, we could then start behavior modification to teach her to behave when you are gone. The method normally used for this is called graduated absences—where you leave the dog alone initially for very short periods, followed by longer times. We include an activity like giving the dog a rubber Kong toy filled with peanut butter to keep her occupied. This approach is gentle and slow. It takes dedication and time, and it is not guaranteed to work.

Our plan contains a lot of "maybes." I can assure you that if drug therapy works, it will be necessary for life. We don't understand why, but there are dogs who are hyperactive from birth. We know that if we can't break through your dog's hyperactivity, our attempts to manage her destructiveness will also fail. Therefore, managing this girl will be a major challenge that could either succeed or force a tough choice.

What if we fail? What if we come to the irrefutable realization that she is a totally unsuitable pet? Could you just hope she works out in someone else's home? If we make a serious attempt to help her and we lose the battle, giving this dog an easy exit from a difficult life may be the greatest gift of love. We really don't hurt those we love. But letting her go and shouldering your own pain could be the right thing to do. It will take real courage, but there are things that are worse than death. If you choose euthanasia, you must know that it is done by painless injection. You can be there with her if you want to be. This is horribly hard. You are in my prayers.

## A Bored Dog Can Become Destructive
*When the family's gone, this Lab chews kitchen items.*

### QUESTION:

I have a Lab who has decided to rearrange my counters when I'm gone from the house. We have tried everything, sprays, scat mats, punishing him by taping the offending article in his mouth, etc. Seems he loves to chew anything with plastic, or anything that might be food . . . just truly a very destructive fit. Any help?

### DR. NICHOL:

Are we having fun yet? Sounds like one of us is. You are not alone in this predicament. Destructiveness is the second most common behavior problem in dogs—right behind biting. But, though your dog may differ with me, I think you have a right to keep your stuff in one piece.

There are two fundamental causes for a dog to embark on a solo mission of home remodeling. The first, and more common, is separation anxiety. This is the dog who has become so highly and abnormally attached to the owner that being alone provokes intense and uncontrollable panic. You will know if your dog has this problem because he watches you with intensity and growing nervousness as you prepare to leave each day. These poor dogs want to be good, but they need serious behavior modification and, in most cases, medications. But Labs rarely fit this group. Instead, the typical happy-go-lucky Lab is so full of energy that he seems to need constant activity. Working dogs by instinct, Labs are bred to toil all day, loving every minute of it. If your dog is home alone . . . well, an idle mind (and mouth) is the devil's workshop.

What your bored Lab needs is more attention: Active play with a ball or Frisbee, a brisk walk or run (you know, exercise for both of you), and obedience training. Each day, you two do your homework by practicing your lessons. Labs are smart and make outstanding obedience dogs. While you're away I recommend wholesome after-school activities like loaning him out to some neighborhood children for rambunctious play. You could also get another dog with whom he can share a few hands of gin rummy. As they age gracefully together, add shuffleboard and golf. Ah, the golden years.

## Chewing on Dolls
*This Lab chews Barbie dolls. Stop her before she chews again.*

### QUESTION:
Our pound pup is facing being returned to the doggie jail and face execution if we can't stop her horrible crime of chewing. Some of her habits we deal with just fine; however, her chewing has gone from misdemeanor to near manslaughter. Today my youngest daughter's "Sleeping Beauty Barbie" and "Prince Ken" met their demise; they are resting in a shallow grave in the backyard. My daughter is in mourning.

### DR. NICHOL:
I think this wayward adolescent can learn to adjust to society. I'd hate to see her take the "long walk" for doll-slaughter. Like any normal kid, she's so full of energy that she doesn't know what to do with herself. My two little boys are the same way. They'll color within the lines for only so long. After that they revert to their basic wild instincts. In the case of your young pup, that means chewing the world.

So, your mission, should you decide to accept it, is to involve the whole family in solving this problem (that is, except for the late Ken and Barbie, of course, may they rest in peace). Start with the kids. Explain the consequences of leaving stuff lying around.

What about big-ticket items like the furniture? That's damage for the adults to prevent by putting your juvenile delinquent outside, or in her dog crate (her den), when she's unsupervised.

Last, and most important, is training. This young girl needs to be watched when she is loose in the house. At these times, all family members must be equipped with dog toys in their pockets. These toys should bear no resemblance to anything valued by humans. Rawhides and Nylabones work fine. As soon as Jackie the Ripper bites the wrong thing, tell her, "No," take it away, then put a "good girl" toy in her mouth. She then hears how excellent she was to have figured all this out by herself. Do this hundreds of times.

It's really pretty simple—but it does require discipline on everyone's part. It's worth it because she will outgrow most of this behavior. But there will be times, as a fully-grown pillar of the community, that she will hanker for a Barbie. Will she kill again or choose the right toy? Better get to work.

## Digging Adult Dogs
### *Learn why they dig and how to control it—before it controls you.*

**QUESTION:**

We got a Shepherd mix (many say with Rottweiler) from the Humane Society last summer. She is approximately 1 to 2 years old and very active. She has dug *many* large holes in our backyard and we need some advice on how to stop this behavior before we spend a lot of money this spring getting our yard back in shape. We both work long days and she primarily stays in the backyard except when we let her inside at night. She has a doghouse and lots of shade available. Please let me know if we can stop her from digging. Any helpful hints you may have would be great.

**DR. NICHOL:**

A dog digging up a nice yard is frustrating. The good news is that it's easier to manage than most behavior problems. That's because in most cases it's not really a behavior problem at all. If you ask well-meaning "dog people," you will get suggestions like filling a hole with water and immersing her head or putting feces in the holes. In response, your dog will act out another way or simply choose a different excavation site. To change the behavior, we must address the cause.

The reason most dogs dig is for temperature regulation. Nearly all diggers are large-breed dogs like yours, and many are dark-haired. In the hot weather (even in the winter), your dog is trying to stay cool. Her holes are most likely in areas that are shaded in the afternoon. Curing the problem may be as easy as adding a cooling device to the afternoon shaded spots. A child's wading pool or a water mister, with an inexpensive timer so that it turns on during the hottest part of the day, work well. Another tactic is to give your dog her own sand box (or dirt box) in the shady area. Put loose dirt in it and dampen it occasionally.

On the other hand, there are youngsters who simply have energy to burn. To make sure your girl isn't just digging as an aerobic exercise, play hard with her. Throw the ball and run around like a nut. It'll be good for you, too, and make you less likely to dig. And all this time you thought she was trying to communicate something else, didn't you? Admit it. You thought she wanted to travel to far off and exotic places—like China.

# Digging Puppies

*Kids dig for somewhat different reasons from their parents—they're bored. Manage an active kid with more appropriate activities.*

### QUESTION:

We have a 5-month-old German Shepherd mix who is digging in our lawn and has one hole that is her favorite. Previously she was digging up and chewing irrigation emitter lines; but she seemed to either have outgrown it or get bored with it. I would rather not use repellent, as it has seemed ineffective and is very costly to apply. Any advice you can offer would be appreciated.

### DR. NICHOL:

Puppies are a lot like kids, aren't they? I remember a "Dennis the Menace" cartoon where Dennis's mother was telling the baby-sitter as she was leaving: "About every 5 minutes just yell 'Stop that!'" While I don't condone destructive behavior, what you have is a kid with energy to burn—not a puppy with a behavior problem.

Knowing that this kid has a surplus of pizzazz, I recommend some wholesome after-school activities. Consider a basic dog obedience class; take the puppy to the class and you both burn off steam by practicing together every day. It's a great parent–child activity that will help you bond like nothing else. As an alternative to training, give this girl another focus. Some bored dogs are taken to doggy day-care at a local kennel, where they interact and play together in a semi-organized way, like kids. Other folks host get-togethers for their dogs to mix it up and run around the yard.

What about your poor yard? Accept that some digging is part of a normal puppy phase. Allow your girl to dig only in her one favorite spot. Do not let her watch you dig in the yard (even if you use a shovel like a human). To prevent her from making the rest of your place resemble a minefield, fill in the other holes and put chicken wire over them to diminish her interest. And forget the Dog-B-Gone. That just seems to spark interest in an inquiring young mind.

# Dog–Human Diseases

## Human Diseases: Susceptibility of Pets

*Our pets are not at risk from mononucleosis and flu. But humans without pets may have more risk.*

### QUESTION:

Here are two families with similar concerns: One of my kids has mono—and the kids were letting the dog lick their faces and lips. Can my 10-week-old Beagle catch this sickness? The entire human part of my family is very sick with the flu. Are our pets at risk of catching the flu if they sleep with us and kiss us? I don't want them to get sick, too.

### DR. NICHOL:

No to mono (infectious mononucleosis) and no to flu. These are viral diseases that occur in humans only. In fact, very few viruses cross species lines—rabies being the big one that does. I suggest you allow as much contact as possible between your sick family members and your pets. Pets have been shown to provide emotional support through unconditional love and affection that leads to faster recoveries. When you're sick, it's hard to find anyone else who'll kiss you and sleep with you anyway. Sometimes pets are better than people.

## Allergies to Pets

*Here are several hypoallergenic dog and cat breeds.*

### QUESTION:

I would like to know if there is any breed(s) of dog for children with asthma. If a child is allergic to cats, does it necessarily mean he or she will also be allergic to dogs?

### DR. NICHOL:

I think you're great to try to find a pet for your children. Pets teach love and forgiveness in ways that no parent can. Peter Rabbit and Raoul (our family dog and cat) have a big place in the lives of the Nichol boys. But asthma and inhaled allergies in children can be dangerous. By far the dog breed most likely to succeed in your home is the Bedlington Terrier because this breed is less prone to release dander into the air. Avoid shampoos because they dry the skin, which increases skin flaking.

Cats and dogs are different species, so your child may have problems with one but not the other. But if your child has trouble with any or all cat and dog breeds, consider a reptile or a pocket pet like a gerbil—or even a Chia pet. But for heaven's sake, get that kid a critter.

## An Endorsement of Chinese Cresteds
*Plaudits for a smooth breed.*

### QUESTION:

In reference to your comment on people with pet allergies, I would like to say that you did not give full credit to the Chinese Crested dog (which I raise). Chinese Cresteds have only a thin amount of nonshedding hair on their heads, tails, and ankles. Otherwise, they are as smooth as the underside of your forearm. I agree that kids should have a pet, but I disagree that Bedlington Terriers are the best.

### DR. NICHOL:

You are right about Chinese Crested dogs. In fact, the same is true of the Mexican Hairless. Not only are they hypoallergenic, but they also make great pets. Regrettably, I neglected to mention dogs without hair. But what I want to know is: How did you find out about the underside of my forearms?

## Heartworms and Human Risk
*We are not the normal host for this parasite, but carrier mosquitoes have infected a few unlucky folks.*

### QUESTION:

Can people get heartworms? If dogs and cats get it from mosquitoes, can't humans?

**DR. NICHOL:**

Cases of human infection with *Dirofilaria immitus* (heartworm) have occurred but are pretty rare. The reason is that the human immune system is very good at killing the larvae because we are not a natural host for this parasite—like dogs are. A dog's system accepts it far more easily. In addition to humans, horses can get it in rare cases. As for cats, they are less commonly infected than dogs—but it is not rare in cats. It is for this reason that a once-a-month tablet has been developed and approved for use as a feline heartworm preventive. If you are concerned about the safety of your cat, ask your veterinarian for more information.

# EARS

## Do-It-Yourself Approaches to Ear Disease

*See the doctor for treatment of ear infections, and do all of the follow-up to be sure it's gone for good.*

### QUESTION:

My 2-year-old male Rottie has had wetness in his ears accompanied with redness and itching and a brown, moist discharge. The moisture is not from an external source. I clean his ears with Solvaprep and then use Solvadry. I use a Q-tip to put antibiotic ointment onto the red areas in his ears. The red areas are not from scratching because they are deep inside. Any help you can give would be much appreciated.

### DR. NICHOL:

Chronic ear infections, believe it or not, are the most common disease treated in veterinary clinics. To understand why ear trouble is more common in dogs than in people, a brief anatomy lesson is in order. Unlike us (most of us, that is), dogs have hairy earflaps. While some dogs have erect ears, most have folded flaps. In addition, the ear canal of dogs is proportionately much longer that its human counterpart. It also has a 90-degree bend. The upshot of all this is that air and light don't circulate very well inside the ear canals of dogs.

Why does this make for ear infections? Another very good question. The inner wall of the ear canal is really just an extension of the skin. Like all areas of the skin, there is a normal population of different bacteria plus a few yeast that live there. They usually mind their own business. The problems start when the environment inside that ear canal is disrupted by factors like water and heat. With a long, bent ear canal covered by a hairy, floppy flap, things stay hot and wet. Anybody here surprised that bacteria and yeasts just love this place? They have a field day. But your poor Rottweiler is itchy and in pain with his swollen, infected ear canals.

The good news is that we can help. We start with a good ear exam using an instrument called an otoscope. Every veterinarian has one. We use the otoscope to look at the swollen areas and the character of the discharge. We also look for foreign stuff like foxtails (little weed awns you may have growing in your yard—if you don't, stop by my house and I'll share a few) and ticks. If we find any uninvited visitors, we evict them on the spot. Then we take a small sample of the discharge and check it under the microscope. After a good flushing of those ears with a disinfectant, we send home medication tailor-made to kill off the nasty little beasts that are causing the infection.

Now all that sounds like a direct approach. But not every bent, hairy, floppy ear responds right away. Most need to be rechecked and have treatment adjusted for at least a few weeks. If the infection has been in residence for a long time, surgery is sometimes the only way to get control.

What about your poor Rottweiler? Because of those long bent ear canals of his, you're getting nowhere with your Q-Tips and treatments. As Ann Landers would say: "Seek professional help."

# Eyes

## Cherry Eye

*Not just unattractive, but chronic eye trouble can result. Surgical correction is best.*

### QUESTION:

I just bought a Boxer and Bulldog mix and he has what is called a cherry eye. What do I do about it?

### DR. NICHOL:

This is a common eye disease, but I wish it hadn't been named after food. It's an oxymoron, like jumbo shrimp or military intelligence.

Okay, cherry eye. It's not an emergency, but it is important. The eyeball itself is fine. The problem is in the pink membrane that sits just below the eyes of our dogs. This structure, called the third eyelid or nictitans, has a bit of lymph tissue on its back side. The whole assembly is quite valuable because of its protective function. Your dog's problem is that the lymph gland has become swollen and has turned the third eyelid inside out. Hence you see this red swelling.

Cherry eye will not resolve on its own. It is not a huge problem if you ignore it, but your dog may develop a low-grade infection because of improper tear flow. In years past, cherry eye was managed by simple removal of the lymph tissue. The problem with this simplistic treatment is that the gland helps produce some of the normal moisture for the eye. Removal of the gland has caused severe dry eye problems later in life. Instead, your pup needs a surgery that permanently tucks the gland back into its normal position. Most good general practitioners are skilled at this. Eyedrops? Sorry, they won't help either. The other eye? It may or may not occur there too.

Two positive points: First, correction is a day surgery. Second, be thankful it wasn't called pineapple eye.

# Eye Discharge

*Extra eyelashes can cause discharge and damage the eyes.*

### QUESTION:

I have a wonderful little female Bichon Frise. She has these really bad leaky eyes that turn the hair around her eyes brown and black. When I look real closely, especially at her left eye, it looks like she has sleep in her eyes all the time. She is not a show dog, just our sweet little pet, so I just wonder how much this bothers her or if it causes her pain of any kind? Is there anything I can do to help her?

### DR. NICHOL:

This is an important question. While a small amount of overflow of tears is normal in this breed, there could be other reasons why your dog has this discharge. Your first move needs to be an exam by your dog's doctor to make sure there are no extra eyelashes that may be rubbing on her eyes. This problem, called dystichiasis, causes continual eye pain. It may also cause permanent damage to the corneal surface of the eye, resulting in blindness. No bueno.

What if your veterinarian gives this girl a clean bill of eye health? No real problem, unless her appearance is your major concern. For good looks, I recommend a small amount of hydrogen peroxide on a cotton swab applied to the discolored hair near each eye. Be extremely careful to avoid touching the eyeball itself, as this can damage the eye. After a few weeks of daily treatments, she'll be so good-looking she can try out for Miss America. Better teach her to sing and dance.

# Fearful Behavior

## Frightened Puppies

*A puppy who hides needs special care and development. You both can win.*

### Question:

Shortly after I got my 4-month-old Scottie puppy, he ran away from home—in the house. It took me 18 hours to find him. I got a crate for him that he dearly loves. I fuss with him, talk to him, brush his coat, and do everything possible to make him outgoing, but I am an arthritic 82-year-old. I love the little rascal. I leave a light leash on him so I can find him and pull him out of corners. Can you help my little peek-a-boo guy come out of hiding? I suspect he was abused by the people I bought him from.

### Dr. Nichol:

The way you love and care for your puppy is a great gift for both of you. But his hiding is really nothing to worry about. Your Scottie is a scared little boy, but for him it's normal. He was born the way he is; it wasn't caused by abuse. Every dog has an individual personality built right in. Some are courageous; others, shy.

It's the nature of a dog to feel secure in an enclosed area—just like the dens that his ancestors called home. Giving him his own den in the form of a crate is a loving way to provide him security. Leaving a leash attached is also smart. Just tug gently on the leash when you call his name. So that he'll feel more comfortable outside of his hiding places, get a plastic-coated cable at the pet supply store. Snap one end to his collar and loop the other end over a doorknob in the room you are using. Give your boy a chew toy and let him enjoy your company in a relaxed, nonthreatening setting. Keep working gently with him. He'll blossom with time.

## A Dog Who Cringes, Runs, and Barks
*"Staring down" an apprehensive dog can damage a gentle personality.*

### QUESTION:
I had never heard of "staring a dog down" before, but a friend said that is what my friend did to my dog. She is from the pound and I am sure she has been abused. Since he did this, she is very scared of him and every time he moves, she runs away and barks. Can this be undone?

### DR. NICHOL:
This is a sad story. Your friend has made a big mistake by intimidating your dog. But before we get to undoing the damage, I'll give you a bit of background on your dog's personality. Dogs and cats are not like appliances; they don't roll off the assembly line as identical items nor are they blank slates. Our pets come preprogrammed with their own personalities—just like you and I. Could she be easily frightened now because of some past abuse? What happened in her past may have added to her fear, but she was built that way from the start. In fact, shyness in some dogs can be traced to a simple recessive gene.

So, undoing the damage: The best thing is for your friend to avoid your dog. Your girl is barking at him out of fear. Allay that fear by putting this scared baby elsewhere in the house when he comes over. If he is willing to acknowledge his mistake, he can help overcome your dog's fear by behaving in a low-key, gentle way. In addition, he can extend a peace offering by giving her a treat. Never again is he to move quickly, raise his voice, have direct eye contact with, nor lean over this dog. To a dog these are dominance signs. Your girl is sensitive—it's built in. Our dogs are very special friends. Don't allow her to be treated this way again.

## Dogs Who Get Frantic When They're Left Alone
*Dogs who got overly attached to their owners as puppies can become destructive and frantic with anxiety when loose in the house. They may become even more frightened if crated. There is a way to manage this fear but it's a long road.*

## QUESTION:

My mother adopted a 2-year-old sweet well-behaved Lhasa Apso named Simba. The previous owners stated that "He does not like to be left alone." So she bought him an airline carrier so he wouldn't tear up the house but he would go completely berserk whenever she would put him in there. He would scream, claw at the door, and drool until his entire body was soaking wet. Finally, after about two weeks, she quit using the kennel and started leaving him alone in the house. Initially he cried and scratched at the door, but now he does fine. The problem is that she is flying here from Dallas for Christmas and wants to bring Simba with her. Is there any way to do this, or would it put too much stress on him, the airline, and my mother?

## DR. NICHOL:

Hmmm. You've heard me say many times how great a crate is for training because of the way dogs feel so secure in their own "den," right? Well, maybe Simba's not really a dog. Allow me to do my weasel imitation so I can wriggle out. I'll start by explaining Simba's not wanting to be left alone.

Dogs are just like us in many ways. They love companionship and affection. But some dogs get so attached that they become literally overwhelmed with anxiety when separated from their loved one. The name for this is separation anxiety.

How did this happen to poor Simba? Did his first owner abuse him? No, but they didn't ask for help either. Dogs with separation anxiety have an attachment so intense that they are unable to follow even the most basic canine instincts when left alone. While dogs like Simba are born with this tendency, some are much worse than others. So right now this boy seems OK. But just wait for the smallest stress or change in routine and little Simba's ability to cope will slip and he will again act out his fear.

For now I will spare you the discourse on behavior modification. But you must understand that the problem lies not with Simba's owners, past or present, but with his tendency to form unhealthy bonds. So instead of Simba spending more time with your mom (which will throw him into a tailspin when they return to their daily lives back home), he should be with her a bit less. It will not work for him to stay in the care of a visiting pet-sitter in his own home. Simba will freak out. Not only will he damage your mom's home, but his anxiety will worsen—making his problem harder to manage. That is why they invented boarding kennels. But won't poor Simba miss his mama? Not if he is occupied by many new and interesting people and pets—away from home. When your mom returns, she and Simba will simply pick up where they left off. They can share photos of how they spent their Christmas vacations.

One last word of caution: If and when Simba returns to his destructive ways, he must be immediately supervised (doggy day care at a good kennel works great) until your mom can get consultation with a skilled veterinarian for long-term behavior modification. If this boy's anxiety is allowed to become deeply rooted, he will face a tremendous uphill challenge.

Oh, the dog crate. Dogs *are* den animals by nature. Using a crate for housebreaking a puppy is great for consistency. It also shows the new baby the realities of adult life with an owner who is gone some of the time. It's fair and effective. On the other hand, puppies raised in constant contact with their owners can have a terrible time adjusting later when they are left alone. Some of these scared kids will become overwhelmed with anxiety and lose all sense of right and wrong, instinct, you name it. Gripping fear takes over and they really do go berserk.

## Thunderstorm Fear

*Patience and perseverance can help a terrified dog. Yes, there is a method for reducing the panic.*

### QUESTION:

I have a wonderful Bichon Frise that is well tempered and healthy. She is a cute little sweetheart; however, she has always been afraid of thunder. I am not, so she is not responding to my fear. Are there any behavior-modification techniques I can try in an attempt to get her used to "Mr. Thunder"? I did mention this to her vet and she was given tranquilizers, which I was not happy with. She is just so frightened and I feel sorry for her.

### DR. NICHOL:

Mr. Thunder, eh? Why not Ms. Thunder? We really don't know what gender to assign to thunder, do we? I didn't think so. Assuming a scary thing like thunder to be male. Hmmmph.

OK, fear of thunder and other loud noises. For dogs who live in a desert, loud noises occur mostly around Independence Day. For a problem that infrequent, heavy sedation is not a bad thing. But if your dog is exposed to repeated loud noises like thunder, there is, in fact, an effective behavior-modification technique. For it to work you must be dedicated and patient—which I think you are.

For starters keep doing what you have been doing. Continue to give that little girl love and support. In addition, provide her a den like a plastic airline crate so she can feel that instinctive security. Ideally you want to start reducing her fear long before Mr. or Ms. Thunder (or the whole Thunder family) visits again. The technique is called flooding. It does not mean leaving the windows open during the storm. What it does mean is that you will buy a tape of the sounds of thunderstorms at your local New-Age sensitive bookstore. Your job will be to play the tape on very low volume in another room for short periods. If your baby acts anxious, move the tape player farther away and reduce the volume. When she acts relaxed after listening for a while, gradually increase the volume. Play the tape for short time periods at first, gradually increasing the volume and length of exposure. Anytime your dog acts frightened, reduce the volume a small amount. Ultimately this girl will become accustomed to the sound and her fear will dissipate. For best results, try to get to the end result before the next storm to avoid a setback.

Tranquilizers: These will only work if taken at least 30 minutes before the loud noises begin. They must be at high enough doses to cause your girl to be in a Zombie-like state—and you know what that is. It's the way you feel by the time you finally get to the end of one of my answers.

## Frightened Dogs and Leash Training

*Some dogs are born shy—it's no one's fault. But you can work with fear.*

### QUESTION:

I have a wonderful 10-month-old Chihuahua. He is such a delight. He will not walk on a leash—I either carry him or have to drag him. He is very shy and is so scared if I take him with me in the car or to the store like Petsmart. What can I do?

### DR. NICHOL:

Take heart. Teach your boy to walk on a leash the easy way. Start by clipping the 4- to 6-foot leash to his collar. (Do not use a harness. You can't steer a dog by pulling him around by his middle.) Let him drag the leash around the house for days, weeks, or years—until it becomes second nature. When it's clear that he's comfortable with a leash, pick up the end of it and walk with him. At some point during this indoor dog walk, your boy will feel the pull of the leash on his collar and panic. Your response will be to allow him some slack in the leash. Encourage him with a small treat and some gentle words until he relaxes. Then pat your thigh a few times and coax him along a little farther. Then drop the leash and let him drag it around the house some more. Do this several times a day. After a week or two he will learn that the leash means fun things.

Next: Shyness. That's a tough problem because it is a fundamental part of who your dog is. It is not because you have failed him somehow. It is a part of the personality with which he was born. But you can influence this trait by allowing him some exposure to strange places—slowly and gently. Like leash training, this must occur in a gradual, nonthreatening way. I suggest calling Petsmart and asking when the store is the least busy. Take your little guy there (after he is leash trained) and walk around a little. If you see another dog, *do not* pick up your dog—instead ask the other dog owner to keep some distance to avoid frightening your little guy. Give your boy a treat. (Eating and fear are inconsistent emotions.) Then walk in a relaxed way back to your car. Keep this up until we all feel better. Don't let him feel threatened, but also do not allow yourself to become anxious. Our pets sense our emotions immediately—every time.

# Feeding and Nutrition

## People Food

*Dogs are the best trainers. Here's how you can be the trainer. Teach your dog to eat dog food.*

### Question:

My dog will not eat dog food; but prefers "people" food. I know this is not good for her, but I don't know how to change her. I have tried giving only dog food until she accepts it. It seems almost cruel to do it that way. She always outlasts me, and I will fix some chicken and rice or beef stew meat.

P.S. I really enjoy the light and amusing style in your writing.

### Dr. Nichol:

My writing is not nor has it ever been light and amusing. I would never poke fun at anyone who has been so thoroughly and reliably trained by their dog. This girl of yours has taught you well. She needs a job in the school system.

Can we get serious now? If you want this sweet little dog to grow old, you must feed her a complete and balanced diet—for a dog. Our pets are so much like us, but they are still members of a different species. If you continue to allow your baby to eat an unbalanced diet, she will be at increased risk of heart and kidney failure as well as obesity. Add degenerative arthritis from the overload to her joints and you end up with a sick dog.

So your mission, should you decide to accept it, is to give this sly little fox *dog* food—only. Can she safely go without eating if she refuses? If she's healthy (an exam by her doctor will establish this), she can easily go several days with no food. This girl's ancestors could generate energy between kills for longer than a week. If you give her a bowl of high-quality, hard dry food (Science Diet, Iams) and nothing else, she will eat. Feed her and she will come.

## How Much Meat Is Too Much?
*Sometimes, you just can't cater to your canine.*

### QUESTION:
Does it hurt to feed a dog boiled chuck roast, rump roast, or round steak daily? I have been feeding this to my 5-year-old mini Dachshund for years. She would rather eat people food than dog food.

### DR. NICHOL:
Me, too. I would much rather eat people food than dog food. But, personally, I gave up the red meat thing. It seemed like the New Age thing to do.

Dogs, like the rest of us, need balanced diets. Meat protein is necessary for your Dachshund, but giving too much is no good. In fact, excessive protein is among the leading reasons for the huge number of kidney failure cases in dogs.

How can we get her to eat dog food? As long as she is healthy, she'll eat when she's ready. Most pets I know on people food have been accustomed to getting a variety of tasty offerings from their doting owners—so much, in fact, that many of them eat way too much and have the waistlines to show for it. If you have short legs like a miniature Dachshund, that could be a real drag. (That was a joke.)

"How boring," you say? Sorry. Dogs really do love to eat. A bowl of high-quality, hard dry food just doesn't look very exciting. But if you want this baby to stay in your life for as long as possible, you must protect her health. Give her one-quarter cup of good dry food (it costs more) twice daily. For fun, instead of allowing her to gorge herself on beef, have a ball game together or take a walk. Exercise—what a concept.

## Begging
*Rewarding this behavior with food will encourage more of it. Avoid the problem and the weight gain that goes with it by putting your pets outside while you eat.*

## QUESTION:

Could you shed some light on giving table scraps like chicken, pork, and beef? I have a situation where some teenagers will give their dog candy because the dog is constantly begging for human food, even though the dog is on the Science Diet program.

## DR. NICHOL:

Your question shows that you are concerned about the health risks resulting from an improper diet. I will first explain how this problem has developed for your family; then I'll tell you what you can do about it.

Let's start with the basic survival instincts of dogs and cats. Despite their centuries of domestication, most of their wild tendencies remain. When they were living in the wild, they knew that they might not survive harsh conditions. To avoid starvation, they learned to be scavengers. And they still do it, even in a home like yours with an abundance of food. Furthermore, we know that there is no better motivator than food. If a pet gets food when he or she does something, that critter will repeat that same behavior, expecting the same reward. So if you feed your pets from the table, they'll be back again for more. Many pet owners enjoy this as much as the pet because it builds a reliable relationship.

Now for the down side. Pets who get table food eventually refuse a complete and balanced diet, even a good one like Science Diet. They just camp out at the dinner table—and they get fat. They also develop problems like kidney failure, liver disease, diabetes, heart failure, and arthritis.

Is it worth it? If pet owners are in denial about the damage being done to their beloved pet's health, they can delude themselves into believing that they are actually helping the pet.

The trick is to never let the problem start. Simply do not let your pets in the room when you are eating. If you already have a pet who eats human food, you must practice tough love. Give all adult dogs and cats two measured feedings per day. Put each pet in a separate room, with the door closed, while they eat. When they walk away from the bowl, pick it up. Your pets are allowed back together only when all of the food bowls have been picked up. There is never food available to them when they are together. This prevents obesity in pets who sneak food from the other pets.

What if you feel sad because this snacking together with your pet has been a source of joy and sharing for you both? I understand the love of shared activities. I love my dog so much I took him to obedience training class. We shared the joy of learning and practicing our lessons together. We also shared a Frisbee, hiking, and good music. Ah, what a life.

## Table Food: What's Toxic and What's Best
*You'll be surprised by what human foods are dangerous to dogs.*

### QUESTION:

Please list foods that may be or are toxic to dogs. I know about chocolate, but my daughter tells me that onions and peanuts should not be fed to dogs even in very small amounts. My dog likes raw carrots, celery, and bananas. I know that your position is to feed them only high-quality dog food, but do other things in small amounts harm them?

### DR. NICHOL:

Are you ready? Is your dog ready? Onions, chocolate, alcoholic beverages (hic), yeast dough, coffee (for some of the same reasons as chocolate), tea (caffeine), salt, macadamia nuts, hops (used in home beer brewing—hic), tomato and potato leaves and stems, rhubarb leaves, tobacco, moldy foods, and some wild mushrooms are all toxic to dogs. I checked with Dr. Jill Richardson at the National Animal Poison Control Center in Urbana, IL (1-800-528-2423). Peanuts did not make the list. I can tell you from experience that while they are not poisonous, peanuts have a lot of fat, like bananas. In short: Please feed dog food only.

Why not give your dog small amounts of other things? High-fiber raw vegetables like celery and carrots can be a good way to help "fill up" an overweight dog because it takes as much calories to digest them as they give. But the problem I have seen is that dogs often really like some of the table food they get from their owners and eventually start to refuse dog food. These dogs end up on unbalanced diets that predispose them to a myriad of health problems.

A good-quality, hard, dry adult dog food is complete and it's balanced. The balance is important. For example, we know that minerals like calcium and phosphorus must be in the proper ratio or a dog will develop bone and kidney diseases. Throwing a diet out of balance by adding to it can only risk your dog's health. Sorry to be the party pooper.

## Vegetables in the Diet
*Great for the humans, but dogs need them predigested.*

### QUESTION:
My little Terrier loves raw vegetables—lettuce, broccoli, carrots, okra, etc.—and fruits—apples and oranges. Will eating these harm her? She eats them in addition to her dry food.

### DR. NICHOL:
Fruits and vegetables are unnecessary for dogs if you are feeding a complete and balanced diet, which most are nowadays. In fact, anything you add to a balanced diet is really just throwing it out of balance and thus lowering your dog's plane of nutrition. While dogs need the vitamins and nutrients in those healthy foods, they have a different system of digestion.

Can we go back to the wild? The free-roaming dog eats game—the whole beast: muscle, hair, intestines, organs, brains, and toenails. Inside those intestines is the food consumed by that other critter: vegetation. This vital source of nutrition is partially digested already, which is exactly the way the canine digestive system needs it to be. High-quality, complete, and balanced dog foods supply these nutrients in a digestible form. The bottom line is that you can give fruits and veggies to your Terrier, but they'll do her little if any good. I recommend feeding your dog, get ready, dog food.

## Supplements
*Feed your dog an excellent diet and forget the rest.*

### QUESTION:
Can you tell me your thoughts regarding supplements for young pups? It seems there are differing opinions as to whether or not they are necessary. He is on Nutro's Natural Choice for dogs not pups, which the breeder (and many others) have suggested.

### DR. NICHOL:
You are an excellent dog owner. I wish everyone loved their pets the way you do. If you feed a high-quality, balanced dog food (not puppy food), then additives are unnecessary. Is it okay to add to the diet anyway, just to

be sure? Please don't. You can cause organ damage if some vitamins are overdosed. The best dog food has the highest price (no kidding). Feed the good stuff and sleep well at night, which I know you are not doing because you have a 4-month-old puppy.

## Overweight Dogs
*Low thyroid function is a factor for some obese dogs.*

### QUESTION:
We have a 4-year-old male Whippet (Echo) with a severe weight problem that we have been trying to get under control for some eight months. We have tried many different diets. With some he was so hungry in about two hours that he would begin crying and trying to open the food container. We even had to put childproof locks on all the cupboard doors because he would open them looking for food. Could there be a problem with his thyroid? He also at times appears to have no energy, which is not normal for a Whippet.

### DR. NICHOL:
Good diagnosis. Hypothyroidism (low thyroid hormone) is a likely answer in part because of Echo's low energy. Other possible explanations for your not-so-streamlined racing dog would include other hormone imbalances like diabetes or Cushing's syndrome (an adrenal problem).

But don't go shopping for hormones yet. First, get a physical exam. (Sorry to sound like a broken record—remember records?) If your boy checks out well on his exam, your doctor will send off a blood thyroid profile. Results should be available the next day. If he comes up positive, once or twice daily tablets should make him right again. But that bit about tearing into the food container: Why not see if you can get him a role in a dog-food commercial?

## Chocolate Candy and Smoking
*Secondhand or otherwise, this stuff is poison.*

### QUESTION:
Hi. My dog, Bruce, is 5 years old. He likes to eat chocolate. I heard that chocolates are toxic to dogs. Is this true? There's one other thing I'm really concerned about. I've been giving my dog candies since he was about 3 months old. I smoke a

lot and I eat candies when I do. After smoking, I give my dog what's left of the candy. Is this going to affect his health in any way? I once asked my veterinarian about that and she said that she encourages owners to give sweets to their dogs. I'm not really sure if that's true. Do I have any reason to be worried? I hope you can enlighten me on these matters. I love my dog so much and I just want him to be in the best possible health.

### Dr. Nichol:

Ahem. What are my chances of talking Bruce out of all the above? I too want Bruce to be in the best possible health, so I will ask him to mend his evil ways.

Chocolate: No good. The problem is that chocolate causes liver damage in many dogs. Our pets' bodies don't handle chocolate or Tylenol or many other substances the same way ours do. Chocolate contains a chemical called methylxanthine that not only damages their livers but can cause seizures. How about other candy? It's mostly sugar, which by itself isn't all that bad. The problem is that when dogs eat sugar, the pancreas releases insulin. If they eat alot of sugar, the pancreas works full-time until it burns out. The permanent result could be diabetes. While diabetes can occur in any dog or cat, I know Bruce doesn't want it to happen to him.

All of this leads us to the last, and perhaps worst, of Bruce's vices: smoking. Did he start this as a teenager? You know, I hate to see young kids like Bruce do this. Not only will it affect his health; it's bad for everyone in the home. The most common result of smoking for dogs is chronic bronchitis—and we see this a lot. Dogs who smoke, or who live with smokers, can't recover until the smoke clears permanently, meaning that no one should smoke in the home—for Bruce's sake as well as yours.

Have Bruce reach for a high-fiber dog biscuit called Fiber Form (available at your pet supply store or your local veterinary clinic) instead of a cigarette or chocolate or candy. A nice raw, fibrous vegetable will be an excellent substitute for your bad habits as well. Now I have a question: Where did that other veterinarian get her degree anyway? Mail order catalog? Sheesh!

## Maintaining Healthy Weight

*Prescription diets r/d and w/d make it easy to help your dog keep that slim figure.*

## QUESTION:

I have my dog on diet food and he is now at his required weight. Should I change to regular food or give him more of the diet food? He acts like he's starving all the time.

## DR. NICHOL:

Good job! Do you know how often I preach my weight-loss sermon to the owners of fat dogs? It's really remarkable. I tell people their dog is overweight. I say it delicately. But I get these looks of disbelief. Then responses like, "Do you really think so?" or "He hardly eats a thing" or (one of my personal favorites) "It's really just a lot of hair, Doc. There must be five pounds of hair on him. He really just needs grooming." Puhleese. It's like they can talk me out of their dog being fat. If a pet owner can plead really hard with me, I won't insist on putting their "baked potato on toothpicks" on a weight-loss diet to save his life. Okay, I'm done now. I'm stepping down from the pulpit.

Yes, you can put your dog on a more enjoyable diet if he has returned to his normal weight. Here is how it works. As the body takes in more calories than it needs for day-to-day functioning, it stores those calories as fat. A moderate amount of fat is good because it gives us a reserve "fuel tank" in case we get sick and need it to survive. But excessive amounts overload organs like the heart and kidneys. It strains our joints and leads to painful arthritis. I hate when that happens.

You, on the other hand, have given your beloved pet the gift of health by correcting his weight problem. The easy and safe way to do this for most pets is to feed prescription diet r/d (your veterinarian has it). R/d is very different from regular or "light" diets because it is very high in fiber and low in fat. It allows an overweight pet to eat fairly generous portions and still lose weight. But when you can feel your dog's ribs with your fingertips (not see his ribs—*feel* them) he is about right. Now that he has reached his goal, you want to stop his weight loss and maintain his now healthy weight. Do this with prescription diet w/d.

Isn't that easy? The truth is that it really is pretty easy for the pets. The real cause of the shortened unhealthy lives of overweight dogs and cats is not the critters themselves but their owners. It's the mistaken belief that we can show our love with French fries and ice cream. But you can share that puppy love much longer by feeding only healthy amounts of a balanced dog food (that's *dog* food), then taking a brisk walk together. Imagine giving that to your dog—and improving your own health and energy level while you're at it. It's good when that happens.

## Corn as the Main Ingredient
*Are you crazy? Dogs don't eat corn in the wild. They need meat, right?*

### QUESTION:
Can dogs digest corn? I know the number-one ingredient in most dog food is ground corn meal, or something like that. If they can't digest it, then isn't most of the dog food you feed your dog just "running through them"?

### DR. NICHOL:
Don't you know that reading food labels can be dangerous to your health? Why, you can become anxious and stressed. Let me help both you and your pets to live a lot longer.

Corn is fine. Heresy, you say? Aren't dogs carnivores? Aren't they supposed to stealthily track cute woodland vegetarian creatures, pounce on them, and then rip them to pieces? Sure they are. So why are vegetables in the diet of your carnivorous pets? Because when inveterate predators like our pets eat their prey, they eat all of their prey. That means the hair, bone, organs, intestinal contents, and a bit of meat (muscle). In other words, they get a balanced diet in the wild by eating what their food ate—vegetation.

Don't get too excited when you read pet food labels. Simply understand that ingredients and guaranteed analyses are regulated by laws that are riddled with loopholes and nuance. There is really no way for you to know the true digestibility or nutritional value of your pets' food by reading the container—except for one clue: price.

During my years in practice I have seen the physical results of feeding every type of pet food. The good stuff costs more, but it results in healthier haircoats and more active immune systems. Your pets will feel better. It's clear from your letter that you want the best for them. You won't get what you don't pay for. Spend a couple of extra bucks and give them the best.

## Bones and Other Table Treats for Dogs
*Feed no bones. Eat without your pets. Table food leads to trouble.*

## QUESTION:

Our 1-year-old female Jack Russell Terrier might have swallowed some fish bones. She seems fine, but I am worried that they will hurt her in her stomach and cause problems. Should I be worried and take her to the vet, or just love her as usual?

## DR. NICHOL:

The reason for your concern is that you love this girl. The good news is that she's not likely to have any real problems from fish bones. Unlike beef, pork, or poultry bones, fish bones are thin and quite flexible. They usually soften in the stomach and intestines and pass without trouble. If they really irritate her tummy, she will vomit and be done with it. What if the bones get stuck? In that case, your girl will stop eating and vomit or wretch often, but unproductively. If that happens, take that garbage-gut girl to the doctor.

A word about dinnertime: Most pets will engulf all the table food you dish out because they believe you are rewarding their begging with those tasty morsels. Once they develop a fondness for turkey, candy, and eggnog, they become more prone to raiding the garbage and swallowing some really dangerous stuff. Don't let your love lead to a life of lard. Put your pets out of the room at dinnertime. Then get the lead out and share a brisk walk. Start now. Put the book down. Grab the leash and get going.

# Pig Ears

*Fine—as long as the pig and the dog aren't related.*

## QUESTION:

I was wondering if pig ears are bad for dogs.

## DR. NICHOL:

I've always thought this should be a matter of personal preference. If a dog has no ears at all, then pig ears are better than none. On the other hand, a guy or gal with a decent set of God-given ears should just be happy and accept themselves as they are.

Now, eating pig ears is a different story. It seems to be quite a delicacy and does no harm, although I have never developed a taste for them. But like all things, especially around the holidays, moderation is best.

## Rawhide Chews

*A great way to keep a dog occupied and maintain healthy teeth and gums.*

### QUESTION:

I have a healthy 3-1/2-year-old female Great Dane. She really likes rolled cowhide chew toys. I let her have one about five times a week. A coworker of my wife's told her that cowhide chew toys are bad for dogs. What's the scoop?

### DR. NICHOL:

You'll hear old wives' tales of all kinds—such as feeding dogs sugar will give them worms or allowing them to stick their heads out the window of a moving car will cause blindness. The truth is that sugar causes obesity, not worms; and dogs leaning out of cars don't go blind, but they often do end up as roadkill.

Rawhide chews, on the other hand, are among the great inventions of the twentieth century. In our home, we liken them to the pacifiers we gave our boys when they were babies. Without rawhides, Peter Rabbit, the 10-month-old Border Collie nutball, would have swallowed Power Rangers and Pokemon instead. I'd have had to install a zipper in his gut just to avoid repeated incisions. Rawhides give chewing dogs a wholesome activity. They also help reduce shoplifting and gang violence—for many dogs, an idle mouth is the devil's workshop.

But here's what I want to know: Are old wives the only people with misinformation? What about old husbands? The truth is that I've heard more nonsense from young single people than anybody else.

## Cheap Pet Food Is No Bargain

*Lower-priced diets boast comparisons with the better brands, but you won't get what you don't pay for.*

### QUESTION:

I read an article in *Consumer Reports* that said some of the lower-priced pet foods are a much better deal than food like Science Diet because the ingredients are just as good but the price is much lower. But you've said that the premium brands are better. Somebody doesn't have their story straight.

## Dr. Nichol:

You're not the first person to raise this point. In fact Hills Pet Products, makers of Science Diet, took issue directly with *Consumer Reports* over its faulty methods of analysis. The editors of the magazine have written an apology to Hills stating that it will do the analysis over more thoroughly and reprint its findings.

It turns out that *Consumer Reports* got into this mess for the same reason many pet owners do: They believed the labels on the lower-priced foods. Isn't it illegal to lie on the package, you ask? Well, in the strictest sense, they are not lying. By the use of parentheses and commas, the order in which ingredients are listed, and the loophole of allowing some ingredient names to encompass many different sources of nutrition, a pet food company can make its product look pretty good. Unfortunately for many pets, the real differences are striking. To make the point, shoe leather has been analyzed for its protein content. The results are around 22 percent—roughly comparable to many pet foods. Too bad you can't recycle your old shoes, handbags, and gloves by feeding them to your pets.

I will conclude my response by recounting my observations of the health of the pets I examine and treat on a daily basis. Cheap food, no matter how low the price, results in poor haircoats, large volumes of soft stool (lots more to clean up), poor weight, and diminished defenses against disease. In addition, the high salt content and excessive quantities of poor digestibility protein add to the risk of kidney failure as these bargain-fed pets age. As the old saw goes: The bitterness of poor quality is remembered long after the sweetness of low price is forgotten. Put differently: You don't get what you don't pay for.

## The Healthy Dog Who Won't Eat

*Frequent dog food changes, gas, and dry flaky skin: This fellow needs a consistent diet.*

### Question:

We adopted Satchmo a few months ago—he was the featured pup in the paper one day—and I'm having a heck of a time trying to get the little bugger to eat. I started him right off on lamb and rice, but he developed patchy red armpits, itchies, and heavy scalp flaking right away. So, I switched him to a new Nature's Choice Hound Formula. He ate it initially, but had some nasty gas and started to refuse it completely. Then, when left at "camp" while we were away, he ate Wayne's Chunks, which is beef-based. He was doing really well, and we're on the beginning of our second 40-pound bag, but since last weekend, he won't touch it, not even with warm water. And I've given him a few sample bags of some food that our neighbor gave us; he's eaten those (but with some gas again). Many thanks for any advice you wish to spare!

## DR. NICHOL:

So I guess Satchmo has a discriminating palate. He also has gas and an armpit and dandruff problem. This sounds like another one for Ann Landers. But this book deals with practical pet care, so I suppose I'm on the hook.

You are clearly a doting dog owner and I respect that. But I want you to know that your pandering to Satchmo's tastes shows what a good trainer he is, and I respect that, too. Each time he tires of the delicate morsels that you offer him, you oblige him with more exotic fare. It's time for you to be the trainer and for Satchmo to be the trainee.

Here is your assignment: Feed Satchmo any high-priced dry food you want. (Cheap pet food is no good—you don't get what you don't pay for.) But if you plan a diet change, do it gradually over a few days. The gut is a creature of habit. Sudden changes cause—you guessed it—gas and loose stool.

Don't food allergies cause patchy red armpits, itchy skin, and dandruff? Maybe. Skin disease can have many causes. For diagnosis and treatment of skin disease, I recommend the services of a real doctor. What if Satch won't eat? Ah, that's the real problem, isn't it? You're afraid that Satch will starve because he doesn't prefer today's menu selection, right? Here is what I would like you to tell Satchmo. Repeat after me: "Sorry, Satchmo, but that mean Dr. Nichol says this food is all you will get morning and night. If you refuse it, I will not feel guilty, but instead I will know that by giving only one brand of high-quality dry food, I am showing my love for you. If you realize that I, your loving owner, have taken charge, you will finally eat when you are truly hungry—even if it takes several days." Now take a deep breath . . . and begin.

## Dogs Eating Cat Food and Cats Eating Dog Food

*Cats and dogs are different species with very different needs. Poor health can result from the wrong diet.*

### QUESTION:

Our 8-month-old Pomeranian-Dachshund sure enjoys eating the cat food! (Although the cat doesn't appreciate it much.) Is this a bad thing? Also, the cat kinda digs the dog food once in a while. What do you think?

### DR. NICHOL:

This reminds me of how much our pets resemble our children. Regardless of how well intentioned our efforts to give them what is right, they want the opposite. And it's tempting to just let it go. After all, pet food tends to look the same anyway, right?

Well, I'm glad you asked. There are significant nutritional differences between cat and dog foods and for good reasons. For starters, the physiology of cats requires that their bodies function at a more acid pH. This necessitates a diet much higher in protein than dogs require. Cats also need more of the amino acid taurine. Insufficient levels of taurine result in a terminal heart condition called dilated cardiomyopathy. So a cat who eats a diet heavy in dog food will have serious deficiencies.

How about a dog eating cat food? Not only do dogs need less protein than cats, they pay a big price if they get too much. By far the most common organ failure disease in older dogs is kidney failure. One big cause for this is, you guessed it, excessive protein in their diets.

The last question has to be: How do you fight this battle and win? First, I'll tell you what does not work. Do not sit your pets down and have a heart-to-heart. Explaining that these species-specific diets are for their own good won't work on your pets anymore than it does on your kids. ("Yeah, right, Dad." No respect.) Also forget the idea of supervising them while they eat. When it comes to food, pets are masters of deceit and diversion. Your only hope is to feed all adult pets twice daily. Give each pet his or her own measured amount of food in his or her very own bowl—and here's the most important part—feed each pet in an isolated separate room with the door closed. When everyone is finished eating, pick up the bowls and mealtime is over.

I know I speak of our pets as though they are devious creatures who love us unconditionally. But they know I'm right, don't they? Naw. But they will thank me later.

## Designer Pet Foods and High Price

*If the ingredients match and the analysis looks as good, why pay more? Because you won't get what you don't pay for.*

QUESTION:

I read an article in last week's paper that got me to thinking about how much money I spend feeding my animals. The article talked about "designer" pet foods and said that regular food like Dog Chow is just as good, but that a lot of people buy the pricier food because it's recommended by their vets. Isn't it really all the same?

DR. NICHOL:

I wish more people asked this question. There is a vast array of pet foods available nowadays. Whether you buy it in the supermarket, pet supply store, veterinary hospital, or health food store, there are way too many choices. With our lives in America getting as complicated and busy as they are, choosing dog food should be a lot simpler. I will make it simpler for you now.

The first point is the type of food. In other words, should you feed hard dry, canned, or the semi-moist stuff that comes in the cellophane packages? The answer to that—unless you have been given a medical reason—is never feed anything but hard dry food. It's healthier for the teeth and gums than soft food and it's much cheaper to feed. If you need convincing, note that dry food is about 13 percent moisture (water), while canned food is 75 percent moisture. Semi-moist is somewhere in between. Add to that the additional cost of packaging (about 25 cents for the can itself), and you begin to see that dry is the only way to go. For those pets who refuse dry food, I would forget about lecturing them on the importance of healthy teeth. Kids these days never listen anyway. They got no respect.

What about senior, less active, and light diets? While there are pets who need a special food for weight loss or for management of an age-related problem, the diets available at the grocery or pet supply store are only slightly different from the regular stuff. Only the prescription foods that your veterinarian has are going to make a significant difference for pets who are overweight or geriatric. What is left is regular dry pet food—in a million different brands and prices.

Now, the informed pet lover feels an obligation to read the ingredients and nutritional analysis on the bag and compare brands. This would seem to make sense, but the pet food manufacturers are way ahead of you. They know that with sleight of hand they can word their list of ingredients to appear to outclass the others and beat the competition on price. If that weren't enough, they also provide you with the nutritional analysis, you know, the percentage of protein, carbohydrates—everything a healthy pet needs in the greatest quantity possible, right? It's enough to give a normal person a headache.

Well, here's how it works. If you are a cheap pet food company bent on making a quick buck, you can design an impressive label listing great ingredients and high percentages of protein. Then you find the cheapest sources possible. Does it matter to the health of pets? You bet it does. In our hospital, we see pets fed every diet you've ever heard of and many whose names we hear only once. Poor-quality food results in rough haircoats, soft stools, poor exercise tolerance, and sometimes the inability to maintain normal weight. On the other hand, the genuinely excellent diets not only prevent these problems, but pets on the better foods stay energetic much later in their lives. They just seem to feel better.

How do you know which foods are worth feeding and which are just a lot of hype? Price. It's really that simple. If a diet is highly digestible with truly good-quality nutrients, it cannot be possible to produce it at a bargain price. You will not get what you don't pay for. Who can afford the highest priced food? Anybody—here's why. One way to make a seemingly good-quality pet food at a low price is to add fillers like wheat hulls. The bag really weighs what it says, but it's not really all food. Since the body knows how many bioavailable calories it needs, your pet will require a lot more volume just to get the necessary calories. So if she's eating more volume, you're going to buy food much more often than if you fed the good stuff. The bottom line is that your expenses for pet food will be about the same over the long term, whether you feed higher-priced, excellent food or cheaper food that claims to be just as good. And while your long-term cost is about the same, the health of your pets will be much better if you choose higher-quality food. Cheap is not better. Better is better—and you really cannot get the best for less. The pet food business is very competitive. If the makers of the better diets could produce their foods for less money, they would.

One last point: With high levels of filler in cheap food, there is a lot more waste—you know, that nasty stuff you shovel up in the yard or litter pan. If you are the pooper scooper at your house, better pet food will improve your quality of life, too.

# Grooming

## Bathing: How Often? What Shampoo?

*With a few exceptions, never is best. Brushing is much healthier.*

### Question:

How often should I bathe my pets? I've heard everything from once a week to never.

### Dr. Nichol:

For almost all pets, the right answer is never. No kidding. Here's why. Unlike humans, pets don't have sweat glands. Without them there is really no hygienic need for frequent shampooing. But pets, especially dogs, do start to smell funky without grooming. This is because, like all of us, they normally accumulate skin flakes and dead hair on their skin. But each time you use shampoo, you wash away an important layer of protective oils that serve as a barrier to skin disease. So the best method is to use a brush on a short-coated pet or a metal comb on a long-haired pet. This stimulates the scalp and pulls loose the dead hair and skin flakes. Dogs smell better, look better, and feel real good, too. Best of all, their skin stays healthy. If they get muddy, you can rinse them with water as often as you want.

# Heart and Breathing

## Annual Heartworm Prevention and Testing
*Treat year-round with once-monthly chewables.*

### Question:
We moved six months ago and our vet there didn't heartworm-test our dog after he was 9 months old because the dog was on the heartworm preventive year-round. Our new vet says that the dog needs to be blood-tested every year. Why? It's so expensive and I'm a senior citizen on a limited income.

### Dr. Nichol:
You have raised an important question. Here are the basic facts you must know to protect your dog. Heartworm preventive tablets are given monthly. They are safe and effective; but like most medications, imperfect. This means that to be sure your dog is not infected with heartworms, he or she needs a blood test annually.

What can happen if you don't have the blood test done? Consider this: If your dog is feeling fine but found to be heartworm-positive on an annual heartworm test, treatment to kill the parasites can usually be done safely. Your dog would suffer no long-term effects. On the other hand, if you skip the annual test and your dog gets heartworm, you would have no way of knowing it until he started coughing (possibly coughing up blood), losing weight, and becoming inactive. In this case, he could also be treated for heartworm infection; but with symptoms like these, the risk is high for complications or death. Long-term effects may include scarring in his lungs from the dead heartworms, which can cause exercise intolerance. The bottom line is that it is much safer to test annually.

The last question we often hear is, why is it important to give the preventive tablets year-round if we don't have mosquitoes in the winter? This year-round recommendation comes from the American Heartworm Society. Research has shown that mosquitoes are becoming better-adapted parasites. This means they have learned to survive indoors in closets, sheds, and garages, even during the winter. The heartworm risk to your dog is somewhat less in the winter, but he is still vulnerable unless the preventive is given nonstop. You are right that all of this can get expensive, but it's still a lot cheaper than the cost of treatment.

# Heartworm Disease

*How to recognize it, how to prevent it, how it's treated.*

### QUESTION:

What are the symptoms of heartworms and is there a cure? If I give my dog a heartworm pill every month, do I have to give him wormer medicine, too?

### DR. NICHOL:

Smart questions. Every dog owner hears recommendations of heartworm prevention, but not everyone knows why. I'm a veritable fountain of information, so I will enlighten you.

*Dirofilaria immitus* (impressive name, eh?) is a stringy, spaghetti-like worm that gets biggest in the heart, but does its worst damage in the lungs. Occasionally, other organs like the kidneys, liver, brain, and eyeballs are also affected. Most infected dogs cough with exertion, lose weight, and become much less active. The reason is that worms living in the vessels of the lungs choke off the blood supply. Badly infected dogs cough up blood. Some arrive at the animal hospital in acute liver failure. Cats can get heartworm, too. It is treatable. An injectable drug called Immitacide works well, but severe infections result in permanent lung scarring—meaning a lot less stamina. Without treatment, many cases are fatal.

That all sounds awful, but it's also unnecessary because the preventives, Heartgard Plus and Interceptor, are very good. Use either of them, whichever your veterinarian recommends. They also prevent two intestinal parasites, so you shouldn't need other wormers. Given monthly, they work against heartworm by killing the microscopic larval worms that pets get from carrier mosquitoes.

One last point: Mosquitoes have gotten better adapted—they can now live inside homes in the winter. So give the chewable tablets once monthly, year-round. Don't stop in the fall. But while the preventives are good, they're not perfect, so get a heartworm blood test once a year just in case. And don't believe that thick-coated dogs are safe from marauding bloodthirsty mosquitoes. We see more heartworm infections in all breeds every year.

## Heart Murmurs in Puppies

*Some abnormal heart sounds are dangerous—but early, thorough diagnosis is key to good outcomes.*

### QUESTION:

I'm a proud owner of a beautiful Siberian Husky who is 8 weeks old and is suspected to have a heart murmur. If that is true, what will happen to my puppy? Will she be able to live a long life? I'm worried to death.

### DR. NICHOL:

I understand how you feel. If you learn more about heart murmurs, you'll feel better. Using a stethoscope, we can hear the extra heart sounds that are called murmurs. It's a *shhh* sound during the lub-dub of the normal heartbeat. In some puppies, murmurs are caused by the flow of blood through a passageway that should have closed before birth. In others, the sound can result from blood shooting through a normal passage that's abnormally narrow.

We see a lot of heart murmurs in our practice, but to make sure you're getting the latest information, I contacted Dr. Larry Tilley, a board-certified veterinary cardiologist. Here's the scoop: Many low-volume murmurs (what we call Grade I) will resolve all by themselves in just 2-3 weeks. These are called innocent or growth murmurs. They mean nothing. These puppies grow to adulthood normally. We become concerned about the future for puppies whose murmurs remain. Dr. Tilley's recommendation is to have that heart examined again in a few weeks. If the murmur is still there, have the doctor take chest X-rays and an electrocardiogram (ECG). If the puppy tests normal, she should be rechecked when she is fully-grown. If her tests are still fine, her future should be bright. If her tests are not fine, other diagnostic work can be done. There are several possible causes; two of them are curable.

For now, try not to worry. Your little girl is having great fun being a goofy kid. Share that joy and take one day at a time. Based on a lot of experience with heart murmurs, I can tell you that the great majority of puppies grow up strong and healthy. Now, throw down this book and run around the yard with that Husky girl.

## Heart Failure

*Medications can have side effects. Know what to look for.*

### QUESTION:

My dog, Comet, is 11 years old with an enlarged heart and liver. She is refusing to eat her dog food. After her bloodwork and X-rays, she was put on Vasotec and furosemide. She will eat rice with some chicken. I have checked several books, and seem to get contradictory information. What would be an acceptable diet, considering she won't eat dog food?

### DR. NICHOL:

Good for you. Because of your conscientious care, we know what's wrong with Comet. Treatment has been started, but now she won't eat. We can help.

A review of Comet's lab work establishes the diagnosis, but it does not indicate a severe problem. Rather than trying to tailor a diet for her, I recommend we find out why she won't eat. If her poor appetite is related to her medications, a dosage adjustment may be all we need. Vasotec is known to cause lack of appetite. Ask Comet's doctor if reducing her dose would be okay, and see if she doesn't regain her appetite. If that fails, tell her doctor. A poor appetite is an important symptom.

## Snorting (You Know, Like a Pig)

*"Reverse sneezing" usually has allergic causes. Antihistamines should help.*

### QUESTION:

I have a 3-year-old female Pug named "Pug." I know we should have come up with something else instead of "Pug" but... Anyway about once a month, she has what I call a seizure, but all I've read doesn't describe what she has. Pug acts like she's trying to "hock up a loogey." It lasts for about 15 to 30 seconds and then she's fine. Sometimes it reoccurs a few minutes later and lasts maybe 10 to 15 seconds. It's not like she's trying to throw up. She's exhaling extremely hard and making a grunting sound like she is trying to "hock one up."

### Dr. Nichol:

Hocking up loogeys? You are so crude. No wonder Pug behaves like a barbarian. Maybe if she had a more refined influence at home, she wouldn't be such an animal.

Okay, I'll take the high road on this one and explain Pug's problem. She is not having a seizure. She has postnasal drip. Just like a person with allergies or a cold, she gets a gob of mucus that hangs off the back of her soft palate. But instead of discreetly expectorating like the actors in the movie *Titanic*, Pug just does her best to gross you out whenever the whim strikes.

So, what do you do about it? If she makes enough noise with all this hocking to keep you awake at night, you can give her an antihistamine like Benedryl at bedtime to dry up those mucus secretions for several hours—or you can join her. A family that hocks loogeys together, stays together.

## Sneezing and Coughing

***Dogs don't get colds the way we do, but they can get some serious upper respiratory diseases. See the doctor.***

### Question:

I have a 7-year-old mixed breed (Lab and Husky). Over the past couple of days, she has been sneezing and coughing. Do dogs catch colds? I'm not sure what to do.

### Dr. Nichol:

Your dog is in good company. I, too, am mixed-breed. I have worked in a lab, but have never been husky, though I have wanted to be. I am no longer 7. I'm 39. Again.

Dogs do not catch colds. When we humans have colds, what we really have is a complex of several organisms that may be different from one cold season to the next. Most of the time, the primary infectious cause is a virus that is specific to humans. Dogs don't get this virus. Thus, what your girl has is not so simple as: Drink plenty of fluids, take extra vitamin C, and wait it out.

So, what could cause the sneezing and coughing? There are several possibilities, including a foreign body like a grass awn stuck in her throat or an infection in her nasal sinuses. If she is unvaccinated, we also need to consider distemper. Antibiotics may be all she needs to get well—but her doctor might also suggest diagnostic work like cultures or anesthesia for a special exam of her nose and throat. My advice is to take this girl directly to your veterinarian. Do not pass "Go." Do not collect $200. She is unlikely to get over this thing on her own.

## Noisy Breathing

*Gradual onset of paralysis of the voice box can be dangerous but it is treatable.*

### QUESTION:

My 11-year-old female Lab's breathing is labored when walking and if there is any excitement at home. X-rays were normal. What are treatments? I competed for six years with Lucy in hunt tests and owe her so much.

### DR. NICHOL:

This must be hard for you and Lucy. Labs are active and playful anyway. But with Lucy also being a working dog, she has to be able to handle exertion without getting winded. Have faith; there is help.

While the lungs and airways are complex with many possible causes for breathing difficulty, the most likely problem is laryngeal paralysis. Here is why. When we are at rest our body's cells need only a small amount of oxygen. When our body works hard, needs suddenly become much greater. But Lucy's breathing gets difficult only when she is active. She's having a hard time getting air inside her lungs fast enough to meet the greater demand. A partial blockage of her larynx (voice box) will impede adequate airflow.

To help this high-energy girl get back to work, we must know the exact cause. Her normal X-rays tell us she has a healthy trachea (windpipe), but her larynx may be a different matter. This complicated little structure in our throats is responsible for making sure we don't breathe our food or swallow air. Special cartilages open as much as needed and close when appropriate. Lucy's larynx may not be opening and closing properly. Lucy needs to be given a light plane of general anesthesia so that her doctor can carefully watch the movement of her larynx. If she can't open her airway wide enough, we know she has a paralyzed larynx.

This sounds bad, and it is. But the good news is that a surgical procedure called a laryngeal tieback can put her right again. The operation would be best done by a well-trained and experienced surgeon. Lucy should end up with enough breathing capacity to enjoy a more active life. She's an excellent dog and an important friend. I say go for it.

## Kennel Cough

***Usually contracted in boarding or grooming establishments, it can be tough to manage. We can help, but it has to run its course.***

### QUESTION:

As an owner of three dogs, imagine my dismay when my vet told me my little one's problem was kennel cough. Their only exposure was at the groomer's. I, of course, hold no one responsible, but am very curious about the disease, its course, and the current preventives. Only my Lhasa mix seems affected. Is it common for some dogs to seem to be immune while others are so sick? Do dogs recover completely? I have gotten them the Bordatella inoculations when they were kenneled, but that has been over a year now, and I am aware that the protective time span is short. Should dogs be inoculated all the time for this disease? Does having kennel cough offer immunity to future infections? These are my babies, and it is hard for me to see the little one sick but unable to let me know exactly how she feels.

### DR. NICHOL:

I'm really sorry your dog has kennel cough. It can be a real nuisance, but is seldom life threatening.

Kennel cough is not a lifelong disease, but it certainly can seem like it when it can go on for a few weeks. Because it spreads quickly by coughing and by contact with surfaces—like contaminated floors and equipment, it is considered highly infectious. So it can be a big problem with groups of dogs, as in kennels and grooming shops. Kennel cough is recognized by a dry, hacking cough (sometimes with gagging and retching) that's most noticeable when there is pressure on the throat. But even though these poor dogs seem miserable, they usually continue to eat well and feel fine.

But that's in otherwise healthy adult dogs. Dogs with underlying health conditions and puppies can develop a severe bronchopneumonia that can be deadly. That's because of the other organisms that nearly always accompany the two main bugs that cause kennel cough: parainfluenza virus and a bacteria called Bordatella bronchiseptica.

All of this sounds pretty awful, but the vaccines are good—with limitations. The distemper–parvo combination given annually also protects against two of the organisms responsible for kennel cough but not Bordatella. The best defense for dogs who are planning visits to kennels and grooming shops is to also give the Bordatella vaccine. This is best administered as drops into the nose, which gives a local immunity. It starts working in just two days—but lasts only four to six months. (The vaccine insert claims one year, but recent independent studies have been more realistic.) And you're right—some dogs who are exposed won't get the disease. Nevertheless, I would protect any dog who is going to be kenneled just to be safe—including those who have had it in the past (there is no permanent immunity).

Finally, treatment for dogs who get kennel cough include bronchodilators (to open airways) and cough suppressants. These help, somewhat. In addition, antibiotics are important in severely ill pets, but the majority of the mildly affected dogs don't get much benefit from them. The bottom line is that regardless of what is done, the coughing runs its natural course and stops in two to three weeks—unless the constant hacking drives the owner around the bend sooner.

# Joints and Bones

## Glucosamine for Arthritis

*Glucosamine is a safe and often effective way to improve joint health and help relieve joint pain.*

### Question:

I have a 9-year-old, very active black Lab who may be developing some arthritis, and will sometimes walk around very stiff if she's been sleeping for awhile after playing hard that day. Would you recommend glucosamine for her? I take it for my old joints, and am wondering if my dog would get the same benefits.

### Dr. Nichol:

Yes, definitely use glucosamine for your Lab. This stuff is not a drug, but more of a nutritional supplement—free of side effects. It works, not like an antiinflammatory, but instead by improving the health of the joint surfaces. Unlike aspirin, it is not useful for occasional "bad days." Instead, it's best given daily over the long haul. Your Lab can take 1,500 mg glucosamine HCl and 1,200 mg chondroitin daily. One preparation is Cosequin, in capsule form. An easier alternative is Glycoflex, which is chewable. Both are available from your veterinarian. About 70 percent of dogs like yours respond quite favorably, although it may take two to three weeks to see the improvement. With any luck you two will be acting like a couple of frisky young pups in no time. Just don't chew up the furniture.

## Arthritis

*More alternatives.*

### Question:

My 11-year Collie, Boo, has arthritis that seems to be located mostly in her hind legs. I've been giving her the prescription medicine Rimadyl, but I'm not a big fan of this drug because of the long-term side effects. I have been taking Boo for Adequan shots with no dramatic improvement. Boo has also been receiving Cosequin. She is a bit overweight and on r/d food, which is not really helping much. She doesn't get so much exercise as I would like her to. Also, would it hurt

Boo to make her go for very short daily walks? It is very difficult to not be able to help her more!

## Dr. Nichol:

I know how you feel. As my Airedale, Juan, got older, I felt a greater need to protect him. It's so unfair that our pets live such short lives. The best we can do is to help them feel as comfortable as we can.

So far, you have done some good things for Boo. Adequan and Cosequin are helpful in many arthritic older dogs because they improve the health of the joint surfaces, which allows better lubrication and less inflammation. But they are not the only answers. Rimadyl is a widely used nonsteroidal antiinflammatory drug that is certainly one of the "big guns." It can make a huge difference. Unlike other drugs in its class, it is almost always quite safe. The few problems that have been seen have involved liver disease, so it's critically important for Boo to have a blood profile before using Rimadyl. (By the way, if you're considering Tylenol, it's only safe for dogs whose livers are okay, and it does nothing to improve the health of joints nor to reduce inflammation. I don't use it.)

But there's more. Want to stay au naturale? Me, too. Go to the health food store or vitamin catalog and get d-l-phenylalanine. Give 375 mg daily. This amino acid, abbreviated DLPA, is a natural part of food. Another alternative is Super Oxide Dismutase (SOD) also available at health food stores. You can also try acupuncture. It won't work on everybody, but it could make all the difference.

My personal favorite: The one thing that makes a huge difference for *every* fat old dog with arthritic pain is weight loss. By allowing your beloved Boo to lug around all those extra pounds, you are accelerating the destruction of her joints. That's because we are asking her skeleton to carry far more load than its Maker designed it to handle. Make it simple. Feed r/d at only one and a half cups twice daily. Pick up her food when she's done eating, finished or not. Don't allow other pets near her when she eats. *Never* give her anything else to eat. Exercise? Sure. It'll be great for both of you. But don't think that an extra trip around the block will reduce Boo's weight. Discipline at feeding time will work better than any drug.

# What to Do If Grandpa Gets Lame
*Older dogs can reinjure an arthritic joint. On-and-off lameness can occur.*

## QUESTION:

Moxie the Wonderdog is faring very well for her 16-plus years, but she has one very curious malady. Every few months she will decide that one of her front legs has gone lame. (I'm not sure if it is always the same one.) We never see her hurt it; there are no stickers or anything in her paw; palpating the leg doesn't seem to cause her any discomfort. But she will spend a couple of days gamely hopping around on three legs. Then the affliction will just as mysteriously disappear and she will be back to romping around like a puppy. Despite her good sense of humor, kidding her about the problem just makes her defensive and morose. Any ideas? Should we be concerned?

## Dr. Nichol:

Well, I'm glad you're going to stop making fun of poor Moxie. There is an important reason for her lameness. Contrary to what some people think, pets do not feign injury or illness just to get attention. If that were the case, she wouldn't be so grumpy.

The reason for Moxie's limping is that she has old joints. After that many years of service, the cartilage surfaces of the ends of her bones are no longer perfectly smooth and well-lubricated. What we call old-age arthritis is really degeneration from wear and tear. With this comes long-term thickening of the supportive structures of the joints. None of this causes any trouble until she plays hard and turns that joint just a little too far. At that point, what had been a slowly advancing change becomes an acute inflammation with pain, so she has the sudden appearance of a chronic problem.

I suspect that you are right—it may not always be the same joint. While it is likely that one or two joints may be a little worse than the others, all of her joints are gradually breaking down. So when this usually chipper girl is carrying a leg, what she is really doing is resting an injury—which is exactly the right way for those parts to heal.

To help Moxie feel better, start by enforcing rest. Like many people with an injury, most dogs don't have the sense to rest the limb after it begins to feel a little better. I advise total exercise restriction for at least two full weeks following a joint injury—no matter how she tries to convince you that she's in good enough shape to play. In addition, give her an antiinflammatory during those two weeks. It must be used consistently for it to be effective. Your choices range from aspirin to prescription nonsteroidals like Rimadyl (available through your veterinarian). Since it happens to Moxie fairly regularly, you could keep some Rimadyl at home for use as needed. But remember to use it for the entire two weeks of rest. The joint surfaces will heal faster and with less permanent damage if swelling and inflammation are minimized consistently.

Now that you know how to manage your little girl during her acute flare-ups, you need to start improving the long-term health of her tired old joints. This is why we have antioxidants like Glycoflex. This stuff is easy to give because it tastes good. It is only useful if given every day over the long term. Best of all, it may reduce the need for heavy-duty drug therapy like Rimadyl. But steer clear of ibuprofen, as this can cause severe stomach ulcers.

I'm glad you're finally taking poor little Moxie seriously. She's been writing to me for a long time. I told her that someday you would change. Now straighten up and stop making fun of your dog.

## When It's Just an Act
### *A rare dog will fake injury to get attention.*

#### QUESTION:

I am responding to your reply to the owner of Moxie the Wonderdog who now and then shows signs of a limp. Your reply of "Pets do not feign injury" is true in 99.99 percent of all cases.

Once in a while an extraordinary animal will feign an injury, as in the case of my Moselle, who passed away in 1978. She had two or three injuries over the years and in each case she relished the attention she received. After an injury healed, I placed a Band-Aid across the top of her front paw. Immediately the paw with the Band-Aid was favored. I tested this sham several times and had the same results. She, of course, was a rare and brilliant Weimaraner.

She was God's gift to me for only eight years. She taught me more than I taught her. She has been gone these many years but never out of my mind or heart. I don't weep in sorrow, but for my luck in choosing this dog who gave me much more than I could ever expect or deserve. Did you know that there are no fleas in doggy heaven?

#### DR. NICHOL:

It's beautiful to hear your feelings about your girl Moselle. I can relate strongly to this. My Airedale, Juan, was the son I had never had. Through years of his patience, I learned the skills that prepared me for fatherhood of human children. Now I know why dogs are called man's best friend. I also know why they say that having children "changes" your life.

While there is certainly a range of intelligence among dogs, at points in our lives we are possibly more ready to learn from them. Our pets, like others in our lives, can be the teachers we are ready to hear. Moselle was clearly a sharpie. But I'm betting that you may also have inadvertently conditioned her. (Don't confuse conditioning with being a "dumb" animal. Most humans are conditioned to the smell of good food, among other things.)

Moselle loved the attention you lavished on her when she was hurt, and connected the Band-Aid with the closeness of your nurturing. No wonder she craved more of your love after she saw the Band-Aid. You haven't lost Moselle. Her love will last you a lifetime.

## Osteochondritis Dissecans (OCD)

*A hereditary joint disease of larger dog breeds influenced by rapid-growth diets.*

### QUESTION:

Today our 6-month-old Golden Retriever was diagnosed with osteochondosis (left shoulder). He's facing surgery and I cannot find any information on the Internet. Can you explain this for us?

### DR. NICHOL:

I'm sad to learn that your happy-go-lucky Golden has a painful shoulder, but pleased to report that dogs with this condition usually do very well. For the skinny on osteochondritis dissecans (OCD), we'll start with some anatomy. Every joint surface in the body is covered by slick, shiny cartilage for smooth, pain-free function. But in the joints of some large-breed puppies, a small area of bone and the cartilage that covers it begin to peel away. This is a bad situation because now the joint has this hard chunk of bone that creates a "stone in the shoe" effect. In other words, your dog can't walk without serious pain. But that's not all. The longer your puppy goes without corrective surgery, the more likely that piece of bone and cartilage is to break free and form a "joint mouse"—moving about the joint causing further damage (not to be confused with Mickey Mouse or a computer mouse). This is where permanent arthritic changes begin.

Your next move should be to have the other shoulder and his hips X-rayed. He could have OCD on both sides, as well as hip dysplasia. You might as well know the whole picture. If he has surgery soon, his shoulder should do great over the long term. Finally, a word to owners of medium- to large-breed puppies: While OCD and other bone and joint growth diseases are hereditary, you can actually increase your youngster's risk by accelerating his or her growth. Rapid bone growth results from feeding puppy food. Feed large-breed puppies adult food only, and you'll promote healthy, normal growth rates.

# Rheumatoid Arthritis
*This crippling disease is manageable, but not curable.*

## QUESTION:
Do dogs get rheumatoid arthritis? What does the treatment consist of?

## DR. NICHOL:
I'm glad you wrote to me about this, but I have to admit that I wince every time I diagnose it or even think about it. Rheumatoid arthritis is a lifelong, advancing disease that destroys multiple joints in the body. Its exact cause is not well understood, but we do know that some of an affected dog's antibodies turn on his or her immune system. The result is inflammation that leads to destruction of the normally smooth, slick joint surfaces of all four limbs. It usually affects small-breed dogs, average age of 4 years. These poor little guys cannot take a pain-free step without medication. It's horrible.

While there are treatments, none are curative. If only a few joints are affected, surgery can be helpful. But in most cases, we use medications like prednisone, cyclophosphamide, and azathioprine. The purpose of these drugs is to diminish the immune system's effects on the joints and slow the progression of the erosive changes. All of these medications are human drugs—with the potential for side effects. We monitor treatment carefully.

I know how rough it sounds, but the truth is that with proper care, most dogs with rheumatoid arthritis can be made pretty comfortable for several months to a few years. Sadly, most do not live out a full life expectancy. Go for quality of life with your dog's treatment and take each day as a gift.

## Severe Hip Pain in Young Dogs

*Large-breed puppies with hip dysplasia can avoid joint replacement and other radical surgery. The TPO procedure can correct bad anatomy early and prevent arthritis later.*

### QUESTION:

I have a German Shepherd puppy I bought about four months ago who's having trouble getting up sometimes. She's 10 months old now and a really sweet dog, but I'm worried that she may be dislocating one hip; if I feel the side of her rear end while I try to help her up, I can feel the bone moving in and out in her hip. Will vitamin C help?

### DR. NICHOL:

I wish a problem like this could be managed with a simple treatment like vitamin C. It can help if started at a really young age, and if given in megadoses, but your puppy has a severe case of hip dysplasia and will only be helped with surgery.

I know that sounds extreme. To help explain, let's start at the beginning. Hip dysplasia is a genetically controlled disease that causes looseness of the hip, resulting in an abnormal shape to the bones of the joint itself. But it isn't a simple dominant or recessive trait, so it's not an all-or-nothing disease. In other words, a dog can have any degree of hip dysplasia, from nearly perfect hips without symptoms to joints that are permanently dislocated. In the case of your puppy, we know that the disease is severe because the support structures of her hips are only strong enough to hold the ball-and-socket joint of the hip together when she is lying down. As soon as she tries to support weight, you can feel the ball (at the top of the thigh bone) pop out of the socket on the pelvis (hip). If you had known when she was a baby that a mild case of hip dysplasia was possible, large doses of vitamin C could have helped strengthen the fibrous support structures of her hips. But your dog's problem is by now so advanced that only surgery will make a difference.

Please don't panic. While hip dysplasia was at one time cause for putting a dog to sleep, we now have methods that can not only eliminate pain but give her normal function. Start with X-rays. By knowing whether the joints are just loose or badly misshapen, your veterinarian can advise you as to which surgery is best. For dogs between the ages of 8 months and about 18 months, a procedure called the triple pelvic osteotomy (TPO) can make a great difference. This surgery involves changing the angle of the dog's hip joints so that the ball of the thigh bone fits better into the socket of the pelvis. While results are usually very good, TPO is not useful for severe cases in which the ball and socket are becoming broad and flat. When hip dysplasia gets that bad, the joint can start to dislocate. That's when a total hip replacement, or an artificial hip, is best.

Joint replacement is a big deal, and it's expensive. But your pup won't be walking much longer without it. If she does get artificial hips, though, her chances of having strong pain-free hips for life are 95 percent.

So what could you have done had you known all of this before you bought your puppy? I'm glad you asked. (Notice how often we talk about prevention?) Since hip dysplasia is genetic and comes in all shades of gray, your best bet is to know the health of the puppy's parents' hips from X-rays that certified them as hip dysplasia free by the Orthopedic Foundation for Animals (OFA). All serious breeders of large-breed dogs do that.

I see you raising your hand. Okay, one more question. What dog breeds get hip dysplasia? It's been seen in every breed, but it is much more common in large breeds. In fact, while the German Shepherd is still among the hardest hit, generally the larger the breed, the greater the risk.

## Hip Dysplasia—The Borderline Case

*A major cause of hip arthritis comes in all shades of gray. X-rays are the key to effective treatment.*

### QUESTION:

I just had my 3-1/2-year-old female Brittany's hips X-rayed so they could be sent to the OFA. She would probably be rated as dysplastic. Should I send these into the OFA anyway and what can I do as far as medications, etc.? She does not show any signs of this problem in her running and jumping. Nor does it affect her hunting in any way.

### DR. NICHOL:

This is a dilemma shared by many owners of purebred dogs. Which do we judge: her ability to work or her X-rays? If she functions normally, why not breed regardless? Let's start with some background.

Hip dysplasia is a genetic disorder that is most often a problem in large dogs, but it's been seen in every breed. The Brittany (formerly called the Brittany Spaniel) has had its share with this potentially crippling disease.

Affected puppies start out with loose-fitting, poorly shaped ball-and-socket components in their hips. Ultimately, those with severe dysplasia become arthritic. The larger the dog, the harder it is for her to walk without excruciating pain.

Now for the gray zone: Hip dysplasia is not an all-or-nothing disease. Some hips are perfect; some are horrible. But many are like your Brittany—somewhere in the middle. That's why we have the Orthopedic Foundation for Animals (OFA), a group of radiologists that rates X-rays of hips and other joints. Only dogs with "excellent" or "good" hips should be bred. That's because even a slight degree of dysplasia in a parent dog can result in severe disease in one or more of the puppies, grandpuppies, or great-grandpuppies.

Send the X-ray to the OFA. Maybe her hips will pass. Either way, you'll know the potential for the next generation. If her hips get a failing grade, have her spayed to prevent an "accidental" breeding and give her Glycoflex chewables everyday to maintain healthy joint surfaces. If she feels good enough to work full-time, then for goodness sake, let her have a full life. Any hip pain she has later can be treated with medications or even joint-replacement surgery.

Finally, a word on prevention: Reduce the risk for medium- and large-breed youngsters by feeding only adult food. Puppy foods drive growth way too fast, making bone and joint problems much more likely.

## The Last, Best Hope for Hip Dysplasia

*Surgical removal of portions of the hip joint can salvage the well-being of a beloved dog. It can be the treatment of choice, but there's no turning back.*

### QUESTION:

When you answered a question about a dog with hip dysplasia, you said there were two different surgeries that could help that young dog walk better. I have a dog who had a different surgery where they took off the ball from the thigh, and he's fine now. What about this other surgery?

### DR. NICHOL:

You raise an important question. First, I will explain the procedure that was done on your dog. This surgery is called a femoral head and neck ostectomy, or FHO for short. It's a pretty simple operation in that the ball of the ball-and-socket hip joint is removed, and nothing is put in its place. How does the critter walk without a hip joint? Mother Nature is pretty industrious. She starts right to work at building up connective tissue around the top of the thigh bone and the vacant hip socket. After several weeks, the dog has a "false joint." A false joint can function pretty well, but it can never carry the amount of weight that a dog's rear end was intended to handle. That's where four-legged creatures have an advantage over those of us with only two legs. Most of them, like your dog, manage just fine by shifting a big part of the load to their other legs.

Why not just do an FHO for every dog with hip dysplasia? Many dogs are just too big. The puppy we talked about, for example, was already over 70 pounds at just 10 months of age. She is likely to end up close to 100 pounds as a full-grown adult. In addition, both of her hips were in deep trouble, not just one. Had we done an FHO on both of her hips, she could only have shifted her rear weight to two other limbs, not three. A big dog missing both hips might not be able to get up. Considering the risk, the safest procedure would be either correction of the angle of the hips or replacement with pain-free, fully load-bearing artificial joints for that big pup.

One final point on FHO: It's a salvage procedure. In other words, it's best considered as a last resort. For example, if the other procedures fail, the surgeon can operate again at a later time and do the FHO as a means of salvaging the dog's life. Also, there is no turning back from an FHO. Once the ball of the hip joint is removed, there is no way for angle correction or artificial joint surgery to be done. If the dog can't walk following FHO, she's out of options.

Is FHO ever a good first choice? It certainly can be in dogs whose adult weight is less than 70 to 75 pounds, whose hip is in good condition, and in cats. In these cases, FHO makes good sense right from the get-go.

## Staggering and Difficulty Rising in German Shepherds

*Degenerative myelopathy is a slowly progressive spinal cord disease. It's not painful, but it is terminal.*

### QUESTION:

My German Shepherd is 8 years old and has degenerative myelopathy. Could you please give me some information about it?

### Dr. Nichol:

This is a tough problem. Your dog's nonpainful disease is caused by a breakdown of the spinal cord. The bad news is that it is progressive and will ultimately lead to his inability to stand and walk. I know how hard this must be for the two of you.

Affected dogs are nearly all purebred or mixed German Shepherds. The average victim of this devastating spinal cord disease is male, aged 9.6 years. Degenerative myelopathy starts by causing a slight stagger in the rear limbs. Gradually, the rear paws begin to knuckle over and cross when the dog walks. Atrophy of the muscles of the rear legs follows. Late stages of the disease are usually seen 6 to 24 months later. In the end, these poor dogs can't stand and may fail to control urination and stool. It's horrible. I'm sorry.

There are a few things you can do. For starters, verify the diagnosis. X-rays of your dog's back and hips will confirm that it is neither disc disease nor hip dysplasia. Once the diagnosis is beyond doubt, do the following: Keep this boy trim—obesity would make it much harder for him. Second, getting plenty of exercise appears to delay muscle wasting. The last hope is to attempt to arrest or slow the advancement of the disease using an experimental treatment combining vitamin supplements with a drug called Amicar. No firm data on the value of this stuff is available.

There may be solace in knowing what to expect. Share every joy you can with your fine dog. Live in the now.

## Dachshund Back Problems
*Vitamins won't help, but you can cut the risk.*

### Question:

I have an 8-month-old miniature Dachshund. I've read that giving them vitamins C and E can help prevent future back problems. Is this true?

### Dr. Nichol:

Close but no cigar. Vitamins C and E are what we call antioxidants. They can help improve the health of arthritic joint surfaces, but they won't prevent the degenerative disc changes that could cause back disease in your Dachshund. Arthritic joints have molecular projections that cause rough, dry surfaces. Vitamins C and E, and other antioxidants, work by attaching to these molecules. If your dog has arthritic joints, antioxidants can help make for smoother cartilage and better lubrication. The end result is less inflammation and pain. But neck and back disease in Dachshunds is not a joint problem; it's a disc problem.

Now, for your dog's future: It turns out that 90 percent of Dachshunds have early degenerative changes in the discs of their necks and backs by age one year. But while this huge majority is genetically preprogrammed, only a few will ever have symptoms. A great many of those who are affected can be spared this pain, but not by antioxidants.

As your Dachshund's discs age, they can become laden with calcium deposits. This makes them hard and brittle instead of cushiony and flexible like those of a normal dog. Even still, most Dachshunds never have a problem. But a dog with bad discs who is allowed to get overweight, to sit up and beg, to jump onto furniture, or to climb stairs is at greater risk. This is because the stresses on those hard, brittle discs make them prone to leak their contents into the space next to the spinal cord. When this happens, the cord gets injured. The result is pain if the injury is minor, or paralysis if it's severe.

The good news is that neck and back disease of Dachshunds is treatable and as you now know, it is largely preventable by proper management. Too bad a simple pill can't help your dog steer clear. Just train that rascal not to use the stairs. If you have a two-story house, install an elevator. And no jumping, no begging, no fast food, and no basketball. So what can he do? Rollerblading, swimming, track and field, and soccer. In other words, all the running around on the ground he wants. Barking and yapping are fine, as well as rooting in the dirt. The more, the better.

## Knee Ligament Rupture

*Anterior cruciate ligament (ACL) rupture: How it's fixed and what happens if it isn't.*

### QUESTION:

Our Lhasa Apso is 6 years old and has been limping on his rear left leg for three weeks. His condition may have improved slightly, but for the most part has remained the same. The doctor diagnosed an anterior cruciate ligament rupture and has recommended a surgical procedure to stabilize it. How successful is this type of surgery?

### Dr. Nichol:

I'm glad you care about that little boy's pain. His attempts to bear weight are causing the bones in his knee to slip. That rear leg is like a rubber crutch. You'll want him well as fast as possible.

A dog's knee is similar to ours; the thigh bone stands directly on top of the shinbone. What prevents those bones from slipping apart is a ligament on each side of the knee plus the cruciate ligaments that crisscross inside the joint. This fragile setup is what makes knees so prone to injury. Your dog probably took a bad turn or stepped in a hole. The wrong forces came to bear and he ripped the anterior cruciate (the more important of the two interior ligaments). Now his leg is collapsing on him.

This joint needs front-to-back stability. His doctor has recommended surgically reestablishing the correct forces. If the surgery is done by a skilled and experienced doctor, your pup should do well. But if his normal weight is less than 15 pounds, you have another alternative: no treatment at all. That's because small dogs bear so little weight on their knees that Mother Nature can thicken the joint capsule enough to provide stability with no outside help. Piece of cake, right? Maybe. Most dogs with cruciate ligament ruptures are overweight. Excessive load will stretch and weaken the knee ligaments, making rupture a high risk. Obesity also cuts a dog's chances of a good recovery. So one real important part of treatment and prevention may be weight loss.

Bigger dogs (15 to 50 pounds) should have the surgery suggested by your veterinarian. Real big dogs (like me) do better with a procedure called tibial plateau leveling osteotomy (TPLO) which is best done by a surgical specialist. Finally, never make your own diagnosis. Without proper management, joint injuries progress to unstoppable arthritis—and man that hurts.

## Rear Leg Limping in Small-Breed Dogs

*Dislocating kneecaps are a common cause of intermittent lameness, especially in overweight dogs. Weight loss and surgery will stop the pain.*

### Question:

I've got a Pomeranian named Sarah. All of a sudden she started yelping (just on occasion) every once in a while. My mother took her to a local vet who said she had dislocated her hind leg in the knee. The vet put it back in place, and Sarah was fine for about a month, and then suddenly she started yelping again. The vet recommended surgery. My mother has scheduled the surgery, but for the last two weeks Sarah has been just fine. We don't want to cause her unnecessary pain by having surgery if we can avoid it. More important, though, we don't want her to hurt if the knee gives her trouble again.

## Dr. Nichol:

Sarah sounds like a great little dog. It lifts your spirits to watch a high-energy, small-breed dog having fun. But when she has leg pain, no one is having a good time. Sarah's problem definitely needs attention.

On again–off again lameness is common in small-breed dogs. It is often due to a problem called luxating patella, or dislocating kneecap. To understand the anatomy, you can use your own knee. While standing, straighten your leg and hold your kneecap. Then bend and straighten your knee and feel the kneecap slide up and down at the end of your thigh bone. It does this because there is a groove near the end of the femur (thigh bone). This groove is like a valley that is formed by a ridge of bone on either side. If the kneecap somehow shifts over the top of one of the ridges, it's no longer in the groove and the leg can't function properly. It is also painful.

Why would this happen? I'm glad you asked. Many small-breed dogs like the Pomeranian, Miniature Poodle, and Yorkshire Terrier are born with bowed rear legs. This allows the kneecap to be pulled out of its groove sometimes; hence the intermittent nature of the lameness. To correct Sarah's problem, we simply need to get the kneecap to stay where it belongs. It does require surgery to move the attachment of the tendon below the knee, but she's in for bigger trouble later if you delay. Each time she dislocates that kneecap, its backside rubs on a bony ridge. Eventually this wears off the normal cartilage surface of the kneecap, and severe pain and lameness result. If you get her knee repaired soon, she should do fine. If you don't, her arthritis will be crippling.

Ask her doctor if she (Sarah, not the veterinarian) is above her ideal weight. If so, get her advice on the proper amount to feed. Reducing the workload on the joints may eliminate the problem. On the other hand, if the doctor reports Sarah's weight as normal, have the surgery done. The procedure will correct her faulty anatomy and allow her sad little kneecap to ride happily again in its groove.

## Screwtail in a Bulldog
*Cursed with funky, misshapen vertebrae, Bulldogs' tails can plug the anus.*

### QUESTION:
Help! My bulldog has screwtail. I'd never heard of such a thing. What do I do?

### DR. NICHOL:
Screwtail is a problem seen in brachycephalic dog breeds (those with pushed-in faces like Bulldogs and Pugs). It's caused by malformed vertebrae in the tail that cause it to grow in the shape of a corkscrew. It's a problem if the tail grows in such a way that it interferes with the dog passing stool from the anus. It has also been a problem in Bulldogs if the tail creates a pit or dimple at the rump, because of the extra skin that Bulldogs have in this area. The result can be a deep severe bacterial skin infection that is sometimes best treated surgically. Like many problems, it is best managed early—under 16 weeks of age. It's just one more reason that I'm glad we humans don't have tails. What a pain.

## Broken Tail in a Puppy
*Fractured and dislocated tails heal without help.*

### QUESTION:
I have a puppy whose tail looks like it has been broken. Should I have it docked or cut off?

### DR. NICHOL:
This is common in youngsters like your little guy. Some cases of crooked tails result from injuries like getting it accidentally stepped on or caught in a door. These heal quickly. Others are simply minor birth defects from malformed vertebrae called hemivertebrae. Either way, your puppy's tail is a nonproblem in terms of his health and comfort.

Should you have it docked (cut off)? If its appearance bothers either of you, why not? You sure don't want this little fellow having self-esteem problems. It may be hard for him to get a date when he's in high school if he has a bent tail.

## Tail Docking in Puppies

*It's just for looks, but have it done early. Doing it when they are 1 to 3 days old is best for safety.*

### QUESTION:

My Boxer just had a litter of the cutest babies I have ever seen. But, as you know, they were born with long tails. We need to get their tails docked to make them look like Boxers, but we don't know at what age to have it done. Our vet's office said 1 to 3 days old, but isn't that awfully young?

### DR. NICHOL:

I am glad you asked. This is a point of confusion for many folks.

Around the age of 3 to 4 days, the blood vascular and nervous systems of puppies become more mature and functional. If we dock (amputate) tails and dewclaws (the thumb-like appendage on the inside surface of the paws) at 1 to 3 days of age, the puppies lose only about one drop of blood—and they have very little nerve sensation. But the procedure is very different on puppies much older than that. In fact, if they're older than 3 days, it's downright cruel.

What can you do if your puppies are older? No problem. You can have the tails docked at the time of spaying or neutering, which can be done as early as 10 to 12 weeks of age. The puppies will be anesthetized anyway and they won't feel anything at all.

Don't feel compelled to have these procedures done. Like ear cropping, these things only serve to make dogs look the way we expect Boxers, Dobermans, Schnauzers, or whatever to appear. Removing these body parts has no other function. So, if appearance counts, have their tails docked and their dewclaws removed between 1 and 3 days of age. If it doesn't count, let them go au naturale. (Boxers are free spirits anyway.)

## Bone Deformities Following Injury

*Damage to areas of bone growth sometimes can't be known until later. Deformed limbs can be corrected if surgery is not delayed.*

### QUESTION:

We have an Irish Setter puppy, about 4 months old. Two weeks ago she got bumped by a car when she got out of the yard. Her name is Beans and she seemed fine after it happened. But in the last few days we have noticed that her front leg is starting to look crooked near her wrist. What's going on? Does Beans need surgery?

### Dr. Nichol:

Beans has premature closure of the distal ulnar physis. What has happened is that the area of active growth of the end of the ulna (one of the two bones of the forearm) has stopped growing. The problem is that Beans is not yet full-grown. Since there is a second bone in her forearm (the radius) that is continuing to grow, her front leg is starting to curve. You see, her forearm can only grow straight if both bones grow at the same time.

It would be easy to assume that since she seemed okay after the injury, no bones had been broken and everything would be fine. The truth is that even if she had been examined by a veterinarian, we would have had no way of knowing if a growth stoppage was in the future for that bone. X-rays cannot show the microscopic changes that started all of this. But with that area of bone near her wrist no longer growing, the curving of Beans's front leg will only worsen unless she has corrective surgery.

Now, let me muddy the waters a bit more. Beans's biggest problem is not near her wrist where you can see the deformity. Both the radius and the ulna are essential to the normal function of the elbow, too—way at the other end of the forearm. The still-growing radius is pushing up on the end of the humerus (the upper arm bone). But, again, the ulna is shorter. So we have an elbow joint that will not only fail to work properly, but could become badly enough stressed that it could fracture all by itself. The long-term, worst-case scenario is severe and painful arthritis of Beans's elbow.

The good news is that there are procedures to correct these problems, but there could be as many as three separate surgeries needed between now and when Beans is an adult dog. Sorry about all that. This may not help anybody feel better, but getting hit by a car can be a lot worse.

## Puppy Lameness: Pain in One Leg, Then Another, Then Another

*Large-breed growing puppies with shifting leg lameness may get well without help.*

### Question:

I have a German Shepherd pup who is 9 months old. He started to limp on his right front leg a while back. After a while, he quit. Well, that was about a week ago.

Starting today, he's limping on his left rear leg. What's the matter with this guy? I keep him with me or in the yard, so I know he hasn't been injured.

## Dr. Nichol:

This sounds like an unhappy puppy. While there are several possible causes, he is likely to have a bone disease called panosteitis. But you don't need to worry. This is a problem that goes away all by itself.

Why does this happen? The truth is that panosteitis has been studied thoroughly and we still don't have definite answers. Here is what we *do* know: Panosteitis is an inflammatory bone disease that, while it can affect any growing puppy, is nearly always seen in large breeds. The disease usually affects specific areas of a leg bone. It is a "shifting leg" lameness in that it can involve different legs, sometimes simultaneously. Each time it strikes, it causes pain and lameness.

The best advice is to have a thorough physical exam followed by X-rays to confirm the diagnosis. Since lameness in large-breed puppies can result in lifelong crippling arthritis, hoping that your pup has panosteitis could be a mistake.

If we are sure of a diagnosis of panosteitis, what can we do for this poor guy to help him feel better until the disease runs its course? The sad answer is that nothing helps much. That still doesn't mean you shouldn't try a few things anyway. But remember this warning: **Do not use ibuprofen** (the main ingredient in Advil and a number of other headache remedies). This can cause severe stomach ulcers. Instead, follow the advice of your veterinarian. There are some new pain relievers available that could help. What is really hard to know, however, is how long the symptoms will last. In some puppies, the pain resolves in a few weeks; others can have an on again–off again shifting leg lameness until they are 18 months old. But take heart. While nothing we do can shorten the course of the disease, rest assured that it will eventually go away.

# Dislocated Hips

*If treated quickly, many can be "popped" back into the socket. If you wait, surgery may be required.*

## Question:

Our dog Nacho is an Irish Setter and he's been scared of hot-air balloons since he was a baby. A couple of weeks ago, he really wigged out and took off. We looked for him everywhere and he finally came home—but not using his right rear leg. His doctor took X-rays and he has a dislocated hip. What can be done for Nacho?

## Dr. Nichol:

You folks must be really relieved to have Nacho home alive. Nacho should do well with his injury, but it may be difficult.

Dislocated hip joints are common hit-by-car injuries. They can be fairly simple to manage if we get our hands on them early. In those cases, we relax the pet with a general anesthetic, then manipulate the ball-and-socket joint back into place by hand. A special sling is then applied that keeps the hip joint together for a couple of weeks to allow time for permanent healing. Those are the easy ones.

On the other hand, if Nacho's injury is more than a couple of days old, it is likely that surgery will be needed to get the ball-and-socket hip joint back together. After one or two days, the muscles surrounding the dislocated joint contract. On a big guy like Nacho, stainless-steel implants such as pins or screws will be needed to keep the joint together for good permanent healing.

The good news is that as long as the joint stays in place during the healing process, he should be able to walk pain-free and normally for the rest of his life. Once he gets home from the hospital, successful healing will depend on your keeping him calm and quiet for three to four weeks.

# Mouth Problems

## A Dog Who Wants to Eat but Walks Away

*Bad breath + tooth and gum infections = weight loss and poor health.*

### Question:

I have three dogs of different ages. All are fine except 11-year-old Chelsea. For the past few weeks, she has seemed like she wants to eat, but does not; and her breath is bad, and she looks thinner. Should I try a new kind of food? Maybe canned food would be easier for her to eat. What do you think?

### Dr. Nichol:

I can tell that you are quite concerned about Chelsea's well-being. We all know that if someone is refusing to eat, we have a serious problem. The best way for us to put her right is to first find the cause, then correct it. If we just hunt around for food that she can eat, her problem could get much worse.

There are many possible causes for failure to eat, but your observation that Chelsea wants to, but cannot, is telling. Breath that could stop a freight train is one more important clue. It's likely that your dog's problem is in her mouth. To complete your diagnosis, hold her head in good light and have a look at her teeth. This is best done by pulling up and back on the corner where the upper and lower lips meet on each side. What you may see is a medium to dark brown buildup on the sides of her teeth. You may also find red gums. If pushing on the gums or teeth anywhere in her mouth causes her pain, you know that Chelsea needs dental care.

Oh, so it's just her teeth, you say? Well, let me say this about that. Poor Chelsea is losing weight not just because she can't eat. Weight loss can also be caused by the continual pain in her mouth that was going on even before she quit eating. In addition, Chelsea has active infection in her gums that may already be damaging the bones of her jaws. So Chelsea stands to lose more than just her teeth.

Now that you understand what Chelsea has known all along, I will explain the cure. While routine teeth cleaning is essential to prevention of mouth disease, Chelsea's problems are much more advanced. In her case, we need to start with some basic lab work to determine the extent of infection, whether her kidneys have suffered significant damage, and if there are other related problems like diabetes. If all of the above have been ruled out, your girl will need pretreatment with an antibiotic called Clindamycin. The next move is general anesthesia and cleaning of the teeth that are in good enough shape to stay. In view of the severity of Chelsea's problems, she is likely to need some extractions. There may also be teeth that are healthy enough to stay but need work. Treatment could include gum surgery or root planing. Any fractured teeth might benefit from root canal therapy.

This sounds like a lot, and it is. Traditionally, dental care has been given a lower priority than other physical needs, in people as well as in pets. In Chelsea's case, if she can't eat, she will die. For her long-term health, she also needs to get rid of that chronic infection that is damaging her mouth and maybe her kidneys, too.

As for your other pets, avoid this whole mess by getting them a thorough physical exam each year. If the doctor sees early tartar buildup on their teeth, get them cleaned before gum disease starts.

Just think, if Chelsea's breath improved, you two could actually be in the same room together.

## Dental Cleaning and Anesthesia

***Advanced infections in the mouth, however, are a greater health risk than carefully administered anesthesia.***

### QUESTION:

My own pets are eating fine, although their breath is less than perfect. Our vet recently said that both our dog and our cat need teeth cleaning, but that they would need anesthesia. Isn't that risky? I've heard of animals who have died from anesthesia. Is it really worth that kind of gamble? We've decided to wait on the teeth cleaning to see if it gets bad enough to be worth having an anesthetic.

### DR. NICHOL:

I understand your concern about anesthetic safety. This is not something to be taken lightly. We are so bonded to our pets that they are like children to us. We want to avoid anything remotely connected to risk.

You should never feel that just because a doctor tells you something is necessary that you are obliged to do it. The decisions as well as the responsibilities of managing your pets are yours. With that said, I will try to give you enough information to make the choice that is right for you.

Chelsea, the dog I discussed with another reader, was in real trouble. Her pain and oral infections were so severe that without extensive treatment, she was looking at an early death. But it never has to be that way. Had her owner gotten the kind of advice you did, routine dental cleaning would have prevented all of her trouble. Here's why: After we eat (that's right—you, me, our pets, everybody), food particles stick to our teeth and form the soft, rough, pasty film we call plaque. You can feel it on your own teeth before you brush. That stuff is important because it starts to turn into tartar on a cat's or dog's teeth in about 24 hours. If you brush it off within that time, tartar buildup is much slower. But sooner or later, tartar always does accumulate on the sides of the teeth. While it causes dragon breath, the worst part is the gum damage—the same chronic gingivitis your dental hygienist scolds you about. It develops because the tartar is thicker at the base of the tooth due to the chewing action. As it cakes on the sides of the teeth, it also builds under the gums where it causes long-term swelling and finally infection. Once the gums are badly damaged, they can't protect the roots of the teeth. Then real pain and tooth loss are just around the corner.

These are the reasons that you've been advised to have your pets' teeth cleaned. It's not that they're in trouble now. As much as you would rather avoid the whole thing, failing to prevent gum disease now will result in the type of major trouble Chelsea has later on. It's not *if*, but *when*.

What about anesthetic safety? Important question. There is no way to hold your pets still for this procedure without anesthesia, so our job is to make the anesthesia safe. We start by doing a routine lab screening—just like the one a person gets at the hospital prior to having general anesthesia. If it all looks fine, we go ahead. (It doesn't always look fine, but it is always good news to catch problems early.) Next, we put a catheter in a vein and dose the anesthetic exactly according to the size of the pet. While they're asleep, we give oxygen and hook them up to a heart monitor, so we can know right away if adjustments are needed in the anesthetic, which is given with the oxygen.

Is it worth the gamble? Since your best plan is prevention, the best approach is to choose a doctor who feels as strongly about safety as you do. Most veterinarians participate in dental month (February) by reducing their fees for teeth cleaning. If your pet's breath can make a houseplant wilt, it's time.

## Teeth—The Baby Kind
*Puppies lose teeth just like the rest of us.*

### QUESTION:
My question is regarding our puppy's teeth. She is a 3-month-old Sheltie mix. I noticed this morning that she lost a tooth (I found it on her bed). Is this something to be concerned about?

### DR. NICHOL:
A baby dog losing baby teeth is normal, but I suspect that she may actually be closer to 16 weeks in age. The emerging adult teeth begin pushing the baby teeth out from ages 4 to 6 months in most pups. As far as being concerned about finding the tooth on her bed, I just hope the tooth fairy is active in your home. Think of the emotional damage to that tender little heart if a yummy biscuit fails to materialize under her pillow.

## Dental and Oral Disease
*Heart disease may be a complication. Thorough care includes a complete lab evaluation, antibiotics, and anesthesia to stop tooth pain.*

### QUESTION:
I have a Yorkshire Terrier who is 10 years old and weighs 5 pounds. He has just been diagnosed with a gum infection. He also has a slight heart murmur, which he has had since birth. I would like to know what antibiotics you would prescribe and at what dosage. My dog's name is Little Foot.

### DR. NICHOL:
Your veterinarian has informed you well about heart and gum disease. Little Foot's heart murmur is likely due to leaky valves that may never cause trouble—unless they get infected by bacterial colonies from his mouth. Antibiotic treatment now could prevent an early death.

There are several antibiotics that may be helpful. Clindamycin (brand name Antirobe) is the most commonly used. The dosage and length of treatment are determined by the severity of the infection. But gingivitis (inflammation of the gums) in dogs doesn't just happen on its own. Usually, severe tartar buildup on the teeth is responsible for the redness, bleeding, and pain. Unless we deal with the cause, the improvement will last only as long as the antibiotic is used.

This is how we help this boy for the long term: Ask Little Foot's doctor for a blood count and chemistry panel as well as a urinalysis to find out if there are deeper infections or organ disease. Chest X-rays, ECG, and blood pressure are also essential to learn the extent of his heart problem. Any underlying diseases that turn up should be managed. When we're sure Little Foot's in good shape, he'll need a safe gas anesthetic and a thorough dental procedure to clean up the infection that's causing his painful gums.

Did I tell you more than you wanted to know? Health care was simpler when medical knowledge was scant. Nowadays we know enough to preserve and improve the lives of those we love. Do what it takes. A Yorkie like Little Foot should live long. Don't let your boy's health cave in on him early.

## Bad Breath in Dogs
### *Tooth and gum disease is the most likely cause. Take it seriously.*

### QUESTION:
We have a pet Shar-Pei who has recently gained a rather bad breath problem. We had thought it was some sort of digestion issue, as we had recently tried a different brand of dog food. We tried a rawhide bone and even made an attempt at brushing the teeth and using a doggy treat. His breath is atrocious.

### DR. NICHOL:
You're not protecting the identity of a human member of your household, are you? You wouldn't be the first to "blame the dog," you know. Okay, I'll play this one straight.

Diet and stomach or intestinal diseases are very unlikely causes of halitosis (bad breath). While respiratory disorders could be responsible, your Shar-Pei's problem is most likely due to tooth or gum disease. Its cause is a part of normal daily life for all cats, dogs, and, ah, their owners: failure to brush.

Here are your instructions: Have your veterinarian examine this puppy. If the diagnosis is gingivitis (inflammation of the gums) and dental calculus (tartar on the teeth), have a preanesthetic lab screen done and schedule a teeth cleaning. In addition to chipping away the tartar with an ultrasonic dental scaler, the doctor will carefully clean the groove between the roots and the gums, polish the teeth, and apply a fluoride treatment to harden the enamel and reduce future buildup.

Is it really that important? Aside from breath that could stop a train, untreated dental disease can damage the heart and kidneys in the long run. And as your dog ages, those gum infections will get bad enough to cause loose teeth—making it painful for him to eat. Finally, his teeth will fall out and he'll never get a prom date. The humiliation alone will devastate his self-esteem.

## Milk Bones, Rawhides, and Pig Ears for Cleaner Teeth.

### Here is what they can and cannot do for your dog's teeth.

#### QUESTION:

I have a question about my animals and their teeth. You wrote about cleaning pets' teeth with an anesthetic. But isn't it true that Milk Bones clean dogs' teeth? How about rawhides and pig ears? I checked my dog's teeth and they have that hard brown junk you talked about, but I would rather get rid of it by her chewing instead.

#### DR. NICHOL:

I thought you'd never ask. The simple answer is yes, anything that is chewed is healthy for the teeth. Pets who chew consistently generally have cleaner teeth and healthier gums.

Now, as Paul Harvey would say, the rest of the story. The rock-hard calculus (tartar) that accumulates on the sides of the teeth will not wear off with chewing—unless your pets chew rocks. That's because tartar is so hard and brittle. It's like a mineral deposit. When we clean teeth in the veterinary hospital, we chip the stuff off using an ultrasonic dental scaler. Milk Bones and rawhides are still excellent because while they can't get rid of hard tartar, they help wear away the soft, pasty plaque that sticks to the teeth after a meal. Plaque is the stuff that begins to turn into tartar 24 hours after forming. We advise brushing a pet's teeth once daily, to wipe away plaque so that it's not there to form tartar.

Isn't handing a dog a Milk Bone or a rawhide a lot easier than brushing? Sure, but while these are good, they can't do the whole job because they tend to clean only the points of the teeth—and our greater problem is the sides. Remember that gum damage occurs because tartar gets under the edges of the gums. Fortunately, preventing gum disease, pain, and garbage breath doesn't have to be a struggle. Most cats and dogs enjoy the chicken- or malt-flavored toothpastes. I've also known a few who declare war on the toothbrush. Other choices are to use a finger brush or to wipe the sides of the teeth using a wash cloth moistened with Nolvadent. These things are available from your veterinarian. They work great for most pets because it's your finger in their mouth instead of a stick. But, alas, there are still a few critters who balk. That's why they invented t/d.

T/d is a prescription diet that slows tartar buildup on the teeth. We recommend feeding it after dental cleaning. Your veterinarian has t/d. It looks like regular dry food and it's nutritionally the same as other good diets. The difference is the way it's made. Instead of shattering when chewed like other hard food, the food is sliced by the cat's or dog's teeth. The result is that t/d wipes the entire sides of the teeth, thus cleaning away the soft plaque.

So, brush, wipe with Nolvadent, or feed t/d. But keep your pet's teeth clean. Give Milk Bones, rawhides, and pig ears because they're fun for your pets and keep them occupied. That's important because we all know that an idle mouth is the devil's workshop.

## Brushing Your Dog's Teeth

*It's the easiest and cheapest way to save the health of your dog's mouth. Start out gradually and don't forget to make it fun.*

### QUESTION:

We've been trying to brush our dog's teeth like you said, but he really hates it. We know it's best, but how do we get him to go along?

### DR. NICHOL:

You are right—it can be a real challenge. While there are alternatives like Nyla-Floss toys and prescription diet t/d, brushing is best. You just need to know how.

The biggest problem with dogs or cats getting their teeth brushed is that the idea is totally foreign to them. Nothing in their instincts prepares them for this, so take it slowly. Rather than a regular brush, use a finger toothbrush. Use flavored toothpaste specifically made for pets and start by brushing just the fronts of the front teeth. Always have a small treat ready and after a 2- to 3-second toothbrushing session, reward your pet's good behavior. Brush just the fronts of the teeth once a day for several days, until your dog or cat seems comfortable with the whole thing. Follow with a treat every time. When your pet is accustomed to this daily routine, start with the front teeth as usual, but move your finger brush along to the teeth on the sides of the mouth, too, then quit and give the treat. As he gets relaxed with this part of the routine, you move further back in his mouth. Remember: Always start in the front and end with the treat.

Be patient, gentle, and consistent. Daily brushing will slow tartar buildup and reduce the need for dental cleaning at the doctor's office. If your dog or cat never does accept brushing, let him play with Nyla-Floss rope toys or Kong toys. These are designed specifically to clean between the teeth. You can also feed t/d, which is made so that it wipes the sides of the teeth and keeps them much cleaner than regular dry food. Your veterinarian has t/d. Keep doing your best to care for your pets.

## How Dogs Get Serious Mouth Disease
### The details on how it starts and when to stop it.

### QUESTION:

Cleaning a dog's teeth is much more of a septic and neurologic shock than cleaning a person's teeth, because the canine gingiva grow over the calculus and tartar, rather than receding as in a person, and have to be cut back. Vets should explain procedures in detail, shouldn't they?

### DR. NICHOL:

This is an excellent question. It is true that no two dental conditions are the same, even among dogs and cats. Calculus, besides being a difficult math class, is another word for tartar. Tartar is the rock-hard, mostly mineral deposit that sticks to the teeth of pets and people. It starts out as a soft, colorless, pasty film called plaque. You can feel it with your tongue on your own teeth. (We assume that our pets can feel it on their teeth, too, but they never mention it.) After it's been on their teeth for about 24 hours, it begins to convert to tartar. As it builds up, the process accelerates. Bummer.

That's the bad news. The good news is that the gums aren't damaged if tartar is cleaned off in its early stages. We look for it carefully at the time of annual physical exams. But when we recommend dental cleaning, some folks say "Nah." When we see the pet the next year, the gums are starting to get swollen and inflamed because the tartar actually gets under the edges of the gums. We often have infections by the following year—and if the growing infections are neglected, the pet starts to have pain when he tries to eat. If the owner still ignores the problem, the pet loses teeth and bacterial byproducts spread to the kidneys. The health of the whole critter goes to pieces.

Is teeth cleaning a septic and neurologic shock? If it's done early, when it should be, it's really no big deal. But when gum surgery and extractions are done to halt runaway infections, you can bet there are ramifications elsewhere in the body. At that stage, we use antibiotics for several days before and after the procedure. We also give pain medication like Duragesic skin patches that provide continual relief. It really can be a shock to the system.

The obvious answer is to never make your beloved pets face this kind of distress. Teeth can be cleaned, polished, and treated with fluoride when the gums are still healthy. You can also feed prescription diet t/d, brush your pet's teeth, and give your dog a Kong toy to chew to keep the plaque off his teeth. All of this will slow tartar buildup and save your pets a whole lot of pain.

## Mouth Pain and Inability to Eat
*Masticatory muscle myositis is a treatable disease of the immune system.*

### QUESTION:

I would like more information on an autoimmune disease our Dalmatian, Sparky, has been diagnosed with—temporal masseter myositis. Please provide any tips, cures, or ideas for the best way to beat this disease.

### DR. NICHOL:

This is a miserable problem and I'm sorry to hear that your Dalmatian has it, but the good news is that if Sparky is treated early enough, the outlook should be excellent. Now called masticatory muscle myositis (MMM), this malady isn't seen real often, but it isn't considered rare. The problem is that your dog's muscles of mastication (fancy name for chewing) are inflamed because they are under attack by antibodies made by Sparky's own immune system. The term *autoimmune* means an immune response against the self. It does not mean that your dog is allergic to your car.

The upshot of all this is that your Dalmatian is unable to open his mouth, has pain when doing so, or both. It's horrible. While symptoms like failing to pick up a ball, inability to eat, or swelling of the muscles of the face would seem like obvious clues, there are other possible causes. That's why Sparky's doctor needs to take a biopsy of the masseter muscle. If the sample is normal, the possibility of Sparky's having an abscess behind the eye, a neurologic problem, or other muscle disease needs to be investigated.

If MMM is caught in time, treatment consists of suppressing the haywire immune response with a corticosteroid, usually prednisone. The dosage is started high, tapered down to a maintenance level, then continued for at least six months. Aren't steroids dangerous, you ask? For one thing, prednisone is a corticosteroid, not an anabolic steroid. Your dog will never hit 71 homeruns by taking prednisone, but should do fine on it as long as your veterinarian is cautious. Even if your dog can't hit the ball over the fence, at least he should be able to catch it pretty soon.

# New Pets in the Home; Loss of Pets and Pet Owners

## Adding a New Puppy to the Home

*It's important to carefully select the right puppy to add to your life.*

### QUESTION:

I have a 2-1/2-year-old female Chihuahua. She is very spoiled. We have ordered a new female Chihuahua puppy to be delivered in a couple of months. I have no idea how to introduce them to each other and am fearful that the older one will try to hurt the puppy. Any advice would be appreciated.

### DR. NICHOL:

You are smart to think ahead on this issue. Small-breed dogs can become very attached to their owners. They get possessive, too. While there are ways of managing disagreements between a couple of jealous dogs, your best bet is proper selection of your new baby.

When we talk about dog behavior, we often assume that a dog's motives would be the same as ours—and often that's a reliable assumption. But while dogs are like us in many ways, they are instinctively quite different in others. One big difference is the dominance order within a dog pack. As soon as you add dog number two, you guessed it, you have a pack.

The idea of social classes is a tough concept for most of us enlightened Americans. We frown on treating some folks in our society as lower-class citizens than others. But with dogs the concept of a dominance hierarchy is fundamental. Any attempt on your part to "enlighten" your dogs to New-Age, sensitive thinking will meet with failure. In fact, the very first thing any dog does when he or she meets another dog is to start jockeying for political position. As soon as your new Chihuahua meets your old one, they will be sending each other signals, communicating where they each believe they belong: "Am I top dog or bottom dog?"

Will it be a major class struggle? Will the new one try to bite the older dog? With good planning and a little luck, you can avoid problems. The trick is to watch your existing dog in the presence of other dogs. Does she behave like royalty, always putting the other dogs in their place, or does she "roll over and play dead"? If she's dominant, try to select a new pup who is submissive. On the other hand, if your girl is a shrinking violet around other dogs, you'll want to pick a new one who is cut from the same bolt as Rambo. Since there is no changing your existing dog's innate personality, temperament testing of the new baby's entire litter is your best hope for picking a compatible personality.

You can stop worrying. It's not hard at all. Flip to Part 1's Chapter 3. If you choose the right puppy, you'll all live happily ever after.

One last thing: Don't "order" a puppy for delivery the way you would order a pizza. One pizza with onions and anchovies is the same as another. But a dog is as individual as a person. Pick out *your* new dog. Then feel good about it and have pizza and a beer too.

## Introducing a New Dog to an Established Group of Dogs
***Give them plenty of distance and take it slowly.***

### QUESTION:

I have a 1-year-old male Chihuahua. He and our female dog got along well until she was killed in a car accident. I just recently purchased another female, approximately 7 weeks old. My male will have nothing to do with her; he growls and tries to fight with her. We gave him plenty of attention and loving before and after her adoption, but he will not even look at her without hostility. Please advise me on how to acquaint them or what to do or not do to get him to accept her into our household. She seems interested in getting to know him. We are not willing to get rid of either one.

### DR. NICHOL:

I bet your male Chihuahua is willing to get rid of somebody. But not to worry. I know this is not only frustrating, but a bit frightening as well. You care for both dogs and you sure don't want anyone getting hurt.

So how could this boy, who has been so loving, be so harsh? Two reasons: The first is that he doesn't like change. The second is that he's unsure of how the family dog politics are going to turn out. Will the new girl let him rule the roost? Remember the dominance hierarchy that is so fundamental to canine instinct. Unlike models of civility like you and me, dogs are snobs. Every one of them is born with a clear concept of his or her rank in the pecking order of life in a dog pack. His dog pack changed with the death of your first female, and now it has changed again. He wants to stay on top of the heap. I'm sorry for how barbaric that sounds. But while dogs share some important emotions and feelings with humans, they have some equally clear differences.

What should you do? Start over. Keep them out of each other's sight for three to five days. Then take them to a park (in separate vehicles, please) and reintroduce them on neutral turf. Don't be surprised if it's not love at first sight. Let them slowly check each other out. When they get home, be sure to give the dominant boy lots of attention in the submissive girl dog's presence, while ignoring her. This will reinforce to both of them that the top dog is still the top dog. Even if your boy growls and jumps on her, he is quite unlikely to hurt her. If the hostilities continue, consider neutering that sexist piglet and/or ask your veterinarian to prescribe (you guessed it) Prozac. Better living through modern chemistry.

# Introducing a New Dog to an Established Group of Cats

*If you take it slowly and carefully, a gentle dog should fit in well— eventually.*

## QUESTION:

Five days ago I got a young dog. I already had three cats. I've let the cats run loose at night and kept the doggie in the bathroom. I let them all sniff under the door. I've taken the dog with me in the daytime and let the cats be able to go into her bathroom to check out her scent. I'm not comfortable letting her roam the house yet with the kitties. The cats are not hiding and are circling around, staring at her when I bring her out on her leash in the house. She appears to want to play; they, of course, are disgusted, but also curious. Soon I need to let the cats get nose-to-nose, with her on the leash in case any fights break out. Do I interfere if they growl or spit? Just hold the leash so they don't chase and fight, and talk to them soothingly? I talk to them all when they're in the same room. I also shut the cats away in the morning and let her roam the house where the cat scent is. None are ever loose in the same room. The dog doesn't bark or growl, other than a small "woof" each time. She seems to want to play and makes a "lunging" movement that appears playful. I expect this routine to last a few weeks at least. Then I'll let them all together with the dog off the leash only when I'm supervising. Am I doing this right?

## Dr. Nichol:

I'm impressed. You have a fundamentally sound approach. Your basic understanding of the fear felt by your cats and the curiosity and playfulness of your young dog are on the mark. I'll make a few recommendations that will help the process along.

Number one: You have added two stresses to your group of cats. One is another creature in their already crowded household. The other is fear. The results of these new stresses may be physical disease. Or they may act it out with behavioral problems like urinating on your walls and furniture. They may also fail to accept this new family member—permanently. But let's work on it anyway; we still have a shot at a negotiated peace settlement.

First, eliminate the fear. Sit with your dog on a leash at one end of your house. Give her a rawhide chewy so she is not focused on the cats. Then let the cats out to explore the house with your dog visible. Repeat these sessions until everybody appears completely bored. Then, the final frontier. Get a 20-foot lightweight nylon cord at the hardware store. Sit with your dog with no toy, and have the cord tied to her collar. Allow the cats to roam the house. Any aggression by your dog is corrected with a sharp jerk on the cord. As her behavior improves, allow her to leave your side, but always with the nylon cord attached. Thus, the cats will learn not to run from her and she will not feel motivated to give chase. Lose the cord when you have confidence that this youngster fails to notice the existence of the cats.

Will it work? Only time will tell. Most dogs adjust well this way. Some are aggressive by nature and can't resist the hunt—and that can be deadly. Use your head. If your dog keeps failing the test, you better leave her outside.

## Pets and Children: Teaching Responsibility

***Carefully consider the maturity of the primary caretaker before adding a new pet to your home.***

### Question:

I'm thinking that a pet is a good way to teach responsibility to my children. One is 5 and the other is 3. Do you think they are old enough for a pet?

### Dr. Nichol:

Do I look like Dr. Joyce Brothers? (Please say no.) The truth is, I see a lot of parents making this decision at various times in the development of their children. And having a couple of bambinos myself, I can add a personal perspective.

Number one: Even some adults lack the maturity to have pets (or children, for that matter). So it depends a lot on the individual child; some mature faster than others. Also consider why children want pets. Let's be honest, it's often for the same reason they want toys—they think it will be fun, which of course it is. But the responsibility part is what takes maturity. If the child is to be the responsible pet caretaker, the best age is 12 to 14 years with some kids being ready closer to age 40.

But what about the little ones? Oh, they can have pets, too, as long as the parent knows that it's not really the child's but actually the adult's pet. This way, the kids have fun helping with feeding, grooming, and trips to the doctor; but they can still be forgetful, which is what they are because, after all, they are little kids. You want pets to be a source of joy to your children, not a point of conflict. If you push responsibility on your kids too early, you may set them up to fail.

## Death of Pet Owner and Its Effect on a Loving Dog

*The loss of a family member can be a major stress on a beloved pet. TLC, time to grieve, and medication can ease the transition.*

### QUESTION:

Our family has a very serious problem. My dad died two weeks ago. He lived alone except for his faithful dog Angus. Angus is a truly great Labrador Retriever. He is 8 years old and physically healthy. The problem is that since Dad's passing, Angus has been really depressed. He barely eats, he won't play, and he hardly moves. Could Angus die, too? Our whole family loves this dog. We can't stand the thought of another loss.

### DR. NICHOL:

I am so sad about your dad and poor Angus. Our pets have become so much like us that it's almost scary. You are right. Angus is experiencing the same feelings of loss as the rest of your family. Like you, he needs special care and understanding. In other words, he needs to feel loved and connected.

While it is unlikely that Angus could die from his depression, his system is truly stressed. This can cause his immune system (bodily defenses) to become vulnerable. If an infectious disease comes his way, he could easily succumb. Can we help him? You bet.

In addition to providing TLC, there are human antidepressants that are effective and safe in dogs. Prozac is one that has helped a lot of people with chronic depression. I have used it successfully in many dogs like Angus. If Prozac doesn't help, there are others. If he starts to act out his fear by barking excessively or becoming destructive, an anti-anxiety medication such as Buspar may work better. The bottom line is that not all grieving pets are the same. Rest assured that medications are usually necessary for only about three to six weeks. None of them will leave Angus addicted or in any way impaired. Stay in touch. You will all make it through this tough time.

## Grieving Pet Loss
*Other family dogs share the loss and the grief.*

### QUESTION:
A few weeks ago I had to put down Sam, one of my four dogs, due to liver failure. The remaining three seem to be grieving—no playing, no barking, not eating. Sam seemed to be the leader. How can I help them overcome their grief when I cannot seem to recover from it? Thank you for listening.

### DR. NICHOL:
Your world has been badly shaken. You and your special family are having normal feelings of loss. The dogs had a unique social structure that needs to repair itself. It will take time. You, too, need time, but you may get through it better with help from a grief counselor. Don't feel silly asking for help because Sam was "only" a pet; he was a family member in every way.

The remaining three dogs in your life share your grief as well as their own. When you feel better, they will, too. In the meantime, your veterinarian can prescribe a medication such as Clomacalm that may ease the transition for your dogs. Thanks for writing.

# Odd Noises and Interesting Habits

## Singing Along
*Good tunes and the dogs who love them.*

### Question:
I have a 1-year-old Bearded Collie who barks and howls whenever I play the piano. My question is, does the sound hurt his ears or is he "singing" along? He doesn't leave the room or try to hide. He barks much less if I play soft or slow; if I play loud and fast, he howls.

### Dr. Nichol:
Gee, if only our pets could talk. Some folks might wonder if your Bearded Collie (they look a lot like Old English Sheepdogs) thinks he's a music critic. I'm betting that he actually likes your playing. At a recent continuing education meeting, the Bayer Company hosted an evening presentation that included a competition of singing dogs. It was great fun; these pets would match the tempo and volume while their favorite tunes were played. The winner was a miniature Poodle who just loved BB King. She especially liked "The Thrill Is Gone." While she was on stage getting her award, BB King himself came out and played and sang right along with the dog. It was a true thrill for everybody. I went out after the meeting and bought the CD—of BB King, that is.

## Sleeping, Dreaming, and a Little Jumping
*REM sleep causes dogs and people to dream and move around.*

### Question:
Is it normal for dogs to jump a little while they are sleeping?

### Dr. Nichol:
Yes, it is. We do the same thing. Like us, dogs have different stages of sleep. The deepest stage is called REM (rapid eye movement) sleep. This is also when we do most of our dreaming.

During this deep-sleep phase, the small movements of the limbs correspond to the dream stage. It is important not to wake your dog, or anyone else for that matter, when you notice the signs of REM sleep. Suddenly waking someone from REM sleep could cause him or her to be frightened and disoriented. Those deep-sleep patterns and dreams are important to our well being.

As much as I write often of the differences between humans and dogs, there are some striking similarities. It's great to feel this common ground with our beloved pets. So share a nap with your dog. A family that sleeps together might start to jump together.

## Licking Caused by Boredom

*This high-energy Boxer puppy (like all puppies) can learn to channel his energy in positive ways. He's goofy, but his heart is in the right place.*

### Question:

Please help me to understand why a little over a year-old (our age) Boxer named Dog goes around in anyone's house and licks the floors and rugs. Dog is well-fed and frisky in a home that loves her. She also has a tendency to lick people's hands, feet, or wherever. She pulls out flowers by the roots and eats them or the blooms. Is the dog lacking a vitamin?

### Dr. Nichol:

How did you know that I was the same age as you are? Are we really just a little over a year old? I have more time than I thought.

The reason your Boxer licks everything in sight is that she is a Boxer. These wonderful dogs are so active that unless you provide gainful employment, most will simply find their own work—in this case, mopping everything in your home with her tongue and defoliating your yard. Is this a problem? Are you fine with a coating of dog spit inside your home and a yard devoid of plant life? You're not? In that case, I recommend channeling that energy into something useful, like obedience training. You two can attend a class together and learn how to behave (I mean your Boxer will learn to behave). Between classes you can work together to perfect those skills. Your large-breed dog will know what's expected and she'll be safe in public.

In the meantime, keep a dog toy in your pocket. Anytime you see this girl licking incessantly, give her the toy to chew and remind her that it's more fun than spreading her spit. Now, dry your hands and get started.

## Pacing, Restless Older Dogs

*Behavioral aging changes, called canine cognitive dysfunction, can be treated.*

### QUESTION:

Sometimes you'd think our 15-year-old Schnauzer was a 6-month-old puppy, but she does sleep a lot and her teeth are in bad shape. The past several months, when she is not sleeping, she is pacing. We would hate to think that it's because she hurts.

### DR. NICHOL:

We get mighty protective of these old-timers, don't we? Start with a thorough physical exam by your veterinarian. If your girl has pain, the doctor may recommend lab work to look for other possible problems or to confirm the safety of the anesthesia necessary to fix her painful teeth and infected mouth.

Beyond pain issues, her pacing may be due to a problem called canine cognitive dysfunction—similar to senility in people. There are several possible remedies; any of them may work wonders. One is a chewable supplement called Cholodin; another is the drug Anipryl. About 50 percent of older dogs improve noticeably with one of these. You can also add vitamin E as an antioxidant, and ginkgo to increase blood flow to the brain.

Is it worth all this for an old dog? If she's in good shape in most other ways, I say give it a try. But I also know how hard it must be to watch her body go back to nature. Aging of a loved one is tough. It will take tremendous courage to let go of her when the time comes. Your veterinarian can make it as gentle as possible for both of you. In the meantime, take every day as a gift.

## Mounting Behavior

*Some dogs who mount want attention. Others are dominant. Rarely is it sexual.*

### QUESTION:

Our question is, what does it mean when our Standard Poodle "humps" my husband when he hugs me or vice versa? He is a very sweet dog who has had obedience training.

### Dr. Nichol:

Ahem, I know this book is meant for family orientation, but I'll work with you anyway. The truth about mounting behavior is that it is rarely sexual; much more often it's an expression of a dog's dominance or, in your Poodle's situation, it's social.

This is the part where I remind folks that while we share a lot of behaviors with our dogs, there are some stark differences. Mounting is not a socially acceptable greeting between most people, but for many dogs it's just their way of being part of the group. Like some humans, though, there are some dogs who need more attention than others—like your Poodle, for example. So while you and your dog share a lot, there are differences—I hope.

Confused? Me, too. But there is a solution. Set aside specific times each day for interaction with your needy dog so he gets his requirements for attention met. Throw the ball, rub his tummy, or whatever. Anytime you notice him minding his own business, give him some love and praise. When he does mount, say "No!" and turn away. Don't push him off because that is physical attention, which will only encourage more unwanted behavior. If he continues anyway, get a handheld foghorn or air canister. Your dog's interruptions of those romantic moments can be addressed by a loud blast. Hey, this could be fun. I only hope that your marriage is strong enough for all this.

## Puppies Who Hump Each Other
*It's not what you think. It's only political.*

### Question:

I have an embarrassing question: How young are dogs supposed to be when they get their sex drive? I have two puppies. They are brother and sister. They are only 8 weeks old and I've caught them humping. What should I do?

### Dr. Nichol:

Don't do anything. It is not sex that is on their little minds, but dominance. Remember that dogs are real concerned with dominance order, that is, who will be the top dog. The mounting behavior you have seen is just one method used by dogs to communicate that the one doing the mounting wants to be the pack leader. It will not warp their personalities, nor will it lead to teen pregnancy. But if you catch them smoking dope, write again.

## Jumping on People

*A dog habit that really annoys some people. It's curable.*

### QUESTION:

I have a 9-month-old Shih Tzu, Goober. He's my new best friend. I can't get him to quit jumping on people when they come to visit. I know he's a lover, but I sure would like to be able to visit with my friends without trying to constantly keep him from being all over them.

### DR. NICHOL:

Goober really does like people. He wants to have an immediate physical relationship with everyone he meets. And why shouldn't he—with his good looks and personality? But he needs healthy boundaries.

Part I: A jumper's behavior can be corrected by the jumpee or by you using a leash. When done by the jumpee, it requires one to wait until the jumper jumps. As soon as Goober's jump begins, one knee is raised quickly to thump his chest. As the correction is made, the jumpee says, "No!" When Goober is back on all fours where he belongs, a treat is given and he is nominated for president (the big reward). Repeat this hundreds of times. If you are consistent, you will have Goober trained not to jump on you. But he may still think it's okay for him to molest your guests. So we move to Part II.

Part II: Have Goober drag a light leash around the house for a few days until he forgets it's there. Next, set up the "sting." With you holding the leash (which Goober doesn't notice), have a friend walk into the house. As soon as Goober starts his jump, jerk back quickly on the leash and say (your catching on quickly), "No!" Of course, as soon as Goober is back where he belongs, he gets a filet mignon and another political appointment. Repeat hundreds of times. As soon as Goober's behavior is perfect, however, he will be unfit for public office and he will have to return to life as a dog.

## Food Stealing

*Break this bad habit early, or just put that thief in the yard at dinnertime.*

### QUESTION:

The shelter where we adopted our puppy Pal believes he is half Australian Shepherd and half Border Collie. He has been an excellent pet, thus far, except that he is a food thief. He steals from the table, the counter, the garbage pail, and our children. Nothing is safe. When we catch him, we take the food away and scold him. He seems remorseful—hangs his head—and occasionally even drops the food himself when he knows he is caught. This behavior can't be because he is hungry. Often there is food in his bowl when this happens. Is there a way we can stop this behavior?

## Dr. Nichol:

My family was really glad to hear me read your letter. You're not alone. Our Border Collie, Peter Rabbit, is a highly accomplished food thief, too. He first becomes very small as he slinks into the shadows. Watching carefully, he bides his time. Silently, he stalks that closely guarded, tender-young corn-dog. It rests in its innocence, never suspecting the danger that lurks. Finally, the corn-dog keeper turns his attention. Quick as a jackal, the predator strikes as he whisks his quarry to the safety of his lair, where he devours it—stick and all. Not a pretty sight.

You would think that a dog who is so well-loved and smart and even beautiful ought to be perfect. But the truth is that Pal actually is perfect. This uncivilized food-stealing habit of his is a genuine part of his basic instinctive personality: Wild dogs are scavengers. But that's not logical, you say. After all, he has everything a dog could want, including an abundance of great food, right? Well, don't forget: We can bond to our dogs just like another person because they are so much like us; but they are also still dogs (uncivilized).

Why do they do this? Why don't all dogs? Number one: Dogs are not people. They are not ruled by the same instincts as humans. Second, some breeds are much closer to their wild plundering roots than others. Border Collies and Australian Shepherds are herding breeds, but they work stock (like sheep, ducks, and bicycle tires) in ways that are predatory in nature. They act much like wolves. Your dog does this because it's part of who he is. He's not a sociopath; he's a hunter, even if it's for peanut butter sandwiches.

What can we do? I'll tell you first what you cannot accomplish. You will never totally break Pal from wanting to steal food. He'll be hatching a sneaky plot on his deathbed. But what you can do is show him, through immediate negative feedback, that it is more comfortable not to steal. In other words, use a Scat Mat or a Tattle Tale. (Aren't those great names?)

Scat Mats can be draped over the edge of a table or kitchen counter, or you could place one on the floor in front of the counter. When Pal steps on the Scat Mat or leans on it on his way to the food, he will get a static-electricity-strength shock—as he is committing his crime. Having the correction occur at the time of the offense is the most effective method of discipline. But, remember: For this plan to work (we'll out-fox your conniving dog), he must be motivated. That means you have to set him up—in other words, plant the bait.

What happens if he starts to recognize the Scat Mat and goes straight until you think you have him cured? That's when a Tattle Tale may work well for you. This gizmo uses infrared light to detect the presence of your dog in the area of the food that you have so devilishly planted for him. When he crosses the light beam on his way to the counter, you hear an audible tone in the other room. That's when you move in and make the bust. (Isn't this exciting?)

Will all of this work? The truth is that there are some individuals who are too strongly attached to the "call of the wild." Peter Rabbit has learned many excellent commands and social skills. But, like Pal, he is an inveterate gourmet prowler. We gave up at our house. Sneaky Pete hangs out in the yard while the kids are eating. Sorry, but sometimes they act just like animals.

Are humans really smarter than dogs? Maybe we are. But I want to know who's sneakier.

## Stool Eating

*There is a remedy for this disgusting behavior. It's not easy, but it's the lesser of two evils.*

### QUESTION:

Help! My Jack Russell Terriers eat their *poo* (yuk!). We've tried saying "No," spraying them with a water gun, putting Accent meat tenderizer on their food, and giving them Deter (two tablets each). They don't always eat it, but I'd rather they didn't at all. They eat Iams dog food. Please help; this is obviously annoying and quite embarrassing!

### DR. NICHOL:

Sorry to hear that your Jack Russell Terriers are eaters of poo. What would Jack Russell say? The name for this behavior is coprophagy. A pet who does this is therefore coprophagic. Maybe knowing this will help with the embarrassment factor.

It is not really known why dogs who are on good diets like Iams would do this. While poor-quality food may cause some dogs to try to regain lost nutrients by eating feces, there is a different reason for your dogs. One possible cause is boredom. Regardless of the reasons, vices like coprophagy can become ingrained behaviors. So whatever you do, do it right away.

Many remedies have been suggested for this habit. Meat tenderizer on the food has made a difference for some. Yelling "No!" and squirting with water help—but only if you are with your dogs every time they snack. The ideal correction occurs whether or not you are there. For this purpose, there is a product called (fittingly) For-Bid.

I've had a lot of experience with For-Bid, not because my pets would ever behave like dogs, but because I have dispensed it many times. You are not the only dog owner who has admitted to this most dark of all family secrets. Most coprophagic dogs change their ways after taking For-Bid. And it's easy to use. Simply mix a packet with each of two meals for two days. Dogs don't seem to notice the For-Bid granules when they eat it with food, but it imparts a nasty taste when it is present in the stool. While a couple of days of treatment seems effective in most cases, a few poop addicts have required a different course of treatment.

What if For-Bid fails to live up to its name? In that case, I recommend taste aversion. This involves a substance that is nasty tasting to a dog—such as cayenne pepper, citronella oil, horseradish, or pepper sauce. Right after your pup has a bowel movement, have her sniff her stool, then immediately squirt about one teaspoonful of one of these substances into her mouth. If you are quick, she will associate the bad taste with the smell of her stool. Then, for a few weeks, watch carefully for fresh bowel movements in the yard and immediately paint the same bad-tasting stuff liberally on the stool. Leave the stool for her to discover in its new "aversive" state. Be consistent, but leave only one fresh stool pile available for her. Then take two aspirin, get a good night's rest, and call me in the morning.

I hope this helps. If your dogs still eat doodies, seek a 12-step program. At least then they will know they are not alone.

## Eating Cat Stool

*This is gross. Here's how to fix the problem.*

### QUESTION:

We have an 8-year-old Collie. Periodically, he will get into the cats' litter and consume their feces. This seems to lead to bouts of nausea or loose stools. There does not seem to be any disciplinary method or physical barrier that effectively keeps him out of the cat litter.

## Dr. Nichol:

The reason your Collie likes to eat cat feces is that they are rich in meat protein. That's because cat food itself is. Not only do dogs not need a high-protein diet, it's also bad for them. While a dog who eats cat stool quickly becomes persona non grata around people, he can also damage his kidneys by ingesting all that extra protein.

So here is my advice: Use an uncovered cat litter pan (so it's easy to know when it's time to empty it), but keep it in a place that is completely inaccessible to your dog. Suggestions include putting it on a shelf where the cats can jump to reach it, or behind a cat door installed in a closet door. Either way, be sure *not* to use clumping litter. If your dog foils your efforts and eats the clumping litter, he can develop a severe intestinal blockage that could require surgical correction.

## Midnight Interruptions to a Pet Owner's Sleep for a Quick Trip to the Yard
*First, rule out urinary disease. Then manage the behavior.*

### Question:

My question is not about a serious problem. My 6-year-old neutered Springer Spaniel has suddenly decided that he has to go out once a night to urinate. There is no doggy door which means all of our sleep is interrupted. I have tried cutting down on his water at night and letting him out before he goes to bed, but it doesn't seem to make any difference. I can live with it if there is no simple solution, but it would be nice to get a full night's sleep.

### Dr. Nichol:

I'd have to say you have a serious problem if your dog is waking you up every night.

Before discussing behavioral reasons for these midnight urinations, we need to establish that bladder problems like stones or infection are not factors. Start by measuring his water consumption for 24 hours. Next, bring him to your veterinarian for abdominal palpation to feel for bladder stones. Tell the doctor the amount of water consumed. And don't let this boy urinate for a few hours before your appointment so that a sample can be taken for urinalysis and culture. If he checks out fine, we'll move to step two.

Step two is to get adequately attired for some quality yard time. When this young man wakes you up, go outside with him and watch what he does. Like any self-respecting male dog, he will pass some urine on his favorite spots. He may also have a bowel movement. Your mission, should you decide to accept it, is to see whether he passes a lot of urine or just a little. If it's a small amount on each of a few trees, followed by a tour of the premises, then we know that he's decided that enjoying the midnight air is just his way of curing his insomnia. But if it's a lot of urine, go back to step one and tell the doctor to do more lab work to look again for physical disease.

Already you have hit on part of a useful strategy. Assuming that your Springer is physically normal, withholding water for a few hours before bedtime is okay. If he's also passing stool at night, be sure not to feed him for 4 hours before bedtime. Now for the simple solution that you wanted: Put him in an airline crate at bedtime and don't let him out until morning. And no, it's not cruel. Dogs are den animals by instinct. They prefer the security of their den and they know not to soil it. But whatever you do: If he complains while he's in the crate, *do not* rescue him. Allow him to get used to it. Remember that we do not have pets so that we can learn to live by their whims. It's supposed to be the other way around. Now go back to bed and get some sleep.

# Outdoor Living and Related Problems

## Porcupine Quills in the Face

*Once stuck, will a dog repeat the mistake?*

### Question:

Recently our dog got a faceful of porcupine quills. It took a general anesthetic to pull them out of her face—she even had them in her throat. Will this teach her to leave porcupines alone, or will she go after them again?

### Dr. Nichol:

This is a truly good example of the predatory nature of dogs. Porcupines are relatively slow moving and easy to catch. Dogs who come home looking like they have a pincushion for a face have usually enjoyed the experience with their hunting buddies (pack members). Will she do it again? If she has the chance, bet on it. But it's not because dogs are stupid. It's really because they love to hunt and they love to be in a dog pack. And let's face it. They love to be dogs.

## Fence Jumpers: An Invisible Fence Is an Almost Sure Winner

*A buried wire sends radio signals to a collar that first warns with a tone, then corrects a dog with a mild static-like shock.*

### Question:

Our dog Millie is a terrible fence jumper. We've tried everything. Are Invisible Fences any good?

### Dr. Nichol:

They are great. The installer will bury a light wire underground around your yard, then fit Millie with a special collar. Next, they will train you on how to teach Millie how to stay in the yard. What Millie will learn from you is that as she gets close to the boundary of the yard, she will start to hear a high-pitched sound that dogs don't like. If she gets even closer to the edge of the yard in spite of this, she will feel a low-level electric shock from the collar. You will learn how to train her to back away from the fence.

The system works because the buried wire puts out radio waves that signal the collar on the dog's neck. Most dogs catch on in a few days and they never have to feel the shock again. I have one for my pets. I'm a real believer.

## Urine Killing Grass
### *Daily vitamin C will provide a healthy lawn.*

### QUESTION:
We have a 6-month-old Blue Heeler, female; she is slowly turning my grass yellow. Is there anything I can do to prevent my grass from dying?

### DR. NICHOL:
Giving her 250 milligrams of vitamin C once daily will acidify her urine and cause the grass to grow lush and green in those spots, instead of brown and dead.

Incidentally, another reader asked whether the vitamin C goes in the puppy food or on the lawn. The vitamin C is definitely for the dog. It is the alkaline nature of urine that kills grass; with vitamin C, the dog's urine becomes more acidic. An added benefit to your dog having more acid urine is the lower risk of urinary infection and most bladder stones.

## Exercise
### *Healthy exercise means more than just "Start out slowly, then taper off."*

### QUESTION:
I have a beautiful 8-month-old Bichon Frise puppy who loves to go running with me. I started her off on 10-minute runs, and she has now done one 30-minute run. (She's always in front of me, pulling on her flex leash!) Am I doing any damage to her puppy joints by having her run with me? How long do you think it's safe for her to run? Could she do 10K with me? Don't tell me I should have gotten a bigger dog—this little sweetheart came into my life from the Humane Society, so I'll just deal with whatever is best for her.

## Dr. Nichol:

This girl sounds like a real gem. The exercise you two share is more than just healthy. You are creating a bond that makes your relationship deeper. I run with my 10-month-old puppy Peter Rabbit. For us, it's also a chance to work on a little training.

How much is too much for your short-legged youngster? Don't worry about her young joints. Running for a dog is low impact because they always have two feet on the ground, unlike humans who fling our entire weight from one leg to the next with each step. As for distance, if this young athlete runs out of steam, she'll lag. So far, you are doing fine. Regarding the 10K (about six miles), you should train your dog's body the same way you train your own. Increase the distance gradually. If she acts winded during the workout or has sore limbs when you're finished, you've pushed it a bit too hard.

One last point on exercise for your dog: Provide water at the start of the workout as well as at the end, but never let her tank up all at once. Take the water away and give her more in ten minutes if you need to. She could twist her little stomach if she drinks a large volume. This is a surgical emergency that not all dogs survive.

You provided a major gift of love in saving the life of this dog. Humane societies are wonderful groups that work hard to find good homes for orphans like your girl. It sounds like they succeeded on this one. By the way, I would never say you should have gotten a bigger dog. On the contrary, I'd say that if she has trouble keeping up on your runs, you can make it easier for her by just having your legs shortened.

## Outdoor Shelters for Pets
### *What's the right size and how much house is enough?*

### Question:

I'm worried about my neighbor's pets because it's getting so cold at night. They have two cats and a dog who huddle up together in a pile each night in a corner of their yard. I told them I would ask your advice—I know they will do what you suggest. They're nice people—I just don't think they know any better.

**DR. NICHOL:**

Thanks for caring. It's actually remarkable how well dogs and cats survive in the elements. As much as they could get through another winter on their own, though, they are sure to feel much better with decent shelter.

Considering how well they get along, they may do very well with one house (pet house?) to share. The pets can start with one, but once they feel more comfortable, they might start getting territorial and somebody may get thrown back out into the night. In that case, they may need one for the dog and one for the cats. Either way, here are the fundamentals for a snug and healthy structure.

Let's start with the floor. It may be more important than the roof because the cold ground literally sucks heat out of the body. A wooden floor is fine, but it needs to be one to two inches above the ground. This clearance will not only prevent direct loss of body heat, but it will also provide the insulation of dead air space if the sides of the house are built to come all the way to the ground. This arrangement will also prevent the wind from blowing under the house and carrying off more heat.

Determine how high the walls should be by standing the tallest pet and measuring his or her height at the shoulders. Multiply by 1.5 and this should be the interior height. Use the same multiplier to determine the length of the house; that is, it should be 1.5 times longer than the longest pet who will call this house a home. Why not bigger? We're not trying to save on building materials here. Aside from keeping these critters dry and draft-free, the house has the essential function of trapping the warm air that is generated by their bodies. Once the air on the inside of the house has been warmed, it will in turn keep their little bodies warm and they will stay comfy. If the house is too big, they will keep putting out heat and will never fully warm the air. This wastes a lot of important calories.

How about a roof? Good idea. A nice pitched roof with shingles works well. However it is attached, be sure to caulk the joints where the roof meets the walls, again to prevent warm air from leaking.

They will also need a door—and this is important. If it's nothing more than an opening, we will have windstorms blowing through. You can simply hang an old piece of denim cloth or a carpet scrap over the opening. This will be fine, but be sure to cut it so that there is a one- to two-inch gap above the floor at the bottom so that they can see outside. This will provide that den-like feel that will give them security. You can accomplish the same thing by designing a vestibule so that after going through the door, the pets must first turn right, and then left through another doorway. With this offset vestibule, no wind can blow through and these little guys will stay toasty.

You could also make this whole project much easier by just purchasing a Dogloo, but you would miss the artistic freedom that comes with playing architect. If you work on building the house with your neighbors, you will enhance your relationship. Just stay out of the cat house.

## Dogs Who Won't Use a Dog House

*Dogs are den-living creatures, but some prefer the great outdoors.*

### QUESTION:

I enjoy reading your column in the *Albuquerque Journal.* You give great advice with a sense of humor I can relate to, since I teach sixth graders. Not to imply you have the sense of humor of a sixth grader—you just seem to have a genuine happiness I often find in children, too. This is a compliment!

Now, to my question. I have a 6-year-old Sheltie, Oliver, who will not use a dog house. Having a heavy coat, he hasn't seemed to suffer being out in the weather in the past. The problem is that he is acting like his hip is bothering him as he gets older, and I wonder if the cold aggravates this problem. Now the complication: We got a puppy, Paco. He has a short coat and the cold gets to him much faster than Oliver. They are both crate-trained, but I don't like to leave them in during the day for more than four hours. Paco won't use the dog house, either. We have tried putting a blanket in there that has our scent on it, but Paco just pulls it out to sleep on it, and then the blanket gets wet when it is raining or snowing. I really care about my dogs and think they would be comfy in the dog house, but they won't use it! Help!

### DR. NICHOL:

You have a real conundrum. When I face problems like this, I try to figure out what would motivate me. So, if your dogs are anything like sixth graders, I suggest putting a Nintendo game in the dog house. Add a big screen with MTV and they'll never leave.

Okay, you wanted real advice, didn't you? Number one: We are going to let your dogs have it their way. The reason they don't use the dog house is that they don't want to. Yes, I remember preaching the virtues of providing dogs a den. Dogs are instinctively den animals. But they are also individuals. Oliver and Paco are in good company. Many canines, including sled dogs in the Arctic, prefer to sleep outside in the snow. What about Oliver's bad leg? Most arthritic joints are more painful in the cold damp weather; but assuming that the best management for joint disease would be a dog house may be a mistake. Instead, I recommend an exam by your veterinarian. Not only do we have ways to keep Oliver comfortable, but we also have an obligation to prevent a worsening of the problem.

Now that we've established what your dogs want, let's talk about what *you* want. You want your dogs to know that you love them enough to give them the best. And if you give it to them, the least they could do is use it. Don't they know you had to walk 12 miles to school in the snow when you were a kid—up hill—both ways? It's okay. Really.

One last point about the indoor crates. Any dog over the age of 4 months should be happy and fine if kept in a crate for 8 to 10 hours at a stretch. They can handle it physically and emotionally. So you have that option, too. But I say let them choose. They're sixth graders, after all, and if you don't let them have some choices, they'll just rebel. Then you'll be sorry.

## Flies

***More than just a nuisance, flies can lead to maggots that destroy the health of an older dog.***

### QUESTION:

My old dog has flies buzzing around. What works well?

### DR. NICHOL:

Go to a feed store and buy a spray or lotion that is intended for horses. Keep it away from the eyes and dilute it as recommended on the label. You'll be fine. Flies are a problem because they can lead to maggots.

# Poisoning

## Chocolate Poisoning

*She may look like a dog, but she's really a pig. Never trust a dog around the goodies. Many will get liver damage from eating chocolate.*

**QUESTION:**

One of my dogs consumed a large amount of chocolate, and I was wondering if this could be harmful? If so, what should or could be done when this happens? I have a mutt and a Dalmatian. The Dalmatian was lying in the other room, whining for no apparent reason. I think she was the one who ate the chocolate. What should I keep an eye open for?

**DR. NICHOL:**

You have a valid concern. Chocolate can be dangerous. It can also be harmless. It's unpredictable. Here is how it works: Chocolate contains a chemical called methylxanthine that is eliminated by the dog's liver. Some can handle it; others can't. If your dog's liver is not built for chocolate, she can have convulsions and die due to severe liver damage. A dog suspected of having eaten chocolate should have vomiting induced. This is best followed by rinsing of the stomach by a veterinarian.

What if your dog has had chocolate in small amounts from time to time without a problem? Can you assume she'll always do fine with it? Again, we can't predict, but we can say that if your dog has a known liver problem, you are taking a major risk by letting her have chocolate.

Here's Dr. Jeff's sound advice on chocolate for dogs: Remember that most (if not all) dogs are chow hounds. They are eating machines. No matter how well trained, they are not to be trusted with food. Protect their health by providing only excellent dog food in measured meals. If goodies like chocolate may be accessible, remember Murphy's law: Any chocolate that can go wrong, will.

## Inducing Vomiting
*Ipecac is best and safest.*

### QUESTION:
I read some advice about making a dog vomit if he swallows poison. I'll bet there's not one layman in 500,000 who knows how to make a dog vomit. Please tell us how to do that.

### DR. NICHOL:
There are several effective methods, including giving oral salt or hydrogen peroxide. Each of these can be dangerous. The safest is syrup of ipecac, which is available in little tiny bottles at any pharmacy. This is an over-the-counter product. The dose is one teaspoonful per 5 to 10 pounds of body weight for a dog. No pet should get more than three teaspoonfuls. (The same advice, incidentally, applies to a cat.) If the pet fails to vomit in 20 minutes, repeat the dose. Any pet owner or parent of small children would be well advised to keep a few bottles on hand in case of accidental poisoning.

## Drywall Eating
*Although not poisonous, plaster can cause intestinal blockage.*

### QUESTION:
Recently my two Lab mixes have gotten into the habit of eating pieces of drywall that I have in the yard. They seem to really enjoy it and will even fight over it! Why do they like it? Could it hurt them?

### DR. NICHOL:
You raise an interesting question about some pretty boring stuff: drywall (plasterboard). Unlike cat stool, which most dogs regard as a delicacy worthy of fisticuffs, gypsum plaster has no taste at all. But Labs and their racially mixed brethren are pretty goofy and love to chew on just about anything. This is not an uncommon pastime among canine connoisseurs of construction scrap. The good news is that it's harmless in that it does not absorb into the body. But once they get started eating plaster, they could end up with a concrete-like blockage of the intestines that can be difficult to eliminate. If they swallow enough of it, they will get pretty badly constipated.

What's a parent to do? My best advice is to prevent their access to it. By the way, what the heck are you doing with a bunch of old drywall in your yard anyway? Get rid of that junk, would you? Hey, wait a minute—you live next door to me, don't you? Want to borrow my truck?

## Strychnine and Seizures

*Highly treatable if caught in time, it's also preventable by "poison proofing" your dog.*

### QUESTION:

I've been worried ever since I saw a TV report of strychnine dog poisonings. I have three big dogs who I need to leave outside while I am away at work. How do I teach them not to eat poison? How will I know if they get poisoned?

### DR. NICHOL:

It's a very serious and frightening situation. Strychnine causes the nerves of the body to fire repeatedly in a high-speed fashion. The result is first trembling followed by convulsions. While it can be fatal, it is treatable if you recognize it early.

The first thing we do for a dog with strychnine poisoning is to give anesthesia intravenously. This quiets the body so that we can pass a tube and remove any poison that is still in the stomach. Then we give fluids IV and other supportive care until the pet begins to recover.

What about prevention? Prevention is my favorite word. You can poison-proof your dog. Like all training, you must be consistent. Poison-proofing involves allowing your dog to eat only after you say his or her special release word. Choose a word other than "okay." Some unusual or invented word is best so that no one else can guess what it is. With a leash and slip-chain choke collar, put your dog's food in front of his or her face. Correct with the leash each time the dog tries to eat—until you say the release word. *Never* allow your dog to eat again without hearing the special release word. If you leave your dog in someone else's care, be sure that person—but no one else—knows the word.

Finally, be a good neighbor. If your dogs are respectful, quiet citizens who stay in your yard, no one is likely to want to cause them any harm.

## Snake Bites

### *What are the risks—and what can you do?*

#### QUESTION:

Last year my friend's dog got bit by a snake. I have a new puppy and we plan to hike a lot when the weather gets warm. What happens if we come across a snake? What should I do if my puppy gets bit?

#### DR. NICHOL:

This is a subject that strikes fear into the hearts of most of us. The type of snakes you might run into has everything to do with the part of the country where you plan to hike. Coral snakes, like those found in the eastern and southern portions of the U.S., are shy and mostly active at night, so they are seldom a problem. Rattlesnakes, copperheads, and cottonmouth water moccasins, on the other hand, are known to be more aggressive.

Which pets are at risk? Most injuries result from a curious dog playing aggressively with a snake. Bites are usually found on the head. The amount of venom injected into the pet is influenced by the size of the snake and just how mad it has gotten. But the activity of the pet after the bite is an even greater factor in recovery.

Remember the old cowboy movies, when they would suck out the venom to save the victim? We have since realized that venom absorbs into the bloodstream much too quickly for this to help. More to the point, allowing the pet to be active after a bite will cause the venom to be carried to other areas of the body faster and increase the risk. So, the best first-aid is to control activity and get the pet to a veterinary hospital as quickly as possible. Knowing what type of snake caused the bite is important because the antidote, called antivenin, is specific to the snake's venom. Most snake bites in New Mexico are from pit vipers like rattlesnakes. In addition to antivenin, the doctor will also treat a snake-bitten pet with intravenous fluids, antibiotics, and pain management. Other problems resulting from rattlesnake bites include shock, bruising of other tissues due to poor blood clotting, tissue death at the site of the bite, and a whole lot of pain.

The best defense against snake bites in pets is to keep them on a leash while hiking. As responsible pet owners, we must use common sense because very often our pets are just too goofy.

# Seizures and Staggering

## When Adult Dogs Have Seizures
*Start anticonvulsant medications early.*

### Question:
I have a Cocker Spaniel who has seizures. His name is Odie and we consider him an important part of our family! He is having seizures more often. I haven't put him on any medication because I fear it will change his personality. What is your advice on this condition? He is 5 years old and in good health other than the seizures. He has a high level of energy except after a seizure. I will do what is necessary to take good care of Odie.

### Dr. Nichol:
Great question. I will start by telling you what will happen if you do not give anticonvulsant medication to Odie: The nerve pathways in his brain responsible for his convulsions will become more deeply ingrained as he has additional seizures. With time, he will have seizures more and more often. When you finally start him on medication, his epilepsy will be much harder to control.

Will medication change Odie's personality? While anticonvulsants affect the brain, they rarely cause a pet to behave differently. In cases where it does occur, we find that they usually go back to their old selves after the first few days on their new treatment. Or we can simply use a different medication. The bottom line: Start Odie on treatment soon. He'll feel much better and he will always be Odie.

## Epilepsy
*Anticonvulsant tablets are inexpensive and nearly always effective.*

### Question:
I have a Golden Retriever. He is only 3 years old. In the last month he suffered two epilepsy crises. The vet told me that there is no remedy, and they will be more frequent until I need to take the decision to sacrifice him. I would like to know if

you can help me. I know it will be difficult because I live in Mexico, but I know you have better services for pets than here. Please help me.

## Dr. Nichol:

I am sorry to learn of your dog's epilepsy. For starters, I want you to stop worrying about having to part with him. In almost every case, epilepsy is controllable with oral medications. There is no reason that your boy should not go on to live a normal happy and active life.

Your local veterinarian is right about one aspect of epilepsy: Without treatment the seizures tend to occur more frequently. While this disease has been recognized for centuries, the true cause has never been fully understood. We do know that there is a hereditary tendency and that it is more common in males. We also know that without treatment, nerve pathways will develop in his brain that will encourage repeated misfiring of neurons (nerves), causing more convulsions.

Want some good news? Treatment consists, in most cases, of giving an easily available and inexpensive drug called phenobarbital. Tablets are given every 12 hours and have few, if any, side effects. For dogs whose seizures are not completely prevented with phenobarbital, another treatment called potassium bromide is also available. Some pets need both.

My advice is to find a veterinarian in Mexico or the United States with training and experience in pet medicine. Simple blood tests will rule out other causes of seizures, leaving epilepsy as the likely diagnosis. Please don't fault your Mexican veterinarian for being uninformed about epilepsy in dogs. The economy of our neighbor to the south is mostly agricultural. Veterinarians there are highly educated in the treatment of livestock diseases. If your pets were cattle and sheep, your veterinarian would be right on the mark.

# When Puppies Have Seizures

*Puppies with seizures need special attention. Don't delay. Babies can get sicker fast.*

## Question:

I have a 3-month-old Brittany. Every once in awhile she has these attacks in which her body tightens up, her eyes get all glassy, and she falls over. I'm assuming it's an epileptic attack, but I'm not sure. What do you recommend we do for her during the attacks? We just hold her, and my husband talks her through it. It's very sad. I'm afraid if we take her to the vet, they will just put her on medication. She's healthy, very active, and *very* hyper. I don't want anything to take away from her playful side.

## DR. NICHOL:

You sound anxious. I would be, too. We love our pets like our children, and it scares the heck out of us when they are sick. Let's start with the possibilities, then we'll talk about what you can do when you have a home emergency.

Your first concern is epilepsy, but this is unlikely as this kid is, well, just a kid. Epileptic seizures are rarely seen earlier than 6 months of age and more commonly not until a dog is 18 months old. So what's more likely in a youngster like your Brittany? Diseases that I would consider first include low blood sugar, a defect in her liver, or encephalitis (inflammation in the brain). I know none of these sounds very good.

Now that I've scared you, I'll give you a little advice. If this baby has low blood sugar, it may be that you just aren't feeding her often enough. If that's the case, simply rubbing honey or Karo syrup on her gums during a seizure will correct the problem in one to two minutes. If this turns out to be the case, you will need to have food available at all times or feed her every six hours until she is 4 months old, at which time you can switch to three daily feedings. On the other hand, your young Brittany may have much more serious problems.

My recommendation is that you take her to her veterinarian. The doctor needs to do a complete physical exam. Have a blood chemistry profile, blood count, and urinalysis taken. These tests will bring to light blood-sugar problems and liver disease. If it all turns out normal, you may be advised to stay observant. If better feeding practices don't fix the problem, a spinal tap and possibly an MRI or CT scan may be necessary.

I know how frightening this sounds, but this puppy is special to you. If you fail to get her the medical attention she needs, she could die young and rob you both of the lifetime of joy that you could share. Don't let your fear of medications and uncertainty stand in the way of saving this beautiful, active baby.

## Sudden Inability to Stand and Walk Straight in Older Dogs

*Dogs don't have strokes. Geriatric vestibular syndrome looks like a stroke, but resolves quickly.*

### QUESTION:

I think my dog had a stroke. She's an 11-year-old Lab named Polly. This morning she seemed to be okay when, all of a sudden, she couldn't stand. Her head is cocked to one side and her eyes are rolling. But she still wants to eat and she still recognizes me and my family. We think Polly's suffering. Do you think it's time to have her put to sleep?

### DR. NICHOL:

I will tell you right from the get-go that Polly will be fine. She has not had a stroke.

The name for Polly's problem is geriatric vestibular syndrome. It is seen in dogs of about her age and is so severe in some cases that dogs not only can't get up, but they also roll uncontrollably. Some of the senior citizens with this disease can stand, but walk in circles. For a long time it was suggested that a brain lesion or hemorrhage was responsible for the sudden onset of these symptoms, but no evidence has ever been found to support this. Dogs simply do not have strokes.

I'm sure that, knowing that Polly is going to be fine, you would like a treatment that will help her feel better and speed her recovery. Despite medical advances in most areas, there is nothing that will make a difference with this problem. Polly will be improved in a few days and has a strong chance of being totally back to normal in about two weeks. Recovery is complete in nearly every case. The only permanent problems have been minor head tilts in a few of these old-timers. Even these pets have gone on to live otherwise totally normal lives.

Please don't even consider euthanasia for Polly. Labradors seem to grow even gentler and more endearing as they age. I'll bet that with the kind of love and care she's had from you over the years, Polly has another 100,000 miles left on her clock. Give her a hug and a kiss. She'll trust you when you tell her that everything is going to be okay.

# SKIN PROBLEMS

## Allergies and Itchiness

*Allergies are a common cause of itching. But don't be a do-it-yourselfer. Overbathing an itchy dog may only make it worse. Get that itch fixed by your veterinarian.*

### QUESTION:

We have a 3-year-old miniature Schnauzer. She has been very itchy lately. Nothing has helped her so far. We tried using different shampoos on her, changed her food, washed all of her bedding, and used dye-free and perfume-free detergent and no fabric softener. We are wondering if it could be something in the carpet. This condition just recently became worse. She will dig and bite herself raw if we don't keep her doggie-sweater on her. We have taken her to the vet several times for this, but everything that was tried has failed. Any suggestions for getting our dog (Sadie) back to normal?

### DR. NICHOL:

This is a common problem. It is miserable for the poor, itchy dog and it can drive her family crazy. There are reasons why it can be hard to control and why it can suddenly worsen.

Veterinarians have struggled with itchiness (in dogs, that is) for a long time. The truth is that when we determine a cause for it, we are usually right. But the reason that some of our patients continue to scratch is that we may have found only one or two of the causes for that dog's itching. In reality, there can be several causes. If we don't diagnose and treat every one of them, we still have a miserable dog and owner.

Ask Sadie's doctor to take "impression smears" of her skin wounds to check microscopically for bacterial or yeast infections. With the damage from scratching and biting, many dogs itch from the "self-trauma"-induced infections. These poor dogs will need antibiotics or antifungal medications in addition to allergy treatment.

Anything else? Sure. There seems to always be something else with skin disease. In your attempts to help Sadie feel better, you have bathed her often. This has caused drying of her skin that has also added to her discomfort. While antibacterial bathing is likely to be important, follow her baths with Humilac (available from your veterinarian) as a rinse. This will moisturize her skin without making her greasy. Be sure to use only the recommended shampoo and bathing schedule. Human shampoos, by the way, are much too harsh for dogs. Also, be sure to continue to follow instructions on the use of oral medications. These are an essential part of treatment.

Finally, food allergies may be an important component of Sadie's itching, but you must remember to use only the specific diet dispensed by Sadie's doctor for as long as eight weeks. It can take that long to learn if a hypoallergenic diet will help. There is no store-bought food that will work. If poor Sadie still itches after all this, give your poor, tired, overworked (but not itchy) veterinarian a break. Ask to be referred to a veterinary dermatologist. In the event that inhaled allergies are Sadie's problem, the specialist can skin-test your girl and start her on a series of injections to reduce her sensitivity.

I know this is a lot of work, but so is typing with one hand while I scratch with the other (which I am not).

## Scratching All Year 'Round

*Food allergies cause nonstop itching. A food trial with a prescription diet can answer the question and help a dog feel so much better.*

### QUESTION:

Dr. Jeff, I have the itchiest dog. Buford is 4 years old and he seems to scratch all the time. I've heard that dogs with allergies only itch in the spring and summer—not Buford. Amazingly, his skin looks fine and normal. Do you think he has allergies? If he does, what can I do for this unhappy pup?

### DR. NICHOL:

It's almost as hard to live with a scratching dog as it is to be the scratching dog. There can be many causes for scratching like this—but with normal-appearing skin and a year-round problem, I suspect that Buford may have a food allergy. While itching and scratching due to inhaled allergens like pollens and molds may be more common, they tend to be seasonal—such as every spring or summer. But since Buford eats all year 'round, he is itching all year 'round, too.

How do we beat this itch? We know that most food allergies are caused by the protein source in the dog's diet. Since most commercial diets supply proteins in the form of horse meat, beef, or chicken, we use diets that have lamb, venison, duck, or—in some cases—beans. The protein source is usually the culprit, but in some cases the carbohydrates are the problem, so we have special diets available with potato, for example. In addition, we have a new prescription diet called z/d that's excellent for dogs with food allergies.

Is this too far-fetched? I can tell you from a lot of experience managing these cases that it is not. When we hit on the correct hypoallergenic diet for a miserable scratching dog, we have a very happy pet and family. Believe it or not, these diets are all available through your veterinarian in dry and canned forms. It is rare that we need to have pet owners custom-cook for their dogs. But don't try experimenting on your own. There is a method to therapeutic dietary trials. If Buford's regular veterinarian is not experienced in this type of skin management, he or she can refer Buford to a doctor who is. When Buford finally stops scratching, he'll say "Ahhhhhh, thanks."

## Hot Spots

*These nasty red infected skin lesions can recur due to allergies.*

### QUESTION:

My dog has an annually recurring problem my vet refers to as "hot spots." His name is Jack and recently he's scratched himself horribly on the side of his neck. He's scratched off quite a bit of hair and skin. Consequently, he spends a great deal of time with a cone on his head. What causes this problem? Is there a treatment to avoid its recurrence? Is there something else I should be doing to help this heal?

### DR. NICHOL:

Jack has a hot spot. It's a nasty, rapidly spreading surface infection of the skin that can attract flies. They lay eggs that hatch into maggots. Are you starting to feel sick? Me, too. Go directly to the veterinary hospital. Do not pass "Go." Do not collect $200.

Hot spot is a term used to describe the sudden appearance of an inflamed surface skin infection that exudes a sticky fluid. They are itchy and they get bigger quickly. When your dog scratches a hot spot, he damages the skin further and it spreads faster. The cone, or Elizabethan collar, prevents him from hurting the wound, but it does nothing to help it heal. What's more important, it does nothing to correct the cause.

Seasonal itching in dogs is almost always a result of inhaled allergens, like pollens and molds, that are in the air only at specific times. A doctor skilled in the management of allergies can prescribe a combination of an antihistamine and fatty acids that could safely prevent all this misery. Allergy testing and a series of injections may also be needed.

I recommend more help for this poor guy. What are his friends saying about him? Will he ever get into college or have a satisfying social life? Will he get dates? How will this impact his puppies? The possibilities are endless.

## Itchy Feet

***Paw licking and chewing can drive everybody crazy. Have your veterinarian do what it takes to understand the cause and get that poor foot-sucking dog feeling better.***

### QUESTION:

Our Dachshund is 4 years old. She began licking her back paws about two months ago, and now does this constantly. Please advise what this could be and any remedies.

### DR. NICHOL:

This is an important question because it illustrates a difference between dogs and humans. While it's annoying when a dog licks her feet constantly, it would be something else altogether if this were your husband instead of your Dachshund. Ponder that, and we'll discuss it in depth later.

Why does your Dachshund do this? Because her paws itch; but only after an exam by her doctor can we say for sure why. Here are the possibilities: inhaled allergies (like pollens or housedust), contact allergies (such as grass), contact irritation (soaps, carpet shampoo), or infection from bacteria or parasites like demodectic mange mites. To provide a truly valuable service for your little girl, the doctor will check microscopic scrapings and might even do a skin culture. If initial treatments fail, further testing for allergies may be needed. I recommend having it managed soon. Some people begin to resemble their pets. Let's hope no one at your house starts to act like this one.

## Surgery Wound Care

***Keep the incision clean for good healing.***

### QUESTION:

We adopted a puppy from a local animal shelter two days ago. She had to be spayed before we brought her home. Do we have to do anything to keep the incision site clean, or put any kind of ointment on it?

### Dr. Nichol:

Congratulations on your new baby! I admire you for sharing your home with this little orphan. You just may have saved her from euthanasia.

I advise gently dabbing her spay incision with a moist wash cloth twice daily until you have the stitches removed—about ten days after the surgery. Do not use hydrogen peroxide, as this tends to be damaging to the tissues. Ointment would seem like a good idea, but studies have shown that—for normal skin—adding oily stuff actually slows healing.

## Dry Skin

*If you treat it yourself, your dog may end up with <u>very</u> dry skin.*

### Question:

Any ideas on skin care? My 3-year-old female Pug named Pug has dry, itchy skin. She loves to be scratched. In fact, she's obsessed about being scratched. Will bag balm help?

### Dr. Nichol:

First, try to determine the cause. For starters, if you are bathing Pug, stop. You may be overdrying her skin. If you have not been bathing her, get her a physical exam. She may be allergic or seborrheic. Her doctor can help her. If Pug needs a skin moisturizer, a spray called Humilac is excellent. Please do not use bag balm. It is quite greasy. This stuff is great if you are a chapped udder on a dairy cow, but not so good if you are a Pug.

## Mange

*It's itchy, miserable, and potentially fatal. Treatment must be aggressive.*

### Question:

We have a Great Dane a little over a year old. He was diagnosed with demodectic mange when he was 8 weeks old. Our local vet says there is nothing we can do except give him a mange dip. He is currently itching and losing a lot of hair. He has severe dry skin with flaking. The skin under his arms is raw, and his coat is becoming patchy. Please let us know if there is anything else we can do.

### Dr. Nichol:

The intense itching plus the skin damage that results from all that scratching has to be unbearable.

You will need to take him to a doctor to reevaluate the diagnosis. It's been a long time. There may be new factors in his skin disease. Have a skin scraping examined microscopically. Assuming that the diagnosis is still demodectic mange, my advice is the following: (1.) Give whole body dips with Mitaban once weekly (*not* every two weeks as directed by the manufacturer). (2.) Give antibiotics. The skin damage caused by all that scratching is worsened by infection. (3.) Give vitamin E. (4.) Give a thyroid supplement. (5.) Say a prayer to St. Francis. I'm serious. Even with all this treatment, your dog's mange may only be improved—not cured. I am a big believer in the power of faith.

Why does it have to be that hard? Demodectic mange is caused by microscopic burrowing mites that live at the base of the hair follicles. It's very tough for the chemicals in the dip to reach that deep. In addition, your dog's immune system is not up to par. The mites responsible for his infection are present in the majority of adult humans and dogs anyway, but this boy is vulnerable. For him to overcome this parasite, he needs all the help and support we can give him. Having said all that, most demodex treatments succeed. Go for it.

## When a Nose Cracks and Bleeds

*Noses shouldn't change. Loss of pigment or blistering of the skin can lead to cancer.*

### Question:

We have a 7-year-old wolf hybrid who has been suffering from a peeling nose so bad it cracks and bleeds for four years. My concern is that it could develop into skin cancer, aside from the fact that she cries when her nose is touched. Our vet's diagnosis was an immune imbalance. He recommended a combination of tetracycline and niacinimide. The problem seemed even worse after five weeks. I apply aloe vera to her nose. Can you help us with any other solutions?

### Dr. Nichol:

While this treatment is the newest and safest for discoid lupus, nothing works on every case. While your veterinarian is probably correct, it would be best to know for sure.

Start by discontinuing the treatment (including the aloe vera) for at least four weeks. Next, have your veterinarian take a small sample of the skin from your dog's (wolf's) nose for biopsy. If the diagnosis is confirmed, you may want to consider increasing the dosages of the tetracycline and niacinimide or adding the corticosteroid prednisone. Is this dangerous? Prednisone has received some well-deserved negative press for its side effects, but in low doses as an adjunct to the other treatment, your dolf (wog?) should do fine.

# When a Nose Turns Lighter
## *Could be a form of lupus, but not to worry.*

### QUESTION:
My dog's nose should be and used to be black. However, it turns a medium to light brown on the tip seasonally. We were told to switch from plastic to steel bowls, and we did four years ago. Now her nose is lighter than ever. What's the cause and how do we fix it?

### DR. NICHOL:
You have good powers of observation. You may be right to be concerned. I'd love to be able to go nose to nose with that nose. Instead, I'll tell you what to look for and what it could mean.

If that nose has ever been inflamed—swollen, cracked, or scabbed—we may have a contact allergy or discoid lupus erythematosis (DLE). That last part sounds like serious business, doesn't it? I'll make it a bit easier.

Contact allergies have already been suspected, but I doubt it as a diagnosis. It is usually seen with redness of the lips also and it is not seasonal. If you want to rule it out completely, use a glass bowl. Now discoid lupus. Do not be frightened by the word *lupus*. This immune-mediated skin disease is not the same as that nasty systemic lupus erythematosus (SLE) of humans and dogs. Both diseases, however, result from foul-ups of the immune system.

First, the anatomy. The nose, like all skin, is made up of layers of cells that are held together by a cement-like substance. What occurs in DLE is that an immune system gone haywire builds antibodies against that cement-like substance. The upshot is that those skin layers slip apart, causing painful erosions. Add to that the more direct impact of ultraviolet (UV) rays from the sun during the warm months, and you can easily have seasonal worsening.

Find a veterinarian who is skilled in dermatology. If an exam shows that your concerns are groundless, then, what the heck, I just taught you some dog trivia. On the other hand, if the doctor's up-close-and-personal exam suggests a serious problem, a biopsy will be the next move. It will require a short anesthetic, but bite the bullet and get the real answer. Even if she has DLE, it can be safely managed.

You love this dog. If her skin disease worsens, she could easily develop skin cancer. Do not gamble with her health.

## The Brown-Nosed Retriever

*Golden Retrievers have a normal nose color change. If it's not inflamed, it's okay.*

### QUESTION:

I have a 10-month-old male Golden Retriever, Casey. I have started to notice that his nose seems to be changing from black to brown. I feed him dry dog food from a stainless steel bowl. Is this normal?

### DR. NICHOL:

Yes, feeding dry dog food to your dog from a stainless steel bowl is completely normal. I do it, too. It is also normal for a Golden Retriever's nose to turn brown as he matures. (That doesn't make him a brown noser.) Contact allergies on the chin of some dogs can result from plastic bowls. Stainless steel and glass are almost always fine.

## Insect Stings

*Know what is dangerous, what you can treat at home, and when to call it an emergency.*

### QUESTION:

'Tis the season and I don't mean Christmas. 'Tis the season for bees, hornets, wasps, and things that sting. My dog likes to chase after and ingest bugs of any type. (Of course, this happens after my vet closes.) What is the best treatment for a sting? What is the best treatment for swelling?

## Dr. Nichol:

I have known many dogs, including my late Airedale, Juan, who have been compulsive bee hunters. Stings inside the mouth seem to cause most of them no harm. But we also see dogs at the hospital with the telltale swollen face indicating an allergic reaction. We know the cause is likely an insect sting but the patient never talks.

The real problem is the risk of a severe allergic reaction. If a dog has no symptoms after getting stung, there isn't a problem. But for those pooches whose faces resemble basketballs after a bee-eating melee, there could be a risk. Here is how it works. Each time a potentially allergic dog is stung, the immune system responds a little more than the time before. In other words, each sting causes an increase in the allergic sensitivity of that dog. Enough repetition and anaphylaxis, though rare, could occur. Anaphylaxis is a serious allergic response that can result in the inward swelling of the larynx (voice box). If this occurs, your dog could suffocate.

Our approach is to take no chances. When we see a swollen-faced dog, we treat with an injection of an antihistamine like Benedryl. If the symptoms are suggestive of an anaphylactic reaction, we also inject epinephrine. You can try giving oral Benedryl at home, but be prepared to wait a while for the symptoms to improve. If your dog develops noisy breathing, go quickly to the doctor.

# Ticks

*Vectors for deadly blood parasites, ticks are actually quite dangerous. Simple home treatment has made them much easier to eliminate.*

## Question:

My dog, a miniature Doberman Pinscher named Morgan, has had two ticks on him lately. I would like to know the best way to keep him tick-free. I use Advantage for fleas, but was told it was not good for ticks.

## Dr. Nichol:

Ticks are not only a source of discomfort for our pets, they are also carriers of some potentially deadly blood parasites. In addition, they are major bloodsuckers. A small-breed dog like a miniature Pinscher can literally bleed to death if he gets enough ticks.

But wait, there's more. The free-living life stages of ticks are largely influenced by the weather. If your area stays dry for long periods, you may not see many ticks. But if it rains a lot, then gets warm and sunny, those bugs will lurch out of dormancy and have a feeding frenzy on any warm-blooded mammal they can sink their little proboscises into. Yuuuccckkkk!

So, how do you prevent or get rid of ticks? Find someone you don't like and turn Morgan's ticks loose in their underwear drawer. Fun, huh? On the other hand, if your life, like mine, is encumbered with personal ethics, you can kill the ticks on your pets using a spot-on product called Frontline. Like Advantage, Frontline comes in little plastic tubes that you open onto the skin between the shoulder blades. Keep the hair parted for a few minutes to let the fluid soak into the skin. The ticks will die within a day or two. Don't use Frontline and Advantage together. Use Frontline instead, because it's effective against fleas as well as ticks. Repeat the Frontline application monthly until the weather gets cold in the fall. However, in the fall, do not stand in the middle of your yard and vigorously rub your hands together in triumph over the dastardly ticks. They do not die off in the winter. They just hibernate and reestablish their intimate relationships again the following spring.

Finally, if you find only the occasional tick, you really don't need heavy artillery like Frontline. You can remove them by hand. *Do not* "unscrew" a tick. They do not have corkscrew mouthparts. Instead, grasp the body of the little beast and pull slowly and steadily until it lets go. Then smash his evil carcass and feel a sense of victory over one of the animal kingdom's worst enemies. Oooo, how sweet it is.

## Ticks, Part II

**Ticks transmit serious diseases. Frontline is a spot-on treatment that works great.**

### QUESTION:

I own a female Lab cross and have been having a terrible bout with ticks this spring. I started her on topical repellents a few weeks ago and have sprayed suspect shrubbery within the lawn, but I still seem to find a few new ticks on her daily. Is there anything I could add to her diet (garlic?) or other precautions I should be taking?

## Dr. Nichol:

You're in good company (with other pet owners that is; ticks are not at all good company). Between March and October, we see a lot of pets with a lot of ticks.

What's the big problem with ticks? How do I hate them? Let me count the ways. Yes, these bloodsuckers are a disgusting nuisance. But they also transmit potentially fatal blood parasites like Ehrlichia and Rocky Mountain Spotted Fever. Ticks in some parts of the country also carry Lyme disease, which infects humans *as well as dogs and cats*. Ticks are not our friends.

The good news is that the fight has gotten easier. A treatment called Frontline is effective for dogs and cats against several kinds of ticks as well as fleas. It's easy to use; just squirt it on a small area of skin near the pet's shoulders. Frontline starts working within 24 hours by spreading through the skin, then being released from the hair follicles onto the hair. Ticks and fleas contact Frontline, twitch and jerk miserably, and die. It's a beautiful thing. Apply it monthly.

Is it really that simple? Of course not. Nothing in life is that simple. Heavy infestations may also require heavy artillery like yard sprays. All of this is available from your veterinarian. Other spot-on treatments can be found in pet supply stores, but they are much less effective.

In most states, county extension agencies also have detailed information about tick-borne diseases, proper tick removal from both pets and people, tick control in the home landscape, and the current local levels of tick incidence. In areas where Lyme disease occurs, some extension agencies also provide tick identification and testing for Lyme disease in the tick that is removed from the pet or owner.

## Schnauzers with Blackheads
### *Antibiotics, prescription shampoos, and vitamin A.*

## Question:

I have an 11-year-old black Schnauzer who two years ago developed the Schnauzer comedone syndrome. I am having a hell of a time keeping it under control. The vet prescribed Soloxine for his thyroid, massages with alcohol twice a week, and bathing him with Oxydex shampoo every week. We are doing all of it, but those nasty sores keep coming back, not so bad as they were a year ago, but we cannot get rid of them once and for all. Is there anything else that you can suggest? The female, who is silver, doesn't have this problem.

## Dr. Nichol:

Such strong language. Hell, blackheads (comedones), nasty sores. Well, okay, it sounds like hell, or heck anyway.

The Schnauzer comedone syndrome is a keratinization disorder of the follicles. This means that bits of dead skin cells make their way down next to the growing hair shafts beneath the surface of the skin. So we try to control this disease, but not cure it. Some Schnauzers are prone to get it, while others, like your female, never do. Underlying causes such as low thyroid function and allergies may contribute to the disorder. It is also common to get secondary bacterial infections, which make them more itchy and "crusty." This little boy may be helped with a three-week course of antibiotics. I also often use vitamin A (not beta carotene) at a dose of 1,000 IU/kg. Oxydex shampoos should help, but make sure there is adequate contact time before rinsing. You can also use the same shampoo on yourself as an oral rinse. At least that's the kind of thing my mom tried in her totally failed attempts to clean up my language. (Just kidding!)

## Hair Shedding

### Dog breeds with continuously growing haircoats shed the least.

## Question:

My friend is going to get a dog for her birthday, but she is having trouble deciding which kind of dog to get. She wants a dog that does not shed and is small. Can you help her decide what kind of dog to get?

## Dr. Nichol:

It's good to know she is thinking ahead. So often it's just an overpowering love of pets that causes the purchase of a new dog on impulse. But cuteness and a fast tail wag are only part of what your friend will live with for the next 13 to 15 years. I think she's being smart to consider what type of dog will fit her life before she commits.

Shedding: The worst are short-coated dogs. Their hair grows to a specific length, then falls out and is replaced. But long-coated dogs have hair that grows continuously so they shed about as much as we do. Longer hair is also much easier to remove from fabric. So which breeds? There are several that make outstanding companions: Poodles, Terriers, Lhasa Apsos, Shih Tzus, and miniature Schnauzers to name a few. But don't forget that, unlike their short-coated brethren, they will need haircuts lest they start looking like the hippies of yesteryear.

# Rough, Cracked Foot Pads
*Home treatment can help those paws feel a whole lot better.*

## QUESTION:

Our 10-month-old Cocker Spaniel has been having trouble with his paws. His pads are very rough and cracked. They seem to be sensitive at times. He gets very upset if we try to touch them, and occasionally we see him nursing them. We live in a fairly urban suburb, so he spends much of his time walking on concrete and pavement. But this seems like it might be more than just normal wear and tear. Any thoughts on how we could treat it or what we could do to help him heal?

## DR. NICHOL:

This little guy sounds miserable. The paw licking he is doing while lying down is a clear sign of pain. His feet hurt even worse than that when he's walking. But not to worry. We can help this boy.

Our first move, as usual, is to figure out what's causing the problem. When a dog's foot calluses become thickened and fissured (cracked), we have to consider things like a recent distemper infection or a disease of the immune system, such as systemic lupus erythematosis or pemphigus. None of these awful-sounding maladies are any fun, but all are treatable. Clearly your Cocker needs to see his doctor. Blood tests and skin biopsies may be necessary to secure an accurate diagnosis.

Does that sound hard? It's no big deal. You can handle it. There is one other possibility, by the way: idiopathic. *Idiopathic* is a great word, and when you hear it you know right away that it means we have a problem, but we have no idea what's causing it. That's okay, though, because it also means that if we just improve the symptoms, everybody will be all right. If your veterinarian reports negative results on all of the tests, do this: Punt. Soak your puppy's feet in plain tap water until his foot pads soften. Then bandage them in nitrofurazone ointment (your veterinarian has this as well as good, safe bandage material). Leave the bandages on for a few days. If the wounds are improved by then, you can maintain these new kinder, gentler pads with daily applications of Panalog cream (you-know-who can also dispense this). Your puppy will feel better and life as you both know it will return.

Is that the end of it? Sorry, but pads like this always require long-term maintenance on an as-needed basis. But the supplies that you will need are fairly cheap and, what the heck, what better way to bond to your dog than daily foot massages, eh? One last thing: Is your dog's name Joe? A young man once brought a Cocker Spaniel named Joe to our hospital and, of course, I had to ask why he named his dog Joe. The kid looked at me as though I had just landed from Neptune and finally, after what seemed like an eternity, said, "Cocker, man. Like Joe Cocker." Boy, did I feel stupid. But that dog couldn't sing at all. I still don't get it.

## Hair Loss and Thyroid Disease

*Loss of hair is a common sign of low thyroid function, which can be diagnosed with a blood test.*

### QUESTION:

Our 12-year-old male Golden Retriever named Buddy has hair thinning in an area about the size of a silver dollar on his upper hindquarter. There is no irritation. It has been on his left side for about a month, and now it is beginning on the right.

### DR. NICHOL:

By far and away the dog breed with the highest incidence of low thyroid function (hypothyroidism) is the Golden Retriever. Hair loss is a common sign. Have Buddy's blood tested. Thyroid tablets are likely to make all the difference. He's a spring chicken, so I say go for it.

## Hair Loss and Eye Discharge

*Low levels of thyroid hormone are common in dogs. Most cases are simple to correct.*

### QUESTION:

I have a little Shih Tzu named Ling Ling. Ling Ling is very cute—but she is losing her hair, she has this beige goop coming from her eyes, and she stinks. I've been to three different vets with her and nothing really helps.

## Dr. Nichol:

I'm sorry Ling Ling has these problems. While there may be only one disease that is responsible for all of her symptoms, skin problems in dogs can result from several causes. Getting her back to good health may require time and patience.

While Ling Ling's skin disease may be complex, I suspect that the underlying cause may be hypothyroidism. As the name suggests, hypothyroidism is a low output of hormone from the thyroid glands. It is quite common in dogs and is often responsible for thinning of the hair. It can also cause the tear glands of the eyes to produce inadequate amounts of tears, resulting in the discharge that Ling Ling has. Finally, the odor you have noticed could well be due to an oily skin condition called seborrhea—also common in dogs with low thyroid output.

Have her thyroid hormone levels tested to determine whether hypothyroidism is the underlying problem. If she is truly hypothyroid, twice-daily tablets should correct most of her problems. But as much as this may resolve the eye and skin diseases over the long term, be sure that her eyes stay moist and free of discharge in the short term. In addition to medications to improve the health of Ling Ling's eyes, antibiotics and prescription shampoos could also be important. Whatever you do, don't let Ling Ling know you think she stinks. Shih Tzus are quite sensitive about their auras.

## Scratching

*Inhaled allergies can cause severe scratching and injury to the skin. Symptomatic treatments can be safe and effective, but the worst cases may need skin-testing. Injection series give the best results for the tough cases.*

### Question:

We have a 1-1/2-year-old Great Dane. For several months now, he has been scratching his underbelly and seems to have an allergy to something. Our vet said he could be allergic to a number of things—Bermuda grass, carpet, cedar bedding (which we have removed), or anything. Our vet gave us a prescription for hydroxyzine. This seems to help some, but not enough. He is still scratching himself silly. His hair on his belly and sides is thinning and his skin is red from scratching. He is so miserable, and we feel so helpless. Do you know of anything else that we can do for him?

## Dr. Nichol:

How unfortunate that your Great Dane is scratching himself silly. My dog has been quite silly. Maybe that's it. Oh, your question: This is a common problem in the spring and summer. I suspect that your veterinarian is correct—it sounds like an allergy. He is also correct in that it can be hard to know the specific cause. Here are a couple of thoughts: While hydroxyzine is a useful antihistamine, it is much more likely to reduce the itching if you add a capsule called Derm-Caps or Efa Tabs. These are specially-formulated vitamin and fatty acid supplements. In combination with an antihistamine, they work great in 30 percent of allergic dogs. If he still itches, a low dose of prednisone can be added. You can also try a different antihistamine like Tavist. (There may need to be a bit of trial and error before you find what works best for your dog.)

It's also possible that while he may be allergic, he could also have an additional skin disease. Dogs often have more than one skin problem. Sounds like a real challenge—often it is, but don't be frustrated; the job of making your dog feel better is your veterinarian's. If you don't mind some trial and error to see what works best, you are likely to succeed. If your dog's allergy is seasonal (just one season of the year), simply managing his symptoms may be the best treatment. On the other hand, with a duration of "several months," he may have additional reasons to itch—like a food allergy or other skin condition.

My advice is to make your dog's doctor fully aware of the long-term nature of the itching. Be sure the veterinarian knows about the partial response to the hydroxyzine (a good sign). Also try to remember when the last diet change occurred, so the doctor can consider the possibility of a food allergy. A prescription hypoallergenic diet could be part of the answer.

If none of this helps, it could be necessary to take your dog to a veterinary dermatologist for skin testing. Once the specific allergens (those things that are inhaled that are responsible for the allergy) are discovered, a desensitization injection can be tailor-made for your boy. The injections would be given monthly to reduce his allergic sensitivity. This is something that you could easily learn to do at home.

Is it worth all this? If your dog scratches to the point of damaging his skin, he can develop other problems, like bacterial and yeast infections. He may also be more prone to ear infections. Besides, how silly do you want him to get?

## A Collar Imbedded in a Dog's Neck

*Puppies can outgrow their collars, just like children outgrow their clothes. Neglected collars can cause infected, open wounds of the neck.*

### Question:

I feel horrible. My Teal is a 4-month-old Malamute puppy, with an awful-looking wound around her neck where her collar dug into her skin. It's my fault because I forgot to check to see if the collar was getting too small. She outgrew her collar. I didn't think about it because she didn't seem bothered. Then it started to smell. What can I do?

### Dr. Nichol:

I know how you feel. You want the best for your new baby and you made a mistake—but take heart. While this oozing wound around Teal's neck looks nasty, it should heal quickly with proper care.

Your first consideration is to manage infection. The hair around the wound needs to be clipped close to eliminate the scabs that hold bacterial contamination in contact with the wound. Electric clippers are a must. Next, scrub the wound with soap and water and rinse it thoroughly. Then keep it clean and free of scabs by washing it morning and night. Depending on how deep the wound is, it could take one to three weeks to heal. Finally, if Teal feels badly or has lost her appetite, she may be spiking a fever. If that's the case, or if all this wound treatment seems overwhelming to you, better take her to your veterinarian.

In the meantime, use a harness on Teal instead of a collar. But don't worry that she will hold a grudge. Most dogs are very forgiving. There will not be any lasting damage to Teal or to your relationship with her.

## Itchy Puppies and Cheyletiella Mange

*Yellow skin flakes and thickened skin are giveaway symptoms.*

### Question:

My husband and I just got a new puppy for our children. The puppy seems to be in good shape, except that he scratches a lot. When I looked at his skin, I saw a lot of light yellow flakes. What's the matter with him?

### Dr. Nichol:

There are a few possible causes, but the most likely is a mange mite called Cheyletiella, a microscopic insect that lives in the outer "dead" layer of the skin. Unlike most other mange mites, Cheyletiella do not burrow beneath the skin surface. But they do cause a lot of thick yellow flaking. The problem can result not only in itching, but also in thickening of the skin and sometimes fever and inactivity.

The first thing is to get this new puppy to your veterinarian for a thorough physical exam. He or she will do a skin scraping that will show the mites under the microscope. Ask the doctor to let you have a look at them, too. These little mites have hooks on their mouth parts and eight long legs. They are pretty nasty. Once it's clear what we have, the doctor will provide a shampoo to get rid of them.

Insecticidal shampoos are effective against Cheyletiella, but be sure to launder the puppy's bedding on the same day of each bath; otherwise, the mites will continue to live in the puppy's environment. In fact, it is this ability to live off the critter's body that allows this parasite to be transmitted through a litter of puppies.

Finally, notify the seller of the puppy. Usually the mother dog transmits this mange mite to her litters. The owners of the mother may have no idea that they have this problem, since adult dogs and cats seldom have any symptoms. By the way, Cheyletiella is not contagious to humans. But don't feel bad, we humans have plenty of parasites that dogs just are not allowed to get.

## Big Active Dogs and Their Big Active Tails

*Wounded, bleeding tails are a miserable mess. Here are some answers.*

### Question:

I have a small problem with my chocolate Labrador. Her tail is hairless at the end and when she wags her tail and hits it on anything, it bleeds. We've tried to bandage it but she takes off the bandages. We are really at our wits' end. Splatters of blood are everywhere she goes. It's not infected or anything like that. Can you help?

## DR. NICHOL:

What a mess. You not only need help getting your dog's tail to stop bleeding, you also need someone who's quick with a mop. Labs are wonderful dogs in part because they are so happy. They're always ready with a tail wag. But many of them are also oblivious to pain. So, when your dog whacks her tail hard enough for it to bleed, she doesn't even seem to notice. You are not alone with this problem. Artful tail painting is common.

Before we discuss your options for treating your poor dog's chronic tail wound, let's first explain how this happens. Labs, Great Danes, and Dalmatians are examples of dogs with long, heavy tails. When they wag, blood tends to accumulate at the end of the tail because of centrifugal force. Happy dogs with no concept of pain smack their tails against walls and fences so often and so hard that minor wounds never get the chance to heal. Just about the time a good scab forms, they knock it off and then pepper the place with blood again. While they appear to be losing a lot of blood, it isn't significant unless a dog has a blood-clotting disease.

To get control of these paint jobs, we'll need to stop the damage to the tip of the tail so the wound can heal. Bandaging can work fine, but it may take a long time. You'll need to replace the bandage every two to three days and prevent your dog from chewing it off. She may be good about this, or she may need an Elizabethan collar (one of those upside-down cone-shaped affairs that will make her look like she's wearing a lamp shade—you know, life of the party). This may prove to be too much of a hassle.

Another alternative used by folks who show tail-beating breeds is to tape an old-fashioned hair roller over the end of the tail. It will protect the end of her tail and allow the wound to be exposed to the air. A hair roller usually works faster than a bandage, but you still have to keep it in place.

Is there an easier way? Yes, there is. It is guaranteed to work, but there is no turning back. Partial amputation of the tail will reduce its length and eliminate that poor bruised and bloody tip. It will heal quickly, and you and your Lab can then pick up the pieces of your lives and go on. I know that many of us see our pets as extensions of ourselves. But if you can get beyond losing your tail, it will certainly solve the problem.

# Stomach and Intestinal Problems

## Parvo

*Symptoms, diagnosis, and treatment of this potentially devastating disease.*

### Question:

Can you explain the disease parvo to me? Our male and female Chows had puppies five months ago and we kept four of the puppies. The mother and father dogs have been fine, but three of the puppies have been sick. The first puppy had some vomiting and diarrhea last week, but got over it. Then another puppy got really sick over two days and died. Will the other puppies get sick and die, too? The vet we took the sickest puppy to said it looked like parvo. Why is it so expensive to have treatment for parvo?

### Dr. Nichol:

I can tell you are frustrated and I can sympathize. Parvo is a horrible disease that can kill some dogs and seems to totally spare others. I will do my best to solve the mystery for you.

Canine parvo viral enteritis is caused by a virus in the parvo family. It is closely related to distemper virus of cats, and it causes similar symptoms. The virus invades the walls of the stomach and intestine, causing severe swelling and inflammation. The result is frequent vomiting and diarrhea, often mixed with blood.

These are very sick dogs. They become dehydrated quickly. Their bodies' electrolytes become imbalanced, bacteria overgrows their intestinal tracts, and their entire physical systems can go to pieces in just one to two days. It's a particularly nasty problem that is usually fatal if untreated. There is a particular smell about the stool of a dog infected with parvo; it's not caused by the virus, but by the death of the tissue of the intestinal wall. These babies lose large volumes of their body's fluids and electrolytes, thus becoming badly dehydrated and weak.

For a parvo-infected dog to have the best chance of recovery, we must start treatment early and we must treat aggressively. If we cut corners to save money, a positive outcome is unlikely. This is tough for some dog owners. To have the best chance of success, you must commit to any treatment the doctor recommends. And it can cost a great deal to beat parvo.

Needless to say, we are serious about prevention of parvo. Fortunately, the newer high-titer vaccines are quite reliable and require a series of only three boosters to give protection to even the more susceptible breeds like Rottweilers. Vaccines administered at home have high failure rates because they are usually of the older low-titer variety. The best protection is not to allow any dog to have contact with strays (or the public places where strays may have been) until two weeks after the third vaccine in the puppy series. Be careful, but don't be paranoid.

So, why did your puppies respond to the virus so differently? The immune system (the body's natural defense) of each puppy is as individual as each puppy's personality. One puppy may have retained the protection from the mother longer, while another may have an immune system that responds much faster with protection of its own. Still another puppy may have had neither advantage and became so sick so fast that his system caved in.

## Flatulence

*Very funny, eh? No laughing matter if it's your dog. Here is how to get it under control.*

### QUESTION:

We have a 7-year-old male Cocker Spaniel who has developed quite a problem with burping and very stinky flatulence. We've tried changing his food to no avail. When he's got gas, his poor little body blows up like a sausage until he burps or farts. Any ideas?

### DR. NICHOL:

He sounds miserable. In fact, you sound pretty miserable yourself. Here's what's going on. All of us produce gas in our intestines as a result of the breakdown of our food by normal gut bacteria. The result is mostly methane—the same "natural gas" that's piped into our homes for cooking and heating. A few reasons for excessive intestinal gas are the breakdown of certain foods, like beans or milk, or an overgrowth of some of the normal organisms in his gut. Or his diet may be too rich in protein.

Start by never allowing this boy around an open flame. Next, have your veterinarian listen to his abdomen for gut sounds (belly growls). Have a fresh stool sample taken. If your dog has parasites, the appropriate medications should make treatment simple. On the other hand, if his gut flora (intestinal bacteria) has an overgrowth of one or more organisms, we can use the antibacterials amoxicillin and metronidazole. After killing off excessive bacteria, his intestines should "repopulate" with the normal balance. Finally, metoclopramide can be tried. This prokinetic agent will speed up the movement of food from the stomach and may cut down the bloating and belching.

What about diet changes or Beano? Be my guest (not my houseguest until this flatulence problem is solved, thank you). Just make the diet changes gradually over a few days. Now, I have a question for you: Is this really one of those "I have this friend" questions? Is this about you? It's okay. I won't tell. But whoever it is, we may have a great entry for the Special Shapes Rodeo at the Balloon Fiesta this year.

## QUESTION:

We have a 9-week-old Boston Terrier puppy who has the most foul-smelling gas problem we have ever encountered. He eats dry Nutro's Natural Choice Lamb Meal and Rice Formula Puppy food. This is different from what the breeder fed him, which was Purina. He has been with us almost one week. His stools are firm and his coat seems healthy, so I do think the food agrees with him—other than the gas problem. What do you suggest?

## DR. NICHOL:

Whoa! How embarrassing. I'm sure all of our readers share your pain. I recommend a support group. On the other hand, if you really want to change the problem, I would suggest a different diet.

There are many good diets available. But just like people, dogs are individuals. A diet that agrees with some dogs may not work well for others. Try another high-quality diet from a different manufacturer, but be sure to read the label—which is really simple. In all my years in practice, I have found only one useful indicator printed on bags of pet food—price. Buy the good stuff. You will not get what you don't pay for.

But wait, if the protein levels are the same and the list of ingredients are as good or better from one brand to the next, shouldn't that mean something? Sorry. The laws governing truth in labeling allow for lots of sleight of hand. Punctuation and disguising cheap ingredients can result in poorly digestible junk masquerading as decent food—quite easily. I know there are ripoffs in our society, but I haven't seen one yet with pet food. Moreover, better food has a lot more useful nutrition in each mouthful, and it lacks fillers. The difference is less stool to clean up and a bag of food that lasts much longer. So, in the end, better food doesn't really cost more.

What to feed? First, I'll tell you the types of food that often cause gas in the first place: canned food, cheap (low-priced) food, and frequent diet changes. But there are several brands that are highly digestible, low-residue diets (little or no filler). A few of the best brands are Science Diet, Iams, Eukanuba, and Nature's Recipe. If one of them causes your boy to break wind, assume that diet to be the wrong one and try another good one.

A word about diet changes: Pick a high-quality (higher-priced) food that works and stick to it. The stomach and intestinal tracts of dogs is a creature of habit. Dog guts are conservative and dislike change. So, if it's necessary to change food, do it gradually. Over a 3- to 5-day period, progressively mix in increasing amounts of the new diet as you reduce the old. And in choosing a new diet, *do not* pander to your dog's taste preferences. He may like it, but it may not like you.

## Recurrent and Unresponsive Diarrhea
*Giardia and intestinal bacterial overgrowth are curable.*

### Question:
Please help us with Babe. She is a full-grown Doberman with diarrhea that has been going on for months now. Her doctor has found a parasite called giardia. Babe has been treated for this, and her diarrhea improved. But, she had it back again a few weeks later. The doctor is now suggesting a different medication. She also says that other tests may be needed. What do you think?

### Dr. Nichol:
Giardia can be a real problem. I sympathize with how difficult it must be to be caring for Babe and the mess.

It sounds like Babe's doctor is on the right track. Here are a few more ideas. For starters, giardia, a single-celled parasite common in the Western part of the country, can be resistant to some medications. The treatment most often used is a drug called metronidazole. Another, called fenbendazole, can be more effective in some cases. While Babe is getting her treatment, be sure that *all* stool is cleaned up immediately to prevent her from getting reinfected. Also watch her carefully after you give the medication, to be sure she is not spitting it out. If you have other pets, they need to be treated too, even if they don't have diarrhea. It is likely that they could be carriers.

What if she still has diarrhea after treatment? It is possible that while giardia has been a problem, it may not be the only problem. Babe may also have other intestinal disease. Other tests may be very important. On the other hand, if Babe still feels active and continues to eat well, you can try a prescription low-allergy diet or antibiotic treatment for bacterial overgrowth. Ninety percent of chronic diarrhea is caused by one of the above, and a "therapeutic trial" can be as good as or better than diagnostic testing. Ask her doctor.

## Pancreatitis

*A severe cause of vomiting and pain, it's unpredictable and sometimes deadly.*

### QUESTION:

My problem is that I'm real scared about my sick dog. Her name is Ginger and she's a 5-year-old miniature Schnauzer. She was vomiting for a couple of days and she wasn't eating, so we took her to the veterinarian. It turns out that she has pancreatitis. Ginger's doctor says that she needs surgery because she has pus in her abdomen. What do you advise? We love this little girl so much.

### DR. NICHOL:

This must be a very hard time for you and your family. Ginger's doctor is right—she is a very sick little girl. Pancreatitis is a serious problem that causes severe pain in addition to Ginger's other symptoms. The problem is treatable—but it must be handled quickly and decisively.

By way of explanation, I will start with what we *don't* know. We don't know for sure why many dogs, and some cats, develop infections of the pancreas. It is clear that it occurs more often in overweight dogs and seems most common after a fatty meal—like after a dog raids the garbage can and eats something like bacon grease. We also don't know why some dogs have a mild inflammation of this gland and others get fatally ill. And when treatment is started, it is very hard to predict who will survive and who will not. To add further to the confusion, while there are several tests that are helpful in making a diagnosis of inflammation of the pancreas, none of them is 100-percent reliable.

Now for what we *do* know. We can still make an accurate diagnosis if we have enough information. We also know that many cases respond well to fluids and antibiotics in the hospital. But there are some cases, like Ginger's, where the pancreas is so severely infected that the tissue of the gland becomes abscessed and drains pus into the abdomen. This leads to septic peritonitis, which can be quickly fatal. When this occurs, as it has in Ginger, surgery is needed immediately to rinse out the contamination and to remove the dead tissue.

But these cases are seldom straightforward. The pancreas, which sits in a loop of small intestine near the stomach, is remarkably fragile. Surgery to remove dead tissue can actually worsen the problem; yet Ginger will not make it without the procedure. If the pancreas is badly necrotic (dead), it can be totally removed. This is very delicate surgery that belongs only in the most skilled hands. It will also leave Ginger a diabetic and in lifelong need of insulin injections and oral enzymes to replace those normally produced in the pancreas.

Is it worth it? Only you can make the call. Despite everything we can do, dogs leaking pus into the abdomen from severe necrotizing pancreatitis have only a small chance of recovery. After they are well, they can relapse. But if you are one of a growing number of pet owners who regard a dog like Ginger as a family member, I would say go for it.

# Diarrhea

*Simple diarrhea can have a simple treatment—but only if your dog is fine otherwise.*

### QUESTION:

What is a remedy for diarrhea? My dog got into the trash and she pooped all over the place today. I don't know what to do! Please help me.

### DR. NICHOL:

Start with a big bucket of soapy water and clean up that mess. I'm sure your dog is embarrassed. Assuming that she is feeling active, eating well, and has no abdominal pain (press gently on the sides of her tummy with your palms and the flats of your fingers to check), give her Pepto Bismol. Use regular strength and give about one tablespoonful (15 ml) orally per 30 pounds of body weight. It will turn her stool a dark tarry character.

If she has pain or has stopped eating, she needs to see the doctor. She may have a bacterial overgrowth from rotten garbage or she may have swallowed a foreign object from the trash. If there is *any* concern that she has more going on than just diarrhea, don't gamble. An exam fee at your veterinarian's office is cheap insurance.

## Rock Eating

*Foreign material lodged in the intestines can be dangerous. A wire-basket-type muzzle is the best prevention.*

### Question:

Our 10-year-old Norwich Terrier is a habitual eater of stones, gravel, twigs, etc. It is a rather serious problem to us because we can't walk her because of this habit. It concerns us greatly because of what the long-term results might be healthwise.

### Dr. Nichol:

Bad dog! (I know that doesn't help, but it felt good to say it.) Here is the reality about rocks: For the most part, if an object can be swallowed, it will pass through the esophagus and move on into the stomach. Some just stay there. But rocks that make their way into the smaller-diameter intestine often get stuck in a narrow passage—and that's real trouble. As the peristaltic waves of the bowel attempt to push the stone further, the object becomes more tightly lodged. Blood gets forced out of the wall of the gut. In a matter of hours, intestinal tissue begins to die from lack of blood. That's when leaks occur resulting in bacterial contamination of the abdomen (septic peritonitis). It can be quickly fatal. Surgical rock removal is best done early.

Have I scared anybody? If you have a rock eater, you must protect that baby. There are no surefire tricks such as painting rocks with hot sauce. It could work, but probably will not. The best method I know is to purchase a wire-basket-type muzzle so that your dog can pant and drink while on a walk. It will take a little getting used to—but much better safe than sick.

## Dogs Who Raid the Trash

*Used diapers, tampons, and bandages can swell inside the intestines, causing blockages. Surgery may be the only path to survival.*

### Question:

I think we have a problem with our Nemo. Nemo is a good dog and we love him. But we also have two small children in diapers. Yesterday Nemo ate a disposable diaper that had fresh stool from our baby in it. Now Nemo won't eat. Will this diaper come out on its own?

## Dr. Nichol:

Oh, brother. This is an important problem and it is not rare. We love our dogs and treat them just like members of our families. So it's easy to forget that they are capable of some pretty disgusting habits. What is going on inside Nemo's stomach and intestines could be real trouble.

Disposable diapers are made of a lot of paper and some plastic. As the eaten diaper absorbs fluid inside Nemo's G.I. tract (stomach and intestine), the paper might break apart, allowing it to move along the way food does. If this happens, it will simply pass with his stool. But the plastic could become elongated like a string in his intestines. If this occurs, it can work back and forth as the peristalsis (the intestinal action that pushes food along) tries to keep it going. This working back and forth can make it into a string-like foreign body. If it saws holes in the wall of the intestine, Nemo will leak fluid, stool, and lots of bacteria into his abdomen, resulting in peritonitis. Peritonitis can kill him.

What you must do for Nemo is to have him examined. If intestinal movement (gut sounds) can be heard with a stethoscope, he may be okay. It would be important to get X-rays of his abdomen. With monitoring and care, he might pass the whole mess and do fine. But if anything becomes lodged along the G.I. tract, it will have to be removed. This can be done either with an endoscope or, if it's too far along, surgically.

Don't delay. He could get much worse if you wait. The fact that he has stopped eating is a major warning sign. By the way, disposable diapers are not the only things dogs will eat. If it's at all nasty and disgusting, be careful. Things that I have removed include used tampons and sanitary napkins, old bandages, underwear, pantyhose, rags, toys, even carpet. The more vile and raunchy it is, the more careful you need to be. Dogs can be such animals.

# Bones: Chewing Them Up and Swallowing the Pieces

*Bone chewing is always a gamble. Swallowed shards can sometimes be removed without surgery using an endoscope.*

## Question:

Porky needs help fast. I think I screwed up. We always thought it was okay to give her steak bones, but since the T-bone we gave her last night, she's been vomiting a lot. I didn't think small dogs could break off bone pieces. She won't eat and she doesn't seem to feel very good. Can we get rid of that bone without surgery? After she's okay, what kinds of bones are safe for dogs to chew?

### Dr. Nichol:

First let's talk about what is best for Porky. It is probably correct to assume that she swallowed part of that T-bone. But it's essential that we know for sure. So the first order of business is to X-ray her abdomen. As long as the bone chip has gotten no further than the stomach or duodenum (the first part of the small intestine), it is likely that it can be removed using an endoscope. This is a long, snake-like instrument with a lens and a light source that allows us to see the interior of the stomach and intestines. We can then get a hold of the bone using special forceps on the interior of the endoscope. The procedure is fairly quick and avoids the need for surgery, but it does necessitate general anesthesia—and it needs to be done quickly. If the bone chip is allowed to move further into the intestine, it can become lodged. This can result in a loss of blood supply to the intestinal wall. If it were allowed to get to that point, Porky would definitely need surgery—or worse, she could die.

What bones are okay for dogs? No bones are 100-percent safe. Even thick, round steak bones can be broken and pieces can be swallowed. Sometimes they get hooked over the lower jaw of a dog's mouth. The worst are bones that can splinter, like poultry and pork chop bones. On the other side of the coin, dogs love to chew. It's also true that chewing is healthy for the teeth and gums. So my best advice is to give rawhide chews or give Gummabones to small dogs and puppies and Nylabones to bigger dogs. These toys are indestructible and flavored. When they eventually lose their flavor, you can toss them into some boiling water with a couple of boullion cubes and jazz up the flavor again.

Are there any exceptions to the no-bone rule? For absolute safety, make no bones about it.

## Bloating of the Stomach

*Large-breed, deep-chested dogs are prone to twisting and swelling of the stomach. A high-risk emergency, surgery is indicated ASAP.*

### Question:

I had my dog Buzzy, a Standard Poodle, boarded at a kennel. When I went to visit him, he passed out. He looked like he was bloated in the middle and they got real concerned and rushed him to a vet real fast. The doctor X-rayed Buzzy and did surgery. He said Buzzy's stomach was twisted and bloated with gas. Buzzy is fine now, but I can't understand how this happened. I know that the kennel where he stayed is a good one. Will this happen again?

## DR. NICHOL:

The disease you are describing is called gastric dilatation-volvulus, or GDV for short. It is a fatal disease if not treated aggressively. It can be a frightening problem because most cases come on without warning. A dog can die from GDV in as short a time as 20 to 30 minutes. I will explain the how and why of it first, then I will tell you how to prevent it.

Although GDV can occur in any dog, it is almost always seen in large-breed, deep-chested dogs. This is the body type of German Shepherds, Great Danes, Irish Setters, and Old English Sheepdogs. It is not rare, however, in a medium-sized breed like the Standard Poodle. The physical conformation is important because in this body type, the dog's stomach hangs in a somewhat different position from that of an average dog like a Beagle, for example. When one of these big rascals eats a large meal of dry food or tanks up on water, the stomach can become too full. While this is not a problem in most dogs, big dogs can lose their ability to expel gas from their swollen, low-hanging stomachs. The worst part is the twisting, or volvulus, of the stomach. This can occur early in the series of events, or later. But it is the 180- to 360-degree twisting that causes loss of blood supply to the stomach wall. It is also responsible for the rapid onset of shock and the deaths of many afflicted dogs.

GDV, or bloat as it is also called, is a genuine emergency. We start treatment by relieving the gas buildup with a stomach tube or trochar. We treat for shock and, as soon as the dog is as stable as possible, we do surgery.

The procedure involves rotating the stomach back to its proper position and permanently attaching it to the wall of the abdomen to prevent it from repeating its mistake. In some cases, it is necessary to remove portions of the stomach wall that have become too severely damaged from loss of blood supply. All of this must be done quickly. The wait-and-see approach for this problem is a formula for disaster.

It all sounds complicated and it is. Many pets have complications. In fact, despite everything we know about this problem, only about 50 percent survive. It is often tragic. So, as usual, your best bet is prevention.

Frankly, the best way to avoid GDV is not to have a giant-breed dog. The bigger the dog, the greater the risk. But if you already have a big dog, this is what you can do. First, feed at least two meals per day. This doesn't mean doubling the amount of food your dog gets. It means splitting his or her daily ration into two or three meals, so that each meal is smaller and less likely to cause excessive swelling of the stomach. The second important rule is to moisten the dry food before giving it to the dog. This is important because if eaten dry, the food will swell from the normal fluid that is already in every dog's stomach. This could cause gas bloating. Let the food get soggy in the bowl for 5 to 10 minutes before feeding so that it won't swell after it is eaten. In addition to not allowing your big dog to eat too much all at once, don't let him drink too much either. Make sure he always has water available so that he doesn't get super thirsty.

Finally, if you want to exercise your dog, do it *before* feeding, but *not* for a couple of hours after. This is important because a full stomach in an active dog can twist from jumping and heavy exercise.

So, why did your Standard Poodle Buzzy get GDV at the kennel? It's an interesting question. It is clear that the stress of being away from home is a factor. This problem is seen more often in dogs who are boarded or hospitalized. While we recognize this risk, we cannot explain it. At the same time, I salute those folks at the kennel for recognizing right away that Buzzy was a dog in trouble. Standard Poodles are excellent dogs. I'm glad Buzzy survived.

But what I want to know is, with all of these Standard Poodles around, why don't they have automatics, too? Write to me if you can figure that one out.

# Symptoms of Sickness

## Anal (Rear-End) Irritation

*Impacted anal glands make a dog scoot or lick his or her rear end. Providing relief is simple but important.*

### Question:

I have a Dachshund (wienie dog, female) about 7 years old. She seems to be trying to scratch her anus, and unfortunately can't seem to reach. She's a tad overweight. She even drags or circles on the floor in a futile attempt to scratch. I do not find the usual suspects of fleas or ticks. I don't see any signs of worms. I have sprayed her for fleas. None of this seems to help. Even baths do not seem to help. I have another dog of the same breed who does not have the same problem.

### Dr. Nichol:

*Dachshund* and *wienie dog* seem to be interchangeable terms for the same breed. Some people call them call *Datsuns*. But this breed came from Germany. How confusing. So you have an overweight wienie dog with itchy buns, no fleas, no worms—other wienie dog okay. Her problem is her anal glands, one of the most common maladies we treat.

What the heck is an anal gland? Anal glands are thoroughly useless structures that lie beneath the skin on either side of the anus in the 4 o'clock and 8 o'clock positions. They are an evolutionary vestige of the scent glands of the skunk. While all dogs and cats have them, the impactions and infections that cause the licking and dragging are seen mostly in small-breed overweight dogs, like your wienie, who can't reach her buns. What she needs is to be taken to her veterinarian to have her anal glands expressed (emptied). If the doctor suspects infection, ointment will be infused into the glands and antibiotics may be given. To prevent more rear-end distress in the future, ask the doctor for healthier feeding recommendations, like prescription diet r/d, to help her to lose weight. A slimmer figure will also help reduce the risk of disc disease in her neck and back.

Finally, it is no surprise that your other wienie dog is free of this problem. It is caused by neither worms nor by other parasites like fleas or ticks. Anal gland problems are not contagious. But do take both wienie dogs to the doctor for routine maintenance. Better to be safe than itchy.

## Tail Chasing

*Anal glands are a common cause of rear-end discomfort. It's usually easy to remedy.*

### QUESTION:

Is it an old wives' tale or a fact that if a dog chases her tail, she will go crazy and have to be put to sleep? This sweet little Spitz of mine also loves to chase her tail. I would appreciate any help in this area.

### DR. NICHOL:

Tail chasing: Sometimes I feel like my life could be described that way. Maybe I'm crazy and will have to be put to sleep.

Don't worry about your Spitz. Take her to the doctor and have her anal glands checked. If they are full of fluid or are inflamed, they may be causing her rear end to itch. It is simple and quick to have her anal glands emptied in her doctor's office. If she still chases her tail, I wouldn't worry. At least she's getting some exercise. Finally, stop talking that way about old wives.

## Hemolytic Anemia

*It's fatal in 50 percent of dogs who have it. It must be treated quickly and aggressively.*

### QUESTION:

What is done to treat hemolytic anemia? My 9-year-old Airedale-Shepherd mix dog has been diagnosed with hemolytic anemia and I am searching for treatment options. Thank you in advance for your help.

### DR. NICHOL:

The problem that has beset your dog is complex and quite delicate to treat. The full name for this disease is immune-mediated hemolytic anemia (IMHA). It means that your dog's immune system is building antibodies against the surfaces of her red blood cells and thus destroying them. The resulting anemia (low numbers of red blood cells) means she has fewer of these cells to carry oxygen to her tissues. Translated into symptoms—this girl will be weak and breathing fast. You may notice pale or jaundiced (yellow) gums. She may start breathing fast to get oxygen into her body. It's scary.

How does all of this happen? Possible causes include blood parasites, infectious organisms, and sometimes certain drugs. In many cases, we just don't know how it starts. What's important is that IMHA is fatal in 50 percent of cases—sometimes rapidly so.

Treatment: The first priority is often a blood transfusion or the use of the newer blood substitutes. Next, we stop the immune system's runaway attacks on the red cells by using corticosteroids like prednisone. Some resistant cases also require more potent immune suppressives, like cyclophosphamide or azathioprine. Cyclosporine with ketoconazole has also been used. In addition, we support these patients with IV fluids and careful monitoring in the hospital. These are tough cases.

I've seen many IMHA cases go well. But while we gradually decrease the dosages of the prednisone and other drugs, we can never be sure which pets will need lifelong treatment. My best advice is to observe your dog's gums and her behavior carefully during treatment. Follow the doctor's orders, and say a prayer every night. Good luck.

## Postoperative Pain

*Pets, without question, feel pain just as we do. Better pet hospitals treat and prevent pain.*

### QUESTION:

I have often wondered about cats and dogs and pain, especially when Skippy, our wonder cat with three legs, had his hind leg amputated at the hip. He came home the evening of surgery, and my wife and I took turns holding him all night. He did not seem to be in pain, but rather out of it or a little crazy from the anesthetic. Isn't pain medication typically given for this kind of thing, and for such procedures as spaying a dog or cat? Don't the cats and dogs feel pain like we do after major surgery? We would certainly be given pain medication. What are your thoughts?

### DR. NICHOL:

I am glad to answer this question. There is a major move afoot among veterinary anesthesiologists to encourage greater use of the many pain relievers that are safe and effective for pets. Until the last several years, many of us didn't think very much about this important issue. We are not proud of this fact. Animals of all species, including humans, feel pain. But our pets don't talk. So, how do we know if and when pain management is necessary? If pets are like us, there are varying degrees of pain among individuals. How can we know when our treatment is sufficient? We are observant, that's how.

According to Dr. Robert Paddleford, in his recent paper on analgesics, the signs to watch for are: increased heart or respiratory rate, unwillingness to move, drooling, poor appetite, restlessness, aggressive behavior, and crying. (I think we already knew that one.) Needless to say, some of these signs are vague, but pets who show two or three together definitely need our help. We can choose from several drugs and methods of giving treatment.

Which is best? This is a great example of the adage that medicine is still more art than science. What is best for a pet is the pain management that is most familiar and safe in your veterinarian's own experience. Different cases require different treatments. In our hospital, we use pain treatments before surgery. For procedures like spaying and neutering that cause only mild discomfort, we use an injection of Torbugesic about one hour prior to anesthesia. The pet is relaxed as he or she goes to sleep and feels a whole lot better for up to five hours after recovery. The injection can be repeated, if needed. For fracture surgery or an amputation for a pet like Skippy the Wonder Cat, we apply a Duragesic skin patch the day before surgery.

Duragesic patches are nifty. Using the same principle as the skin patches for people who are trying to quit smoking, they provide a continuous through-the-skin release of the drug for three to five days. We send the pet home wearing a patch and recheck the pet's comfort level a few days later, replacing the skin patch if needed. This way, no one has to give pills and the pain relief is continuous. Everybody's happier.

We welcome interest in pain relief. Let's face it—most injured pets will get well even without our helping to relieve their pain. But we love these little guys like our children. Which of us would knowingly deny pain relief to a hurting child? To help every pet with pain, we need observant pet owners. Be aware and be the voice for your pets. Alleviating the suffering of animals is a responsibility we can all share.

## Fainting

*Severe flea infestations can cause blood-loss anemia. Shock and death are two big risks.*

### QUESTION:

I have a small dog who has been passing out! She comes out of it when I pick her up. Yesterday she went into convulsions, but again snapped out of it when I picked her up. The fleas are really bad this year. The dog was okay for one day after bathing. I sprayed the carpet, and all was okay until she went outside and again was covered with fleas. Is it possible this can be caused by a reaction to the flea bites?

### DR. NICHOL:

Your little girl is lucky to have an owner who cares about her. She has a serious reason for fainting, which may or may not be related to her flea problem. Let's start with an understanding of fainting and convulsions; then we'll talk about fleas.

The truth is that the list of causes for convulsions and fainting is quite long. The possibilities I would consider first are: low blood sugar, anemia (low number of red blood cells), epilepsy, heart disease, and liver disease. There may be other considerations depending on her physical exam. How does that fit in with fleas? A large number of fleas can drain a small dog of a lot of blood. This could cause her to feel weak and pass out just because she would not have enough red blood cells to carry oxygen to her brain. The physical stress of all those parasites could also be making her blood sugar drop, resulting in seizures. Her seizuring is also a great concern all by itself.

Here is the best way to proceed: Explain your dog's history to her doctor, in detail. Be prepared to have some lab work done, like a blood count, a blood chemistry profile, and a urinalysis. These will answer most questions regarding the severity of blood loss and the function of her internal organs. While the hospital's technician is working on the lab tests, the veterinarian will be starting treatment. Given the number of fleas you describe, I suspect that a blood transfusion may be necessary. She may also need IV sugars. This should get her stable.

Your girl's fleas are also a major priority, but they must be eliminated carefully. Potent insecticides would kill the fleas, but could also be the physical stress that pushes your frail little girl over the edge. Medical management of this puppy must happen fast and it has to be done carefully. Your mission is to save your dog's life. Please do not delay in seeing your veterinarian.

## Addison's Disease

*Poorly functioning adrenal glands produce low amounts of the body's cortisol. Learn the signs of this disease. Also know how to recognize trouble with medication dosages.*

## QUESTION:

My 5-year-old mixed-breed dog was diagnosed with Addison's disease last August. He is currently on 5 mg prednisone and 5 mg Florinef daily. Since he started these medications, he has been experiencing excessive urination, mostly when he is asleep. Is there something I can do to control this? I have several other pets, so reducing his water intake would be difficult. Any suggestions you might have would be greatly appreciated.

## Dr. Nichol:

I'm glad you wrote in with this question. Excessive drinking and urination are not only important physical signs, but can be downright tough on your floors.

For the uninitiated, I will start with an explanation of Addison's disease. This is a condition of the hormone-producing glands that sit on either side of the abdomen just in front of (or in the case of humans, just above) the kidneys. In addition to producing the hormone adrenaline, the adrenals turn out cortisol (the body's own form of cortisone) plus aldosterone. The functions of cortisol and aldosterone are many and they are essential to normal physical function. But most important, a dog with untreated Addison's disease will tend to be lethargic, will eat poorly, and may occasionally vomit and have diarrhea or constipation. Since these are pretty vague symptoms, Addison's disease can easily be mistaken for other problems. I salute your veterinarian for making a difficult diagnosis.

Because Addison's disease is really an underperformance of a hormone-producing gland, replacing those hormones in your dog's body is the treatment of choice. Hence, the deficiency of cortisol is replaced by the drug prednisone, while Florinef is used in place of the deficient aldosterone. The only question remaining is dosage. Since bigger dogs need more, these replacement hormones are usually dosed according to weight. While you did not include your dog's weight in your letter, I will assume that an overdosage of prednisone is responsible for his excessive drinking and urinating.

What should the dosages be? My recommendation is that you connect with your veterinarian and report the problem. The best course might be to repeat the tests used for diagnosis of Addison's disease—the ACTH stimulation test plus serum electrolytes. These tests will confirm whether your dog still needs these medications in the first place. Second, they will help the doctor know how severe the deficiencies are that need to be corrected. The last test is the one that may be more useful than the others: How is your dog feeling, and what are your observations at home? Any dog who produces so much urine that he is losing control while he sleeps definitely needs an adjustment in his dosage.

Finally, if you have a pet who drinks a lot of water, *do not* restrict his intake. Excessive thirst is a sign of a critical physical need. Water deprivation can only lead to dehydration and possible death. Pets who drink a lot of water need a lot of water. They also need a doctor.

## Swelling of the Abdomen, Weight Loss, and Yellow Gums

*Advanced liver disease can be deadly, but many cases are manageable.*

### QUESTION:

Our beautiful old dog is getting a little weak. Her stomach is getting big, but when I feel her head and her back, she's skin and bones. When you push on her stomach, it's soft and mushy. She still feels pretty much okay, but I also notice that her gums are a little yellow. Why is her belly big?

### DR. NICHOL:

I'm glad you are getting advice. This old girl needs help for what sounds like liver failure. Let me explain.

The liver does many important things. In one sense, it acts like a filter for the blood, to strain out harmful particles and bacteria. A major portion of the blood is carried through the liver. When it becomes swollen due to infection or cancer, it can't filter the blood efficiently. That forces some of the fluid portion of the blood to seep out into the abdomen. Chronic (long-term) scarring of the liver does the same thing. The fluid in your dog's abdomen (called ascites) could be caused by other problems as well.

This will be hard for you to hear, but these are very grave symptoms. The yellow color of her gums (jaundice) is also a result of her liver getting behind in its work. The plumbing inside her liver is swollen internally, and the normal bile pigment (yellow color) isn't being pumped into the intestines where it belongs, so it's ending up in her blood instead. Hence, you see it in the tissues of her mouth.

What you must do for your old friend is to find the cause(s). Have your veterinarian examine her. Blood and urine tests will answer many questions. X-rays of her abdomen as well as ultrasound evaluations will tell whether cancer is a likely cause. Finally, a biopsy of that liver is essential for showing exactly what's ailing that poor old organ.

It all sounds terrible, but a lot of pets with abdominal fluid and jaundice can be helped. With special diets, medication, and possibly surgery, you may improve her quality of life for a while. Have her checked out soon while there is still time.

## Car Sickness

*Dramamine or a prescription medication given before a car ride will prevent nausea.*

### QUESTION:

My 6-month-old Silky Terrier is plagued with car sickness. We have tried traveling on an empty stomach, to no avail. We've also only taken very short trips—so far 10 to 20 minutes of traveling time. Part of our reason for getting a small breed was so he could join in on family vacations. Is there anything we can do to prevent the car sickness, or a medication that will help?

### DR. NICHOL:

Sorry to hear about all that terrible traveling terrier trauma. The motion sickness that is hounding your dog is likely to be something that he will outgrow. Here is why: The vestibular apparatus that manages our sense of equilibrium can take a while to develop and mature fully. Located in the inner ear, this essential part of our nervous system tolerates more in some individuals than others. So there are a few dogs who, like some people, can never enjoy sailboats, roller coasters, and automobile rides. But the great majority of dogs simply mature beyond this problem by the age of 8 to 10 months.

What can we do in the meantime? Acepromazine, a mild tranquilizer available from your veterinarian, should help. In addition to its sedative properties, "ace" will also overcome the nausea. Another good drug is Dramamine; but this stuff may be impossible to dose safely for that little guy of yours. What about those short trips? Forget it. You won't train motion sickness out of this boy. You'll just have to be patient until he matures and keep "traveling on an empty stomach, to no avail." Hey, I think I've been there.

# Training

## Puppy Exuberance and Wild Jumping

*A combination of obedience training and good manners will help tame the wild beast.*

### QUESTION:

I'm trying . . . but it's so-oo-oo hard and tiring! I think I'm the one who needs training, not the doggie! I'm hearing lots of strange advice on how to get her to calm down and not jump at people meeting her. I've read that the knee in her chest is not good. Tugging on her leash is pointless when she's wild, and she nearly hangs herself with the leash which doesn't even phase her when she meets people. It's gross. She flops around and flips herself. As soon as she calms down, she's great. She just sits there. Is this a puppy thing, or plain old bad manners? She's not hyper around the house.

### DR. NICHOL:

It sounds like you're talking about landing a fish. On the other hand, maybe this is a question for Miss Manners. Okay, I'll give you my best shot at improving the social graces of this youngster.

Let's start with all that puppy energy. It's normal. You can't get rid of it, but what you can do is direct it. Puppies are like children. They need an outlet for all that goofy stuff and if you don't provide some wholesome activities, you will end up with graffiti on your walls. Here is what I recommend: Call your local dog obedience club and ask about puppy class. Your little girl will learn the fundamentals of good behavior—things like come, sit, stay, down. (Maybe I'll take my kids.) Like any form of schooling, you will get results commensurate with the energy you both put into it. Between classes, you two can practice your lessons, giving the young and restless a chance to burn up some energy. Be sure to have a ball or Frisbee ready for some fun after each practice. This reward will help keep her focused.

Now that we have her education covered, what are we going to do about the body slams? That's a problem that is best managed at home. You will succeed at this because your girl will have the security of knowing that the corrections for this behavior will be consistent. It's not going to be harsh— just effective. Here's how it goes: Start by doing something that is likely to cause your puppy to jump on you—like walking in the door. Be ready before she jumps. Stand with your weight on one leg and have your other knee bent. As the puppy is launching herself off the ground, bring your knee up quickly and "pop" her in the chest and say, "No!" This will surprise her. As soon as she is back on the floor, tell her how good she is, as though she has always been perfect. Then resume your stance and be ready for her next lesson. She will continue to jump on you as though she is spring-loaded. The more, the better. She is giving you an abundance of training opportunities. When she stops, have a treat for her—and, what the heck, have one yourself.

I know how hard this sounds. No one wants to hurt a dog. But what you are really doing is startling her. Putting your knee in her chest is totally safe. But to be effective, it must be quick and somewhat forceful to get her attention. Most important, the correction must occur *every* time she jumps on you—*every* time.

So, what about when your friends come over? Training your puppy not to jump on you will not prevent her from doing it to them. Here is your assignment: Attach your puppy's 6-foot training leash to her slip-chain choke collar and let her drag the leash around the house until it becomes second nature. When it's clear that she no longer notices it, have a friend drop by and knock on the door. The puppy will get there first because pouncing on people is her favorite joke. You will be right behind her, with the end of the leash in your hand. Open the door and, as the puppy is in the act of catapulting herself into your friend's chest, jerk back quickly on the leash and say (you guessed it), "No!" As soon as she's back on all fours, remember to tell her how awesome she is. Then repeat this several times—and be ready anytime somebody comes over. Never miss a chance to make the correction. Consistency is the key. Are we having fun yet?

## Puppy Training Class

***Even small-breed dogs need good manners. Taking a puppy to school gets you both trained—and your lives together will be better.***

### QUESTION:

We just got a brand new puppy and are we ever excited! She is perfect. She's a miniature Poodle and she's 12 weeks old and she's already making potty outside and she comes to us when we call her. I think dog school would be a great idea, but my husband says that she's just a little dog and we can train her at home—and why would we want to take her to a place where they have other dogs who could give her diseases? What do you think?

## DR. NICHOL:

This isn't the first time I've been asked to settle a family argument, you know. I feel like Dear Abby. I have to find a win for each of you in this.

Now that I have you feeling sorry for me, here is the answer. Take that prized puppy to training class. Many people have trained their dogs beautifully at home, but when they have needed those skills on a busy street, their dogs have panicked in the chaos and lost control. The tragic result can be that you lose your dog. On the other hand, if your pup is trained by you as part of a well-managed obedience class, she will learn to work for you (her prized possession) in the presence of a zillion distractions. She will also learn that she can pay attention with a bunch of goofy classmates, and that learning is fun.

That's what's in it for your dog. Here is what *you* get: the detached third-party observation and guidance of a trainer who thinks bringing out the best in dogs and their owners is the highest calling. No kidding. People who teach obedience classes love dogs, and they yearn to see those dogs please their families.

What if you've been through obedience training before? You already know how to train a new dog, right? If you want great results, do what the experienced obedience handlers do. The most accomplished and knowledgeable trainers all take their new puppies to classes, because they know that a good teacher will watch them work their puppies and offer tips that will improve their performance and their enjoyment.

Do I sound like I love this stuff? My Airedale, Juan, and I trained when he was a baby, and we stayed with it because he learned early to love his work. We forged a bond that made our lives together the very best.

If you don't take that little girl to school, you will both miss out. I say go for it.

## Training Collars and Head Halters

*There are several useful tools. Each has its place; all are safe if used properly.*

### QUESTION:

Do you know of any health problems related to either prong or pinch collars or head halters? I am doing some research for our training club.

### DR. NICHOL:

I'm glad to get this question because there is a great deal of concern and misinformation about training methods and devices like these. The truth is that, yes, they are safe, but there is always a way to misuse and mistreat a dog during training. Most often these problems occur as a result of genuine ignorance from a loving owner.

In addition to prong collars and head halters, regular leather or woven collars and slip-chain choke collars are still widely used. Any and all of the above are legitimate and have their place. For youngsters, like my puppy Peter Rabbit, training with a leash and a regular collar is still best. Babies need to have the joy of learning instilled first. There is no place for firm corrections when they're less than 6 months old.

Choke collars are the old standbys. The principle here is simple. When the dog is behaving correctly, he or she feels nothing. (This is when you praise.) A quick tug on the leash gives the correction by tightening the collar on the dog's neck. It works because it's uncomfortable. But dogs are individuals. A very minor correction is all it takes for some. I've seen other cases when it looks like the owner is trying to pull the dog's head off, and the dog doesn't even notice—literally. Prong collars were invented for these dogs. A prong, or pinch, collar has smooth metal prongs that poke the skin when the collar is tightened. The collar is designed so that there is no way to harm the dog's neck by "overcorrecting." They are safe for adult dogs and a godsend for some owners. Even a light flick of the wrist will get the immediate attention of the most unfocused canine trainee. But while they work great on the tough cases, prong collars are unnecessary for most dogs.

Head halters: My favorite use for this tool is with the aggressive dog who needs to be reminded that his owner is his boss. They work well for most routine training, too, because they steer the dog by the head rather than by pulling the dog by the neck. Nothing about a head halter causes discomfort. It sounds ideal—but for training, it may not be the best tool for every dog.

How do we prevent overly harsh use of these gadgets? Take your dog to a class at your local obedience club. Let the instructor be your guide. But for goodness sake, have fun. Make sure your dog looks forward to the rewards, rather than dreading the corrections. If you and your dog aren't having a good time, *you* may need to wear the prong collar.

## Hitting Pets in Training

*Hitting will worsen any behavior problem. Other training tools are humane, are easy to use, and work effectively.*

### QUESTION:

Is it ever a good idea to hit a dog or cat? My pets seem a little hard-headed and a friend has said that hitting is sometimes the only thing they understand.

### DR. NICHOL:

The best communication with animals is learned from the way they "talk" to each other. In other words, teach pets in ways they can understand. Studies of dogs and cats in the wild have never found that they yell at or hit each other. They do keep each other in line physically, but it's done with control of the neck and muzzle. So it should come as no surprise that collars and head halters work great for training.

Can it do any harm to hit your pets? Not only does it teach them to fear you, but it can work against you, too. Aggression training for guard dogs is done by "agitating" with hitting motions to make them angry. If you want to be your dog's or cat's friend, never agitate—teach instead. Be firm and consistent. Use food rewards and praise. Remember that the best trainers ever found are unconditional love and kindness.

# URINARY PROBLEMS

## Urinary Disease

*Frequent urination often means infection. Left untreated, this often leads to bladder stones.*

### QUESTION:

I have an 8-year-old Sheltie and she seems to be urinating more frequently. Normally she will sleep all night without having to go out. Last night she needed to go out twice. Can dogs get bladder infections? If so, what are the symptoms? Should I take her to the vet?

### DR. NICHOL:

I wish every pet owner were as perceptive as you are. Dogs absolutely do get bladder infections and, yes, you are seeing those symptoms in your dog. Take this girl to the doctor.

Your powers of observation are essential to the proper care of your Sheltie because she can't say "Wow, does it hurt when I try to urinate!" Here's how it works.

The bladder, an expandable pouch in the lower abdomen, is the holding place for urine after it's produced by the kidneys. With infection, the wall of the bladder gets thickened by inflammation. The nerves in that thick bladder wall then send a message to the brain that says "Hey! (the brain doesn't get much respect) There's something inside this bladder!" Well, of course the poor brain thinks it's urine, so it sends a message back that says "Okay, go ahead and cut loose." Then your dog tries to urinate. But that bladder's not so smart. While it felt full, it didn't really have much urine. What it did have inside was a very thick, inflamed wall. So when your girl tries to urinate, she only passes a small amount and still feels like she has to go. What's more, it hurts when she tries. Take the poor kid to the doctor. If it's not clear on examination whether the bladder has mineral stones or just infection, X-rays will be needed. Next, a urine sample will be taken for chemical tests, a microscopic exam, and culture. The lab can then recommend an antibiotic.

What happens if you don't take her to the doctor? Untreated infections usually lead to bladder stones. It's bad when that happens because bladder stones usually require surgical removal.

# Bladder Stones

*Crystals in the urine can form stones, which might pass with the urine. Carefully save these so your veterinarian can have them analyzed. This is the key to effective treatment.*

### QUESTION:

I have a real problem with my dog Emily. She's been a healthy girl, but the last few days I've seen her straining to urinate. I watched closely yesterday and she passed a small round stone with blood on it. What the heck's going on?

### DR. NICHOL:

You do good detective work. Number one: Grab that little stone and run it and Emily down to your veterinarian. Emily's doctor will send the stone out for analysis and culture. (Specifically, it requires quantitative analysis; best done by the University of Minnesota.) Next, the doctor will do a urinalysis and urine culture, as well as take X-rays of Emily's abdomen. Don't wait—get after it today.

What's going on with Emily is that she has developed bladder stones, also called cystic calculi. In most cases (about 70 percent) the problem starts with a bacterial infection of the bladder. But if that weren't bad enough by itself, minerals can start to accumulate around the bacterial colonies. As the minerals (in most cases a combination of phosphate salts called struvite) build on each other, they form a crystal-like structure that finally gets big enough for us to call it a bladder stone. In some dogs there is just one stone that continues to grow in size, but in most cases there are several. Don't believe that Emily is fine now that she has passed one little stone. You can bet she has plenty more, and that the rest are much bigger.

The good news about all of this is that in some cases, bladder surgery can usually be avoided. Feeding a special prescription diet called s/d can dissolve many struvite stones—as long as the correct antibiotic is used to kill off the bladder infection.

It sounds easy, but be sure to follow instructions carefully. Rechecks are needed to be sure the infection is under control and the bladder stones really are dissolving. What if the diet and antibiotics fail? In those cases, surgical removal is the only way to go. But fear not, the procedure is straightforward and safe. Either way, Emily should be fine.

# Urination and Defecation Behaviors

## Defecating Inside the House
*Eliminating odor plus careful retraining will resolve the problem.*

### Question:

I have a problem with Duchess, my 2-year-old Queensland Heeler mix. I recently had my carpet cleaned and Duchess has taken to pooping in the dining room. Not only does she continue to go in the same spot, but she is stinking up my house! We are crating her at night. We hate to do this to her, but her recent behavior is disgusting!

### Dr. Nichol:

Now stop candy coating it and tell us how you really feel. Seriously, I'm glad you wrote in. If we don't correct this soon, Duchess will develop an aberrant pooping habit.

Duchess's problem is change. She isn't trying to "tell you something"; she's just confused. Get a product called Equilizer or Outright from your veterinarian or pet supply store. These have no smell to them. Instead, they contain an active organism that literally consumes the organic matter left behind when you clean up the stool. Continue crating Duchess when you are not there to supervise her.

Watch her like a hawk when she is loose inside so that you can tell her "No" when she starts to defecate. Then take her outside and throw her a party to show her how delighted you will be when she gets it all figured out again. Finally, stop hating it when you put her in her crate. It's her nature to be in a "den." She's a dog—but do keep treating her like your child.

## Defecating Inside the House: Part 2
*The problem could be lack of exercise, or lack of access to the great outdoors.*

### Question:

We have an 8-year-old Collie. Periodically, he will get into the cats' litter and consume their feces. He has used the guest bedroom as his poop field. Why is he suddenly defecating in the house when he is clearly housetrained? There has been a change in our exercise schedule since January.

## Dr. Nichol:

Indoor bowel movements: Your poor Collie is probably as embarrassed as you are infuriated. The reduced exercise schedule may be partly to blame for this. Your Collie is holding his stool too long. He needs to get outside more often to relieve himself. One reason that most dogs pass stool during a brisk walk is the physical activity. Also, his system balks at that rich, nasty cat stool. So, when he feels the sudden need to pass that loose stool, he has no other place to go but your guest room. Correcting the problem is simple. Walk him daily, prevent access to cat stool, and install a dog door for him so that he can get out of the house as needed.

# Urinating Inside the House

*Correct by retraining. Here are the tools.*

## Question:

We have a 5-year-old neutered Tibetan Spaniel named Sparky. He continually marks by urinating in every room in our house. How can we get him to break this annoying habit after all these years? He has been caged, blocked off from rooms, and reprimanded for his nasty habit, but all to no avail. Except for this one *really* bothersome habit, he is a great dog whom we love very much. Can you help Sparky learn not to be Marky?

## Dr. Nichol:

You were right to get Sparky neutered. But he has reasons for marking other than just being a macho man. For example, he may be doing it when visitors use the furniture, or as an advertisement of his self-confidence or his dominance in the household. Maybe he's a graffiti artiste. Whatever the reason, I take it you don't enjoy living in a dog latrine.

To correct this, we must return to some of the basics of housetraining. Until we succeed, never leave Sparky unsupervised inside the house. If you can't watch that bad boy like a hawk, put him in his crate (his den) or in the yard. When you are on supervisory duty, attach a bell and a light leash to his collar so that you can always find and catch that rascal. As soon as he starts to lift his leg, blast him with a foghorn or air canister to startle him. If your timing is good, Sparky will associate the loud noise with the act of hiking his leg indoors. With diligence you should win. Ah, but life is not always fair, is it? If the problem persists, drugs may be helpful. Sometimes there *is* better living through modern chemistry.

One last point: Do not make a fuss over Sparky when you put him in the crate or when you release him from it. If you do, he will begin to believe that maybe it's not so natural. This can lead to separation anxiety, which is much harder to manage. Remember my mantra: We bond to our dogs because they share so much with us, but they are not like us in all ways. They are still dogs.

## House-training

*Teach the lesson once and for all. Stop struggling and do it without anger.*

### QUESTION:

I am so frustrated you can't believe it. I have this 4-month-old Springer Spaniel puppy who will not learn to stop peeing and pooping in the house. I've tried everything. First, I scolded her, then I pushed her nose in it and hit her on the rear end with a newspaper. She still kept doing it, but started to get sneaky about it—whenever I was watching, she didn't go. But when my back is turned, she sneaks off and soils the carpet. So a friend suggested that I take her outside after every meal and wait for her to go, but that doesn't work. So now I'm tying her up on the end of a rope out in the yard until she goes. Will this work? Another friend said I should try putting her in a cat litter pan to shame her. I'm about to lose my mind.

### DR. NICHOL:

It sounds like you and your puppy are both at the ends of your ropes. I know how frustrating training a puppy can be. Having trained a few dogs of my own, I have learned that an outside perspective can help. To get a fresh look, we'll view the situation through the puppy's eyes.

When you got your puppy, she only knew what instinct had genetically imprinted and what her mother had taught her. While none of this includes knowing what not to do on your carpet, there is one basic that will make the difference for you both. Dogs by instinct are den animals. This means that, in good times and in bad, all dogs love the feeling of security they get from a snug enclosure with a roof and some type of window. (To convince yourself of this, watch what any dog does when she is frightened; she'll crawl under a piece of furniture, a porch, a shed, whatever.) What's more important is the instinct not to "soil" their den. In other words, except in rare cases, dogs will respect their den by neither urinating nor having a bowel movement in it.

So how does this help you and your puppy? I'm glad you asked. First understand that while your efforts up to this point have been well-intentioned, they have failed because even though they make sense to you, they mean nothing to your puppy. Your Springer has no idea of what you are trying to accomplish because you have not explained yourself in dog language. If you want to get along with anybody, you must communicate effectively.

Start by showing this baby how much you love her. If you follow Dr. Jeff's advice, you *will* house-train your puppy—I promise. So relax and stop training for a few days. Play ball, roll around together, and enjoy each other. As you forge your new bond with this child, you will also establish the most important piece of the puzzle—trust. When you can feel the relaxed energy between you and your baby, we can start to train.

We will begin by realizing that while house-training is the most important skill any indoor dog will ever have, it is also her first exposure to learning human skills. Human skills? Sure. Dogs in packs never tell each other where to go to the bathroom, when to come, sit, stay, or heel. That's people stuff, not dog stuff. You are asking your baby dog to learn a foreign language. So be real patient—this is hard for a first lesson. Next recognize that your puppy really wants to learn this because you are the leader of her pack. (I talk a lot about the pack dominance order because your puppy already understands this—it's dog stuff.) So your first lesson is to be patient and low key. Be willing to repeat, repeat, repeat. Never lose your patience. She will catch on.

So, let's get a den. You can buy one (called a dog crate) at any pet supply store. Be sure it's big enough for your puppy when she is an adult; it could be useful anytime she needs security through her entire life. Next, make it comfy. Add a nice fluffy pad (if she's a cloth chewer, use newspaper). Throw in a few toys and some food and water. Next, leave her den, with its door open, where she likes to play. Let her go in and out as she pleases.

Training starts by allowing your puppy loose in the house *only* when she is watched closely by an adult. When you are not at home or you are sleeping or busy, she must be in her crate or in the yard. There will never again be an opportunity for her to make an unsupervised indoor mess—*no way*. What if you're busy and you have only 20 minutes each day for this type of constant supervision? No problem. The key is consistency. You can watch, play, or do anything you want. But as soon as that young whippersnapper squats, you make your move—*quietly and low key*. You are going to correct this puppy. You are not going to punish. You must also remember to neither frighten, shame, nor hurt your puppy—not even her feelings. You want her to enjoy learning this house-training thing so she will believe that learning is fun. In fact, you want it to be so much fun that when she has finished learning this, she will want to learn many other human skills like reading, driving, and using a word processor.

So, here is how it goes. When she squats, you walk to her quietly and relaxed. You pick her up *as she is passing the stool or urine* and you say "Pipsqueak, NO!" (The firm tone is on the word *no*.) Don't shout. Next, you carry this baby outside, dribbling all the way. When you put her down where you want her to go (even if she has stopped dribbling by then), you lavish her with praise as though she thought of the whole thing herself. Make a big party of it, then let her go. That's it—until her next indoor mistake; then you repeat the process the same way. You will repeat this charade hundreds of times, never raising your voice, always showing your puppy love and patience. She will catch on, even though it feels like this could truly bore you to death.

Is it worth all this time and energy? Well, you can house-train a puppy using negative reinforcement, but then you must accept that her first and most important exposure to training will be fear-based. On the other hand, if every repetition of this training reminds her of your love, the future for you two will be so bright that you'll have to wear shades.

By the way, forget the kitty litter. Your puppy will run away to join the merchant marines and you'll only embarrass your cat.

## House-training in Reverse

***If you are unclear on the concept, your puppy may train you instead.***

### QUESTION:

I am in dire need of your advice. My 1-year-old female Dachshund, Xena, refuses to become housebroken. I put her outside immediately after she eats, about two hours after she eats, as soon as she's awake, and whenever I hear her gulping water. She cries during the night and I let her out. But often she'll urinate and defecate right after she comes in from outside. I have never caught her in the act. I've taken her to the spot and yelled at her and spanked her. But it just doesn't sink in. We love her and we don't want to give her up.

## Dr. Nichol:

You're right about one thing. You are in dire need of my advice. But before I advise you, I will explain what has happened. You have been trained by your dog. She has you jumping all the time. So, let's start by turning things around. From this moment forward, you will do the training.

Next item: *Stop yelling and spanking!* Nobody's having a good time and it doesn't work anyway. Here is what I want you to do. List the specific times of day that Xena (warrior princess) will be allowed inside. Then get a commitment from every member of your family that Xena will be supervised at all times when she is inside.

Now for the training: When Xena (urinator princess) is in the house, she is never out of the sight of her supervisor. As soon as she starts to squat, she is gently apprehended, picked up, and hears the words "Xena, No." Xena is then carried out the door and put on the spot where you want her to go. She next hears, "Xena, good girl!" You will then throw a party.

Easy, right? Here is what most people miss. They are inconsistent. Sometimes they catch the felony as it is being committed; other times, not. This is unfair to the dog. The truth is that she really wants to do it right, but she's confused. So your mission, if you choose to accept it, is to never miss a chance to correct her. Repeat the training hundreds of times. Consider her house-trained when she has gone four solid weeks without incident. And for heaven's sake, stop getting out of bed when she calls you.

## House-training Using Newspaper

*Dogs are den-living creatures by instinct. Never teach a dog to use any part of your home as a bathroom.*

### Question:

Thank you so very much for explaining about how to housebreak a puppy. I am glad to hear that I am not the only one with this problem. But I have two other questions. You said that I should wait until Curly (my puppy) starts to wet or dirty on the floor before I carry him outside. But I don't want all that mess on my floor. How about taking him out when I think he needs to go and then praising him when he does it outside? Isn't that easier? Or, a friend suggested that I train Curly first to go on some newspapers (but not the page with your column on it). Would that make it easier?

## Dr. Nichol:

These are great questions. You want to make this process easier and I am all for easy. Since house-training is the first lesson young Curly will learn, simple and easy are the keys to his success.

From the point of view of Curly's young brain, he actually needs to learn two lessons. He needs to learn where not to make his messes as well as where he should make them. It is easy for us humans to assume that he already knows that it's a bad idea to soil the inside of your home. Just show him how happy you are when he goes in the yard and he'll quit doing it on the rug, right? Sorry, but that's way too complex for a kid. Remember, puppies don't know *anything*. You have to teach him everything. Your job starts by correcting the mistake and then showing him what to do instead—and how delighted you are after you have shown him. Don't forget that the praise doesn't start until you have taken him to his outdoor bathroom—not a moment sooner. If you prevent Curly from making those indoor mistakes, he may think it's okay inside as well as outside. All dog training is basically the same: Correct the mistake, show him what you want him to do instead, then make a big party about it—and make sure the praise is the high point of every repetition. Young Curly loves you. All he wants is to see you happy. If you show him how good he is *every time*, he'll catch on much faster.

How about that half step of paper-training first, then moving on to the great outdoors? This approach actually works with some puppies, but a lot of puppies get confused. To understand their confusion, consider how dogs think. For example, if you trained Curly to come when called at the age of one year, then waited ten years to ask him to do it again, he would have forgotten the lesson. On the other hand, almost all dogs need house-training only as puppies. Once they catch on, you never need to reinforce the lesson. Why is that? The reason is that as a puppy matures, he or she begins to regard the entire house as his den, not just the area surrounding his bed. At that point, the instinct not to soil the den prevents indoor accidents anywhere in the house. So it confuses some puppies to learn that making stool or urine is okay, on newspapers in part of their den, only to be taught later that while it was okay before, now it is not. The bottom line is: Teach only one house-training lesson—over and over and over.

One last point: How do you know you can trust your puppy? In other words, when is all this supervision and repetition finally over? The best rule is that when a puppy has gone a full two weeks without an indoor mistake (with plenty of supervised opportunities to make mistakes), you can have a graduation ceremony and go on with life. Oh, and yes, I do give commencement addresses for these events, but you'll have to talk to my agent.

## Older Dogs and Urine Dribbling

*Aging problems are manageable in some cases. It's worth some investment in diagnostics.*

### QUESTION:

My 12-year-old female dog, 85-pound Shepherd mix is starting to "dribble" and is kind of incontinent. My vet seems to feel there isn't much that can be done about it. It's hard to believe that, in this day and age, there isn't a pill or shot for this condition. Is my vet correct?

### DR. NICHOL:

Depends(?). This is an important quality-of-life question. If this senior citizen lives inside the house with you, it's about *your* quality of life, too. Assuming that she is dropping stools in addition to urine dribbling, you have a dog who is as bothered by this as you are. I have known this problem to offend the dignity of dogs this age. Sometimes we see this in pets who seem quite functional otherwise. Depending on the cause, there may be a couple of treatments that could help.

A few diseases seen in older Shepherds can cause loss of control of urine and stool. One of these is a progressive condition of the spinal cord called degenerative myelopathy. It's tragic in that it also causes loss of control of the rear legs. There is no treatment. Two other possibilities are spinal cord injury from disc disease and a lower back problem called lumbosacral instability. While these last two are painful, they are treatable with surgery or with medications that could help her to control her urine and stool.

But sometimes this happens just because of age. It has a name, of course (medical people have to name everything), canine cognitive dysfunction. A prescription medication called Anipryl might work for your dog, but it's expensive and not a sure thing. You can also try acupuncture. Finally, a supplement called Cholodin, available from your veterinarian, has helped some older dogs. By replacing the depleted building blocks of the nerve transmitter acetylcholine, Cholodin can make the difference.

My last thought is this: Whether your old girl's incontinence responds to treatment or not, it's a sad reminder of the reality of aging. We love our pets like children who age way too fast. It never fails to break my heart to see older pets with sharp minds fail physically. If none of these treatments helps, you can try to make her comfortable as an outside dog. But know that with her life nearing its end, you can still make the most of every day you have together.

## Urination with Excitement

*Hyperexcited dogs can lose bladder control. Here is how to train better habits.*

### QUESTION:

We have a beautiful little Shih Tzu female (8 months old) who is driving all of our friends away as she jumps on them and then proceeds to pee all over their shoes. Woe is me! How do I break her of this nasty habit? Each time the doorbell rings, she goes ballistic! Any suggestions? I am putting the training collar and leash on her when the bell rings, but that doesn't seem to do the deed.

### DR. NICHOL:

Your friends must be pretty exciting people. Maybe if they understood that your girl is paying them a big compliment, they would be flattered. On the other hand, if you really want her to stop, she will need some training. In addition to a leash, get a dog treat pouch to wear on your waist like the ones trainers use. You'll need to be ready when this foot-washing event is likely to occur, so you can help this baby learn a more socially acceptable greeting.

Start by having your pup drag a 6-foot lightweight leash around the house for a few days until she forgets it's there. Next, have a friend ring the doorbell. Even before your baby has a chance to react, calmly sit her down and feed her a small treat. If she gets excited again, repeat the sit and give her another treat. Then put her in the other room and let your friend in. Repeat this hundreds of times.

Why are we doing this? First: Urinating and eating are incompatible in the brain of a dog. Second: By rewarding her when she is calm, we are showing her what we really want. We repeat this process hundreds of times because we must alter the nerve pathways that are already becoming established in her little brain. We put her in the other room because if you don't, she'll keep pestering your friends until you don't have anyone left to use as a straight man. Last, the long view: When she's finally relaxed with the doorbell, we'll let her greet your friends, *but* they must have a treat ready and they must be quick to offer it. The pup needs to be munching on the treat *before* the urine flow begins. Or you could just give your friends firefighters' boots and live with it.

## Urination Around Just One Family Member
*A dog with a submissive personality may dribble urine with every exposure to the "Leader of the Pack."*

### QUESTION:
We have a female spayed short-hair Collie, 1 year old, whom we love dearly. The problem is that whenever my husband gets near her, she gets so excited (or nervous) she'll squat and pee right there. She is fine when I go near her, no problem. We can't keep her in the house for obvious reasons, and I am the one who ends up walking her, feeding her, etc. She has been like this ever since we got her as a puppy. Is there anything we can do or give her to stop her from being like this? We really would like her to come in the house if she wouldn't act like this. I have noticed that she'll also do this around strangers sometimes. *Please help!*

### DR. NICHOL:
I am wondering if your husband is that charismatic around all females. (Just kidding.) We'll start by explaining what's going on in your dog's head.

While I often answer questions from folks whose dogs are too dominant, yours may be a bit too submissive. To understand her, first remember that while there are significant similarities between the behaviors of humans and dogs, there are also some big differences. In this case, we're talking about pack dominance.

For those who are new to our chats about how to get our pets to act more civilized, pack dominance is second only to eating on the list of what matters most to dogs. They are born with a permanently ingrained mindset about their place in the "pecking order" of life. The big take-home point here is: There is no way to change a dog's mind on this, unless we talk brain transplant.

So, if your Collie regards herself as low dog on the totem pole of her pack (which includes dogs like you, your husband, your friends, etc.), she will communicate in dog language that she acknowledges your superiority. And, you guessed it, she'll say it with urine. But take heart, we can still get her to be socially acceptable.

As much as your girl truly loves your husband and worships the carpet he walks on, the lead dog in her life can stem the flow by making a few minor adjustments. It will be easy for him because he loves this dog. For starters, he needs to know how lead dogs communicate because that is how your Collie is interpreting his body language. Cues that cause your girl to act submissive are the following: leaning over her (squat down next to her instead), making direct eye contact (look next to her and use peripheral vision), speaking in a loud booming voice, and walking up to her quickly. A good general rule is for your husband to allow your dog to approach him, rather than the other way around. When you have friends over, consider putting her in another room. The less submissiveness she feels, the less pronounced the response will be. In other words, if it happens less often, it may become less of a habit. Your husband (as well as your friends) can help manage the problem by being intentionally low key and relaxed around your dog. This will be most important when she is excited to see him. In fact, when he comes home, he can give her a dog biscuit before she has a chance to get too excited. It's hard for a dog to do two things at once, like eating and urinating.

You can make this better. But, remember, it is neither a house-training problem nor willful disobedience. Correcting or punishing your dog for this won't help; in fact, it will make the problem worse as she will feel even more submissive and fearful. Besides, if you think this problem is embarrassing to you, consider how your dog must feel.

## Nighttime Urine Leakage in Female Dogs

*A few spayed girls will leak urine while sleeping. Management of the problem is simple and inexpensive.*

### QUESTION:

This is regarding my spayed 5-year-old female dog, Mia. She has developed spay incontinence and I am very upset about it. She will now be on medication the rest of her life. If I had been told this may be a negative side effect of being spayed at such a young age, I would have let her cycle at least one time. My question is, why are pet owners not warned about the negative side effects of early spaying?

## Dr. Nichol:

You are right; your dog will need lifelong management to prevent urine dribbling, And it is true that it is because she was spayed; it is not, however, a result of "early" spaying.

Early spaying and neutering is a hot topic right now. Humane groups around the country are having these surgeries done on pets as young as 6 weeks of age. The rationale is to avoid reliance on these pets' owners to prevent unwanted litters later. It's a good idea that is working well to help curb the tragic pet overpopulation problem. But the urinary incontinence (urine dribbling) seen in a small percentage of spayed dogs is not related to the age of spaying.

Spaying a female dog is the same as an ovariohysterectomy in a person. Removal of the ovaries along with the uterus causes these girls to have a lot less of the female hormone estrogen. The problem your dog is having relates to the need for a small amount of estrogen to help the muscle at the base of the bladder control urine flow. While there is still some estrogen produced by the adrenal glands, for a small number of spayed bitches (there's that naughty word), it's not quite enough to prevent a small dribble of urine during sleep. Fortunately, the problem is simple to manage. We can give estrogen tablets or a drug called phenylpropanolamine, abbreviated PPA. Either is likely to work for your dog. Both are inexpensive.

I know this is a drag and an embarrassment for the whole family. Frankly, it would be best if all veterinarians mentioned this possibility to dog owners. But while it is an uncommon down side of spaying, the benefits far outweigh this problem. Spayed dogs have no chance of infection of the uterus and almost no risk of breast cancer. Both of these life-threatening diseases are common in the unspayed girls. Is there an alternative to drugs for Mia? Depends. (Sorry, I couldn't resist.)

# Vaccinations

## Vaccines Administered at Home Have High Failure Rates

*Old-fashioned, improperly stored, mail order or feed store vaccine often misses the mark. This leaves the most vulnerable puppies open to severe infections.*

### Question:

My 6-month-old Rottweiler puppy was doing great, then got to throwing up and having diarrhea with blood that turns out to be parvo. How did this happen since I vaccinated him when he was younger? The vet said it's because two of the vaccines I gave myself came from a feed store. How can they sell vaccine that doesn't work?

### Dr. Nichol:

I can promise you that no one intends to sell worthless vaccine. But there may be several reasons why your puppy got sick. With parvo being such a serious and painful disease, providing iron-clad immunity is a high priority.

There's a lot that goes into stimulating a protective antibody level. First, understand that the purpose of vaccination is not to give an immunity, but to stimulate the body to make its own protection. Not all vaccines are equally good at it.

Most of the stuff available to the general consumer is the old-fashioned, low-titer variety. For this to be at all useful, a series of four to six vaccinations is needed. Rottweilers are especially vulnerable to parvo, so boosters every three weeks have been recommended, starting at age 6 weeks and continuing until age 20 to 22 weeks. Many puppies still fail to respond to low-titer vaccine. On the other hand, if you have your veterinarian give the vaccinations, you can have the newer high-titer vaccines that require a series of only three boosters. Protection rates this way are close to 100 percent—even for Rottweilers.

I know that most folks who give vaccinations themselves are doing their best to care for their pets and save money, too. But it's not a risk worth taking.

# Distemper in Dogs

*This horrible disease of the nervous system is still with us. Vaccinate, vaccinate, vaccinate.*

### QUESTION:

A couple of weeks ago my wife and I adopted a beautiful Labrador Retriever-mix puppy from an animal shelter. Everything was great for the first week, then he stopped eating, had pus in his eyes and nose, and quit playing. Our veterinarian said that little Brandy has distemper and that he may die. We thought distemper was all but wiped out. How could this happen?

### DR. NICHOL:

Brandy's story is both tragic and fairly common. Young puppies are the least likely to survive distemper. Be sure to follow his doctor's advice: Keep his nose and eyes clean, keep his antibiotics on schedule, and be sure he eats; force-feed him if necessary. Good nursing care is essential. I recommend weekly rechecks by the doctor; changes in treatment are sometimes necessary.

How could this happen to your puppy? This disease has become less prevalent since the advent of distemper vaccine in the past 30 years. In recent years, however, its incidence may be increasing—especially in animal shelters. Even the best-run shelters have large volumes of dogs coming through, many of them carriers of this deadly virus. Not only does it cause symptoms like those that Brandy has, the distemper virus can also ultimately reach the nervous system, causing muscle twitching, convulsions, "chewing gum fits," and death. It is a horrible disease. The only good news is that prevention works well.

All puppies need a series of three vaccinations starting at 6 to 8 weeks of age. These are usually given in combination with a few other vaccines, parvo being the other vaccine of serious importance. Adult dogs are also susceptible and need vaccination boosters annually.

In Brandy's case, it sounds as though he was exposed while still at the animal shelter. It took several days for his symptoms to develop. Vaccination *after* exposure has little value, if any. Right now, you are doing the best for him that anyone could possibly do. If he survives, he will be immune to distemper for life. Keep your hopes up. I share your concern.

## Vaccine Reactions

*Our best methods of disease prevention have a down-side risk. Here are the facts.*

**QUESTION:**

Last year, my Standard Poodle had a very severe reaction to her annual vaccinations. In fact, she almost died. She was literally unable to move without a great deal of pain, and her eyes were glazed. She was treated, but barely survived. They told us they give the same dosage of vaccinations to all dogs, whether Chihuahua or Great Dane. I find that hard to believe. Now I am extremely reluctant to chance it again. Why is it necessary to vaccinate every single year? She's had shots for eight years in a row, surely she has enough immunity to last the rest of her life.

**DR. NICHOL:**

I can tell from your letter that you're still upset and maybe a bit angry that this happened. I understand. I'll do my best to give you some answers.

First, let's face it: Vaccinations and other medical advances don't come cheap to the consumer. Why aren't they safer? The truth is that nothing in medicine is 100-percent risk-free. But the great majority of our work, including vaccinations, is quite safe—for almost everybody. Vaccine reactions like what your pet experienced are truly rare.

Regarding dosage, your veterinarian is right. The vaccine manufacturers recommend the same dose regardless of weight because it has long been believed that every dog has the same "size" immune system. It has also been an official recommendation that dogs receive annual boosters throughout their entire lives. If a doctor breaks those rules, he or she can be held liable if the pet gets that infectious disease. The veterinary profession has felt that it's been doing the right thing to keep pets healthy.

Recently the immunology and internal medicine folks have been taking a fresh look at these issues. Soon the American Veterinary Medical Association is expected to provide new canine vaccination protocols. We're waiting for the experts' advice partly because we don't want to underprotect dogs. But I don't blame you for your reluctance to repeat your dog's vaccinations. At age 8 she may have a lifelong protection. At the same time, I would ask that you trust your veterinarian to stay up to date with new developments.

# PART 3

# All Your Cat Questions Answered

# BASICS

## Silent Dog Whistles and Your Cat

*Cats can hear them, but—like most things canine—they lack dignity.*

### QUESTION:

If a silent dog whistle is blown around my cat, will it bother her?

### DR. NICHOL:

It is likely that your cat will ignore the "silent" dog whistle. The fact is that they aren't silent—to dogs, nor to cats for that matter. The reason they hear the whistle and we inferior humans cannot is that these two species can detect higher pitched sounds than we can. What's nice about this type of whistle is that if you train your dog to come to you when you blow it, you can retrieve him without yelling or making other noise that might disturb other people. This means that when you use it, other dogs and cats will hear the sound as well. But like most noise we all hear everyday, the majority of it is meaningless unless one is conditioned to respond. Thus, your cat will view this high-pitched whistle as another of life's little mysteries to be pondered while waiting for the next lame mouse to hobble by. If your cat is the fussy type, she will make an annoyed cat face and tolerate more human absurdity like so much else. But don't expect her to come running and panting after you like a dog. She has far too much dignity for that. Why should she anyway—you're only human.

## Cats with Bells On

*The noise doesn't cause hearing loss.*

### QUESTION:

I recently read in a cat magazine that you should not put bells on your cat's collar. The ringing, although an alarm for the birds and a locator for the owners, is very irritating and disorienting to a cat's sensitive hearing. Should I remove the bells from my cats' collars?

### Dr. Nichol:

While cats haven't figured out how to remove the bells from their collars, it's clear that at least one of them has learned how to write for a cat magazine. Nice try, Fluffy, aka cat columnist.

I have found no information in the veterinary medical literature to suggest any health issues associated with cat bells. My experience in general practice (and as a feline audiologist) confirms this. Cats seem to adapt well to wearing a bell.

Why doesn't the noise drive them crazy? Remember that cats are not dogs with short ears. They are different. They are not constantly on the move. Cats by nature sit and wait most of their lives. In waiting, there is silence.

## Microchips and Tattoos for Pet Identification

*Each has its place, but microchips are the latest and greatest. They are quick to implant and highly reliable. Worth the modest expense.*

### Question:

Are doctors trained to look for identifying tattoos and microchips? A friend of mine recently lost her Labrador Retriever—a very valuable show dog as well as a beloved pet—when he broke through the gate and took a walk. She hired the services of a search-and-rescue dog, advertised in the local newspapers, put up flyers all over the area, visited the humane society every day, and *faxed* information about the dog and his identifying tattoo to *every* veterinary clinic in the area. When she located this Lab after three and a half weeks, she was told that the dog had been neutered just a few days previous. This vet was told that the dog was a "stray." I hope that vets understand that a pet is a very important family member and that they should assist in attempting to reunite a lost animal with its family, much the same as we would work to reunite a lost child with his or her parents.

### Dr. Nichol:

Wow. What a harrowing story. Your friend must not only have been worried sick, she must also have been frustrated. Unless her Lab shows in obedience or tracking, being neutered takes him out of the game completely. You are right about the feelings we have for our pets. They are just like our children. Most of us work very hard to get the family back together when this kind of thing happens.

I will provide a bit of education for those who are not knowledgeable about microchips and tattoos. Both methods of identification are permanent and each has its advantages. A microchip is implanted by a quick injection of an inert glass encapsulated-encoded devise about the size of a grain of rice. It has no power source but will relay its unique code back to a "scanner" on a digital display. High tech. Microchips have been around for several years now and they have enormous value *if* the person who finds a pet gets him or her scanned. Since there is no way to know if a pet has a microchip under the skin, animal shelters are usually given free scanners by the manufacturers so they can scan every pet upon arrival. Pretty slick.

What about tattoos? You don't need fancy electronic gadgets to find them. (Ask anyone born after 1970.) But if you find one, who do you call? Unless your friend's dog had his owner's phone number on his inner thigh, the veterinarian may not have known where to go next. But if the doctor got your friend's fax but forgot. . . . What can you say.

So what's better? I say both. If your local animal control facility has each of the different scanners and uses them all on every pet, plus looks for tattoos (and every veterinary hospital does, too), more lost pets will get home. But to make these systems work, we need a greater awareness. Here is what can be done: Call the National Dog Registry at 1-800-637-3647. Tell them you want information brochures that you can distribute to all area veterinary hospitals, shelters, boarding kennels, and grooming shops. Next, have your pets tattooed and/or implanted with microchips. Lastly, register their permanent identification with the National Dog Registry (they do cats, too). Then, if your lost pet's chip or tattoo gets called into these folks, they will provide your name and phone number to the caller. If you're real lucky, your dog or cat will arrive home still in possession of the family jewels.

# A Single Cat in a Household
### *If he or she is a happy kitty, leave well enough alone.*

## QUESTION:
Our 7-month-old kitten spends approximately 12 hours a day alone. I worry that she gets lonely. I have been thinking about adopting another cat to keep her company. The kitten does get (demands, actually) plenty of attention from the dogs and people when we are all home. One of the dogs has a wonderful time sparring with the cat and chasing her up and down the stairs. So, do cats like feline company or are at least as happy on their own?

### Dr. Nichol:

Cats by instinct are loners. That knowledge is based on a huge volume of observation by the behavioral and medical sciences. In addition, cats have been domesticated longer than any other pet. So, we feel strongly connected to our cats. But that sense of kinship and unconditional love causes us to make other assumptions that aren't always true. One false assumption is that cats enjoy a continuous party. Oh sure, a cat will shake his booty once in a while. But the truth is that cats actually live a more monastic existence, often pondering the meaning behind all life.

So here are the harsh realities of life with more than one cat: If a cat feels crowded (many do with as few as one other cat in a home), they are more prone to urinating in places other than the litter pan. They are also at risk of physical illnesses like urinary and upper respiratory disease. And if they really hate each other, they are likely to always want to mangle the other—meaning that they will spit and howl at the most intriguing times of the day or night. Oh, how interesting the next 15 years will be for you and your husband if that happens.

You folks have one well-adjusted cat right now. You, your husband, and your dogs give this active youngster lots of attention and play. To give her even more stimulation, you can get a cat-climbing tree with carpet-covered houses and platforms. You can add a feathers-on-a-stick toy. She can race up and down, rip at it with her claws, and bat the feathers on a stick around. You're doing fine. Don't mess with a good thing and flirt with disaster.

## Social Interactions

*Even though cats are truly solitary creatures, they can still have social bonds. A great story of loving cats.*

### Question:

A couple of weeks ago you wrote in your column that cats are political, not loving. It sounds like the people where I work, but it doesn't describe the cats I live with. I have two cats, Felix and Arthur, who treat each other with tenderness and concern.

Arthur tends to Felix when he is sick. Arthur will cuddle Felix for hours, with his paws around him. I've seen Felix approach Arthur to get his head licked. Of course sometimes these lickings turn into chewings, but no harm is done. So, if you saw my cats curled up cheek to cheek in a heart shape on the bed you would see that cats do have the ability to love.

## Dr. Nichol:

This is an excellent perspective on feline behavior. Your life with Felix and Arthur clearly shows the complexity of the social interactions among housecats.

Cats are capable of many behaviors, sometimes serving as a model of caring, but in other cases causing injuries to each other or damage to their homes. In explaining the reasons for the problems, I often make generalizations. Cats are truly solitary and territorial by nature because they hunt that way in outdoor settings. But that does not mean they can't have social structures like a dominance hierarchy. As usual, it's easy for us to see their lives as an analogue of our own, as though they were an outgrowth of their owners. But that way of thinking leads to misconceptions. Cats are very unlike humans in many ways because they are a different species.

Your cats have an established relationship. The deference Felix shows Arthur means that Arthur is the likely dominant cat—which is OK. Human interaction that involves dominance smacks of office politics. But for our cats this structure forms the basis of the way they behave. Fortunately for everyone in your home, the social order of your cats, as well as that of the humans in the group, allows for the caring and nurturing that you get to share.

You have a truly beautiful family. We can't control the personalities of others, but we can foster love and bring out the best. Now, try that at work.

# Biting and Fighting

## Biting During Play

*How could a well-loved cat bite you while having a nice time? How to correct it.*

### QUESTION:

Two years ago I acquired a Calico cat named Tiny. She is now 13 years old. (I love her.) She's sweet but when most affectionate, she bites. She also goes against the wall and seems to be crying—her tail goes almost straight up and it wriggles. Is she telling me something that I'm not getting?

### DR. NICHOL:

We love our pets like children, but we forget that they are a different species. What Tiny is telling you is that she is a cat and you are not. Most humans neither attack and bite during play nor pretend to urinate against the wall. Tiny has a complex personality. She doesn't understand English, but she does communicate. Lucky for you, Tiny is not repainting your home with cat urine, but only going through the motions of normal territorial marking behavior.

Now for that naughty biting: Most cats who were weaned too early, then hand-raised by humans, were never taught self control by their mothers. If Tiny nursed too hard, she would have been quickly reprimanded. Worse still, some cats stalk their owners and bite and claw as though they were hunting. Because the predatory stage in kitten development occurs right after they learn social play, a human-raised kitten never gets the lessons that only a mother cat can teach. Bummer. You live with a wild child who is lacking in social graces.

Rather than correcting the biting, we'll prevent it. Watch carefully as you play with Tiny. As soon as her ears begin to lay back, her claws extend, her tail switches, or her pupils dilate, startle her—but don't overdo it. I find that a strong cat-like hiss works well. As soon as she backs up a step, reward her quickly with a kitty treat or play gently with a feathers-on-a-stick toy to divert her attention from the aggressive attitude that you just derailed. Every time you play together, be ready to repeat this sequence—hundreds of times. Here is what *NOT* to do: *DO NOT* swat her on the nose. Her response will be an escalation of aggression that will damage your loving relationship. Tiny is a cat and not a person. She will only understand a cat-like correction. If you're firm and quick—and you don't get carried away—Tiny will eventually catch on.

## Harassment Between Cats
*A cat returning home from surgery can spark serious hostility.*

### QUESTION:
We found a stray kitten in our yard in early September. We couldn't find her owner so we kept her. Our 9-year-old neutered male cat Frodo has not been happy about this. Iggy, the kitten, is rambunctious and constantly harasses Frodo. Poor Frodo is constantly on guard, wondering when she'll get him next. Sometimes she is downright mean to him, and she frequently chases him from his favorite spots. This week, Iggy was gone for a day and a half to be spayed. Frodo was absolutely elated. He purred and played (which he hasn't done for a long time). When she returned he growled and hissed even more than when we first found her. He's really upset.

We don't know what to do. We'd like to keep Iggy, but not at the expense of Frodo's sanity. We'd appreciate any suggestions you could give us.

### DR. NICHOL:
Bummer, man. These two are acting, well, like a couple of cats. Now that I've stated the obvious, I'll try to help.

While we already know what Frodo would suggest, we can go back to the beginning and reintroduce these two—very slowly. To break the behavior pattern they have already established, Frodo and Iggy must be totally separated for two weeks. Then start the reintroduction by having one person hold each cat at opposite ends of a large room. While the cats are held, they will need a positive and enjoyable distraction like a game of "feathers on a stick." (Feathers on a stick is a cat toy sold in pet stores and some veterinary hospitals.) The idea is for each cat and handler to play individually. Do this for about ten minutes a couple of times a day. When it's clear that both cats are comfortable, move the games a few feet closer together. Play this way for several days or until both cats are relaxed, then move the play a little closer. Ultimately, if all goes well, they'll be playing side by side. When this close, but individual, playing has worked successfully for several days, try having them share one feathers-on-a-stick toy. If they are still doing well, you're still not done. (Sorry.) Your last big step will be to play with both using one toy for a few minutes, then remove the toy and watch. If they mix it up together, separate them and go back to the shared toy, or even separate toys, if necessary, to get them to relax again. But remember that, except for the training sessions, Frodo and Iggy must remain isolated from each other until it's clear that they will get along.

When they finally play nice together, you may be done. But if Iggy goes back to harassing poor Frodo, you may have to consider having their union annulled or maybe having Frodo take an assertiveness training class. But be optimistic. Many cats will buy into this behavior-modification plan. Admittedly some don't. If it fails, you know you have done your best. Yes, you can find a good home for Iggy.

## Aggression Toward Other Cats and Skin Crawling
*Complex problems may have multiple causes. Careful diet changes and management of medications are essential.*

### QUESTION:
I care for homeless cats (that's how I got five of my own—I love animals in general). One of my cats is Shanti who I got five years ago. He was so aggressive toward my other cats that he's been taking Megace for the last three years. It has helped immensely. He has another problem and that is of twitching along the spine. When this happens he licks his sides frantically. He runs through the house still licking as though something was stinging or biting him. He calms down in less than five minutes. One vet said he has hyperesthesia and put him on vitamin B complex. I tried this for a year and the problem remains, though it seemed to help. Any help you can give would be greatly appreciated.

### DR. NICHOL:
You are definitely an animal lover to care for all those cats. I'm glad you found a way of managing Shanti's aggression. Now the poor guy has a different behavior problem. Let's see what we can do to help him.

Going back to Shanti's aggression with your other cats, it's no surprise that he improved on Megace. Megace is a synthetic form of the female hormone estrogen. It's quite reliable for this problem in male cats because of the direct connection between hormones and behavior in that species. (The truth is that all of us are influenced by our hormones, but we won't get that personal here.) While the Megace will continue to help Shanti be the sweet guy we all know him to be beneath his gruff exterior, there is a long-term risk. Cats given Megace for more than a few months may get malignant breast cancer—even a male. What's worse is that breast cancer in cats is nearly always a very nasty malignancy. But there are alternatives, so keep reading.

Poor Shanti also sounds like he really does have feline hyperesthesia syndrome. But before treatment is started, we need to be sure that it's not a result of excessive thyroid hormone levels instead. This problem, called hyperthyroidism, results from benign tumors of the thyroid glands and can also cause hyperactivity as well as a potentially fatal heart problem. So the first thing for Shanti to get is a thyroid test. If it's normal, we'll treat him for hyperesthesia.

There has been a bit of controversy about hyperesthesia in cats. Among the causes that have been considered are food allergy, epilepsy, and inflammation of nerves. There may be other causes, too, and more than one of them may be responsible in a particular kitty like Shanti. Because it's difficult to pinpoint the cause, different treatments may need to be attempted until the right one works in your cat.

Let's start with diet. Since food allergies are usually due to the protein source, prescription hypoallergenic diets for cats have meats like venison or duck. (Sounds pretty good, doesn't it?) The brand name that is most recommended by veterinary dermatologists is IVD—your veterinarian can get it for you. To do what's called a therapeutic trial, give Shanti the IVD diet for eight weeks allowing him *nothing* else but water. To accomplish this, you'll need to feed all of your cats separately. If he's better, you have a diagnosis. What if it doesn't work? We can do another therapeutic trial, but with a drug called phenobarbital which is often used for treatment of epilepsy. If that fails, we can try diazepam, Buspar, or even prednisone. One way or another, we are very likely to manage Shanti's hyperesthesia.

While you can be confident that we can help your kitty stop chasing himself around your house, the best possible result would be to find that the same treatment would also manage his aggression. If you continue with the Megace, you could end up losing him to breast cancer. Instead, ask his doctor to start him on diazepam for his aggression and stop the Megace. Then try the diet or another medication. When both problems are under control, try quitting the diazepam. When it comes to drug therapy, less is more.

## Aggressive Mother Cat

*Behavior toward the kittens can change after weaning and spaying. Improvement must come with skill and patience.*

### QUESTION:

Last summer our 1-year-old female cat had a litter of kittens. We wanted her to have the kittens, we had already found homes for them, except for the two we wanted to keep. She was a very good mama and we had to force her to stop nursing the two we kept. A couple of months after the babies were born, we had mama spayed. At first she was fine, then she started growling and spitting at the babies and us, too, which almost a year later she still does. Also she will bite. Sometimes she acts fine and other times she's acting like she has PMS. I had her checked over by our vet and he can't find anything physically wrong with her. She's quite the Bitch—what can we do??

### DR. NICHOL:

Mama cat has two separate problems. For one thing, she is responding to the increased number of cats in your home. Since cats are loners by nature, she is feeling stressed by having so many other adult cats in her territory. While this may seem illogical since the additional cats are her babies, remember that after she raised them, she assumed they would be leaving home to attend college, find jobs, or at least get married. (No wonder she's grumpy.) Second, she also has what's called redirected aggression, that is, aggression toward people. This latter problem is related to the first in that she is simply feeling overwhelmed. Now that I've confused you with what's wrong with Mama, I will help you fix it.

For starters, avoid all activities that might trigger Mama's aggression. If it might get her honked off, don't do it. Next, separate her from the other cats. To help her calm down and to speed the process, it would help to temporarily give Mama an anti-anxiety drug like amitriptyline or diazepam. Following this we'll do counterconditioning and desensitization, which in English means that we will allow Mama and the other cats to see each other only from long distances at first. While they are glowering at one another, we will feed them little tidbits to show them that the pleasure they feel as they eat may really be associated with their former enemy. As they become a bit more civilized in their regard for each other, we will shorten the distance between them as we continue with the delectable morsels.

But what about you—the one who's making all of this possible? You get to play a game called feathers-on-a-stick—but not yet. First, do nothing until Mama comes to you. Then rebuild your friendship with her by tossing little bits of food to her. When she starts to feel like you might be an OK human after all, glue some feathers to the end of a stick (you can actually buy a toy like this) and gently play with her until she really warms up. As you play, gradually reduce the distance between you and her until she rediscovers the deep wonder of your magnetic personality.

Will this work? I can say with confidence that it will. I have employed these methods in other cases and they are sound. So get out there and whip those cats into shape—and enjoy the feathers.

# Breeding and Reproductive Organs

## Reproduction in Cats and Kittens
*When the hormones hit and what to do about it.*

### Question:
At what age can a kitten become pregnant? My kitten is 4 months old. I am baby-sitting a male kitten who looks about 8 months old.

### Dr. Nichol:
Gee, the girl is 4 months old and the young stud is 8 months: sounds more like puppy love to me. Should you be worried? Is this "age appropriate"? Is it even legal? What if a pregnancy resulted from this tawdry little affair? Would it be "Kittens having kittens"?

OK, let's not take this too seriously. Here is the rest of the story: Most male and female cats reach sexual maturity at about 6 months of age. And because of the reduced number of daylight hours this time of year [autumn/winter], your young flower may not come into "heat" until early spring. In addition, cats—as well as rabbits—are "spontaneous ovulators," meaning that they do not release an ovum (egg) on a set schedule like most other mammals. For example, we humans have a female reproductive cycle of 28 days, dogs about 6 months, etc. But cats, on the other hand, won't ovulate until they are bred by a lothario such as that visitor of yours. This means that nearly every breeding with cats results in more kittens.

Do you need to be worried about this? At 4 months your little girl still thinks boys are yucky. But if these two are still an item in a couple of months I would recommend one or more of the following: (1) spay your kitten, (2) neuter the male, or (3) send your girl to live at a convent.

## Different Fathers for the Same Litter
*Because each sperm (even from different fathers) fertilizes a separate egg, there can be a different father for each kitten in a litter. But that mother cat can have other litters of kittens all fathered by the same male.*

## QUESTION:

Our purebred Siamese cat came into heat last week and we bred her to a male Siamese. But as soon as she came home from being bred, she got out of the house and we found her hanging out with this nasty-looking alley cat. Her name is Rosie and I know that her purebred kittens would be beauties, but what if she got bred by this alley cat? Will he ruin the whole litter? Could having mixed-bred kittens once ruin her for purebred litters next time?

## Dr. Nichol:

Your cat Rosie is typical of cats in heat (that time of the female's reproductive cycle when ovulation occurs). The hormone levels in her body not only cause the release of several ovum (eggs), but hormones are also responsible for causing her to attract male cats as well as to go out in search of them. If Rosie were bred by both tomcats, you may have some kittens in the litter with different fathers. Here's why.

Since it requires one ovum (egg) and one sperm to make an embryo (the earliest stage of development), there will be as many embryos as there are eggs that get fertilized by sperm. If Rosie releases six ovum and they all get fertilized, there will be six kittens. But the ovum are not released all at the same time. So if she releases the six eggs over a few days, and she is bred first by the Siamese tomcat and later by the alley cat, you are likely to get some kittens who are purebred and some who are half Siamese and the other half mixed bred. Of course, they all have genes from Rosie because she is the mother of all of them. But some will have genes from one father while others will have genes from the other father.

What about future litters? There is never any lasting affect from the genetic input from a previous father. So you can breed her to any male you want after this. But you are not the first cat owner to notice how *badly* an in-heat cat wants to get bred. Even cats who have been frightened of the outside will throw caution to the wind when in heat.

By the way, you shouldn't have trouble placing the mixed-bred kittens in good homes. A "Free to good home" ad in the classified section of the newspaper should get the job done. But I would advise that you leave out the part about their mother being a floozy.

## Spaying an Indoor Cat

*What's the point if they never go outside? Surging hormones cause major behavior changes in cats. When nature calls, your kitty will find a way to reproduce.*

### QUESTION:

My cat Misty really means everything to me. She stays inside all the time. There is no way for her to get pregnant, but I am told that it is still a good idea to get her spayed. How could it be so important? She is like a child to me. I am really afraid that she might not come through the surgery.

### DR. NICHOL:

I understand how you feel about Misty. You are not alone. It turns out that 70 percent of pet owners consider their pets as children. Most veterinarians feel just as strongly. First, I will tell you why spaying is important, then I will tell you about the risk.

As much as Misty is strictly indoors, she may have a major attitude change when she comes into her first "heat" period. The hormone changes make many of these girls suddenly want to go out and find a tomcat as fast as possible. No kidding. But even if she simply cannot get out, remaining unspayed puts her at risk of breast cancer later. This tumor is malignant 90 percent of the time in cats—and it's remarkably aggressive and fast growing. The bottom line is that spaying makes sense.

How about the risk? This is a real important question. First, there is never a guarantee. But her chances of a healthy recovery are very close to 100 percent if she has the following. First, a preanesthetic lab profile to be sure that her internal organs are working fine. Second, high safety gas anesthesia given with oxygen. Third, be sure to ask the doctor if there will be an IV catheter in place (just in case), and lastly a heart monitor for the staff to know that Misty is doing well throughout the procedure.

The real question is: Do the benefits outweigh the risks? If done properly, the answer is a definite yes.

# Pregnancy in Cats
*Do the right things early to ensure a healthy mama and babies.*

## QUESTION:

My 1-1/2-year-old cat is pregnant (about two months). I just wanted to know how long pregnancy will be and is there any prenatal care that should be given. I also believe she has a tapeworm.

## DR. NICHOL:

Pregnancy in cats lasts 63 days (about two months). Most signs like a swollen tummy and development of the mammary glands don't appear until the last two to three weeks. The best diet for your girl is a high-quality dry kitten food because it will provide the optimum calcium/phosphorus ratio as well as a bit of extra protein. The best is Health Blend by Hills available from your veterinarian. While you're there, have her thoroughly examined.

Tapeworms: Your cat has them either from fleas or from eating rodents. They cannot pass directly to the babies. Fleas can. The babies can be at risk from the fleas because they can be bled to death by these blood-sucking insects. If you see fleas, get a flea powder with carbaryl from your veterinarian's office for use on mama and the babies. Do not use tapeworm treatment before the babies are weaned. Tapeworms are worth treating, but are not really a significant risk. I would suggest having a stool sample checked for other parasites. Vaccinations should also wait until after the babies are born.

Now my questions for you: Who is the father of this family? Does he have a good job or does he just spend his time chasing mice around? Is he this "tapeworm"?

# Cancers, Lumps, and Masses

## Vaccination-Related Cancers

*The risks and rewards of vaccination. Now we know that less may be better.*

### QUESTION:

Our 12-year-old cat has developed a pea-sized lump at the site of the vaccination she got last November. We have since found out about postinjection fibrosarcoma and are afraid she now has cancer. Should we have it biopsied? We've heard that a biopsy may cause it to spread more rapidly if it is cancer. We're concerned about the risk of having her under general anesthesia.

### DR. NICHOL:

Oh, brother. This is a tough one. For the past 40 years veterinary medicine has heavily lobbied the American public to protect their pets against every disease possible. Recently, more vaccines have been added to the "distemper combination." These have been repeated year after year in cats like yours. It sounds good, but there is more to the story.

While modern medicine is great, there are risks. Annual repetition of the same vaccines can make rare sarcomas (cancers) more likely in some cats—and these malignancies can be aggressive. Proceed quickly. Ask your veterinarian to do a geriatric health screen first. If it's normal, move ahead with anesthesia and have that mass removed and evaluated to make sure it's been totally eliminated. Want to avoid anesthesia? A needle aspirate of the tumor can give us useful information—but you're right, it could cause a malignancy to get "fired up" and spread faster. But if you act quickly with surgery, you can cure your kitty of a potential killer.

Recently it's becoming clear that with vaccinations, more is not necessarily better. For many adult cats it might be wise to vaccinate against a different infectious disease each year rather than every disease every year. Your veterinarian can recommend the safest protection.

Don't take this to mean that cats are better off without vaccinations—the risk is small. An annual exam may be the best way to make sure your pets do well long term. We'll keep doing our best. I'll keep you posted.

## Leukemia Virus

*What are the risk factors? How to avoid trouble.*

### QUESTION:

I have two cats who I've had vaccinated against leukemia who come into contact with other cats. There are two neighbor cats who had been diagnosed positive for feline leukemia and neither cat has been put to sleep. How dangerous is it for my cats?

### DR. NICHOL:

Ready for a complicated answer? Feline leukemia virus (Felv) is a contagious cancer-causing organism. It can also lead to several other diseases that are potentially fatal. But it's not highly infectious except in some circumstances.

An infected cat carries Felv in the blood, saliva, stool, and semen. During active infection, it can spread to another cat through a transfusion; breeding; mutual grooming activities; shared food, water, and litter pans; and—most important for your cats—fight wounds. Some cats die from it and some get over it on their own. Others can be lifelong carriers or latent cats where the virus moves back and forth from the blood to the bone marrow. Confused? Good.

Those neighbor cats are a threat to your cats only if the virus is active in their blood. But your two are vaccinated, right? That's good, but until recently leukemia vaccination has been only about 60-percent effective. A new vaccine just released claims 95-percent efficacy, but time will be the judge. Real protection for your cats depends on their relationships with these local pariahs. Do they physically feud or just call one another ugly names? Do they know them in the biblical sense? Will these other hoods submit to random blood testing? Would your cats be happy staying indoors? Avoidance of a known risk is the best protection.

## Skin Lumps on Cats

*Do not "wait and see." Most are malignant. Early surgery can save Fuzzball's life.*

### QUESTION:

I am writing you today to ask if you can help with any suggested treatment for a member of our family. His name is Fuzzball, a 13-year-old male cat who looks like

"Sylvester" the cat. Some months ago we noticed Fuzzball was walking with a slight limp favoring his right arm. The limp persisted and did cause him pain. A visit to our regular vet could find no problem. He was put on Tolfedine. This helped the pain. A few days later I noticed a small sized lump on his right elbow. X-rays were taken as well as a fine-needle aspirate. Diagnosis: Mixed inflammation with prominent eosinophilic component.

Fuzzball was given a Depo Medrol injection and put on Cephalexin. It was thought we would notice a change, but it has remained the same and his arm hurts. Our doctor cannot offer any further treatment other than "wait and see." We feel an operation is not an option as the lump looks like it is interfering with either a nerve, muscle, or tendon. Doctor, with your experience and the information given, can you offer any suggestions for treatment or know anyone to whom you can refer me? Thank you so much for your time. Fuzzball really means a lot to us.

## Dr. Nichol:

I can tell this is very hard for you. After 13 years most of us would be just as attached to such a precious friend as Fuzzball. With that kind of emotional commitment, it is nearly impossible for you to be objective enough to make good treatment decisions. So, let me be the detached third party for you. Your cat Fuzzball has a serious problem. Not only is he in pain, but his leg is not functioning properly.

The medications that were tried were logical choices based on the pathologist's diagnosis from the needle aspirate. They were intended to manage infection and inflammation. Why didn't they work? First, understand what a fine-needle aspirate is and what it is not. The procedure is simple. The needle is inserted into the interior of the mass and a few cells are "aspirated" (sucked) into the inside of a syringe. The cells are put on a glass slide and sent to a pathologist who simply reports what is seen under the microscope. It sounds like an easy way to get a diagnosis. But remember that the needle aspirate is nothing more than a blind stab. What if the inside of the lump isn't consistent throughout? What if that tiny sample showed cells that didn't truly represent the whole tumor? Yes, it may be a tumor.

Poor Fuzzball is still in trouble, so we have to put this boy right. It's time to consider the worst-case scenario and make whatever decision is needed. Consider that 85 percent of all skin tumors in cats are malignant—usually aggressively so. Even if you act quickly, you may find that the mass is too advanced to be completely eliminated. But if the mass is surgically removed, the pathologist can examine the whole thing and provide an accurate diagnosis. If the report shows that there is more cancer still remaining on Fuzzball, there may still be options like amputation (cats do remarkably well—believe it) or chemotherapy (they handle that with few complaints). On the other hand, surgical removal alone could be curative.

I know how hard it is to digest this kind of advice. What about anesthetic safety on an older kitty? What if the tumor involves a nerve? For you to save your beautiful Fuzzball, you will need to be brave and accept some risk. Ask your veterinarian for a referral to a trained surgeon. Go for the gold. Save your cat.

## Fuzzball's Saga Continues...

### QUESTION:

Thank you for taking the time to reply to my questions about Fuzzball. Here is an update. Fuzzball went in for surgery to have the mass in his elbow removed. The mass had grown around a nerve and artery and was not possible for our vet to remove without the fear of him ever being able to walk on that limb again. A biopsy was taken. The diagnosis: adenocarcinoma, possibly metastatic.

Please, if you have any suggestions, or know of anyone who could help, let me know. We don't have anything to lose. Fuzzy came home from surgery the same day and immediately started chasing birds off our lawn. He eats well and shows no signs of discomfort, but I know he will get worse and that's unbearable for me to accept. I was told radiation or chemotherapy would not help and only cause him discomfort and stress. I just cannot sit back and do nothing. I have to try and find some way to help my friend. Thank you again for your time.

### DR. NICHOL:

It's great to hear that Fuzzball is up and around and active. While it's excellent that he is feeling well, as you know, we are not done with his cancer yet. The information from the biopsy is invaluable. We now know what we must do to give Fuzzy his best shot at survival.

Adenocarcinomas by definition are malignancies that are derived from glandular tissue. The cancer Fuzzball has may have started with a sweat gland. Because the entire tumor was not removed, the pathologist can't tell us everything about it. While the elbow tumor may have already spread, this mass by itself could be a cancer-spread lesion. But that's worse-case scenario. Best case is that the malignancy is still confined to Fuzzy's elbow.

X-rays of his chest and abdomen as well as aspirates of his lymph nodes may show cancer spread. But if they all show negative, I say go for broke: Amputate the leg.

Holy smoke! Isn't that drastic? There are two essential points here. The first is that this is the only way to save the life of your beautiful cat. If you back out now, you can count on losing him soon. Second, cats do just fine with three legs—honest. Fuzzball will be happily chasing birds on three legs.

Anything else? Once the entire mass is removed, the pathologist can examine every bit of it. The cancer will be methodically described and graded as to its degree of aggressiveness. Chemotherapy following surgery may be useful. This is not to be feared. While people often have a bad time, cats and dogs seldom have any complaints at all. The key to all of this is putting Fuzzball in the hands of a doctor who is knowledgeable in cancer surgery and treatment. If there is no such veterinary facility nearby, ask Fuzzy's doctor for a referral. Last, act quickly. Time is not on your side.

### Fuzzball: The Final Frontier...

#### QUESTION:

I wanted to bring you up-to-date on Fuzzball's condition. He underwent surgery to remove the forelimb with the cancerous elbow. He has some adapting to do, but I know he will do fine. Thank you again for your encouragement, and I look forward to receiving any suggestions you have for after surgery and future care I can provide.

#### DR. NICHOL:

Thanks for the update. You and Fuzzball have shown great courage in committing to his longer life by having the amputation done. I know it was a hard decision. Fuzzball will adapt quickly all by himself. Cats are remarkable this way. Could this tumor show up elsewhere in his body? Yes, but it's unlikely. It's a reminder to us all to live life to the fullest every day. God bless you both.

## Breast Cancer in Cats

*An aggressive killer, breast tumors in cats must be removed ASAP. All lumps on kitties need immediate attention.*

### Question:

I have a cat and her name is Katy. Katy is 13 years old. She has always stayed inside, so we never got her spayed. A few weeks ago I found a lump under her belly and I thinks it's getting bigger. Does Katy need a vet?

### Dr. Nichol:

It sounds like you and Katy are very close and that you have taken good care of her for a long time. With the problem she has now, you must act quickly.

The first thing Katy needs is a complete physical exam. My greatest concern is that she may have breast cancer. If the mass you describe is located on one of her breasts (mammary glands), it must be surgically removed immediately. The reason is that breast cancer in cats is malignant in about 95 percent of cases and it is remarkably aggressive. These are the basics, but there is a bit more to it.

While surgery is Katy's best hope, it's important to understand the possible advancement of the disease first. The place to begin is with three X-ray views of her chest. This is essential to check for spread of the cancer to her lungs. If we don't see any tumors, we may have a fighting chance. Next, a complete blood and urine screening is necessary to make sure her organ function is good. If this checks out as well, we go to surgery with the plan to take a wide area of tissue surrounding the cancerous gland. We also remove the other mammary glands, usually taking some of the normal ones two to three weeks later.

Will this save Katy for you? That's a tough question. If the pathology report shows that her cancer is an aggressive malignancy, chemotherapy should follow the surgery. While this approach will extend her life expectancy, she may still die from this ugly disease. On the other hand, if the pathologist feels that the entire disease was removed at the time of surgery, Katy may be home-free.

I know this sounds scary. Be brave and have your beloved Katy examined right away. It's her best hope. My last point is for other cats you may have. Don't assume that spaying is only for outside cats who are likely to get bred and have kittens. Spaying every cat when she is young is highly likely to prevent this angry cancer.

## Second Opinions and Chemotherapy

*Anxiety, fear, and doing the right thing for a beloved pet. Where to start and what's right for you and your kitty.*

### QUESTION:

My cat's 13 years old and she's been losing weight and eating poorly for a few weeks. My husband and I have no children and this little cat means the world to us. Yesterday we took her to her vet who did some tests. She said that Spider has cancer and that she needs chemotherapy. This is very upsetting. We want a second opinion. But who do we see? Are there specialists?

### DR. NICHOL:

I am so sorry about Spider. You are not alone in your feelings. News like that is hard to take. Maybe the first veterinarian is wrong, maybe not. Those of us who consider our pets as children never want to hear the word cancer. I know how frightened you must feel.

I will try to give you some perspective. Number one: Please do not feel that you are betraying your veterinarian when you want confirmation of a diagnosis or treatment plan. On the other hand, try first to understand whether it is a need to be sure, or the possibility that you never trusted this doctor in the first place. Or consider that maybe you liked the doctor until you were given bad news. Either way, your feelings are legitimate.

Are there specialists? Yes. To know where to turn, consider asking the first veterinarian. If she is a true professional (and most of us are), she will understand that you are speaking from your heart when you ask for more help. Tell her that it is your love for your pet that motivates your need for consultation. Since Spider's doctor's first concern is for her patient's well being, she is duty bound to help you find a knowledgeable second opinion. In addition, she is obliged to provide copies of records for the second doctor.

Two final points: Try hard to put aside your anxiety over Spider's condition when talking to her doctor. Veterinarians have feelings, too. Be kind. Lastly, ask the doctor to send or fax the records directly to the other doctor rather than insisting on taking the copies yourself. This will preserve your relationship with the first doctor by showing her that you trust her. Good faith really counts.

# Cat–Human Diseases

## Allergies to Pets

*Here are several hypoallergenic cat breeds.*

### Question:

I would like to know that if a child is allergic to cats, does it necessarily mean dogs, also?

### Dr. Nichol:

I think you're great to find a pet for your children. Pets teach love and forgiveness in ways that no parent can. Peter Rabbit and Raoul (our family dog and cat) have a big place in the lives of the Nichol boys. But asthma and inhaled allergies in children can be dangerous.

Cats: Glad you asked. What good is life without a cat? The best breeds are Sphinx and Rex cats because they have less hair. Of the three varieties of Rex cats—Cornish, Devon, and Selkirk—the first two are better for cat allergies. While Sphinx cats are less hairy and nonflaky, they are also quite oily and need frequent baths.

The species of pets are different. If your child has trouble with any or all cat and dog breeds, consider a reptile or a pocket pet like a gerbil. Or even a Chia pet. But for heaven's sake, get that kid a critter.

## Hantavirus

*A disease of pets and humans, the human risk is low—mostly.*

### Question:

I live in the Four Corners area and camp in the mountains in the Flagstaff area. The hantavirus has been reported in Arizona and I am concerned about our pets. Can they catch the virus and/or transfer it to humans?

### Dr. Nichol:

I'm glad you're concerned about hantavirus. This infection has actually been around for a long time. It infects about 150,000 humans each year in Europe and Asia—with 5 percent of those cases being fatal. The West was introduced to this sneaky virus during the Korean Conflict when our soldiers became affected in the Hantaan River valley.

Sounds pretty ugly—but there's more. Most of what has been learned about hantavirus relates to rodent populations and accidental human exposure to their urine and feces. What has happened to the Navajo people in your area largely seems to have resulted from exposure to accumulated dust mixed with the dried urine and droppings of deer mice in confined areas, like a seldom-used shed. Accidentally disturbing these rodent nesting areas releases the virus into the air. Thus, a person who inhales the virus can easily get pneumonia-like symptoms. But the fatal part of the equation is often from the spread of the virus to the kidneys. It's a real serious disease.

So what's the risk to you and your pets when camping? Not much. Yes, you may have a chance encounter with an infected deer mouse while you commune with nature—and cats, dogs, and humans can get hantavirus. But you will need to inhale a pretty strong concentration of the virus to get sick. To avoid this disease, just don't you or your pets go sticking your human and pet noses (literally) into accumulations of mouse urine and droppings. Dogs and cats will hunt rodents. If they raid a rodent nest, they might become infected. Ultimately that could put you at risk if you contact their urine or stool. The risk is small. Be safe and keep your pets under control and don't hassle those poor deer mice. Those poor dears had it rough with all the media attention they've already had over this thing.

## Heartworms and Human Risk

***We are not the normal host for this parasite. But carrier mosquitoes have infected a few unlucky folks.***

### QUESTION:

Can people get heartworms? If dogs and cats get it from mosquitoes, can't humans?

### DR. NICHOL:

Cases of human infection with *Dirofilaria immitus* (heartworm) has occurred, but it is pretty rare. The reason is that the human immune system is very good at killing the larvae because we are not a natural "host" for this parasite—like dogs. Cats are less commonly infected than dogs, but it isn't rare in cats. It is for this reason that a once-a-month tablet has been developed and approved for use as a feline heartworm preventive. If you are concerned about the safety of your cat, ask your veterinarian for more information.

# Destructive Behaviors

## Chewing

*Chewing and sucking on fabric can be prevented by providing wholesome after-school alternatives.*

### Question:

Our 9-month-old kitten has one bad habit. She chews holes in things like the comforter cover, my sweat pants, and socks when no one is around. Do you know why she would be doing this and can you recommend action we can take?

### Dr. Nichol:

Is this "Stump the Expert"? Like many cat behaviors, destructive chewing may be manageable by any one of several changes. What will work on your kitty depends partly on how motivated she is to destroy your home.

For starters, keep the stuff she has already chewed away from her. Closing doors into bedrooms while you're gone would make good sense. Next, provide her plenty of wholesome activities like a cat-climbing tree. Attach a feathers-on-a-stick toy. In addition, hard dry food helps deflect domestic destruction by giving the cat something useful to chew. Lastly, you can provide her some catnip toys and a kitty herb garden. The plants in the herb garden are healthy if she consumes them and cats think they're fun to destroy. If all that fails, get her a computer game and let her play with the mouse.


## Furniture Wrecking

*Clawing upholstery is taboo. Declawing is one option—but there are some good alternatives.*

### Question:

My cat Willie is turning into a real problem child. I have had this boy for over a year and we have gotten quite close. But more and more he is destroying my furniture. He seems to know everytime my back is turned. Then he sneaks off and claws the new sofa. I've tried a squirt gun and throwing keys at him, but he seems to thinks it's a game. Is declawing the answer? It sounds cruel.

### Dr. Nichol:

You have raised an important question. I'm sure you have considered making Willie an outdoor cat. Many cats make this transition well, but I would not push you to make this decision: Outdoor cats have a shorter life expectancy. Instead, let me give you some options and you can choose.

In terms of negative reinforcement, you have another choice. It's called a Scat Mat. These are available through a couple of mail-order sources and come in a few different sizes. You put it on the sofa and plug it into a wall outlet. It will give Willie a low-voltage, static electricity-like shock when he touches it. It won't work on every cat, but it could eliminate the need to declaw Willie. It's much better to have a device like a Scat Mat punish Willie than for you to do it. As much as he thinks it's a game, you don't want to damage your relationship with your cat. Besides, a gizmo like this is faster than you are and will catch him every time.

What about surgery to declaw Willie? It is actually not a bad option. If you find that this little weasel outsmarts your Scat Mat (not likely, but possible), declawing could make the difference between keeping Willie or finding him another home. Is it painful? Young cats seem to have discomfort for only one to two days postoperatively. This will not be significant given the pain relievers that we use right after surgery. If you feel that Willie will need these at home, too, be sure to ask his doctor to dispense tablets. For this procedure we like to use Torbutrol tablets in our hospital. They are safe, reliable, and free of side effects.

Whatever you do, stay away from aspirin, ibuprofen, and especially acetaminophen (Tylenol). This stuff is truly deadly in cats.

## Chewing Plastic and Other Nonfood Items

*Indoor cats get bored and need healthy activities. Provide wholesome activities or say goodbye to your nice stuff.*

### Question:

I have two young cats, ages 1 year and about 9 months, and a third, nearly geriatric. Of the young cats, the older one chewed a lot of plastic when he was around

6 months old (including a portable phone!), but he wasn't particular—he also chewed cardboard. Now the younger one has been caught chewing plastic (including the cord to my carbon monoxide detector!). My old cat isn't a problem. Is this because their permanent teeth are on the way? Will cats take a liking to those dorky plastic pork-chop dog toys or should I spray catnip on one of those rawhide things?

## DR. NICHOL:

Your questions are important. Aside from the damage to your phone and other appliances, there are some definite risks to your cats if this continues.

Why do they like plastic? Number one: Since the adult teeth in kittens are already in place by age 6 months, I doubt this is a result of new teeth. But until kittens are over 1 year of age, they have a great deal of energy. Like little kids, they get into trouble unless you provide healthy after-school activities like sports or arts and crafts. Otherwise, they join gangs and chew plastic.

What's so bad about plastic? Aside from pieces of it getting lodged in the stomach or intestines, the act of biting the electric cord on your carbon monoxide detector is most worrisome. Cats who bite electric cords can get severe burns of the mouth that can cause their tongues to slough. So it's definitely a habit worth stopping if only to prevent a smoldering cat from generating more carbon monoxide.

To manage this deviant behavior, start with a good diet. Remember that you will know the good stuff by the price. Cheap food is poorly digestible, causing a cat to chew things other than cat food. Next, get some really fun toys like a cat tree. This is a carpet-covered, multileveled playhouse affair. I recommend one that is tall enough to reach the ceiling. All of your cats will enjoy scampering around and playing hide and seek. In addition, you can hang other toys like feathers-on-a-stick from the platforms. But while these things are good fun, there's still nothing like the taste of plastic.

So, what can you do if you provide the greatest alternatives, but they still go after plastic? Hide the plastic. If the object is immovable, put a Scat Mat in front of it. But break that habit. Don't wait for them to quit on their own.

Oh, about those dorky plastic pork-chop dog toys? Forget it. If you're a cat, *everything* dog-like is dorky.

# Declawing

*Concerns about post-surgical pain are important. We can help.*

### QUESTION:

Victoria Louise is a 7-year-old, pretty fat tabby who is an expert furniture shredder. She's just smart enough to know that she will be sprayed with water and shrieked at if she claws in our presence. I have heard that a cat will not walk the same, might have a personality change, and will certainly be in major pain for weeks if her claws are removed. This cat is precious to me, and I don't want to warp her for life. I hope I will not end up with a psycho.

### DR. NICHOL:

Ah, the well-loved problem child. You needn't worry; she can have an excellent recovery. For adult cats a Duragesic skin patch, applied the day before surgery, will give three to four days of pain relief. Any follow-up pain can be easily managed using Torbugesic mixed with tasty VAL syrup and given orally. Lose the guilt trip. Our pets are in our lives to share our love, not to destroy our stuff. Besides, Victoria Louise will like you better if you stop trying to extinguish her like a forest fire.

[*Note:* I believe it's best to avoid declawing, and I've often advised cat owners on different methods of discouraging destructive behavior. But while many cats can be trained, a few are not amenable to any changes. In fact, there are cats who scratch members of their families, including children. Sometimes declawing is the only way to prevent a cat from being taken to a shelter. All things considered, it isn't a bad last resort.]

# Ears

## Earflap Swelling

*Head shaking/ear scratching can damage blood vessels in the earflaps, forming a blood pocket. Treatment of the disease of the ear canal is priority one.*

### Question:

I have a 5-year-old cat. He had been holding his ear down, and when we looked at it, the *entire* inside is swollen. It looks like a bubble. I don't want to take him to the vet for something that will clear up on its own! It doesn't seem to bother him at all, not even when we touch it! It just looks *awful*! Please help!

### Dr. Nichol:

You are describing an auricular hematoma. It is a nonpainful pocket of blood that has filled the space between the cartilage and skin of the pinna (earflap). As much as it is abnormal, by itself it's not a major problem. The greater concern is its cause. This hematoma, or blood pocket, has formed because your kitty has ear pain and has been doing some serious head shaking and ear scratching. So much, in fact, that the tiny vessels inside the earflap have broken and leaked enough blood to cause a swelling. The reason for his pain is a problem way down inside the ear canal close to the eardrum. The usual causes are things like bacterial or yeast infections, ear mites, ticks, and foxtail awns. The bottom line is that you will need to make that dreaded trip to the veterinarian. If left untreated, the pain and infection will only worsen.

Now, back to the hematoma of the earflap. This part does not require treatment. If you get the ear canal managed, you can ignore the flap if you want to. It'll heal by itself if you do nothing about it, but it will be permanently rumpled like a leaf of iceberg lettuce. The alternative to this vegetation of the head is a minor surgical correction that will preserve your cat's boyish good looks. You make the call on the earflap.

## Ear Infections

*They can recur time and again. Get serious. End the misery for the kitty and protect long-term health.*

## QUESTION:

My father's cat has a problem since birth with his ears. He seems to have what we thought at first was some sort of ear mite and now believe to maybe being some sort of a yeast infection in his ears. He will constantly shake his head and stuff does come out and his ears are very sensitive. My father has tried various products and it seems once it gets cleared up, the problem comes right back.

## DR. NICHOL:

Well, I'm glad to get this question. I can tell you from a lot of experience (25 years) what a major problem ear infections can be. It's the most common disease we treat. But when they get deeply rooted and advanced, they can be difficult to cure because of permanent changes in the anatomy of the ear canal caused by chronic inflammation.

Your dad's cat sounds like he's been miserable for a long time. And his infections may be due to more than one cause. Foreign material like ticks, mites, and foxtail awns could have been the inciting cause. But after the initial damage, bacteria and yeast can become the bigger danger. Not only that, he may also be suffering from kidney damage due to accumulations of inflammatory materiel from those uncontrolled ear infections.

Have I made a case for taking this kitty to the doctor immediately? Treatment may require anesthesia to remove all that nasty discharge. Microscopic evaluations plus cultures will be useful. Injectable and oral antibiotics may also help. This sounds like a lot—it has to be to get this boy back to the health he deserves. Please don't wait any longer.

## Ear Mites

***Nasty little creatures drive cats crazy. Injections from your veterinarian are easier for you and your cat than pet store ear drops.***

## QUESTION:

We have three cats at our house and all of them are scratching their ears. This has been going on for a long time. We took them to the doctor and she said that she saw ear mites. She even showed them to my kids and me in the microscope. The doctor said that she could give the cats injections to get rid of the mites, but with three of them, I picked up ear drops at the pet store instead. It's much cheaper. The problem is that the cats fight with me every time I try to put the ear drops in. How can I make them hold still?

## Dr. Nichol:

You have two common problems. One is ear mites and the other is cats who won't hold still. Try to see it from a cat's point of view. There are these actively running and scurrying insects in your head driving you crazy. Then this person shows up and tries to wrestle you down and squirt medicine in—that by the way irritates the heck out of the ear tissue. (They don't tell you that on the label.) Cats are no dummies. If they already hurt, they have no interest in adding to their pain. But don't lose faith. Your cats will love you again.

First, I will address the question of expense. As you continue your well-intentioned treatment attempts at home, the ears get worse. Not only are the ear mites (*Otobious Megnini*—the dreaded spinose ear tick) multiplying, bacterial infection is also on the rise. That's because the mites are damaging the walls of the cats' ear canals and bacteria are setting up housekeeping. The longer the ear mites stay, the worse the secondary infection. By the time you finally surrender to the attack of the ear mites, your cats and their health will be paying for it. When you take them back to the veterinarian for treatment, you will pay a bigger price because by then they will need not just the injections for the mites but treatment for their ear infections, too.

Your second concern needs to be your relationship with your cats. If you treasure the trust you have with those pets, make it easy for them. The injection, called Ivermectin, is essentially painless. Bring them in together, then return for a repeat in two to three weeks. Then you are done and your cats will thank you. They will also act more civilized if they don't have bugs in their heads.

## Head Shaking in Cats Can Mean Foxtails in the Ear

*A sudden onset suggests a grass awn (foxtail). Have it checked out soon.*

### Question:

I have a head problem with Schnapps. Schnapps is our cat and she is a female. All of a sudden two days ago she's been leaning her head to the right. Sometimes she sort of shakes her head, too. She seems OK in other ways. What's wrong with Schnapps? Will this problem go away by itself?

## Dr. Nichol:

I'm glad you are asking for advice on Schnapps's problem. While it will not go away by itself, it also may not be serious.

There are a few possible causes for Schnapps's head tilt. Middle- and inner-ear infections can do it as well as dental disease. Even a brain tumor is a possibility. But considering that it came on suddenly and that she is doing well in other respects, I would suspect first that Schnapps has a foxtail awn stuck in her ear canal.

What is a foxtail awn, you ask? Foxtail is an aggressive weed that grows in fields and in many yards. The branches of the weed look like the bushy tail of a fox—hence the name. Stuck to the shaft of the branches are dozens of awns that break loose and blow around the yard. The awns are shaped like the birdie used in the game of badminton. They are pointed at the tip. "Feathers" project away from the tip. Each of the feathers has tiny barbs like a fish hook. If you have weeds in your yard, you have probably found foxtail awns stuck in your socks after walking through the weeds. As your ankle and your socks move, the foxtail migrates further and further into your sock until it starts to rub your skin. The more you walk with a foxtail stuck in your sock, the worse it bugs you. That is exactly what is happening in Schnapps's ear. A foxtail has found its way to the opening of her ear canal and, as she moves, it works its way further in. No wonder her ear is bothering her.

What poor Schnapps needs is to have the foxtail awn removed using instruments called an otoscope and an alligator forcep. Most cats hold still for the removal of foreign material like this. If she gets wild on her doctor, Schnapps may need to be sedated.

The question I often get at this point is "Won't it just come out by itself?" This almost never happens. Because of the shape of the awns and the barbs on their feathers, they tend to just keep moving in. So if you don't get it removed soon, it can continue its movement until it reaches Schnapps's eardrum, penetrates it, and possibly continues into her brain. That is the worst part of the problem. Foxtail awns have been found in every part of the anatomy of dogs and cats. Not only have they been found in brains, but spinal cords, livers, lungs, you name it. They can travel anywhere in the body if given enough time. So the moral of the story is: Get this type of problem managed fast to avoid advanced foxtail migration.

## Sores on the Ears of White Cats

*Lacking protective dark skin pigment, white cats are vulnerable to skin cancer.*

### QUESTION:

Our cat is 8 years old and we've noticed that he has little red sores on each of his ears. They've been there for a few weeks and they don't seem to heal. I don't know if it's important but Bronson is a white cat and he is outside most of the time. Do you think this is a problem?

### DR. NICHOL:

Yes, it is important. It is likely that Bronson has a malignant skin cancer called squamous cell carcinoma. This form of skin cancer is quite common in people as well as critters living at high elevations.

What can we do for Bronson? Since the problem sounds like it's in its early stages, the simplest treatment would be amputation of his earflaps. Since squamous cell carcinoma does not spread to other parts of the body, surgery should be curative. On the other hand, if the lesions are still tiny, he can keep his earflaps by having them treated with radiation instead. So the news is actually pretty good. But you may object to the idea of amputation of Bronson's earflaps, knowing that his friends will start calling him 'E.T."

# Eyes

## Eye and Nose Discharge

*Infectious upper respiratory diseases can linger and run rampant in multiple-cat households.*

### QUESTION:

I have a litter of white kittens who are approximately 3 months old plus six cats. They have never been outside, but they have developed a discharge from their eyes and scabs around their noses. Only two of them are infected. They have not had any shots as of yet. Their behavior has not changed, and they run and play and eat really well. And now another cat is getting the same symptoms. I am concerned it might be distemper, even though they never go outside.

### DR. NICHOL:

I think I can help you with your herd health problem. Herd health? A herd of cats? Sounds absurd, doesn't it? In a way it is. Think about dogs running in a pack or birds on the wing in a flock or livestock being moved as a herd. But cats don't behave that way, do they? The reason that cats don't exhibit group behavior is that unlike most other species, cats are not community animals. So when they are kept in a group such as yours, they are in an unnatural living arrangement. The result is stress that, in the case of your cats, shows up as physical disease.

This is not to say that cats kept alone live more meaningful lives. For indoor cats to have symptoms of infectious disease, someone sometime brought it into the group from the outside. That someone has had a smoldering infection for a while—what's called a carrier state. No symptoms, no discharge, no scabs. Then along comes a litter of vulnerable kittens and one after the other they start to get sick.

Now that you understand the problem, let's help your kitties out of this mess. The infectious cause of the upper respiratory symptoms is likely to be a virus called feline viral rhinotracheitis. Other complicating organisms may include calici virus, chlamydia, and bacteria. Drugs like antibiotics can be helpful in controlling the bacteria (the "groupies" of upper respiratory infections of cats). But for the most part your best defense will be good nursing care, like keeping their little noses free of snot, and providing ginger ale and videos until they feel well enough to go back to school. In other words, it has to run its course.

I know I make it sound easy—just wait it out. The truth is that if you continue with this crowded living arrangement, you may never be rid of it. I mean *never*—remember the carrier state in a herd of cats? So the moral of the story is: Find homes for all of the kittens where they will each be the only pet. Next, give your adult cats more space—that is, keep only one indoors. The forces of nature are at odds with your cat management. And you know that it's not nice to fool Mother Nature.

## The Third Eyelid

*Third eyelids can be visible with stress, infection, or foreign material. A good exam is important and essential.*

### QUESTION:

I must say that I am very worried about my Maine Coon kitten. This morning, when we woke up, we found that one of her eyes had an off-white coating on most of the eye. It doesn't seem to bother him (he's not scratching at it or grooming it or anything else) but it really worries me. It looks like the stuff that is usually in the inner corner of his eye. My daughter has said that when other cats she has had developed this condition, they died. Can you tell me what causes this condition and what can or should be done about it?

### DR. NICHOL:

I'm glad you and your daughter have taken this cat's symptoms seriously. Here is the long and short of this situation: What you describe is called a protracted third eyelid. The third eyelid is actually a normal structure that all cats and dogs have. It also goes by the name nictitans or nictitating membrane. What's important about it is its protective function. On the back side of the third eyelid is a patch of lymph tissue like a mini lymph node; thus, it helps clean up infections and debris. In addition, the third eyelid can easily slide up over the entire cornea (the clear front part of the eye). Most people never notice that their pets even own such equipment because the third eyelid normally sits tucked neatly in the inside corner of the eye. In this position it can move up to shield the eye from injury or help heal it if it gets injured. Pretty nifty. Too bad we don't have them. If you look closely at the inside corner of your eyes, you will see a small pink tissue that is an evolutionary vestige of a third eyelid. It's all we have left of ours. Maybe we humans have just gotten too good for such things. Oh, how I yearn for simpler times. . . .

Enough nostalgia; back to your question. What does it mean when you actually notice that your cat has a third eyelid? If it's visible on only one side it suggests an infection or injury to that eye only. On the other hand, if both third eyelids are protracted, we need to be concerned about internal disease. We call it a sign of systemic illness because a disease in some other part of the body is responsible for the symptom. Diseases that can cause protracted third eyelids in cats include any physical or emotional stress as well as severe problems like feline leukemia and feline infectious peritonitis (FIP) infections. The entire list of possibilities would be quite long. Suffice it to say that any stress can do it.

Here is my advice: Have your daughter take this kitty to a veterinarian with lots of experience with cats. A thorough physical exam alone could answer the question. If not, screening lab work like a blood count, chemistry panel, and urinalysis are in order to look for indicators of internal disease. In addition, testing for leukemia virus is essential. The last big concern, FIP virus, can be investigated if physical signs and initial lab work suggest it.

So, how sick is this kitty? The truth is that without a good exam and lab work, I can only guess. Her problem may be as simple as a minor stress or as severe as a terminal illness. But like any possibly serious disease, early diagnosis and treatment are your best hope. Good luck.

## Uneven Pupils

*It may be normal, or maybe not. Get a good physical exam.*

### QUESTION:

We have recently acquired a new cat to our household. She is an odd-eyed white. The pupil in the blue eye is always larger than the pupil in the yellow eye. Is this normal? She seems to be in good health otherwise.

### DR. NICHOL:

Congratulations on your new kitty. You were smart to examine her carefully. Actually there are lots of white cats with eyes of different colors. Many with one or both blue eyes are deaf. That part's really OK. But differing pupil size (called anisocoria) may or may not be normal. There could be several possible causes including cancer, glaucoma, infections, or nerve damage.

This girl needs a thorough physical exam. It should include an evaluation of the interior of her eyes using an ophthalmoscope as well as measurements of the pressures inside her eyes. These procedures plus a few neurologic tests will hopefully show negative for disease. Last, ask for a feline leukemia test. This potentially fatal infection can cause spastic pupil syndrome. (This sounds strangely like descriptions of me in grade school.) The blood test is fast and reliable.

I know it sounds grim but the truth is that most cats with anisocoria are actually fine—what we call a variant of normal. But don't gamble. Your girl sounds special. Get her checked out for your peace of mind.

## Eye Discharge

*Don't goof around at home. See the doctor fast.*

### QUESTION:

I just noticed today that my cat's eyes were tearing and one was infected with green pus. Is there any way I can treat her myself? She is kept indoors.

### DR. NICHOL:

Please do *not* monkey around with eye disease. Discharge coming from just one eye suggests a possible injury to that eye. Without thorough diagnosis and appropriate treatment, she could end up with big-time pain and blindness. Go directly to the nearest veterinarian. Do not pass "Go." Do not collect $200.

# Feeding and Nutrition

## Milk for Cats

*Kitties love milk—but it's not part of a balanced diet, unless you're a calf.*

### QUESTION:

I am in first grade and have an assignment that is asking why cats like milk. Why do they like milk?

### DR. NICHOL:

Cats enjoy milk for the same reasons people do: It tastes great. That's because it has plenty of animal fat and protein. Cow's milk makes a fine diet for baby cows—not really for cats. The best thing to feed a cat is cat food. But you like milk and so does your cat. So I think you can each have some—just don't let it spoil your appetite for your real dinner.

## Varying the Diet—Changing Brands of Pet Food

*Variety is the spice of life, but cats can get gas and diarrhea. Pick a good diet and stay the course.*

### QUESTION:

I live alone and my cat is my constant companion. I know I spoil her, but I can't help it. She's 4 years old and I have noticed that she seems to grow tired of a particular food after a while. So, like the doting cat mother I am, I give her something different. The problem is that I often find loose or fluid stool in her litter pan. She smells gassy, too. What can I do?

### DR. NICHOL:

What you are describing is something very familiar to most of us cat owners. They can be finicky. But you can allow your kitty to be fussy and still enjoy good health.

To manage this problem, you need to first understand that the stomach and intestinal tract of cats is truly a creature of habit. In other words, most cats do best eating the same diet every day, long term. With frequent changes in the diet, the intestine has to change the way it manages the differences in fiber, proteins, and fat. Bloating with gas and diarrhea can result. When these problems occur, you are also likely to notice your cat making urgent, more frequent trips to the litter pan. This problem is not only unpleasant for you, but uncomfortable for your cat.

The best prevention for the loose stool and gas problem is to use the same diet. Your best choice is one of the higher fiber cat foods. While not all cats have this problem with changes in diet, those who do usually need more fiber. Ask your veterinarian for a recommended diet. Prescription diet r/d is a good choice.

What about the enjoyment? Use cat treats. Be sure to limit your kitty to two per day. Treat her like a child (our pets are really just furry children anyway). Give her one cat treat after she finishes her breakfast and another after dinner. If you stick to that structure, she'll go along, too.

## Finicky Eaters

### *What's good, what's junk, why it matters.*

### QUESTION:

For most of my cat's 12 years she would only eat canned food. She got cat acne and our vet suggested it was due to the wet food. We have tried many varieties of semi-moist and dry foods and she seems to hate them all. She seems to always be hungry, yet she often won't eat the food we give her. Recently I noticed her eating our dog's food quite often. As the cat has lost weight, I am worried about her.

### DR. NICHOL:

Your cat's quirky appetite isn't unusual. Aging cats get so set in their ways that some would prefer a hunger strike to following their doctor's diet advice. So let's accept realities. If this girl forgets to clean those sticky bits of canned food off her chin, then I say let's wipe her face for her. I do it for my kids everyday. (Shucks, I wipe food off my own chin, too.) A clean, dry chin should prevent the feline acne that prompted the diet change in the first place.

So, how about canned food? Like all types of pet food, there are excellent canned diets on the shelf right next to the bargain-priced junk. Get the good stuff like Science Diet or Iams. But also be sure she isn't eating poorly and losing weight because of dental infections, organ failure, or cancer. If your feline senior citizen hasn't had a thorough exam in the past six months, she may have serious reasons for failing to eat. Ask your veterinarian for a geriatric lab and X-ray profile. If we catch age-related problems early, we can extend the excellent quality of life that your loving care has always given her.

Cats are special creatures, aren't they? It's really true that their behavior is fundamentally different from dogs and humans. My cat Raoul has seen me through good times and bad over our 15 years together. I love him intensely. He doesn't spend his life trying to please me, but he's always my friend.

## Poor Eaters: When Cats Lose Their Appetite

*Elderly cats who fail to eat may have serious illness. But we can help many.*

### QUESTION:

We have a 20-year-old female cat. She will not eat canned cat food from the pet stores. I have tried many brands, but she will go many days before finally eating a little. My wife wanted to know if there are any recipes available she could cook up that our cat might eat. We are worried she is not getting enough food.

### DR. NICHOL:

Thanks for writing. You are right to be concerned, but please do not try to manage your feline senior citizen's poor appetite by trying new foods. What is truly important is to understand *why* she is not eating. Possible reasons in a 20-year-old cat include painful infected teeth, organ failure, and cancer. Frankly, this mature lady is on borrowed time. There is much wear and tear by age 20. That does not mean she should be written off. There may be a few good miles left for you to share. But be careful. If you allow the cause of her poor appetite to continue without treatment, she is likely to crash suddenly.

Get this girl the care she needs. Have her examined soon. Get a thorough geriatric lab screen so her doctor can find the age-related problems that can be managed. Do whatever it takes so you three can enjoy those golden years. It sounds like she is well loved.

# Overeating

*Most hungry, overweight cats are just bored.*

### QUESTION:

My 8-year-old cat, Nelson, was placed on IVD special diet three years ago. I have noticed that giving him the same measured amounts of food have recently caused him to gain weight. He always acts famished, so I am reluctant to reduce the amount. Being a housecat, he is inactive and cannot burn off the calories. Can you recommend another limited diet plan product for him to try? He is my firstborn, after all, and I want to keep him around at least another eight years.

### DR. NICHOL:

Does Nelson threaten you with action from Animal Humane? Does he stagger into the room with the back of his paw against his forehead and flop unconsciously at your feet—even though he can barely fit through the door? I think I know this guy. I've met him a thousand times.

I know how you feel about Nelson. My cat Raoul always insists that he's never been fed. Cats are such con artists. The only viable treatment is finding this bored teenager wholesome after-school activities. If he already owns a cat tree with feathers-on-a-stick toys attached, get him a window-mounted birdhouse or a fish tank. If his gluttony continues to haunt your relationship, I suggest offering raw carrot wheels. If he won't eat them, maybe he'll chase them and burn off a little fat.

# How Much to Feed

*Being overweight is unhealthy. Here's how to get it right.*

### QUESTION:

How much should I feed my cat? I thought I was doing the right thing by following the recommendations on the bag, but when I took Shalako for his shots, he weighed over 12 pounds. Now I feel guilty that he may not get old because his doctor said that overweight cats usually don't. How much is the right amount?

### DR. NICHOL:

This is a very good question. Please don't feel guilty for trying to do the right thing for Shalako. There are many things in life that we cannot change. Be thankful that body weight is not one of them.

Your veterinarian is right. Extra weight puts extra strain on the heart, kidneys, and joints. In cats we have the added risk of a potentially fatal liver disease, too. So thin is in. What's the right amount? Remember that pets are a lot like us in that they have differing individual needs. But the average adult cat does fine on a quarter cup of dry food morning and night. This amount should help Shalako maintain a weight of around 8½ to 9½ pounds. You say Shalako is just big boned? Even a big framed cat has no business weighing more than 10½ pounds. Because Shalako is male, be sure to add some water to his dry food to help prevent crystals from forming in his bladder.

Here is how I determine if a pet's weight is healthy. With the pet standing, feel for the ribs with your fingertips. If you can count the ribs with your fingers, but you cannot see the ribs individually, that critter is about right. If you can't find the ribs with your fingers, your pet needs to lose weight. Use the above feeding recommendations as a starting point. Then adjust the amount fed as needed.

So the last question is: Why did Shalako get fat following the manufacture's advice? Shouldn't they know best how to feed their diet? The answer is that the manufacturer's advice is based on cats and dogs who live in research colonies—a very different life than your pets. Pet food companies are also in the business of promoting pet food sales. Your veterinarian is in the business of promoting pet health.

# Grooming and Skin Care

## Skunked Pets

*Tomato juice or a new mixture can make a pet worth having back in the county.*

### Question:

Do you have any suggestions on how to deodorize a skunked pet?

### Dr. Nichol:

I hate it when that happens. There are a few products on the shelves of pet supply stores that claim effectiveness for pets who have tangled with the business end of a skunk. But the best treatment still seems to be tomato juice.

Start by bathing your cat (don't do it like a cat or hair will stick to your tongue). Next, plug the drain in the sink and sponge tomato juice onto every square inch of your kitty, allowing him or her to soak for a good 15 minutes before rinsing. Do not shampoo after the tomato juice.

Don't expect this approach to totally eliminate the odor, but you will at least be able to share the same county. Lastly, your pet won't "learn a lesson." Cats already know everything.

But wait, there's more. Don't touch that dial. A new and exciting way to deskunk your skunked pet. Paul Krebaum, a chemist at Molex, Inc., advises: one quart 3-percent hydrogen peroxide, one-quarter cup baking soda, one teaspoon liquid soap. Make the solution fresh just before use. Rinse the pet with tap water after soaking. I'm so excited I just can't wait for one of my pets to give me a chance to give it a try.

## Haircuts

*Shorter hair is easier to manage, but be careful to keep the skin protected.*

### Question:

I have a 22-pound cat with very long fur. He gets ticks and thorns, etc., caught in his fur every day. I brush him the best I can, but he still accumulates debris and pests when he goes outside. My question is, could I shave off his fur?

**DR. NICHOL:**

Yes, it's a great idea to give this boy a haircut. Be sure that it is no shorter than one-half inch or his skin may be unprotected. If you make him look like a Marine recruit, he will not only be fat, but sunburned—and quite mad.

## Soft Paws Instead of Declawing

*These glue-on nail covers are a reasonable alternative, but they need to be maintained.*

**QUESTION:**

My husband wants me to declaw my 7-month-old kitten and I don't want to do it. There are supposed to be some kind of plastic nails to place over their nails. What are they called and where do I find them? HELP!

**DR. NICHOL:**

I share your apprehension about declawing. Who wants part of their cat's God-given anatomy in the trashcan if there's an alternative? Not me. I have *all* of my claws.

For those unfamiliar with the onychectomy (spiffy name for declawing), the surgery amounts to removal of the end of the toe including the nail. In other words, we separate the last joint of each toe, then use surgical glue to close the wound in the skin. A new technique utilizes laser surgery, but it's expensive and the equipment is largely unavailable. While it sounds tough on the kitty, pain medications help a lot and recovery would be quick with a youngster like yours. But I still wouldn't do it unless your indoor kitten is shredding your furniture or your body.

There is an alternative: Soft Paws. This nifty product includes individual silicon rubber nail coverings. The cat's nails are trimmed, a drop of special glue is applied, and the nail covering is fitted over each of your cat's claws. They even come in colors so your cat can make a fashion statement—just like you. Isn't that easy? Yes, but the nails will grow and sometimes the Soft Paws fall off, so you'll have to fiddle with these for a lifetime. I've found most cats to be a bit fussy about their feet, which can make the whole exercise a bit arduous. You can have your veterinarian order them and do it all for you or you can buy them at a pet supply store and do it yourself. Simply a must for all stylin' cats.

# Heart and Breathing

## Breathing Difficulty

*Persian cats can have a simple surgery to correct their narrow nostrils.*

### Question:

We have three Persian cats. Two are just fine, but one of them (2 years old) has trouble breathing. Her nostrils are very narrow. Can anything be done to help her breathe a little easier? I thought maybe tubes can be inserted.

### Dr. Nichol:

This kitty has stenotic nares; it's as though her nose is being pinched. Persian cats have pushed-in faces that, in some cases, make the sides of the nostrils cave-in on themselves. You are right about it being difficult for her to breathe. It's especially tough for her when she runs, because the faster she tries to get air into her lungs, the more those nostrils collapse. If she needed to move really fast, being unable to get enough air could cause her to panic. She needs help.

The good news is that there's a pretty simple fix. A wedge-shaped piece of tissue from the side of each nostril can be surgically removed. Stitching the edges of the nostril across the gap created by the missing wedge will allow those nostrils to permanently stay open big enough for her to breathe normally. But while it's a basically straightforward procedure, not every veterinarian will want to handle it. Those of us who have helped brachycephalic (pushed-in faced) dogs like Pugs and Pekingnese could do an artful job. Cats, in general, are known for their vanity. But Persian cats, well, they're like royalty. For her it better be a purrrfect nose job. But tubes? No way. Only punk cats have tubes in their noses.

## Heart Disease

*Cardiomyopathy can cause blood clots. Severe pain and paralysis can be debilitating.*

### Question:

My cat has just had his second thromboembolism. My vet has treated him with heparin. Does he need anything else?

### Dr. Nichol:

This is a tough problem. The blood clots in your cat are caused by a heart disease called cardiomyopathy. It is a severely debilitating condition of the heart muscle. Sludging of the blood in the left atrium of the heart leads to clots that can stop blood flow—most often to the rear legs. It's extremely painful.

Depending on your cat's ECG, cardiac drugs may be needed. Anticoagulant "blood-thinners" like heparin and Warfarin are often helpful. But these are risky. Warfarin is the active ingredient in rodent poisons. It must be dosed and monitored carefully. Aspirin, on the other hand, may be sufficient—and it's much safer.

Your cat's doctor may also prescribe blood pressure medication. These are hard cases. The long-term prognosis for your kitty is not great. Enjoy every day with this boy.

## Coughing Cats

*Asthma is common in cats, but it's not the only cause of coughing.*

### Question:

Hunter is my 6-year-old kitty and she's been coughing lately. I take really good care of her and she stays inside all of the time. She eats fine and plays. Could Hunter have asthma?

### Dr. Nichol:

Yes, she could, but it's not the only possibility. I know I'm starting to sound like a broken record, but before you assume anything, get Hunter thoroughly checked out. Other causes could include pneumonia, F.I.P., heart failure, heartworm infection, or even foreign materiel in her airways or lungs. A clear diagnosis is needed.

I would start with a good exam. Of course the most important part of it is listening to Hunter's chest. What kind of lung sounds does she have? Is there a nice quiet movement of air or harsh dry sounds, wet sounds, or noise on only one side? What about a heart murmur? Armed with these answers, we will take chest X-rays next. Lung tissues can have many different appearances on X-ray. Asthma cases look pretty typical. With asthma, we expect only slightly dry sounds with the chest X-rays confirming our suspicion.

Can we help Hunter feel better and stop coughing? Feline asthma usually responds well to treatment. There are a few medications that work well in individual kitties, so we can do what we call therapeutic trials to see what will help. Many cats do best on prednisone, a corticosteroid. Not only is it reliable but cats handle it safely long term. Most important, *no smoking*.

# INTESTINAL AND STOMACH PROBLEMS

## Vomiting

*Never considered normal, it occurs more often over time. Early diagnosis and treatment prevent bigger trouble later.*

### QUESTION:

Our 14-year-old male cat seems to be in good health and has a good appetite, but vomits almost daily. I changed his diet to Science Diet Hairball Control for Adult Cats. I took him off wet food. That has not stopped the problem.

### DR. NICHOL:

This is miserable for your boy. Every time he vomits, stomach acid is forced into his lower esophagus, causing weight loss and more pain for this poor little guy. Over time his chronic vomiting will occur with increasing frequency. By the time it's happening daily, we know there's more to it than just hairballs.

So, let's get started on finding the cause. Following a thorough physical exam, he needs a complete blood, stool, and urine workup plus abdominal X-rays to check for problems like kidney, thyroid, and liver diseases as well as some cancers. If he clears these hurdles, we're going to need information taken directly from the site of his vomiting: the inner walls of the stomach and small intestine.

Surgery? Naw, we're much too high tech for that. Using a long snake-like instrument called an endoscope, we can see the interior of his esophagus, stomach, and upper intestines. More important, we can take a dozen or more tiny scrapes of tissue for biopsy while we're in there.

Should vomiting be this complicated? Your cat's body is sending strong signals that there are serious problems. This little guy feels rotten. Diet changes won't do the job. But I can tell you that most persistently puking pussycats are manageable with medications for problems ranging from parasites and chronic inflammatory disorders to intestinal malignancies. But the longer you delay, the more deeply entrenched his problems will be. Get going now.

## Tapeworms

*Simple to kill, tapeworms are carried by fleas or rodents. Fleas are much worse than tapeworms. Declare war on fleas. Careful with the chinchilla.*

### QUESTION:

I was recently adopted by a young, female, seal-point Siamese who has tapeworms. I understand that tapeworms come from fleas. I didn't see any fleas on her. Now that I have given her the medication, how long should I expect it to take for the worms to go away? Are they contagious to other animals or even humans? I also have a chinchilla, which I am worried about getting the worms, since my cat likes to antagonize the chinchilla by sticking her paws and tail in the cage. Are there any other things I should do to insure the demise of these creatures?

### DR. NICHOL:

Tapeworms are pretty creepy, aren't they? Let's start with a few fun facts. Tapeworms are made up of a series of segments that are each nearly complete parasites unto themselves. As the segments mature in the intestine, they fall off and show up on the fur around the rear end of the pet or in the stool. The segments contain eggs. But tapeworms cannot be passed directly from one critter to another by simply being swallowed. An intermediate host is needed. This creature eats the eggs and allows the development of a larva inside its body. When the real victim eats this middleman, she gets the worms themselves.

So the plot thickens. We have two types of tapeworms in our part of the world. One has the flea as its intermediate host and the other requires the services of rodents like mice. If your cat or dog has fleas, he or she can get tapes. If you have a rodent eater, it can happen. Now the truth about tapeworms themselves: They are worth killing, but they don't do much harm. They are not responsible for weight loss except in huge numbers. What's more important is the intermediate hosts. If it's rodents, toss a biscuit to that hunter or huntress and say "good job." But if your pet has fleas, you'd better declare war. Fleas are much more than a cause for itching. They can carry other serious diseases like plague. Don't take the cheap route and buy flea stuff off the shelf. See your veterinarian for the heavy artillery and win. Lastly, the tapeworm treatment: Droncit. It's a great drug. It does the job with only one dose. The chinchilla: Careful there. Your cat is doing more than playing. She's rodent hunting.

# Eating Cat Litter Can Cause Intestinal Blockage

*Avoid clumping litter for these cats. Pelleted newspaper litter is much safer if eaten.*

## QUESTION:

I hope you can help. My 4-year-old tabby is in the hospital for eating kitty litter. He got several blockages in his intestines. My question is, how do I keep him from doing it again?

## DR. NICHOL:

This must be really hard for you. It's unpleasant for your cat to have surgery to remove this stuff. As much as we love our pets and care for them, it's too bad we can't teach them good sense. I've heard pet owners ask if a disaster like this will be a lesson, but our pets just don't make the connection.

In trying to prevent a recurrence, it would be useful to understand why your cat would eat litter in the first place. Could his diet be lacking? Is he getting enough to eat? Is he bored? The likely answer is boredom. In addition, it's possible that he has developed a compulsive habit of eating the stuff.

Here is my advice: Set up a permanent hobby or healthy athletic activity for this guy. Try any of these ideas or a combination of them. Buy a tall scratching post with two or three carpeted little houses. You can add a few feathers-on-a-stick toys to it for him to bat at. Consider getting another cat as a playmate. Even a fish tank could work in that it would keep him occupied. These diversions will help but I wouldn't stop there. Just in case this fellow thinks your brand of litter tastes yummy, change brands. Not being a connoisseur of cat litter myself, I can't say which brand tastes the worst, but there is one that won't clump together and block his intestines. It's called Yesterday's News because, you guessed it, it's recycled newspaper. We use it at our animal hospital. It's pelleted, but it softens up when it's wet. We've had no odor problems with it.

The specific type of litter to be avoided is clumping litter. While there has been no definitive study, there is anecdotal evidence that litters that stick together when wet in the pan do the same thing when they reach the fluid in the stomach and intestines—and it's normally plenty wet in there. Since the best prevention of urinary disease in cats includes access to fresh unused litter, I always recommend cheaper throw-away litters anyway. A small amount in each of several pans around the house makes it easy for a cat to urinate often and avoid bladder problems. Pelleted newspaper absorbs well and falls apart when wet.

Sorry your boy had to undergo surgery to survive his dietary indiscretion. But know that by bringing this issue to other cat lovers, you have helped keep other kitties off the surgery table. Thanks.

## Diarrhea in Kittens

*Parasites and diet are major factors. Get a stool exam, feed an excellent kitten food, and prevent dehydration.*

### QUESTION:

I rescued two abandoned kittens at my workplace one week ago. They are approximately 5 weeks old. One of them has bad diarrhea. I'm feeding them kitten biscuits, kitten tin food, and weetbix mushed up with milk. What should I do about the diarrhea? Should I take her off wet foods and only give her water and kitten biscuits?

### DR. NICHOL:

You are smart to be concerned. Diarrhea should never be considered acceptable, especially in youngsters. Severe dehydration could be just around the corner. Kittens can die quickly.

The best diet for babies this size is a high-quality, moistened dry cat or kitten food. There is no need to add canned food, milk, or anything else for variety. The better diets are both complete and balanced. This means that if you add to it, you will throw it out of balance. Your well-intentioned attempt to improve on a good diet has actually reduced its value. So, in answer to your question, the diet may be a factor in the diarrhea. But there may be an even more important cause: parasites.

Take a fresh stool sample to the nearest veterinarian. Do not pass "Go." Do not collect $200. A microscopic exam will show any parasite eggs. The correct medications can be started right away and the diarrhea should resolve within one or two days. In the meantime, provide plenty of fresh water and coax a teaspoonful of Gatorade into this baby every few hours to avoid electrolyte depletion. If she stops eating or acts weak, get emergency help.

You have done a very fine thing to help these homeless babies. Once the diarrhea is under control and they are on a steady diet, you can assume them to be free of physical stress. Start vaccinations when they are well. A good age for the first in the distemper–upper respiratory series is 6 to 8 weeks. They will need a booster three weeks later; another, three weeks after that. Rabies vaccine can be given with the last booster. Thanks for caring. You are a gentle soul.

## Vomiting and Poor Appetite in an Overweight Cat

*Fatty liver disease occurs in fat cats. Any stress that makes them stop eating can throw a kitty into liver failure.*

### QUESTION:

I have an 11-year-old cat named Frank who recently started to vomit. He quit eating, too. He's always been kind of pudgy, but his doctor told me that being overweight may have caused him to get a sick liver. He's not doing very well. Can you help?

### DR. NICHOL:

What you are describing in Frank is called feline hepatic lipidosis—or fatty liver disease. It's a real serious problem and Frank needs to start taking in food soon or he may die from this. I will explain.

Hepatic lipidosis, while not only seen in fat cats, is more common in cases of obesity. Often the problem starts with some minor cause of loss of appetite. But soon the body starts to shift its fat stores, the cat loses weight, and begins to vomit. The end result can be failure of Frank's liver and death.

To get a handle on this problem, Frank's doctor will need to follow blood tests with a biopsy of his liver. This is done with a high-safety general anesthetic allowing the doctor to take a small scrap of liver tissue for microscopic examination by a pathologist. Knowing that it is truly hepatic lipidosis allows the doctor to give the right medication. But the most important treatment for Frank will be implanting a tube into his stomach so that a liquid diet can be given three times per day for several weeks. This is done either through the nostril or through the body wall using an endoscope (called a P.E.G. tube). Even if Frank is still overweight, he must take in nutrition or his liver will fail and you will lose him. Fortunately, these cases often do well if they are treated early. Prevention is the best medicine: Never allow a pet to become overweight. Any pet with a weight problem needs a veterinarian's advice on safe methods of managing it.

## Cats Who Play with String—High-Risk Behavior

*Yarn, string, fish line can move through the intestines lengthwise. Multiple saw holes result. String and yarn can kill.*

### QUESTION:

Last week I was playing with our cat Flossy. I was having her chase a length of yarn. Well, when I was looking the other way, she up and swallowed the yarn—about 18 inches of it. I brought her to the veterinarian and they tried to get her to vomit, but she wouldn't. Finally, they took the yarn out of her stomach with an endoscope. Why was it so important? Couldn't she have just passed it in her stool?

### DR. NICHOL:

Maybe that would have happened. But what also can happen is that the yarn can move into the intestine lengthwise. As the peristaltic (milking) movements of the intestine try to move it along like food, the yarn can start to saw holes in the intestinal wall. These holes leak bacteria and fluid, causing septic peritonitis which can quickly lead to death.

Swallowing yarn or string sounds innocent, but often it is not. Flossy's doctor acted quickly. The endoscope was a great choice of instruments. It saved Flossy from having to undergo surgery. It is quick and risk free. Good doctor.

## Feline Distemper

*The hallmark signs are vomiting and diarrhea. It's highly infectious and deadly. But vaccination is safe and effective.*

### QUESTION:

Four months ago we had a young cat who started vomiting and having diarrhea. We took him to the doctor. He was hospitalized and treated. We know that everything possible was done for him, but we lost him. It broke our hearts. The doctor said that little Homer had feline distemper. We kept meaning to get him vaccinated, but never got around to it. We're finally ready to try again to get a new cat. Is our home safe for a baby kitten?

## Dr. Nichol:

It is difficult to lose a young kitten like Homer. Kittens are so full of life's energy. We bond so strongly to them. I know you don't want to go through that again.

Feline distemper's real name is infectious feline panleukopenia. It is caused by a virus in the parvo virus family. This organism is closely related to the parvo virus that causes such horrible disease in unvaccinated dogs. In fact it is likely that the virus that infects dogs was actually a mutation from the feline panleukopenia virus. While vaccination in cats is effective at prevention, it must be given in a series of two to three injections *before* your new kitten is exposed.

Your home is safe for a new kitten if you have properly disinfected it since the loss of Homer. The virus can be a resistant organism, so I recommend the following: Mix Clorox bleach and water in a dilution of 1 part Clorox to 30 parts water. Wash all areas that Homer was exposed to—most important, food and water bowls as well as his litter pan. Anyplace where vomit or diarrhea occurred needs special attention. Next, take the new kitten to the doctor for a thorough physical exam *before* you take him or her home for the first time. Be sure the new baby is healthy and be sure that the first vaccination is given. Follow through on the series and I think everyone will be fine. Vaccination, by the way, needs to be started at age 6 to 8 weeks.

## Constipation in Kittens

*Know what to do and when. Also see Constipation in part 4's Emergency Home Care.*

### Question:

My son found a 6-week-old kitten. She has a healthy appetite, she drinks a few ounces of kitten milk a day, but she is constipated—she only moved her bowels three days ago. We tried to stimulate her anus with a wet tissue, but she still doesn't go. Please tell us what to do. Thanks.

### Dr. Nichol:

What I'm about to tell you is something that gives most folks that pinched expression that tells me they want our staff to handle the chore for them: She needs an enema. Eeeeewwww!

If you're tough, you can easily do it at home. First, go to your local veterinary hospital and ask for a stool-softening enema containing dioctyl sodium succinate (DSS). They are simple to use. They come packaged in a soft, pliable plastic syringe. Just spread Vaseline generously on the nozzle and insert it into the kitten's rectum, then push the plunger. Do not stand directly behind the kitten as you do this. Put her in her litter pan right away and stand back. That's all there is to it. You are now an expert. Or maybe you're not. If not, take the kitten to the hospital and return in a couple of hours. Just don't brag about this to your friends. (*Caution:* Do not use phosphate enemas on cats—they will kill.)

## Constipation in Adult Cats

***Many older cats have recurring problems. Here are some short-term and some long-term solutions.***

### QUESTION:

I'm worried about my cat Scratchy. Lately he's been going back and forth to the litter box a lot. Sometimes he cries when he's in there. I've looked to see what he's done and I can tell that he's making a good amount of urine but I haven't seen any bowel movement for a while. He's not eating very well either. What should I do?

### DR. NICHOL:

I'm glad that you are concerned enough about Scratchy to check his litter pan so carefully. While most of us pet owners have a pretty good idea of how well our critters are eating, it makes a lot of sense to be aware of their stool and urine, too. Since our pets can't talk to let us know if they are feeling sick, we must be observant.

Scratchy is a constipated kitty. It may be an advanced problem for his appetite to be affected. If he has hard stool that has backed up through his entire colon (large intestine), he may need the help of his doctor. But you can try to manage it for him on your own—just don't let it get to the point where he completely stops eating.

For home management, you will need to administer enemas. That's right, this is rear-end stuff and I meant it when I said more than one enema. You can use the old-fashioned enema bag with soapy water, but unless your cat has nerves of steel, you are both likely to get very wet—or worse. Instead, get a syringe-type disposable enema with a liquid stool softener called dioctyl sodium succinate (DSS). To give the enema, have a willing assistant hold Scratchy on a table with one hand on each of his shoulders. It'll work best if your helper pushes down gently on his shoulders so that Scratchy is lying on his chest. Your job is to lubricate the nozzle of the enema, grasp Scratchy's tail at the base, and hold it straight up. Then slide the end of the enema into his rectum—all the way to the wide portion of the syringe. (If you don't get the liquid DSS as far into the cat's rectum as possible, you won't do much good.) Then depress the plunger on the syringe and let go of one very surprised cat. (Do you still want to try this at home?)

How well will this work? Depending on how much hard stool there is, it may need to be repeated several times per day over three to four days. On the other hand, if the constipation is not severe, only one or two enemas may be enough.

As much as relieving a cat's constipation is really pretty straightforward, the bigger issue is avoiding a repeat performance. Some causes include diet changes, hair swallowed from grooming, chronic intestinal disorders, and old age. Here, too, you can try prevention at home. Oral lubricants like Laxatone or Petromalt are good, but messy. You can try adding Metamucil to his food, but many cats would rather file their knuckles with a cheese grater than eat Metamucil. Instead, what works well for many cats is mixing one tablespoon of Libby's canned pumpkin with the food. You only need to do this once daily. It works because the amount of fiber is just about right for many cats. Other brands of canned pumpkin don't work. If none of this prevents constipation, better appeal to the court of last resort—your veterinarian. In some cases, special high-fiber diets work while other cats need in-depth diagnostic work like endoscopic biopsies. Be sure you take a constipated cat seriously—he could die.

Just a couple more points. *Never* use a Fleet or other type of phosphate enema on a cat. Because these can upset the electrolyte balance in cats, they can actually kill a cat. (They are OK for big dogs and humans.) Oh, and don't stand directly behind Scratchy while you give him the enema. You could learn a whole new meaning of graffiti art.

Long term: The truth is that many older cats will continue to have worsening problems with constipation. A surgery called a subtotal colectomy can permanently eliminate the problem. While there is some infection risk postoperatively, the great majority of these old-timers walk away from all that straining and never look back. If your cat has had more than a few bouts of serious constipation, talk to your veterinarian about the procedure. If he or she is not qualified to perform the operation, ask for a specialist referral.

## Hookworms

*A nasty parasite, they can also infect humans.*

### QUESTION:

What causes hookworms and what are the symptoms? Can my kitten be reinfested with them? (She is strictly an indoor cat.)

### DR. NICHOL:

Hookworms are passed between cats and dogs by microscopic eggs and through the skin. They bite into the inside wall of the intestine and suck blood. They cause weight loss, diarrhea, and anemia. If you fail to dump out your cat's litter pan after every use, your girl can become reinfected as you give her the medication to eliminate those worms. The good news is that your veterinarian can make short work of them.

Human infection: More folks are getting roundworms and hookworms from their pets. These parasites are the greatest risk to first-trimester unborn children, diabetics, the elderly, cancer patients, and those with HIV. To prevent risk to humans, every pet should have an annual stool exam.

## Intestinal Parasites Can Put Your Cat at Risk—and You, Too

*Have a stool check done for the kitty's health. Have a new kitten wormed for yours.*

### QUESTION:

We got a new cat last week and took him to the vet for his first shots. After the doctor gave him the shot, he said that we need to bring in a stool sample to check Teka for worms. He also said Teka needs to be wormed anyway even if they don't find worms in his stool. Why not just worm the darn cat in the first place and forget the stool sample?

### DR. NICHOL:

That piece of advice is really more about you and your family than about Teka. First, though, let's talk about Teka and his health.

There are about a half dozen different internal parasites that can infect pet cats in the United States. Some parasites are more dangerous than others, but any of them can cause weight loss, diarrhea, poor haircoat, and sometimes death. For the most part, each parasite requires a different medication to safely eliminate it from the cat's body. A fresh stool sample is important because it is examined under the microscope for parasite eggs. Since the eggs have a distinctive appearance, we can identify the type of parasite when we find eggs in the stool. Then we send home the right medication, get rid of the little creeps, and we all live happily ever after.

So, if it's that easy, why do we also give a wormer? That's the part that's for you. (No, you don't take the wormer.) It turns out that two of these parasites, roundworms and hookworms, are transmissible to people. An otherwise healthy adult would have little problem, but babies can suffer damage to their livers, brains, or eyes. But while stool exams are important, no lab test is 100-percent accurate. In fact, it is not rare for a pet with a belly full of worms to have a day when no worms lay eggs, thus showing us no evidence of the worms in the stool.

All of that being true, the experts in infectious disease have issued this advice. For the health of the pet, check a stool sample and treat for any parasites found. For the health of the family, make sure there is no risk of roundworm or hookworm infection by using a wormer that is effective against both.

Fortunately, we have one. It's cheap, totally effective, and even tastes good. (No, I haven't tried it—but I don't get any complaints either.) It does need to be repeated in three weeks, but so does Teka's vaccination. Its name is Strongid. Ask for it.

# Joints and Bones

## Loss of Use of Rear Legs

*Severe heart disease in cats can send blood clots to the arteries of the rear legs. A problem of sudden onset, it is painful. Have a full diagnostic workup done ASAP.*

### QUESTION:

My cat Button has twice lost use of her hind legs. My vet had suspected something parasitic going on, inflaming the disk space, and Button has now tested positive for heartworm exposure. She was not tested for this during last year's episode, as it is uncommon in this area. My vet says there are no approved methods of treating heartworm, and this is a very uncommon attack. I figure someone somewhere is working on this, and an unapproved treatment is better than none when death is the alternative. Button is only 3.

### DR. NICHOL:

This is upsetting. There is no "approved" treatment for heartworms in cats but there are effective ways of managing most cases. My greater concern for Button is that her symptoms are not suggestive of heartworm disease because she does not have the typical signs of coughing, vomiting, and shortness of breath. Instead, her history is more consistent with a heart disease called cardiomyopathy. This can cause blood clots to the rear legs that may improve over time, only to repeat later. Cats with cardiomyopathy often drag their rear legs and cry out in pain. It's a terrible disease, but it's manageable in many cases.

The heartworm-positive test means that Button was exposed. To know more about this possibility as well as cardiomyopathy, have her chest X-rayed. In addition, a special ultrasound examination called an echocardiogram will determine not only which problem she has, but also help her doctor learn how best to treat it. I hope this helps.

# Amputation

## *When is it the right thing to do?*

### QUESTION:

Our cat is 5 years old and we love her a lot. Yesterday she was run over by a car and the veterinarian said that her leg is so badly mangled that there is no way to fix it so she can walk normal again. The doctor told us that it's best to amputate Freckles's leg. We don't want to do this because we feel this is cruel for Freckles to be handicapped this way. Would it be kinder to have her put to sleep?

### DR. NICHOL:

It is so upsetting to have a pet get so badly hurt. You want what is best for Freckles, but you want her pain to end. You can relax—the choice is much easier than you think.

Number one: With the exception of giant-breed dogs, almost all pets do just fine with three legs—especially cats. They simply shift some of their weight to each of the other legs. They develop their other muscles and learn to rebalance the load. But best of all, three-legged cats learn quickly to run, play, and climb trees.

Amputation sounds like an intensely stressful and painful operation for recovery. We give pain medication to our amputation cases, and they heal remarkably fast. They go home the day after surgery.

In terms of pluck and the resolve to play the hand they are dealt, pets—especially cats—can be an inspiration to us all. I say go for the amputation.

# Mouth Problems

## Bad Teeth in Cats
*Careful treatment and prevention at home. Better health and no mouth pain.*

### Question:
I just had my 6-year-old male cat, Sam, to the vet for a checkup. Two of Sam's small, lower teeth have cavities, and they'll probably break off. What can I do to improve Sam's dental health? I don't think he'd let me brush his teeth.

### Dr. Nichol:
I'm glad you're taking your cat's mouth seriously. My cat Raoul has a very nasty mouth, but in his case it's his rude comments more than anything else.

Start by having Sam's doctor clean his teeth and apply a fluoride treatment to harden the enamel. Teeth that are badly weakened or have exposed root canals may need extraction. On the other hand, they may be OK to be treated with tooth varnish or fillings. If he won't tolerate brushing, I would recommend feeding prescription diet t/d; your veterinarian has it. T/d is different because the teeth slice it when it's chewed unlike regular dry food, which shatters when a cat bites it. It'll slow down tartar buildup. Lastly, keep in mind Sam's vulnerability and have him examined every six months. To me, you sound like a cat's best friend.

## Age, Teeth, and Anesthetic Safety for Cats
*Special lab profiles just for cats can uncover most concerns.*

### Question:
At what age is it too old to allow my cat to have anesthesia? Our veterinarian is suggesting that we have Odie's teeth cleaned, but he's 14 now. I don't want to take a chance that Odie might not wake up.

### Dr. Nichol:
I am glad to get this question. I hear it a lot from concerned pet owners at our hospital. The answer is that anesthetic safety has no direct relation to the number of birthdays. Instead, anesthetic safety is influenced by the following factors: physical condition; the type of anesthetic used; and the experience, training, and care of the personnel who administer the anesthetic.

Here are the things you can do to make it safe for Odie: Insist that he have a thorough lab screening first. This should include a blood profile, blood count, and urinalysis as well as chest X-rays and ECG. Since many older cats have benign thyroid tumors, I advise a TT4 also. Assuming that Odie's lab work checks out fine, he should be a safe candidate for anesthesia as long as he is given a gas anesthetic accompanied by fluids IV.

Is it worth all that? As long as he is healthy and anesthesia is given safely, the answer is yes. If you neglect the need for dental cleaning, he'll pay much bigger later with infections, mouth pain, and maybe kidney trouble, too. Besides, I bet Odie doesn't think of 14 as "old."

## Anesthetic Safety for Dental Cleaning

*Oral health is too important to neglect. Lab profiles help make it safe.*

### QUESTION:

I have a 2-year-old cat, Livvy, who has never had her teeth cleaned. I have been told by my vet that this should be done annually, but I am terrified that Livvy will meet the same terrible fate as my friend's dog and my other friend's cat—they both died under anesthesia during dental cleaning. How necessary is it to give dental cleaning to a cat who eats dry food? Are there any checking questions I can ask of a vet to assure they are using the safest methods of anesthesiology?

### DR. NICHOL:

You are right about anesthesia. If not done with great caution, it is not worth the risk. Livvy is mighty important to you. It's your job to keep her safe. So, what's the big deal about dental cleaning? Cats and dogs can get chronic gingivitis just like us. Tartar buildup will force Livvy's gums away from her tooth roots. She can get infections, loose teeth, cavities, and pain when she tries to eat. Imagine pretty Livvy with no teeth: No prom date. Tragic. Dry food is excellent, but tartar will still accumulate—just more slowly. But without anesthesia for the cleaning, your veterinarian will need anesthesia for facial surgery. Wide-awake kitties get upset when alien instruments go buzz in the mouth.

Livvy needs a thorough physical exam, a preanesthetic lab profile, safe gas anesthesia with oxygen, cardiac monitoring, and, most of all, a well-trained staff to watch her like a hawk while she slumbers through her dental cleaning. At our place we do it right and the pets go home with a pretty smile.

# New Pets in the Home; Cats Who Leave Home

## Pets as Gifts

*It may be a great idea, but the surprise of a real live, long-term responsibility wears off fast. Talk about it first and be sure everyone's ready for the real investment of energy and expense.*

### Question:

My fiancee has said that she might want a pet and I'm running out of time to get her a birthday present. I really love her and I want to see that look of joy on her face when she opens the wriggling box. What kind of pet do you think I should get her?

### Dr. Nichol:

Boy, am I glad you asked this question. A major recent survey of pet owners showed that a full 75 percent of us regard our pets as children. Now that I have two human children, it's like having two more kids (or is that two more pets?). They touch your heart in the same way. The answer to your question is *do not make it a surprise*. Our emotional lives are complicated nowadays. If the object of your love gets a pet she is not ready to care for, she may keep the critter anyway because she won't want to hurt your feelings. But it takes time, commitment, and expense to manage pets properly (except maybe goldfish).

Here is what you do. Tell your heartthrob that you love her and that you want to share the joy and responsibility of raising a wild and crazy young dog or cat. (You can get her a gerbil or an iguana, but cats and dogs are easier to bond with because they have emotions that are much closer to ours.) Give her a chance to say, "Not now, later." If she decides to pass, don't feel rejected; instead, take it as a sign of her maturity and ability to know when to commit and when the time is not right. On the other hand, if she gushes with enthusiasm, read her Chapter 2, on selecting a pet that will end up as your firstborn (I hope).

Finally, I will tell you what you can do if you *really* want to share the commitment with your fiancee. Present your fiancee with a birthday gift certificate for the vaccination series and the spaying or neutering for your new pet. Now we're talking true love.

# Roaming

*Too many cats in a home may cause some the need to get more "space."*

### QUESTION:

Is this true that even if your female cat has been spayed, she still goes looking for a male? We have five cats and one of the females escapes. We live where coyotes come down off the mesa at night and hunt.

### DR. NICHOL:

I understand what a frustration this must be. I couldn't bear the thought of losing my cat to a coyote. But to understand why this is happening, we must recognize the realities of who our cats really are. A spayed cat has no drive to mate. Your girl is no floozy. She comes from a good family, darn it. But there are two reasons for her to look for adventure away from home. First, cats are natural hunters. Second, they are not really community creatures but loners. While some tolerate sorority life, this one needs "her space."

To stay inside, she must have her natural needs met at home. Provide her a tall indoor scratching post with little carpeted hideouts and dangling funky toys to stalk, maim, and disembowel. It may be necessary for her to live with no more than one other cat. If she can live what is "normal" for her indoors, she shouldn't need to prowl the streets and have anyone question her moral character.

# A Wild Cat Who Leaves Behind a Loving Home Life

*How can a well-loved house cat leave home—for good?*

### QUESTION:

I had a long-haired Calico who was with me for eight years. We moved to a new house and two days later she dashed outside and I never saw her until ten months later. I tried to capture her; I did manage to grab her once and I ran back to my house, but she scratched me and I dropped her and she ran away. She had never been an outside cat before. She's not hungry, but she just doesn't want to be with me. She doesn't want to come home. Is there anything I can do or is this just her choice? I am at such a loss.

**Dr. Nichol:**

This must tear your heart out. We invest heavily in the love of our cats, but we can easily forget that there are some huge species differences with them. While your cat loved you in your home, you saw only one side of her personality. Because cats are not truly community creatures like most other mammals, they can easily revert to a solitary free-living existence. The apparent sudden change is what's hard. Behaviorists have learned that cats mature "socially" around 2.5 to 4 years of age. For your cat, this maturation amounted to a need to live her other life as a loner. The move to your new house provided the right stress and opportunity. Your girl's "call of the wild" was not your fault. Keep the memories in your heart alive, but let her go.

## Choosing a Kitten? Be Careful When Considering a Manx

*These cute pets with funky tails can develop nerve damage.*

**Question:**

I just love Manx cats—especially the ones with no tail at all. I had one as a child and I would like to get another. Any advice?

**Dr. Nichol:**

I share your love of cats. I cannot imagine living without at least one in my life—and you're right about Manx cats. They usually have great personalities. But there is an important problem to bear in mind and that is the reason for their interesting tails.

The tails of animals are really an extension of their vertebral columns (the backbone). It starts just behind the skull and is made up of a series of bones that are mostly block-shaped with a tunnel through the middle for the spinal cord (the bundle of nerves that supplies different parts of the body). In Manx cats, the vertebrae are the normal block shape from the skull to near the rump. Then their shapes can get bizarre and irregular. This is why some Manx tails are different lengths—often kinky in shape. For most Manx cats, the abnormally shaped vertebrae cause no problems. But in some it can mean trouble.

If the odd-shaped vertebrae develop in the lower back instead of just in the tail, the nerves that branch off the spinal cord can become pinched as the kitten grows. If the nerves that supply the bladder are pinched, the kitten loses the ability to control its urine flow. The result is not only a mess, but urine that stays bottled up inside the bladder. This leads to infection and often kidney failure.

There is no way, when choosing a Manx kitten, to know if it will end up this way. You will need to either accept this gamble or choose another breed of kitten—or best of all, a mix.

## Death in a Family of Cats

*Do cats in group mourn the loss of one of their own? This is how the survivors react.*

### QUESTION:

I know this might sound juvenile, but when you have three cats like I do, if one dies, do the other cats know that one of them is gone? And if they do, how long does it usually take for them to adjust?

### DR. NICHOL:

I don't think your question is juvenile at all. While our pets are part of our families, they also have their own social structure. Your cats know when changes occur, but they respond differently because they are a different species.

When cats behave like a person, it's because they recognize the leader and they allow that individual (you) to set the tone. But among your household cats, one of them is dominant. That cat has a heavy influence on the behavior of the others. If that cat leaves the group, you may see one of the others become much more assertive—maybe acting in new ways. It's also possible that with the loss of one kitty, there may be no changes.

How could that be if the hierarchy is upset? Most animal species, including humans, are highly social, meaning that removal of one member results in someone else filling the void. But cats are not really very socialized. They are loners by nature. In fact, a whole bunch of cats in one home may cause stress that can be manifest as physical disease. So the death of one of your cats may have no effect or it may bring out the "true" personality of one or more of the others. One thing that's unlikely is that the others would mourn the loss. Cats are not usually into weddings, birthdays, and funerals. There are never wakes but the political deck does sometimes get reshuffled.

## "Found" Cats May Really Be Beloved Pets
*Watch the paper, post signs, and have that cat scanned for a microchip.*

### QUESTION:

I've had my cat Pancho since he was a baby 12 years ago. He's been through a lot with me. Now I have small children who love him too. Even though he's a real independent cat, he likes to spend most of his time outside, he always comes home every day. But he disappeared three days ago. I'm real worried and my kids are waking up at night crying for Pancho. He never goes near the road. I've talked to most of our neighbors, but nobody has seen him for three days. They usually see him every day. What can I do?

### DR. NICHOL:

I know how worried you are. The same thing has happened to me and my cats. I know Pancho never intended to break your heart and sadden your children, but he is a cat. Needless to say, cats have minds of their own.

Statistics and experience show very clearly that outdoor cats are less likely to reach old age. The perils they face include altercations with dogs, automobiles, and other cats. All that catting around puts them at greater risk of infectious disease, too. So, it makes a lot of sense to have only indoor cats—unless your cat will *not* stay in. Pancho sounds like a pretty street-smart cat. Surely he's learned to avoid dogs and cars by now. So, where is he? I will suggest an answer based on my years of experience of seeing "new" cats.

Here is how it goes. I walk into the exam room to see an adult cat brought in for its first visit to the doctor. The family is proud as punch of their new cat. I ask, "Where did you get this good-looking, well-cared-for healthy adult cat?" The answer comes back: "He just showed up" or "We found her on the road." Or the best one: "She followed the kids home from school." But the reality may be that this was not a stray cat at all, but someone else's beloved pet who also happens to be an adventurous opportunist.

Assuming for a moment that Pancho is enjoying the adulation of another family, it does not mean he loves you any less. It's just that most cats are perpetual teenagers. Thinking of it this way may cause you to resent folks who, in effect, steal pets. You're right. It is selfish. But the way the new family sees it is that they are saving the life of this homeless waif who would surely starve or be consumed by evil forces were it not for their generosity.

So here is my advice: Make some fliers for your neighbors. Include a picture. Point out that Pancho's children miss him. Also place a classified ad in the paper. Put his picture on milk cartons. Do whatever it takes to get the word out. As soon as he returns, be sure he has a tag with your name and phone number. And have a microchip implanted by your veterinarian (it takes a few seconds in the exam room) so that you can prove he is your cat.

To cat lovers who feel a duty to take in homeless pets: Consider the feelings of others. Any cat who seems remarkably tame for a stray may not really be stray. If you find a cat, show compassion for the cat *and* the heartsick family who doesn't know how to find their pet. Print fliers, place an ad, and take kitty to the Animal Humane folks to have him scanned for a microchip (this takes a second). For every pet who has gotten love, there is a person who has given love.

## A Strong Case Against Multiple Cats in the Household

*Having cats who get along well is a godsend. Gambling by adding more cats invites behavior problems in the group.*

### QUESTION:

We have two beautiful cats who are 2 years old. They are brother and sister indoor cats. The male is mellow, alert, and protective of both of us. He gets along very well with his sister. She does not like strangers. Quite the opposites, but both incredible cats! The question is: We would like to get another kitten, possibly two. What is your advice on this major decision? We do not want to disrupt the wonderful relationship we have with our animals, but would like to have more so they can have someone younger to be playful with and we would have younger ones when our original cats, unfortunately, pass away.

### DR. NICHOL:

I wish more people would seek out this type of counsel. You know how we are. If we get pets who turn out badly, we are still in love with them. In other words, you can get stuck in a bad situation.

First and most important: Cats are *not* community animals. Unlike people, dogs, birds, and livestock, cats are naturally loners. So when we put cats in groups, weird things can start to happen. Most often this amounts to urinations on beds or countertops, but can also include fighting and reclusive behavior. Some multiple-cat households develop group infections. The bottom line is that community life for cats is stressful.

But wait. There's more. Your cats are established in your household. Newcomers may never be accepted. Howling and caterwauling may ensue and destroy your happy home. You could tear out your hair. You could lose your mind. Or it could work out fine—but that is a major gamble. Remember what I have said before: We treat our pets as children because they are so much like us. We share so many emotions and feelings with them. But there are some essential and striking differences. Don't try to fool Mother Nature. What you have now is working. If it ain't broke, don't fix it.

# Odd Noises and Interesting Habits

## Hyperactive, Yowling Older Cat
*Hyperthyroidism can cause behavior changes. It can also be dangerous.*

### Question:
My 15-year-old, spayed female, Siamese-mix cat walks around the house yowling constantly. She sounds just like a cat in heat. She does it day and night. She is otherwise completely normal: eating, drinking the same amount of water, using the cat box, the way her fur looks, etc. It is getting on our nerves so badly that my husband is threatening to have her put to sleep. Any ideas on what might be causing this?

### Dr. Nichol:
I can appreciate why you need help. Without a solution to this yowling, you may want yourself put to sleep. There are a few plausible explanations for this behavior, but by far the most likely is hyperthyroidism. It's caused by benign tumors on the thyroid glands, which produce too much thyroid hormone. Aside from their bizarre behavior, these poor old cats often lose weight in the face of excessive appetites. Severe heart damage is also a common result of this disease.

The good news is that hyperthyroidism is quick and easy to diagnose with a blood test. Treatment is usually quite safe and effective. Call your veterinarian.

## Constantly Meowing Unspayed Cat
*She'll be in heat most of her life until she's spayed.*

### Question:
I have a cat who is not in heat who meows *constantly*. She is not deaf. This started about five months ago after her kittens were given away. The meows are deafening! It sounds as if she is in heat, but she is not (again, this has been going on for months). She does not seem to be in any pain as the meowing will subside for a few hours, then start up again. Any help would be appreciated for the cat's sake.

### Dr. Nichol:

It's good to know that your cat is not deaf, although with her constant meowing I bet you wish you were sometimes. Let's fix this not only for the cat's sake, but for yours, too.

The reason your cat is meowing constantly is because she is in heat—constantly. Cats are usually in heat or pregnant at all times. The reason is that unlike the rest of us mammals, daylight is a major influence on their reproductive cycles. Between March and October these girls are, well, waiting for gentlemen callers.

Won't she finally stop being so obnoxious and just cycle out of heat? Yes, but only when she is bred. Cats not only stay in heat during the warmer months; they stay that way until they find Mr. Right. (These are deeply meaningful relationships. but only for a few minutes.) At the time of breeding, they ovulate (release one egg for each kitten) and immediately go out of heat and shut up. Thus, almost every breeding with cats is a fertile one. They tend to have big families.

Your girl is talking about this all the time—not because she is in pain—but because she wants something done about her reproductive issues. What she is saying, in cat language, is "Have me spayed!" I know this. I'm a veterinarian and I talk to the animals.

## A Family Cat Has Started to Wage War on the Dog

*Look for changes in the dog's health that cause the cat's aggression.*

### Question:

My cat and dog were the best of friends and then all of a sudden they are fighting like cats and dogs! My dog starts screaming this high-pitched bark/scream every time I walk out of the room and leave her alone with the cat. Her private area is swollen and looks sort of blackish in color around the opening with some leakage that smells and keeps matting up her fur. I've never owned a female dog before and I'm clueless.

### Dr. Nichol:

Sounds like a pretty scary cat. The truth is that your kitty had grown accustomed to the normal smell of your dog and now look what's happened—he's living with an alien. The real issue is the health of your girl dog.

The list of causes for this discharge includes infections of the vagina, uterus, or bladder. Or she may simply be in heat. Occasionally a thick-coated dog like a Pomeranian can get an infection of the skin folds near the genitals. How do you figure out which of these maladies is besetting your dog and upsetting the delicate political balance in the animal kingdom you call home? As Dear Abby would say: Seek professional help. Take her to her veterinarian. She may need urine and blood tests as well as X-rays to learn the real cause. Treatment may range from antibiotics to an ovariohysterectomy to remove an infected uterus. If you wait, she could get very sick.

Now about that cat: He needs to learn to accept others as they are. Maybe he should get in touch with his female side. We'll work on him later.

## Nighttime Activity

*A yowling inside cat will keep you awake. There are ways to reset a cat's clock.*

### QUESTION:

About a month ago, our 6-year-old Birman male (neutered) started waking up in the middle of the night and wandering around the house yowling. I had his thyroid tested, and it was fine. I have also tried a program of keeping him awake during the day, but what an impossible task that is! Any suggestions?

### DR. NICHOL:

You sound tired. I bet the reason you're having trouble keeping this boy awake is that you keep falling asleep.

The trouble with this party animal is that he's an active indoor cat who's trying to get you to pay more attention to him. While you're gone during the day, he's sleeping soundly. Being a naturally nocturnal guy anyway, 2 A.M. seems perfect for some quality time together. If you chase him off when he yowls your name, well, you just rewarded his behavior by paying attention to him. If you feed him, he'll learn even faster to wake you even earlier. What he really needs is gainful employment. A few useful ideas include a large scratching post with enclosures, ramps, and tunnels. Add a couple of feathers-on-a-stick toys and a good time will be had by all. If he still craves attention during the wee hours, consider getting another cat as a playmate. If that doesn't feel right to you, an alternative would be to make him an indoor–outdoor cat. But if you go this way, be aware of the potential for disasters like auto injuries and fight wounds.

Last, if none of this works, you can give him the over-the-counter antihistamine chlorpheniramine (brand name Chlortrimeton). Two to four milligrams at bedtime with a late dinner and all could be peaceful—unless you start yowling around the house and pestering your poor Birman cat.

## Growling and Hissing at Neighbor Cats Through a Window

*Gradual introduction to another cat will help overcome fear of strange cats.*

### QUESTION:

We have a kitten who's about 5 months old and stays indoors. She is the only pet we have. Her only problem is that whenever another cat comes to the sliding glass door, our cat hisses and yowls and throws herself at the window. This wouldn't be so bad, but it always seems to happen at night when I'm trying to sleep. What can I do to make her stop this?

### DR. NICHOL:

With the help of folks like you who write in, we may be able to save a few lives. I'm serious. Behavior problems are the leading cause of death in pets because it is the biggest reason that pets are put up for adoption at animal shelters. Only 40 percent of dogs and 25 percent of cats in shelters find homes. The bottom line is that only one in three pets are in the same home two years after adoption. A great number die from euthanasia because their owners did not know how to live with them. If we can help fix a few behavior problems, we can make a dent in this tragedy. So keep the questions coming.

Understand first that the reason your cat does this is that she hasn't had enough exposure to other cats to feel comfortable when they visit. She feels threatened. Her aggressive behavior suggests that better social skills would help. Knowing this, one might assume that the more visits she gets from other cats, the more relaxed she will be. The opposite is true. So, handle this problem now and avoid worse trouble later.

To help your cat learn to play nice with her friends, we can use a behavior-modification technique called "flooding." Don't get her a boat. Instead, it means that we can introduce other cats to her gradually and nonthreateningly. The ultimate goal is for her to learn that she can be a cool kitty around other felines and not jar you from your sleep. The easiest way to do this will be to adopt a second cat (preferably a congenial kitten).

Start by keeping the new kitten in a separate room for a couple of weeks to allow him (or her) to adapt to your home. At the beginning, do not allow the two cats to see each other. When you are ready to start, give your cat her regular feeding, then sit at the other end of the room while gently holding the kitten. Your cat is sure to notice the other guy, but will continue eating. When your cat is just finishing her meal, sneak the kitten back into his private room and you are done with lesson number one. Easy, right? For your next trick, you will do the same thing, but you will sit or stand with the kitten a little closer while the grumpy one eats. You will do this at least a few times each day. Each time try to move a little closer. If the big girl starts to growl or hiss, you have moved the process along a little too fast; so you will need to back away a little. With me so far?

Things will go OK until old Sour Puss acts put out and just walks away from her dish. And this is good because now you can start to have a little fun. You will just whip out your feathers-on-a-stick toys (available at some veterinary clinics and pet supply stores) and start to entertain your cats by having them jump around and act goofy with their individual toys as you wave them one in each hand. This part of the process will take several sessions also because cats are, of course, resistant to change. Be sure to start out with the toys at the ends of your outstretched arms. As they begin to learn to play close to one another, you can move the toys closer together. Eventually, they may learn to share the same toy, fall in love, get married, have kittens of their own, contribute regularly to a 401(k) plan, and live happily ever after. Go ahead, admit it, you're getting a little teary-eyed, too.

What about other suggestions? Oh, they're much too easy. You could close the blinds so your cat can't see her visitors or put a Scat Mat in front of the window to discourage her from going near it. Things that don't work include spraying Cat-B-Gone or other repellents near the outside of the door. You could also develop your own neurotic habits, but you might end up at Animal Control yourself.

## An Outdoor Cat Who Moves Inside a Small Apartment

*Yowling, clawing, pacing, and generalized anxiety are common after a move to confined quarters. A snug den, fun indoor activities, and anti-anxiety medication should make the difference.*

## QUESTION:

My coworker recently moved to a small apartment where she has to keep her 5-year-old cat indoors. He used to be indoor–outdoor and is not happy. At night he wakes her with yowling, furniture-clawing, pacing, etc. She's getting pretty worn out after two weeks. I suggested she confine him in his carrier for short periods during her sleeping time when he goes nuts. The apartment will seem large compared to the carrier when he's out the rest of the day. Also, he can't scratch furniture when she can't squirt him. I figure he'll grow out of his anxiety if she does this. I told her to just quietly put him in the cage—no yelling, hitting, etc.

Do you think this will work for my friend's cat? I hate to see her get rid of this guy because he's making her life hell!

## Dr. Nichol:

Such strong language. You want to know hell, try answering tough questions like yours. And one more thing: Is this really about your friend's cat? Is this really your cat? Or maybe he's not a cat at all. Getting rid of a guy who's making your life hell. . . . Is this about your boyfriend? See my picture? Do I look like Dear Abby?

OK, let's assume this is about your friend's cat. This little fellow has just gone through a life-changing experience. He has moved to a new home with no outside. That's tough for cats. These guys don't like change. His yowling, pacing, and furniture clawing simply means he's scared and anxious. There are three things that will help him adjust. (If we're talking about your boyfriend, add a lobotomy to the list.)

For starters, remember that cats are instinctively den animals. They naturally find comfort and security in a snug enclosure. Using a carrier (not too small, please) or a heavy plastic airline crate may give this boy the security he needs. She can make it comfy with a nice thick pad, some food, water, and a few kitty toys. Will this be enough by itself? Maybe. For most cats it will help; a few may get even more anxious. Give it a try.

The second ingredient for kitty adjustment is short-term use of an anti-anxiety medication called Buspar. Cats do very well with this because it's gentle. It has no tranquilizing affect. After a few weeks he should be fine and will not end up at the Betty Ford Center. The third factor in the success of this adventure is time. Patience will pay off.

Now, back to your boyfriend: Do you really squirt him when he gets on the furniture? Yelling and hitting before putting him in his cage? Maybe you just need a support group.

## Inactive and Bored
*Adding a second cat could be a disaster.*

### QUESTION:
I have a 10-year-old female indoor cat who is largely inactive and possibly bored. Do you think it would be a good idea to get her a cat companion? It's been just the two of us living together for over nine years. Would she welcome or resent another feline? She refuses to say!

### DR. NICHOL:
This must be lonely-hearts day for pets. I don't want to sound like a broken record (nor a geezer for using that expression) but no, don't get another cat as a companion for your older cat. Only do it if you want one for yourself.

May I repeat my mantra? We are highly bonded to our pets because we share so many emotions—but they are different in some important ways, too. Cats, in particular, are not community creatures. Unlike people, they are meant to be solitary. If your girl cat were still a kid, she could learn to accept another kitty. But cats are conservative, and as they age, they just become even more stodgy. Be warned. If you get another cat, she'll hate his guts.

## Licking People
*Yucky. Is it normal? Why do some cats do this?*

### QUESTION:
Over the last couple of years my 14-year-old cat, Pita, has developed the habit of licking me on the hands, arms, and face as if bathing me. She also does this with cotton T-shirts I have worn. I have been wondering if there may be something lacking in her diet, or that she's getting senile.

### DR. NICHOL:
I bet that rough tongue drives you crazy. Is the name Pita code for sandpaper mouth? Poor Pita may have been weaned too young and thus never matured out of the normal kitten behavior of mutual grooming and sucking. An easy experiment would be to give her a rawhide chew or a bone with a bit of meat still attached. If she relishes the experience and stops

treating you like a Popsicle, your problem is solved. But I'm concerned that for Pita, there may be more to the story.

Behavior changes in older cats are often due to a problem called hyperthyroidism. The benign thyroid tumors that cause these excessive hormone levels are found in as many as 30 percent of cats over age 10. High thyroid levels can also cause serious heart disease and weight loss. A simple blood test will make the diagnosis. If Pita has hyperthyroidism, she's likely to do just fine with medication or surgical management.

What if Pita is physically normal? She may have a form of obsessive-compulsive disorder (OCD). One of several medications may be useful in turning off the abnormal chemical balance in her brain. Regardless of its cause, Pita isn't licking you to ingest missing nutrients. The human body is not a normal food group for cats.

## A Dental Problem—or a Need to Roam?

*A two-pronged analysis of a male cat's meowing.*

### QUESTION:

I have a 5-year-old neutered male cat. At a checkup at the doctor's office in October they told me he has two teeth that should be removed. My concern is that he meows constantly in the evening and frequently in the early mornings. I live in a small studio apartment. When I take him out on the balcony, he stops meowing. He is driving me nuts. Can I make him stop this?

### DR. NICHOL:

It's real easy to see how your kitty's complaining could make you crazy. Maybe you need family therapy. Just kidding. I have two recommendations.

First: Those teeth. I applaud you for getting him examined recently. Most pet owners recognize the value of annual vaccinations, but few understand that frequent checkups are even more important. Our pets age much faster than we do. By watching carefully we can diagnose problems sooner and keep our pets healthier and living longer. If your boy has infections and tooth pain, he has plenty of reason for his misery. Start by having that dental procedure done for him. Relieving his pain could make all the difference in his grousing.

If he is still a chatterbox after his smile is fixed, he may simply need broader horizons. While some cats are content with life inside a small home, others require outside time. Cats are normally more active at night, but as we approach springtime, the increasing amount of daylight is another factor that could make a guy more active and want to be a part of that big world out there. For safety, add chicken wire to the balcony rail so he can't jump off. Plan his outside time each evening so that he can rely on his social hour. Mix him a drink and, hey, have one yourself, too, and join him on the balcony.

## Cats Who Cover Their Food
*Feline instincts influence protection of food resources.*

### QUESTION:
How can I get my cat to stop dragging rugs to cover the cat food dish? Is he hiding it from the other two cats to eat later?

### DR. NICHOL:
Yes. Cats are loaded with instincts from their wild heritage. How could this be, you ask, given that they are the oldest domesticated pet? We don't know. Despite thousands of years of living with humans, cats seem unchanged from historical reports of the ancient Egyptians. They don't really live with us anyway. We live with them.

## Anxious Cat Prowls the House at Night—"Meeping" Keeps Family Awake, Causing "Insanity"
*A recent move to a new home upsets the routine for this frightened cat. Time and modern medicine will ease the transition.*

### QUESTION:
We have a neurotic cat. Turtle has always been a touch compulsive and she's very meek. Always the low cat on the totem pole. We have a total of three. The latest problem: We just moved into a new house, and she's driving us insane. The first few hours, she explored and seemed OK, and then she started hiding in crevices and wouldn't come out for hours. Every morning now, for four mornings, she has woken up at 4:30 and wandered through the house "meeping," as we call it. Constantly crying out with short meows. Nothing we do comforts her. Is there anything we can do to calm her down (not only to make her feel better, but so that we can sleep until it's actually time to get up)?

### Dr. Nichol:

I have known other meepers. While none of my behavior references list anything under "meep" or "meeping," this is a not-uncommon problem. What you have, of course, is a very anxious cat. Considering the conservative nature of most cats, it's never a surprise to hear about those who have difficulty with change.

In addition to having a hard time with an event such as moving to a new home, Turtle is easily frightened. This fear and anxiety are really just a function of her personality. Many cats are like that from birth and there is nothing you can do to make it better—except what you would do for anyone going through a difficult change. Be gentle and supportive—and give drugs.

Did I say drugs? If you want to improve everyone's quality of life in the short term, it's your only hope. You can just give Turtle's anxious meeping plenty of time, but you're getting sleepy. In time Turtle will finally adjust, but who knows how long it will take? In the interim I suggest Buspar. This is an anti-anxiety drug that works well in most cats. The usual dose is one 5-milligram tablet every 12 hours. Ask Turtle's doctor for a prescription. It should start to help in one to two weeks, maybe sooner. While it won't cure Turtle's anxiety, it will diminish it until she adjusts to this big change in her life. This will also help you folks sleep better. Don't you dare take it yourself.

Lastly, here is what will *not* work: Tranquilizers. While the most commonly used and safest tranquilizer in cats is acepromazine, it won't help Turtle. Using it will cause her to stagger through the house while she slurs her meeping. This will only serve to embarrass her in front of the other cats.

## Cats Who Hunt Compulsively

*Predators by nature, cats can sadden their loving owners with the corpses they deliver to the door. An Ultrasonic Mouser can keep the mice at bay and prevent their demise at the paws of a pet cat.*

### Question:

Miss Kitty is really a mister, but since I wanted a loving, cuddly cat, I named her Miss Kitty. She adopted us about 5 years ago, and I would guess her age to be 5 to 7 years. She is a nocturnal creature during the warm weather, and is constantly bringing home "presents" of birds, mice, rabbits, etc. Is there any way, short of confining her, to make her stop the hunting?

### Dr. Nichol:

Perception is reality, isn't it? To you, Miss Kitty is loving and cuddly. The birds, mice, and rabbits would describe her differently. The bottom line, of course, is that Miss Kitty is a normal cat. It bears repeating that we bond to our pets because of the common emotional ground we share. They have feelings and needs just like we do. We are so bonded, in fact, that we can forget that cats are very different in some ways. Even though you give Miss Kitty an abundance of good food, she still feels compelled to act out her predatory instincts. All the same, it always hurts my feelings when I see a wild creature injured or killed by a pet cat. So here is an alternative besides a bell on the collar or just keeping her inside. I was made aware of it by one of my readers from Santa Fe.

"Another device is my Haverhill mouser (1-800-797-7367). I do not sell these things but I was plagued (pardon the pun) with mice in the garage. I did not want to kill the mice, so I bought a Have a Heart trap. I was catching a mouse each night and could not find how they were getting in. I even painted a few on their bottoms so I could verify that they were not coming back. I installed the Haverhill ultrasound mouser and during over a month of operation I have caught only a single mouse so I am convinced that this thing works."

So there you go. There is no end to what a true animal lover will do. Just don't get caught painting the rear ends of field mice as you may get busted for some crime against nature. But you can tell me—your life with mice will be our little secret.

## Plant Eating

*There is no way to stop plant eating. Give the gift that keeps on giving: a Catnip Garden.*

### Question:

We have an 8-year-old purebred Manx who seems to really love to eat plants. It was always a problem for the geraniums in his grandma's house when he lived there (she's happy to actually have plants now, since he would eat them all), and now he goes completely crazy when my husband brings me flowers. It seems he loves the baby's breath and the ferns that accompany the roses. We've heard that there are plants that are actually okay for kitties to chew on. Could you recommend some that we could purchase and leave on the floor for him to nibble on? Or is there a change we should make in his diet to satisfy his craving?

### Dr. Nichol:

Aren't cats sneaky? Here your husband, new-age sensitive guy that he is, brings you flowers and your cat goes crazy. Maybe they were never your flowers in the first place.

Let's start with diet. It's not his diet. Cats aren't really vegetarians. There is nothing about house plants that he needs. But I do believe your cat is bored. To help him lead a more balanced life, I recommend a hobby. Go to your local pet supply store and purchase a Catnip Garden for $1.99. You grow the stuff yourself and your kitty can enjoy his own botanical delights, leaving you and your husband to share the ferns and baby's breath. Catnip is perfectly safe. In addition, you can provide other healthy activities such as a ceiling-height cat tree with carpeted little houses. Cats love to run up and down and play hide and seek in the enclosures.

Of course, there are alternatives to providing your cat with his own garden. In other words, something to bring out his gentler side—like rodent mauling. (Believe it or not a new kitten owner recently announced, with great pride, that she had purchased a pet for her new baby to keep him occupied. You'll never guess—a hamster. I suggested that the hamster may not fair well, but I was assured that the kitten is quite gentle and that the hamster is oblivious. Oh, brother.)

Now, back to boredom: If you leave out the catnip all the time, your cat will get bored with it. Instead, bring it out whenever you expect your husband to show up with a bouquet. This way your cat can go completely crazy over his catnip (something all cats do), leaving you to enjoy your roses in peace.

# POISONING

## Tylenol Poisoning

*Cats can die quickly from just one dose. Emergency medical attention is needed fast.*

### QUESTION:

My 2-year-old cat, Bebe, swallowed an Extra-strength Tylenol a couple days ago. I took him to a vet and he's currently undergoing treatment. The test results show no signs of kidney damage, but they say his liver has been damaged. Can he continue to live an otherwise normal life? Would it mean constant medication? If you could shed some light as to what's to come, I'd really appreciate it.

### DR. NICHOL:

You did the right thing in getting your cat to the doctor fast. It turns out that over-the-counter drugs are the fourth leading cause of poisoning in pets, with Tylenol (generic name: acetaminophen) topping the list. It's potentially deadly in cats and can be nearly as bad for dogs. The problem is that we get so connected with the feelings we share with our pets, we forget that there are some major physical differences.

As safe and useful as acetaminophen is for people, it is a horrible poison for cats. Even part of a tablet can kill. As soon as acetaminophen is absorbed into the bloodstream of a cat, it damages the red blood cells. About one to four hours later a poisoned cat will become physically depressed and breathe rapidly. This is usually followed by vomiting, drooling, and brown-purple gums. Often their faces and paws will swell. But that's only the beginning. Cats can't eliminate acetaminophen from their bodies the way we can. Instead, they release a toxic substance that damages their livers, lungs, and kidneys.

This is really horrible—and treatment, while sometimes successful, can be prolonged and expensive. The first priority is to rinse out the poisoned cat's stomach. A medication called acetylcysteine is given IV along with fluids and other supportive care. A few cats have full recoveries, but most need long-term treatment for liver fibrosis.

The future management of your cat will depend on the severity of his liver damage. A prescription diet plus daily medications and periodic lab tests could be necessary to keep him going. I wish the best for you and Bebe.

[**Note:** The above is the response I sent to this worried cat owner. But afterward I received an update saying that Bebe's health had turned for the worst and he passed away. By Saturday night, an X-ray showed that his liver had shrunk to one-third the normal size and X-ray images of his lungs were cloudy, probably due to fluid buildup. Though he was not expected to survive more than 36 hours, he fought on for six days. "I would appreciate it if you would use my question in your newspaper column," the owner wrote me. "I had no idea one little Tylenol tablet could be so harmful to a cat, and I'm sure a lot of pet owners out there don't know either." I told this man that I would do my part to alert caring cat owners. I ask everyone who reads this to spread the word!]

## Antifreeze Poisoning: A Risk for Outdoor Cats

*Malicious or accidental disasters: Cats who roam can break your heart. An Invisible Fence can keep them safe in your yard.*

### QUESTION:

Our cat Samson has been a healthy outside cat for a long time. Suddenly, about a week ago, he stopped eating and started to throw up. Since then he has begun to eat a little bit but he is drinking a lot more water than he ever has. Thinking back, the only thing different that happened was that he seemed to get sick right after we changed the antifreeze in the car. Can you tell us what's wrong with Samson?

### DR. NICHOL:

It sounds very much like Samson was poisoned by the antifreeze. Even though he has begun to eat again, he is still very sick. When you take him to his doctor, blood and urine tests will be done that are likely to confirm ethylene glycol toxicity (antifreeze poisoning). With this diagnosis Samson will be treated for kidney failure. This will involve several days of hospitalization for IV fluids and medications to prevent nausea and vomiting. If treatment is started quickly, Samson should improve, but he will always have kidneys that are prone to failure. Lifelong medications and a special diet will help him live as long as possible.

This is a very serious and common problem. In the fall many of us change the antifreeze in our cars. Even a small amount (two or three teaspoons for a cat; two or three tablespoons for a 50-pound dog) will kill. We see it a lot because of the sweet taste—these little guys will race for it and lap it up quickly. Within 20 to 30 minutes after being drunk, the ethylene glycol in the antifreeze forms crystals in the kidney tubules. Symptoms include trembling, vomiting, seizures, coma, and death. It is treatable, but because of the rapid action of this poison, we have to start fast—before symptoms appear, if possible.

Is it OK to just watch a pet who was seen drinking only a small amount—just to be sure that treatment is necessary? Unfortunately, this is not a good option. Even minute amounts of antifreeze will cause permanent kidney damage.

Bottom line: If you plan to change your own antifreeze, lock up your pets and thoroughly clean up any spills. Or better still, use Sierra-brand antifreeze. Sierra has propylene glycol instead of ethylene glycol. It is nontoxic as well as harmless to our environment. Regular antifreeze is unsafe on both counts.

## Beware of Mouse and Rat Poison

*D-Con and other rodent bait stops normal blood clotting. Death can occur quickly.*

### QUESTION:

I'm worried about my cat and I hope you can help me. He's a cat who goes outside a lot, but sleeps in the house at night. Yesterday he started acting kind of sluggish and today he has a lot of blood in the litter pan. So I looked in his mouth today and his gums look real pale—almost white. I call him Mouser because he catches lots of mice. What can I do for him?

### DR. NICHOL:

I share your concern for Mouser. I suspect that he may have been poisoned. He is in grave danger and he needs medical attention fast. The reason you need to move quickly is that he may be bleeding internally.

We know that Mouser catches a lot of mice. It is possible that you have a neighbor who uses a rodenticide (mouse and rat poison) to get rid of the mice on his property. These poisons kill rodents by damaging their normal blood-clotting mechanism. Every one of us (including critters) needs normal blood clotting because throughout our day we often bump ourselves without noticing it. Little blood vessels are damaged and we bleed internally very slightly. But because our blood clots normally, that little vessel stops leaking right away and we don't even get a bruise. But what happens when a mouse or cat or anyone can't clot normally? We just continue to leak blood—until we bleed to death.

Rodenticides are poisons that taste good to rats and mice—and to cats and dogs, too. You may have some of this stuff at home. D-Con is the most common brand. When the D-Con starts to act on the rodent's body, internal bleeding occurs and they get weak and easy for a cat like Mouser to catch and eat. In recent years this poison has been made far more potent. There is easily enough D-Con in the body of a dying mouse to kill a large dog. When a pet like Mouser eats a poisoned mouse, the poison is absorbed into the pet's body and begins to damage his blood-clotting mechanism, too. The result is a cat with internal bleeding. The tipoff in Mouser's case is the blood in the urine and the pale gums.

What can we do? First, we can check his blood. If he is severely anemic (low numbers of red blood cells), he will need a blood transfusion. Next, we will need to get his clotting factors functioning normally again. Fortunately, there is an antidote: vitamin K-1 injections (*not* vitamin K-3). Once he is stable, he can go home on an oral form of K-1 for three to six weeks. The tablets are expensive, but without them you will lose Mouser.

This problem is frightening. The moral of the story is: Don't use mouse and rat poison. Pets are too easily made accidental victims. If your cat is a mouser like Mouser, talk to your neighbors and ask them to avoid rodenticides. Offer to share your cat if you have to. Give your neighbors their own cat. Use a neutron bomb. Do anything. Just don't let anybody in your area use poison.

# SAFETY TIPS

## Garage Door Openers
*That "safe" door might not be.*

### LETTER:
I received this input from grieving cat lover, Tanya Gross: "I sure wish I'd asked about the safety of garage door openers before my cat, Big Louie, was fatally crushed by my 'safe' garage door. My new opener had sensor lights but they were set too high off the ground (at 8-1/2–10 inches). Louie limboed under the sensors as the door was moving downward. The back-up safety feature, auto reverse, was never adjusted, so the door came down with crushing force.

"The recommended setting for the sensor lights is 4 inches to protect pets. Folks who set sensors at bumper height could be inviting disaster for small children and pets. The auto reverse should be tested monthly using a board or a crushable cardboard box. For more information, you can call the Genie Company at 1-800-654-3643."

### DR. NICHOL:
Tanya, thanks for sharing this essential protective tip. I can speak for every one of our readers in sharing the pain of your loss of Big Louie. By spreading the word you may be saving the life of another pet or even a toddler.

## Cats and Clothes Dryers
*The warm enclosure invites cats. Inadvertently starting the machine leads to a terrifying death.*

### LETTER:
This letter is to warn other cat lovers. My 2-1/2-year-old cat, Katie, died in May 1996. She had always loved to lie on the clothes coming out of the dryer. I should have paid closer attention to her habit. One morning I was going to refluff the towels in the dryer. I shut the door and turned it on. I heard a thumping noise but rationalized it in my mind as wet towels. Twenty minutes later I found my precious baby—she was gone.

I have two cats now and Daisy has gotten into the dryer several times, but I was there and got her out. Check everything—the oven, the dishwasher, the washer, even the recliner and hide-a-bed. Cats find the most secluded and comfortable places to sleep. I'd hate for anyone to go through what I've gone through.

### Dr. Nichol:

You have endured a terrible loss. It's clear that you still feel the pain over the death of Katie. Know that her passing was not in vain. By making other cat lovers aware of the hazard of clothes dryers, you have prevented the loss of other beloved pets.

Fortunately some cats are discovered in the dryer in time. But the injuries can be tough to manage. Not only do they suffer from severe heat exhaustion, but multiple skin burns as well.

## Fanbelt Injuries

*Cats love a warm, cozy spot on cold winter nights. Horrible trauma occurs when the car is started.*

### Question:

Our neighbor's cat got stuck in the fanbelt of his car last week. How common is that? How do I make sure that doesn't happen to my cat?

### Dr. Nichol:

Great question. I'm delighted to hear you thinking about prevention. The truth is that automobile fans and fanbelts kill and maim many cats every fall and winter. It is tragic but preventable. It happens because it takes awhile for a car engine to completely cool down even on a cold night. Cats naturally love snug enclosures anyway. So if it's a warm and cozy spot, your kitty may find it downright inviting. Often a cat will spend a whole night snuggled up against an engine. Then, when you start the car the next morning, the cat is suddenly hit by the spinning blades of the fan or cut or burned by the friction of the fanbelt.

The injuries are frightening. These kitties sometimes don't survive. Those who do usually have wounds of the face and rear end that sometimes include broken bones. The best way to keep your cat safe is to either keep her indoors at night or scare her out from under the hood before turning the key. You can do this by thumping on the hood a couple of times or blowing the horn. When the weather gets warm again, you can stop worrying. Thanks for caring this much for your cat.

# Seizures

## Staggering, Rolling, and Yowling
*Vestibular disease is actually harmless. Affected cats recover.*

### Question:
Recently we had to bring our 10-year-old cat in for symptoms that later showed she had vestibular disease. Our veterinarian was unable to tell us very much about it, because there wasn't really that much information available. My family and I are just trying to understand better what's going on with our cat, and how long it lasts.

### Dr. Nichol:
This is a really scary problem when it suddenly appears. But the good news is that it should start to improve on its own in just three days. Cats with idiopathic vestibular disease (impressive name) are usually normal in two to three weeks. Treatment is seldom necessary.

So, what is this disease? There are things we know about it and things we don't know. We know it's caused by an abnormal flow of fluid in the part of the inner ear that controls the sense of balance. Cats with vestibular disease get disoriented, roll on the floor, howl and yowl, and get frightened when picked up. If they could talk, they would tell us how scared they are. We don't know what causes it. Those cats who recover from it are unlikely to get it again. It does not appear to be contagious.

But knowing that your kitty will be fine still isn't enough. She needs to feel better. We like to manage them at home unless they are too disoriented to eat or drink on their own. In those few cases IV fluids, sedation, and feeding tubes may be necessary for a day or two. Otherwise I prefer home care: a darkened, quiet room, and soothing music. Minimize the rap.

## Seizures and Circling
*Brain tumors in cats are usually treatable. Acting early can return an older kitty to her old self.*

### Question:
I am really worried about my cat. She's been sleepy and inactive for awhile. Lately she's walking like in a circle. She acts blind. She even had a fit. Our vet has

done tests and X-rays. The vet said she might have a brain tumor. She wants us to take her for a scan. It sounds horrible.

## Dr. Nichol:

You are right to be concerned, but your kitty may actually do quite well. My first advice is that you follow the doctor's recommendation. Take her to the neurologist (a specialist in diseases of the nervous system) for a CT scan of her skull. They will be looking for evidence of a brain tumor called a meningioma. If they find a mass on the outer surface of her brain, they will recommend surgery.

Is this risky? Believe it or not, in trained hands, it is not. In fact, cats respond very well to this surgery and are usually much better within a few days. But time is of the essence. Your veterinarian has given you sound advice. Move ahead quickly to prevent further brain damage.

# Skin Problems

## Fly Larvae Under the Skin

*Harmless larvae can mature beneath the skin, drop off, and then move on to their next life stage. Your cat as a mule.*

**QUESTION:**

How do you get a wolf worm to come out of a cat's neck?

**DR. NICHOL:**

Wolf worms. I've been a student of parasitology for a long time and I can find no reference to this name. We do, however, see bott fly larvae imbedded under the skin of cats. These go by the scientific name of Cuterebra and they're actually pretty interesting. It's a parasite that's related to the stomach botts of horses and cattle.

The larva that's stuck in your cat's neck can also infect rabbits, squirrels, mice, and dogs. Quoting from a recent text: "The eggs are laid in rodent burrows. The larvae penetrate the skin and in about one month, develop into stout grubs two to three centimeters long and beset with large black spines. The female fly uses a slave to carry her eggs to a prospective host. She captures mosquitoes or stable flies and glues her eggs to their abdomens. The eggs ripen in one to two weeks and the larvae inside them stand ready to disembark when the slave fly alights upon the skin of a warm-blooded animal to feed." And you thought your life was weird. You could have been born a bott fly destined to spend your life searching for slaves upon which to glue your eggs. Far out.

What your cat has is a swelling of the skin with a small hole that, believe it or not, is used by this spiny larva for breathing. You can wait for it to get bigger and drop out on its own or you can have it removed by a minor surgical procedure—a local anesthetic and a quick prep. If I were your cat, I would choose the latter.

## Fleas

*Here is how to get rid of them and stay rid of them.*

### QUESTION:

I have been treating my cats with Advantage. Now they have worms from ingesting a flea. I have a dog who apparently brings the fleas into the house. I have been treating the worms with a medication called Droncit. Is it safe for my cats to be treated with this medication often? The fleas seem to be returning.

### DR. NICHOL:

You are struggling with some of the toughest, meanest, wiliest, most low-down, no-good varmints that a pet can ever have: fleas. On the other hand, the tapeworms the fleas carry are almost totally harmless. The Droncit that your veterinarian has prescribed is quite safe and effective against tapeworms. But your primary pest priority is those darn fleas.

As chemical warfare has improved, so has the ability of fleas to adapt. These cunning bugs can survive most over-the-counter insecticides. If you use a truly effective treatment like Advantage on your pets, the fleas will live off skin flakes and dander in your pets' bedding. If you attack on the bedding front, the fleas just migrate outside. Your only hope is to move on all fronts using the following: Frontline Plus (which now includes a "growth inhibitor" to eliminate fleas from your home) on your pets' skin, and Dursban yard spray. Give Program tablets monthly for long-term management. I like Program because it's inert in the body of our pets. But inside the flea larvae it inhibits formation of "chitin" which they need to cut their way out of their eggs. Without their chitin "teeth," the larvae stay inside their nasty little eggs and rot.

So your dog is the "Typhoid Mary" of the household? All that means is that your family fleas don't care what mammal they suck on: dogs, cats, humans—no problem. A blood meal is a blood meal. Have your veterinarian provide the full array of weaponry and get tough.

## Cat Fight Wounds

*Abscesses are common result of cat fights. Know how to treat them at home and when to see the veterinarian.*

## QUESTION:

My cat is a boy about 5 years old who gets into a lot of cat fights. He's been neutered but we have a lot of cats in our neighborhood, so I guess he's just going to keep coming home with these wounds. Here's my question: Should I be using hydrogen peroxide to clean out these wounds? It sure seems to fizz up and make the pus go away.

## DR. NICHOL:

Good question. The answer is no. Do not use hydrogen peroxide. Here is why.

This stuff works because it breaks down degenerate organic matter by oxidation, hence the foaming—in other words, those are oxygen bubbles. But while it's doing that, it's also harsh on the normal tissue in the wound. This delays healing and causes pain. But the worse part is the risk of embolism. While it is not common, open bleeding vessels can take in oxygen from those bubbles. If those bubbles reach the brain or heart, you could lose your kitty. So lose the hydrogen peroxide.

Clean those wounds, but use soap and water. Gently soak off the scabs at least three times daily. Do *not* let the wound heal on the skin surface for at least three days so that any discharges on the inside of the wound can escape. What you are preventing is trapped bacteria inside a wound. This would result in an abscess that can lead to severe tissue death.

But while it's important to apply first-aid, also know that if the wound swells, drains, or smells badly, you should see your veterinarian. It's OK to play doctor with your cat. Just don't get carried away.

# Losing Fur in Clumps

### *With short but normal hair beneath the clumps, a cat may just be overdue for his spring shed.*

## QUESTION:

When I moved [to New Mexico] last summer from Massachusetts, I brought with me my 12-year-old female domestic long-hair cat. Recently, I have noticed that her fur is coming out in handfuls. I looked closer and found that I could easily "pinch" out a gob of hair by gently pulling on the base of the hair. (I didn't do this much though.) She does not, however, have any bald spots, but I did find a small spot that looked as though a different textured and darker colored hair has grown in. Could this be disease, age, or is she adjusting to the new drier, warmer climate? (Also, hairball production has been greatly reduced lately.) What should I do for Reggie?

## Dr. Nichol:

Reggie's situation is common and we get this question often. But I'm still glad you asked. Some people might have just started using Rogaine.

I will start my answer with a qualifier: Without an up close and personal physical exam, it won't be possible to be certain of my diagnosis. Having said that, the diagnosis is: normal. Here's how I know. Reggie is a girl who has come from a different climate—that's one factor. In addition, she is a long-haired cat who, through the past fall and winter, may not have fully shed her summer coat. Shed her *summer* coat? Yes, ma'am.

Many folks don't realize it, but our pets shed their coats twice yearly; that is, they shed a winter coat each spring and a summer coat each fall. With long coats like Reggie's, it's easy for the hair that is shed in the fall to get tangled and matted in the new undercoat of the winter. Now that the daylight is getting longer with the approaching spring, Mother Nature is saying, "OK, let's get rid of that old winter coat." So the whole works comes loose at once. And since most of that old matted dead hair has long ago been released from the skin, it pulls away from her new crop of spring hair with ease. That's why there are no bald spots underneath. That's also why she doesn't need Rogaine.

As far as reduced hairball production is concerned, I'm glad. To help Reggie along with this, get a "slicker brush" from your pet supply store or veterinarian's office. This is a brush with rows of claw-shaped wire bristles mounted in rubber. You can bear down pretty hard on Reggie's coat and get a whole bunch of dead hair loose. She'll enjoy it. But understand first that without her dread locks, she'll need to join a different clique in school.

## Constant Irritation of the Tail and Amputation

*A severely self-destructive problem that can drive a cat crazy.*

### Question:

Our cat's tail was oozing bloody fluid and the surgeon amputated, leaving about a 2-inch stub of a tail. She is perfectly adjusted to it now. While we never had the tail specimen analyzed, we do have it at home in formaldehyde.

## Dr. Nichol:

I, too, have seen cats who have suddenly begun to lick and chew their tails to the point of severe damage. While cleaning and bandaging the wound can be helpful, some of these cats will continue to go after their tails with a vengeance. In some cases, only amputation of the tail eliminates the problem.

The severe pain and irritation that drives some cats to do this has always been confined to the tail. The destruction of the tail is an interesting disease. I have made a search of the neurology literature and I have failed to find it described as a specific diagnosis. Yet, I know other veterinarians who have encountered this. While none of us wants to remove part of a kitty's body, the damage and infection that result from this problem can get so bad that tail amputation becomes a welcome alternative. In my experience every cat whose tail was amputated has gone on to do just fine.

So, in the case of your kitty we could have a pathologist examine the tail specimen and provide some answers. On the other hand, your cat may feel an attachment to her tail—even though she has lost her tail over this problem.

# Symptoms of Sickness

## When to Go to the Veterinarian
*How sick is that kitty anyway?*

### QUESTION:

My cat has had all of his shots plus a recent tapeworm shot. He has been lethargic and drool has been pouring from his mouth. He has not lost his appetite and is currently drinking more water than usual. Should I take him to the vet $$$ ?

### DR. NICHOL:

I think I understand your problem. Your kitty is eating, but not feeling well. Clearly his drooling and excessive drinking are not normal. But is he really sick enough to justify the expense ($$$) of a visit to the veterinarian? Or, put differently, will he get better on his own or will he just get sicker if he doesn't see a doctor?

Cats are special to those of us who love them and share our homes with them. They're different from dogs and people in that they complain less; maybe that's part of their appeal. It's also what makes it hard to recognize when they are in trouble. Typically a cat who is sick just lies low and tries to be inconspicuous. There's a good reason for it considering the instinct of self preservation. Only the strong survive in the wild. A kitty who advertises his illness by grousing about it is more than a nuisance—he's somebody's lunch. Your cat may be sicker than you think.

We have special challenges in veterinary medicine because our patients can't tell us what's wrong. We rely heavily on the observations of the pet's family. Cats make it harder still in that they tend to hide their disabilities by being less active. So, here are some important questions that will help you decide if your boy is really sick. Does he go outside? Does he chew house plants? Any vomiting or diarrhea? Is he passing more urine than normal? You said that he has had his vaccinations and an injection for tapeworms. Did his symptoms start the same day?

Now that I've added more uncertainty, I'll try to provide a few answers. If this boy goes outside, I would be concerned about antifreeze poisoning. This sweet-tasting toxin can quickly damage kidneys, causing drooling and increased thirst. On the other hand, if he's just sucking on the bitter leaves of indoor plants, I would shake my finger at him and explain that he has just reaped the consequences of his bad behavior. How about other symptoms? If he has vomiting and/or diarrhea, he may have other serious trouble. Important concerns here would have to include intestinal disease, organ failure, and maybe diabetes. Lastly, if he got his injections the same day, he may just have a stress reaction. But whatever you do, do not give him an aspirin and call the doctor in the morning. Aspirin, ibuprofen, and especially Tylenol will make for a much sicker kitty.

So what about the expense? I wish money didn't have to be a factor, but let's face it—it is for a lot of folks. You love this guy and want him to have the very best, but if he'll get better anyway.... Here's what you can do. Call your veterinarian's office and ask for a little telephone advice. Provide all the information you can. If they say that they better take a look, do as they suggest. No way do they want your kitty to take the wait-and-see approach if they think he'll be at risk. And if you take him to the doctor, remember that you're the boss. The veterinarian has two jobs. First, to diagnose and make treatment recommendations. Second, to do as you ask. I say you are smart to be concerned. Just don't gamble with the health of your cat.

## Wet Noses

*Wet nose, dry nose—no big deal.*

### QUESTION:

Should my cat have a wet nose? In the mornings, his nose is wet. He did have an upper respiratory infection when I got him at the shelter.

### DR. NICHOL:

Assuming the infection has resolved, your cat can have a wet nose because of excessive tearing. Are you making your cat upset? Does he read romance novels in bed? Some of my best friends have wet noses and I'm not complaining.

## Butt Dragging

*Anal gland disease and the itchy rear end.*

### QUESTION:

My indoor pet Siamese cat has recently begun dragging her butt across the floor. She has never been outdoors, and I really am clueless as to the cause of the problem. What could be causing this?

### Dr. Nichol:

Mmmmm. Sounds like me after a tough week at the animal hospital. Maybe she just needs a vacation. Oh, I forgot—cats are always on vacation.

OK, let's talk about physical reasons for this rather socially unacceptable behavior. For starters, I'll tell you what is *not* going on: She does not have worms. The type of worm associated with anal irritation is pinworms. There are two species: one is a parasite of horses; the other, a cause of unending embarrassment for the parents of elementary school children. I will avoid that subject because the Nichol boys are elementary school children who, for the record, are not behaving like your cat.

The reason for your kitty's itchy rear end is almost certainly her anal glands. Now, this is not a pleasant subject so you may want to finish your lunch before you read on. These nasty little structures are similar to the scent glands of the skunk. For cats and dogs, they are nothing more than a pain in the . . . you know what I mean. There is one anal gland on either side of the anus. They secrete a foul-smelling fluid that normally flows out by itself as the pet goes about its daily life. But your unlucky cat has anal glands that have become full and may even be infected. If we don't empty them for her, she may develop a drainage of pus as her body tries to rid itself of this mess.

Your job is to take your kitty to her doctor soon to have those glands emptied. If they are infected, an ointment will be infused and antibiotics will be dispensed. Then, life will go on and, hopefully, she'll never look back.

## Diabetes

***Learn about this difficult disease and how best to control it.***

### Question:

My 13-year-old cat has recently been diagnosed with diabetes. My doctor has me injecting him twice a day with insulin before his meals. I feed him one-quarter small can of w/d in the morning and one-quarter can at night with some crunchy food on the side. I have talked with another cat owner who only gives her cat one shot a day and less food at night. Do you recommend one method over the other? I would much rather only have to give him one shot a day. He would prefer this, too, I'm sure!

## Dr. Nichol:

I know exactly what you mean. As far as I'm concerned, less is more when it comes to injections. But diabetes mellitus in cats is a creature unto itself. I can tell that your veterinarian is savvy about this awful disease. While once-daily insulin injections are easier for everyone, every 12-hour administration may be best for your cat.

Those of us lucky enough to have a normally functioning pancreas never think about insulin. But we all need it to survive. Here's how it works: The pancreas in cats is a few inches long and sits next to the small intestine near the stomach. When we aren't eating, it rests. But as soon as food arrives in the stomach, the pancreas goes right to work and secretes the hormone insulin. As the sugar from the digesting food absorbs into the blood, the insulin is already there to carry that sugar into the body's cells. But a diabetic is in trouble. The diabetic's pancreas has little or no ability to make insulin. Sugar builds up in the bloodstream, but has no way of getting into the cells. The cells cry out to the brain "Hey, we're starving out here!" So the brain turns on the hunger. Meanwhile, there's a whole lot of sugar in the blood. This causes the kidneys to let go of a lot of water in the urine. So the diabetic needs to eat, drink, and urinate more.

So we give insulin by injection. If we give it just once a day, there has to be food in the stomach when the insulin reaches its peak blood level, usually several hours after being injected. If the insulin and the blood sugar are at their highest levels at the same time, things work fine. But the rest of the day your cat may eat food that does nothing but cause trouble. If you give insulin twice daily you have a cat who feels better and whose body functions better much more of the time.

I know it's hard. But the needle on the insulin syringe is really tiny. Pinch the skin a few times before injecting to make it a little bit numb. Then feed your kitty as soon as you're done with the injection. Most cats go along with it just fine. Some even salivate when they see the syringe because a meal always follows. Thanks for loving this kitty. He's lucky to have you caring for him.

[**Note:** There are many reasons why a cat can become a diabetic, and sometimes it starts with overactive adrenal glands, a condition called Cushing's disease. The adrenals' job is to make cortisol (like cortisone). Adrenals that make too much cortisol will give continual big orders to a pancreas. That poor little pancreas then gets overworked and burned out. Thus, it fails to produce enough insulin. Sometimes a kitty's trouble begins with Cushing's disease, which damages her pancreas—and she ends up with diabetes, too.]

## Excessive Sleeping

***A grumpy, sleepy cat with fleas is also anemic and sick. Frontline Plus should do the trick.***

### QUESTION:

My cat of eight months recently has been sleeping a lot, and every time I pick him up, he gets mad and bites me. My cat is normally very active, and doesn't mind getting handled. My cat right now is experiencing a lot of fleas. I don't know if that has to do with anything.

### DR. NICHOL:

You make the diagnosis simple. Those fleas are a major nuisance to your cat and, in large numbers, will cause grumpiness. But more important, his fleas are sucking his blood and he may be getting anemic (low numbers of red blood cells). Anemia will cause weakness that might be responsible for his sleeping more. Lastly, not only is your grouchy cat biting you, I'll bet his fleas are as well. Are you getting sleepy and grumpy, too?

Take this baby to the doctor. Have him examined to be sure that he doesn't have other problems in addition to fleas. Fleas have become hardy and adaptable while treatment has gotten more effective and easier. Ask for Frontline Plus, a liquid that you "spot-on" on your cat just once a month. Nothing you can get at a pet supply store will come close to prescription treatments for your cat, your home, and your yard.

## Postoperative Pain

***Pets, without question, feel pain just as we do. Better pet hospitals treat and prevent pain.***

### QUESTION:

I have often wondered about cats and dogs and pain, especially when Skippy, our wonder cat with three legs, had most of his hind leg amputated to the hip. He came home the evening of surgery and my wife and I took turns holding him all night. He did not seem to be in pain, but rather out of it or a little crazy from the anesthetic. Isn't pain medication typically given for this kind of thing, and for such procedures as spaying a dog or cat? Don't the cats and dogs feel pain like we do after major surgery? We would certainly be given pain medication. What are your thoughts?

## Dr. Nichol:

I am glad to get this question. There is a major move afoot among veterinary anesthesiologists to encourage greater use of the many pain relievers that are safe and effective for pets. But until the last several years, many of us didn't think very much about this important issue. We are not proud of this fact. Animals of all species, including humans, feel pain. But as many of us animal lovers often observe, our pets don't talk. So, how do we know if and when pain management is necessary? If pets are like us, there are varying degrees of pain among individuals. How can we know when our treatment is sufficient? We are observant, that's how.

According to Dr. Robert Paddleford in his recent paper on analgesics, the signs to watch for are: increased heart or respiratory rate, unwillingness to move, drooling, poor appetite, restlessness, aggressive behavior, and crying (I think we already knew that one). Needless to say, some of these signs are vague. But pets who show two or three together definitely need our help. And we can choose from several drugs and methods of giving treatment.

Which is best? This is a great example of the adage that medicine is still more art than science. What is best for a pet is the pain management that is most familiar and safe in your veterinarian's experience. Different cases require different treatments. In our hospital, we use pain treatments before surgery. For procedures like spaying and neutering that cause only mild discomfort, we use an injection of Torbugesic about one hour prior to anesthesia. The pet is relaxed as he or she goes to sleep and feels a whole lot better for up to five hours after recovery. If needed, the injection can be repeated. But for fracture surgery or an amputation for a pet like Skippy the Wonder Cat, we apply a Duragesic skin patch the day before surgery.

A Duragesic patch is nifty. Using the same principle as the skin patches for people trying to quit smoking, they provide a continuous through-the-skin release of the drug for three to five days. We send the pet home wearing a patch and recheck the pet's comfort a few days later and replace the skin patch, if needed. This way no one has to give pills and the pain relief is continuous. Everybody's happier.

We welcome interest in pain relief. Let's face it—most injured pets will get well without help with pain. But we love these little guys like our children. Which of us would knowingly deny pain relief to a hurting child? But for us to help every pet with pain, we need observant pet owners. Be aware and be the voice for your pets. Alleviating the suffering of animals is a responsibility we all can share.

## Stiff-Legged, Weak Cat

*Low potassium causes poor muscle function. Get a thorough health evaluation to rule out other problems. The right supplement will make it right.*

### QUESTION:

Blinken is my 9-year-old cat and he's been acting funny lately. He's always been pretty healthy, but for the last few weeks he seems weak. He doesn't want to walk around the house much, and when he does, his legs are kind of stiff. But the part that I really noticed is that his head is down. He won't look up. What's wrong with Blinken?

### DR. NICHOL:

Blinken has a serious problem—I'm glad you wrote in. You did not mention what diet you feed Blinken or whether he goes outside. This is important because his symptoms could result from thiamine deficiency or poisoning from antifreeze or certain insecticides. But assuming that Blinken stays inside and that you feed him a decent diet, I would have to suspect low blood potassium. We call this feline hypokalemic polymyopathy or hypokalemia for short. While it can lead to death, the good news is that it is almost always manageable, although not curable.

Here's how it works. Hypokalemia occurs when the kidneys allow too much of the electrolyte potassium to slip out into the urine. Because potassium is important in the normal functioning of muscles, cats with this problem get weak and may walk with a stilted gait. They lack the strength to keep their heads up. To help Blinken, we first would need to check a blood sample to confirm our suspicions. If his potassium is very low, it would be corrected intravenously. If it's only moderately below normal, an oral supplement called Tumil-K should work fine. Tumil-K is a powder that is mixed with the food. Most cats don't seem to mind taking it. Because hypokalemia is a long-term problem, Blinken is likely to need Tumil-K for the rest of his life.

Can hypokalemia be prevented? Some cases can be. Not every cat with this disease is losing potassium through the kidneys. Low blood levels can also result from feeding a deficient diet. But don't bother to read the labels on the packages. Just know that deficient diets are cheap diets. When it comes to pet food, the good stuff costs a bit more. You don't get what you don't pay for. Besides, Blinken isn't a cheap cat anyway.

# Excessive Drinking in Older Cats

*Always a serious sign—move quickly. A thorough exam plus lab work may uncover age-related kidney failure, a disease that may be treatable.*

## QUESTION:

Our cat Bugsy is 17 years old and she seems to be acting like the years are catching up to her. For the past two or three weeks she's been drinking more water and she's hardly eating. My sister thinks her breath smells like urine, but I say it's because her teeth are bad. How could a cat's breath smell like urine?

## DR. NICHOL:

You are right to be concerned about Bugsy. At age 17, there are several age-related problems that could cause her to drink more water and reduce her eating. Diseases to consider include kidney failure, thyroid tumors, diabetes, liver disease, and possibly cancer.

What about the urine smell to her breath? This is an astute observation on the part of your sister. This symptom is often seen in kidney failure in cats as well as in dogs. The reason is that worn-out, failing kidneys are falling way behind in their work. One of the important jobs they do is to eliminate what's called nitrogenous wastes (the stuff that gives urine its smell) from the body. When the kidneys are unable to handle that job, the body tries desperately to get rid of these wastes some other way. In Bugsy's case, her body is excreting some of it through the membranes of her mouth.

I know that it's hard to hear this news, but your Bugsy is a pretty sick old kitty. Her kidney failure is advanced. It is likely to have been going on for a long time. But please don't feel like you have neglected her. Symptoms like hers really do present themselves suddenly, even though her problem has been gradual in its development. While organ failure like this is a slow process, other organ systems are remarkable in their ability to compensate for the shortcomings in her kidneys. Finally, though, her system is starting to collapse.

Can we help Bugsy? It is possible. What you must do immediately is to get her to her doctor for an exam and some lab work. If her kidney failure is confirmed, but is not too severe, treatment with fluids intravenously and medications to manage her nausea and mouth pain may help a lot. If she responds well, she may do well at home for quite a while on a special diet and oral medications. Even at 17 she may still have a few good miles left on the clock. Whatever you do, don't allow this old friend to go any longer without help. Her poor appetite is caused by her nausea. She feels pretty badly.

By the way, for younger kitties whose kidneys have run into serious trouble, kidney transplants are available. Finding suitable donors is much easier than other species—any cat with the same blood type could be a kidney donor. They generally do well long term with easy-to-live-with antirejection medication.

## Feline AIDS Can Cause Chronic Disease in Cats
***Many different long-term symptoms can suggest AIDS. Infected kitties must be handled carefully to allow them to live as long and as well as possible.***

### Question:
My cat Jessie has been sick on and off for a long time, so I got worried about him. He's had a snotty nose and a fever and then he starting losing weight. So I took him to the vet who did some blood tests and he came up AIDS positive. Now I'm really scared. Will Jessie die soon? What about my kids and me—are we going to get sick, too?

### Dr. Nichol:
I know how worried you are. It's true that Jessie is a very sick kitty, but he may do OK for a while. Rest assured that you and your family are not at risk of getting AIDS from your cat. Not only has it never happened; it really can't. The virus that causes feline AIDS has no way of infecting people.

While people can't get AIDS from a cat, there are some striking similarities with the human disease. AIDS in cats is a lifelong disease, there is no vaccination against it yet, and while we can help an infected cat feel better, we can't cure it.

I know this is bad news for Jessie, but he could do well for quite a while with good supportive care. For example, with upper respiratory symptoms, like his nasal discharge, oral antibiotics can make a world of difference. To be sure the right antibiotic is used, a nasal culture will be important. In addition, if he is dehydrated and malnourished, fluids intravenously and feeding through a special P.E.G. tube could save his life. As long as the AIDS infection in his body is not in its terminal stages, he should respond very well.

While AIDS in cats is scary for us cat lovers, we could all do well with some good information. Here it is: This infection is found all over the world. Infected male cats outnumber females 3 to 1 because the majority of infections are contracted through fight wounds; the virus is present in large numbers in the saliva. While other methods of transmission include lactation (kittens nursing from infected mother cats) and breeding, infections from these sources are rare.

When do we suspect AIDS in a sick kitty? Often the tipoff is signs of AIDS-related complex (ARC). This really just means chronic infections that have occurred for months or years—similar to what has happened to Jessie. This includes infections of the inside of the mouth, diarrhea, skin problems, urinary infections, anemias, weight loss, and respiratory infections like Jessie's. When a cat with AIDS gets real sick, weight loss becomes severe. In addition, they can also have behavioral changes like pacing, twitching, or hiding.

I know how horrible this sounds. Fortunately, we can spare a terminal cat the fear and indignity of a wretched death by humane injection. Know that you may be able to keep Jessie comfortable and happy for quite awhile. By taking the time to write to me with your question, you have helped increase public awareness of feline AIDS. The bottom line is this: Do your best to prevent feline AIDS by keeping your cats indoors. And neuter your male kitties to curb their desire to fight.

## Complications in Infant Kittens

*Problems develop fast. Learn to correct low blood sugar and hypothermia.*

### QUESTION:

My cat just had kittens two weeks ago and one died yesterday. I found him off by himself moving slowly and crying. It broke my heart. I didn't know what to do for him. Any ideas? The other six kittens seem OK but I'm worried that it might happen to another one.

### DR. NICHOL:

That is so hard to take. The excitement of raising babies is great until you have a disaster. I will give you an understanding of what works in many cases.

First and most important, be sure not to blame yourself. There can be many reasons why young puppies and kittens die in the first few weeks.

Sometimes there are birth defects, but infections, dehydration, and failure to take adequate nutrition are also common causes. In fact, only 70 percent of puppies and kittens survive to weaning age. But like most disease states, knowing how to recognize a problem early can make all the difference.

Here are the common early signs: Crying, slow activity, diarrhea, and isolation from the littermates. Once you notice any symptom like these, move quickly. Start by putting a small amount (4 to 6 drops) of 50:50 honey:water or Karo Syrup on the baby's gums. We do this because most sick babies under the age of 16 weeks have low blood sugar as part of the problem. Next, warm up the little guy. You can do this many ways, but what's best is to put the little rascal in your shirt right next to your skin or on no fewer than three layers of towel on a heating pad set on low. At this point if he starts to move a little faster, you're on your way—but you must get some real food into that tiny tummy or his blood sugar will plummet even lower after that first dose wears off. The best real food for kittens is KMR; for puppies, it's Esbilac. Your veterinarian has them.

If the baby gets even more active, you can heave that big sigh of relief—but you still need one more thing from your veterinarian—a diagnosis. You need this because these things seldom happen all by themselves. If the cause is not corrected, it can occur again to the same kitten or to the entire litter.

There is nothing like saving a life. It's my favorite part of my job. But please don't feel badly about the kitten who died. You have learned to save another by asking for help.

## Feline Infectious Peritonitis (FIP)

*A contagious disease, it is always fatal. Our best success is helping some cats feel OK.*

### QUESTION:

My cat Roger is real sick. He's only about 1 year old and for the past three weeks he's not been very active, and not eating very much. I think he has a fever, too. Then his belly started to get kind of bloated looking. His doctor said that Roger might have FIP. Can we try antibiotics?

## Dr. Nichol:

I am sorry to hear about Roger's illness. He truly is quite sick. Unfortunately, while there are a few medications that could help Roger, antibiotics will only help a little. First, I will explain FIP.

FIP stands for feline infectious peritonitis. It is caused by a virus that is often transmitted to kittens by their mothers or by other adult cats. Cats at greatest risk are those who live in multiple-cat households or in breeding catteries. Kittens born in these groups are at greatest risk. The worst news of all is that FIP is a fatal disease. It causes a severe inflammation of blood vessels. It can affect many internal systems like the kidneys, eyes, brain, and liver. But the symptoms most often seen are like those that Roger has; that is the effusive or "wet" form of FIP. "Effusive" means that fluid accumulates in the abdomen or chest causing a bloated tummy (like Roger's) or difficulty breathing (fluid in the chest). Although the fluid buildup is not usually painful, these kitties run fevers, feel badly, and have poor appetites.

What can we do for Roger? Since FIP is an inflammatory disease with involvement of a cat's immune system, drugs, like prednisone, that suppress the immune response could help Roger to feel better and live longer. Drainage of the fluid in his belly and a blood transfusion will also help. Most of all, you need to prepare for losing Roger some day. I am sorry—FIP is not curable.

Lastly, there is a preventive for cats who are at risk. The FIP vaccine, which is given by nosedrops, is moderately effective. It is best started when kittens are 16 weeks old, then boostered three to four weeks later. Since we don't see much FIP, except in multiple-cat households and catteries, an average housecat has no real need for vaccination. On the other hand, purebred kittens purchased from breeding operations or pet stores should be tested right away to be sure they are free of the disease. Adult cats intended for breeding should be tested first, then vaccinated before being introduced into a group.

# Traveling Cats

## Car Travel and Frightened Cats
*Dramamine or Acepromazine is helpful if used before the trip.*

### Question:
A few years ago when I moved across country, my vet told me to sedate my cat by giving him half of a Dramamine tablet. I've since heard that this is not a good idea. I'm taking an extended vacation this spring and want to take my cats with me. Is it OK to give them the Dramamine?

### Dr. Nichol:
Sure, your cats can have Dramamine. It's a safe and effective way to induce a stupor and prevent motion sickness. The dose is 12.5 milligrams every eight hours. Just break the over-the-counter 50-milligram pill into quarters. Start the trip by giving one-quarter tablet about 30 minutes before hopping into the car. That's because it works a lot better as a preventive. If a cat is already on the road and upset, it's not likely to work. Feel better now? Good. Please don't take Dramamine yourself before traveling. It doesn't matter if you get carsick and vomit; we just don't want an unsafe driver with cats onboard.

## To Drive or Fly . . . That Is the Question
*How does your cat relate to the carrier?*

### Question:
I have two Abyssinian cats. We're moving, but I'm not sure if we're going to fly—which would take about six hours—or drive, which would take four or five days. I was wondering which way would be better to transport my cats and what means would we use to move them for each (i.e., I heard that you tranquilize the cat to fly)?

## Dr. Nichol:

I don't think tranquilizing a cat to fly will work. I've tranquilized lots of cats and not one has ever taxied down a runway and . . . oh, maybe that's not what you meant anyway.

Traveling with cats: You can go either way. If these cats are calm inside a carrier crate on car rides, I would send them by air and get the trip over quickly for them. On the other hand, if they are frightened and noisy in the car, they will absolutely panic in the plane. So, if they're bad riders in the car, my best advice is to drive them—and tranquilize them. Get a tranquilizer called Acepromazine from your veterinarian and use it liberally while driving. (On the cats, that is.) Dramamine works fine, too. (See previous question and answer.)

While the car trip is longer, you will have the peace of mind of having your kitties with you. You can comfort them and repeat the tranquilizer tablets as needed. But, you don't want them to freak out in the baggage compartment of the plane. Even with tranquilizers, they can get pretty scared if they are all alone.

# Urinary Disease

## Recurrent Urinary Disease

*Cats with frequent bouts of painful straining to urinate can find relief—but an accurate diagnosis is needed first.*

### Question:

I have a Maine Coon cat who is over 8 years old. She is very prone to urinary tract infection. My vet has her on special foods as well as Methigel. She gets better, then flares up again within a few days. Is there any cure? What will be the long-term effects for my cat? I need help desperately.

### Dr. Nichol:

Yes, this disease is curable in most cases. Your kitty's problem is that there is another, yet undiscovered, cause for her symptoms. The other causes include feline leukemia infection, feline AIDS, bacterial infection, or stones inside her bladder. In rare cases there can be cancers or malformations of the wall of the bladder. Ask your cat's doctor to culture her urine and do blood testing for leukemia and AIDS. X-rays of her bladder and possibly an ultrasound examination will also be helpful in uncovering the cause(s). Most important: Do not give up. Your cat is miserable. If left unmanaged, her problem could progress to a blockage of the outflow of her urine. This could end up fatal.

## Frequent Urinations

*Frequent attempts to urinate may signal serious disease. Do the right thing first.*

### Question:

I have a 12-year-old male cat who has a bladder infection and it is not getting better even with antibiotics. I see him going to the litter box, all day long. In our backyard, he has dug little holes where I see him urinating or at least trying to. After he uses the litter box he drops blood all over the house. I don't know what else to do other than to put him to sleep because I know he must be in pain. He has lost a lot of weight and seems to cry all night long.

## Dr. Nichol:

This sounds just miserable. I completely understand that you want to end his suffering. But please don't have him put to sleep. I think we can put him right.

Your kitty has what we call feline lower urinary tract disease. It's an inflammatory problem that causes thickening and sometimes bleeding of the bladder wall. Infection is responsible for only about 3 percent of these problems. Many are caused by a combination of crystals and mucus that can block the flow of urine. The bottom line: Your kitty may be unable to empty his bladder. He's in constant pain.

Have him tested for feline leukemia and feline AIDS virus. If he's negative, he'll need a urinalysis and culture as well as X-rays of his bladder. His weight loss worries me so I would also check a blood pressure, blood count, and chemistry profile to look for kidney damage. It's time we fill in the blanks in this boy's health.

He may need a different antibiotic; but if he can't pass urine, he may also need surgery. In males, the urethra (the tube that carries urine from the bladder) narrows as it passes through the penis. Many urinary blockages occur at this location. Surgical correction will provide a wider urethra that will allow crystals to pass normally and painlessly. But if his longstanding disease is in the bladder wall, he may only get the relief he needs from anti-inflammatory and antispasmodic medications. In addition, the anti-anxiety drug amitriptyline may also be helpful. The good news is that we know more now than ever about how to help a cat like this. Don't give up. Invest whatever it takes to give him his health back.

## Repeated Bouts of Inability to Urinate

*Kidney damage and severe pain mark these repeated episodes. Surgery of the penis and urethra can be the best way to assure quality of life.*

### Question:

I live in Japan and recently, for the fourth time, my male Siamese was not able to urinate. The doctor has shown me the fine crystals found in his urine when he was forcibly voided. The fourth time, about two weeks ago, the doctor couldn't dislodge the crystals from his urinary tract and had to put him out and clear the tubes. The cat, Puyi, is 5 years and 4 months old. He eats everything including a steady diet of sewer rats when he can catch them. I have looked at different books in English and some say this is caused by too rich a diet; others say it is caused by ash and magnesium and my doctor says it is caused by too much salt and has given me Science Diet's s/d formula. The vet also said cats with this do not live past middle age.

I wish to know *if* it is *just* diet and what can I do about it? Puyi gets four to five Pounce treats a night. Besides a proper diet, I love my pet very much, but I am wondering how much medical treatment I can afford to give him. I have spent $350.00 this month and dread to think of future costs and yet, think I will do anything for him. He is a loving wonderful pet with a perky and friendly personality—the life of the neighborhood. Children are starving all over the world, do I spend hundreds, even thousands on him? Is it myself that I am spending the money on? There are two separate issues here: actual diet and health care; and the psychological guilt I feel even wondering about money. Any words of advice and encouragement will be most welcome.

## Dr. Nichol:

You have raised several important issues; some medical, some quite personal. The emotional distress you are feeling is the essence of why we have pets in our lives. You have struck to the very center of the love and caring felt by my readers and me. Without the gift of unconditional love from cats like Puyi and the joy felt in giving it back, there would be no knowledge of problems like feline urinary disease. No one would have bothered to discover its treatment.

Now that we're clear on why you spent the time to write, let's fix poor Puyi. The sudden inability of some male cats to pass urine results from a mixture of crystals and mucus in the urine. There are several reasons why it happens almost exclusively in male cats. The first reason is chemical. The crystals that cause the blockage are composed of mineral salts called struvite. There are three primary ions involved, but the most important is magnesium. Diets low in this mineral (but still providing the trace amounts required for normal health) help prevent the problem. Another reason is anatomical. Female cats have short wide urethras (the tube that carries urine from the bladder to the outside). If a female cat makes crystals, she is unlikely to even know it because they simply pass right through. That's because the crystals rarely stick together to form a stone like in people and dogs. But the problem in male cats is their narrow urethras. With their smaller passageway, the crystals can form a plug and suddenly the poor guy can pass only a few drops of urine or none at all. Without immediate treatment, death can be imminent.

There is no doubt that Puyi's doctor did the right thing. By getting that plug of crystals out of the urethra, Puyi's plumbing could start to function normally again. But why does this keep happening to this little fellow? Each time Puyi has gotten a blockage of his urethra, he has been left with more inflammation and scarring. The result is a more narrow urethra, making it even easier for clumps of struvite crystals to block his urine flow. Each time Puyi can't urinate, he has tremendous pain and back pressure on his kidneys. Much more of this and he won't get past middle age because his kidneys will fail. What he needs is serious prevention.

Tell the doctor that you want an operation called a perineal urethrostomy for Puyi. It is essential because it will remodel his urethra, resulting in a short wide passageway like that of a female cat. It's also important to continue the s/d food in that it will help reduce formation of more crystals. Lastly, and this goes for *all* indoor cats, provide several fresh unused litter pans. Cats have a much better sense of smell than we have. In addition, they are very clean creatures. Even if his litter pan smells OK to you, if it has been used at all you are asking your cat to step around in a stinky soggy mess. Many cats would rather hold their urine than face this indignity. That stagnating urine in their bladders greatly increases the risk of urinary disease. Oh, and the Pounce treats and sewer rats—no problem. Like a glass of good scotch, they are fine if taken in moderation.

It is very clear from your letter that you love your cat with intensity. This is not only OK—it is part of what makes you a healthy and loving person. Puyi helps bring out your best. Love is the reason we are in this life. Invest whatever resources you must to ensure his long life. If you draw the line on Puyi's value, you are also limiting what you bring to others. Yes, children are starving. But if spending less on Puyi could save them, we should all forego everything but food and water. All else is luxury. Spending less on our pets won't reduce world hunger. Everyday we create wealth both emotional and monetary. It is not a finite thing. Follow your heart.

## Kidney Transplants

*A highly successful way to save the life of a beloved cat with failed kidneys.*

### QUESTION:

What can you tell me about the success of feline kidney transplants? One of my cats has been diagnosed with chronic renal failure, and my wife and I are considering renal transplantation. We would like to know the best clinics or schools of veterinary medicine to contact.

## Dr. Nichol:

What once sounded bizarre and impossible is today not only feasible, but highly successful. Cats who are in otherwise good health can be fairly easily matched with suitable donors and go on to live normal happy lives.

Interesting, isn't it? Here is how it works. Unlike most other species, the feline immune system can avoid rejection of donated organs as long as both cats share the same blood type. Following successful transplant surgery, the recipient must take the immune suppressant drug Cyclosporine for life. That's because while blood type assures a close match, it's never perfect. The drug is safe, relatively inexpensive, and given at home in pill form.

But while this surgery enjoys great success, it's highly specialized. Two veterinary teaching institutions carry out the procedure: The University of California at Davis and The University of Florida. Since the system was developed first and is carried out in greater numbers at Davis, this may be the better hospital for your kitty.

Cool, huh? Actually it's truly fortunate that the Maker gave each of us two kidneys. Cats, in particular, have a high rate of kidney disease and kidney failure. Each of us has plenty of function in just one normal kidney to carry us for a lifetime. So a kitty with two bad ones can be saved with a donation of just one kidney from another cat—usually a healthy stray from animal control. That means that the donor can also go on to enjoy a normal life expectancy. Thus, the last requirement is for the family to adopt that homeless donor cat. You feel great love for your pets. If I were a cat on death row, I'd be the first to volunteer when the call came.

# Urination and Defecation Behaviors

## Litter Box Problem 1: Pooping Outside the Pan
*Learn the ways of the feline and master the problem.*

### Question:

I have an 8-year-old male Russian Blue cat. I clean out the box every day. My Gray Boy will poop on the carpet in my living room and on the bathroom floors. It is very frustrating. He is in good health, and there has not been any changes in the house, physically or emotionally. Yet he is doing this deliberately and for no apparent reason. My vet can give me no other explanation for this rude behavior.

### Dr. Nichol:

Whoever said cats were delicate and fastidious creatures? Not me. Oh, yeah, it was me. But I wasn't talking about your cat and, come to think of it, I wasn't talking about mine either. Hmmm. Must have been a cat I met in a previous life. But I will commend you for doing a lot right.

Your kitty may have an aversion to the types of litters you've tried or to the location of the pan; or he may have a physical reason such as impacted anal glands, chronic constipation, or abdominal pain. Start by asking his doctor to repeat his physical exam with special emphasis on these possibilities. Bring a fresh stool sample (not in short supply at your house) so that this juvenile delinquent can be checked for intestinal parasites. If all of the above is fine, we'll move on to the next space on the gameboard—behavioral issues.

So why do some cats do this? He isn't being rude on purpose; he's a cat and cats can be like that anyway. It's happening because this guy has bathroom preferences built right into his little brain. On top of those preferences he has developed bad habits that are becoming more deeply engrained with each passing day. Act decisively. Get a few more litter pans (no roofs, vents or filters, please) and put them on the places where Gray Boy has defecated. Use a different type of litter in each. Your options include clumping, clay, Yesterday's News (pelleted, recycled newspaper), fine-grade playground sand, and no. 3 blasting sand. Try filling the pans to varying depths. If you carry out this experiment methodically, you are likely to determine the exact preference of this sociopath. If you still have trouble, let me know and we'll discuss making it a negative experience for him to practice pooping in prohibited places.

Is this fun or what? Actually, if clumping litter works out well, consider getting a Litter Maid—a self-cleaning pan. We have one at our animal hospital. You never handle the used litter and your cat always has a fresh pan. Besides, watching the Litter Maid work is cheap entertainment.

## Litter Box Problem 2: Urinating Outside the Pan
*Behavior management is the key.*

### QUESTION:

I have an 8-year-old female Siamese cat who has chosen to urinate on a chair or bed—always in the same places. I have covered them with plastic, but she still does it. She has always been an uptight cat. She knows this is inappropriate behavior because she will run and hide. I have tried punishment, ignoring, anything else I can think of. I took her to the vet who found her in perfect physical condition and ordered Prozac, which is not working. I realize this is probably "spite," but I give her a lot of attention and she has been doing this for five years with an increase as time goes on. It seemed to start at the time of my divorce. Please help—I'm at my wits' end!

### DR. NICHOL:

I'm glad you wrote in. It's when people are at their "wits' end" that I know they are desperate enough to follow a whole new method of behavior management. Correcting your cat's urination habits will require patience and time.

I will begin by reminding you of the big reason some folks find it easier to love pets than people. The love we get from our critters is pure. In other words, forget about spite. Honest. I've had a bunch of formal training and a heap of experience in managing and preventing behavior problems in pets. They are like us in many ways, but unlike us (in fact, better than us) in a few others. So why does she act guilty? Because she knows that you'll be angry when you find the urine, but she has this darn habit and she doesn't know how to stop. Now you're both unhappy. Here's how to both get happy.

First, get rid of the odor. While household cleaners can reduce the smell so that you don't notice it, your cat still does. Get a product called Equalizer or Outright. These liquids have no smell. They work because they contain an active organism that literally consumes the organic matter from the urine. Use it exactly as the label instructs. Next, make that chair and bed really weird places to urinate by laying a sheet of aluminum foil over them. If you want to really spoil the fun, put a Scat Mat over them.

But this is only the start. If we don't help your kitty change her behavior, she'll just do the same thing some other place. Manage this by providing her a totally fresh, unused litter pan at all times. It's easy. Just keep three or four pans each with a small amount of cheap fresh litter. Check the pans twice a day. Dump, rinse, and replace the litter in any that have been used. If she always has access to a fresh litter box, she will prefer that.

Last, but not least, think about your poor uptight kitty's being so darn uptight. Remember that it was a major change in your home (your husband leaving) that got her wigged out in the first place. To get her to relax and accept life a little better, you have a few choices: (1) you could take your husband back, (2) you could take Prozac yourself and you wouldn't care that your cat is uptight, or (3) you could give her a drug called Buspar for one to two months. The correct answer is (3) because Buspar is an effective anti-anxiety drug for cats that works especially well for this problem.

## Litter Box Problem 3: Half In, Half Out
### *Litter Maid may be the solution.*

#### QUESTION:
I have a cat I adopted from the pound. She's several years old and spayed. She's a good cat except for her bathroom habits. She gets in the litter box except for her rear end. Needless to say her "business" is outside the box. Help!

#### DR. NICHOL:
We've all heard the expression "Think outside the box," but to get your kitty to think inside the litter box, we must first understand why she doesn't just jump right in with her whole self and make a commitment.

Cats are fussy. They won't scratch and relieve themselves just anywhere. When outside, they select that perfect place with great care. I believe they see this process as an art form. Indoor cats are really outdoor cats who live indoors. The aversion this girl feels for the litter is shown by her unwillingness to settle into it and get comfortable. Your mission, should you decide to accept it, is to provide this little princess with the perfect bathroom.

Start by keeping her pan purrrfectly clean at all times. Forget the deodorizing crystals. Products meant to pass the human smell test mean nothing to cats. Your girl has a sense of smell that's ten times as acute as ours. Like her outdoor-living counterparts, your cat needs a fresh place to go every time. Your assignment is to experiment using a few pans each with different types of litter. When you learn which is her favorite, experiment again with different depths of litter in each pan. Once you gain her favor, you can also provide her with two identical pans, as she may prefer a different one for each bathroom function.

Too much work? I'll make it simple. Try clumping litter; the finer, softer stuff is most often preferred. To make life easier yet use it in a Litter Maid—a self-cleaning litter pan. This is also safer if you have a dog. Litter pans are a cornucopia of special "dog treats." Those who indulge in this gourmet delicacy with clumping litter can get a horrible intestinal blockage.

## The Clean-up Challenge

*Here are some products to use—and how.*

### QUESTION:

We recently put in new carpet a month ago and by doing a "sniff test" have discovered one of my two cats, Bill or Hillary, has been urinating on it. I am very interested in the products you listed and would like to know where I can purchase either of them. Then is it OK to shampoo it after it has been treated?

### DR. NICHOL:

For the odor eliminators, Equilizer or Outright, check with your veterinarian or with a pet supply dealer. Or you can call Foster and Smith, a mail-order house, at 800-562-7169 to order these or a Scat Mat. Remember that while these products are useful, they are only part of managing the cat who has forgotten where the bathroom is. Also be sure to provide plenty of fresh unused litter in several locations.

Regarding your question about shampooing the carpet. Yes, do it after you have eliminated the odor. If you shampoo first, you will only dilute and spread out the organic matter in the carpet, making it more difficult to eliminate. If you plan to bathe your cats, I say go ahead with that, too—just try to avoid getting a lot of hair stuck to your tongue.

# The Cat Who Wet a Roommate's Bed

*A cat can be a very bad ambassador of goodwill. It takes work, but it can be managed.*

## QUESTION:

My daughter's cat, April, is urinating on furniture. She has been fixed and is an indoor cat. She's been doing this since she moved in with new roommates over a year ago. She especially does this on her roommate's bed. She also acts a little "crazy" at times. What do you think is wrong? My daughter is desperate as she is considering giving up the cat.

## DR. NICHOL:

It does my heart good to know that April means enough for you to ask for advice. Since this behavior started with the move (and those new roommates—hiss!!), it's pretty clear that April has responded badly to change.

First, here is what is *not* going on: April is not demonstrating her negative feelings toward the roommate by urinating on her bed. Cats and people do have some emotions in common, but we are not identical. Only humans are low enough for that kind of dirty trick. Why would a cat do such a disgusting thing? Because when a cat urinates someplace other than a litter pan, she is marking that thing as her territory. So, if that's the case, why is she still doing this over a year later? Because yet another nuance of cat behavior is the habit of returning to the same scent to urinate again. And the more she is allowed to repeat this behavior, the more ingrained it becomes. So we need to stop it soon.

Your mission, should you decide to accept it: Prevent April from having access to the roommate's bedroom. Also, provide at least three litter pans, always keeping them in the same places. Use only a small amount of litter in each pan and check them twice daily. Anytime you find one that has been used, dump it, rinse it with water, then replace with a small amount of litter. This will make the litter pans more appealing to her. To discourage her from urinating in the same bad places, start by eliminating the odor of past urine with Outright or Equilizer. Then lay aluminum foil on those spots. Lastly, get a prescription for Buspar from your veterinarian. This will help her abandon old anxieties.

## The Untrained Kitty
*There's probably a way to make him litter literate.*

### QUESTION:

Our new tabby, Pata Grande, has turned into a most loving kitten. Pata was not trained by his mother as a kitten to use a litter pan before being abandoned. Phoo Phoo, the senior animal and 12-year-old cat, is litter trained, but is not about to teach him. How do we train this newest member of our household to use the litter pan?

### DR. NICHOL:

Cats really can't be litter trained; it's a behavior that develops in kittenhood. But you can encourage it by taking Pata Grande to the litter pan often, waiting for him to make you proud, and then throwing a party. Something like an inaugural bash will do nicely. When you catch him going in the wrong place, you can startle him with a handheld foghorn, but you must be quick—do it just as he is beginning the vile act in the wrong place.

What if this fails? Plan B: Confine Pata to a restricted area and continue to encourage his bid for the presidency each time he exhibits good bathroom behavior. As he improves his litter box performance, you can expand his access to the rest of the house. Do this gradually. It takes a village to raise a kitten.

## Habits of an Unspayed Cat
*If she holds her hind end in a funny position, don't shrug it off.*

### QUESTION:

My 5-year-old female cat has been urinating everywhere for the past six months. She has not been spayed, she always stays inside. She has lost some weight, but is very playful, runs, and plays with the dog. She doesn't act sick. She eats about the same as always. However, she's starting to hold her hind end funny. I hope you can help me.

### DR. NICHOL:

Being unspayed and holding her hind end funny are likely to be related. In other words, your little girl is about to go into heat and develop a social life that could make you a grandparent. Regarding her "urinating everywhere," this may be behavioral or it may be a sign of important physical disease. Start by getting her examined by her doctor. Have a urinalysis and urine culture done to rule out infection or other bladder disease.

## Cats Defecating in Flowerbeds and in the Children's Sandbox

*Aluminum foil will foil the cats. But give them their own outdoor litter pan.*

### Question:

We have two acres of property, yet our cats insist on using our flowerbeds and the children's sandbox (it has a lid, but sometimes the kids forget to put it down) for the potty. I have tried commercial preparations, mothballs, and red pepper mixed with mustard (not in the sandbox) to keep them out. We even dumped some kitty litter at a "good location" in a far corner. Do you know of any way to redirect them?

### Dr. Nichol:

This is an important problem for a couple of reasons. First, it's disgusting. Second, and even more important, it's a possible health risk because intestinal parasites from your cats can infect your children. Are your cats trying to tell you something? Do they secretly resent you for giving your human children more expensive gifts than they get? Are they plotting escapades that are so evil that pooping in the sandbox pales in comparison? Naw. They don't even care what you think. They just think your flowerbeds and sandbox are interesting outdoor litter pans. And two more things: These places now smell like latrines to your cats and this aberrant pooping has become a habit.

Let's fix this bizarre bathroom behavior. You already understand the concept. Not only must we make the wrong locations undesirable poop places, we must also give your kitties a new lavatory that they will like even better. First, get rid of the odor of urine and stool by replacing the soil in your flowerbeds as well as the sand in the sandbox. This is important because cats have a superior sense of smell. Besides, they won't be fooled by products like Cat-B-Gone and mothballs. (Your cats are insulted that you think they resemble moths—they eat moths.) Next, make sure the sandbox stays covered when not in use. Make the flowerbeds unfun by laying aluminum foil on the dirt. (Cats do not like urinating on foil as their outfits might get mussed.) Then provide them a new outdoor litter box. I suggest a simple wood-frame box filled with the original dirt from the flowerbeds. This way the new litter box will feel and smell like the flowerbeds used to. When they start using this new bathroom, you can gradually drag it farther out into the back 40.

Sorry it's so hard. Don't lose your patience and try to correct their habits with squirt guns or land mines. It won't work and they'll only retaliate. Cats are cunning. You have no idea of the creative locations they can find if they really want to. It could get ugly.

# Vaccinations

## Vaccinations for Solo Kitties

*Some vaccines may be less important for cats without exposure to other cats.*

**QUESTION:**

I have chosen not to vaccinate my indoor cat. I take my cat outside in the backyard a couple times a day while he is supervised by me every minute.

From the research I have done I don't think there is any chance of him getting feline leukemia or rabies, but I need to know about the four diseases that are contained within the feline distemper vaccine, which are rhinotracheitis, panleukopenia, chlamydia, and calicivirus/herpesvirus. Are these airborne viruses, and if so, is there much chance of my cat catching any of these while he is outside? How long can the virus survive in the air? Can the viruses get into dirt or flies or mosquitoes or even other animal's urine or feces?

**DR. NICHOL:**

You are asking some educated questions. Let's start with the basics. Vaccines work by stimulating the immune system with a virus that, in most cases, is more of a distant cousin than the true infectious organism. What results is the production of protein complexes called antibodies that will glom onto the virus itself if it ever finds its way inside the body. This concept of customizing somebody's defense system is pretty remarkable, but it may have a down side. These vaccines contain a variety of components that can cause allergic reactions and sometimes cancers.

With risks like that, who would bother? Well, let's face it; every day we all take risks. Just getting into your car is a gamble. But for the very small risk attendant to vaccinating, we can drastically reduce the chances of death due to infectious disease.

OK, your cat is extremely unlikely to ever confront these ugly bugs, right? Well, let me say this about that. Consider the stray alley cat. Not only has he never had a vaccination, he can't even spell veterinarian. (Not to be confused with vegetarian, which is plant doctor.) Believe it or not, feral cats rarely if ever get sick from contagious disease. That's because of the frequent "natural boostering" they get in small doses each time they share a cigarette or wine bottle with a colleague on a street corner. These guys are almost bulletproof. Your boy, on the other hand, is downright vulnerable. If his immune system never gets a stimulus of any kind, i.e., by vaccination or "natural exposure," he could get sick and die quite easily with a minor exposure. Even if you take full charge of his social calendar, he could need hospitalization for an unrelated illness and get exposed. In a weakened state he would succumb fast.

Which vaccines are most important? Start with rabies. It's a human disease, too, and failure to vaccinate could get you busted by Animal Control. For safety make sure he gets a killed vaccine. The vaccine risk is close to zero. Next are the combination of panleukopenia (feline distemper) and the upper respiratory viruses. I vote yes to these because without them he is a sitting duck if he has even the slightest exposure. Feline leukemia: It's unnecessary for your cat. He would need to get bitten by an infected cat or share a home with one. Leukemia, by the way, is the vaccination with the greatest risk of causing cancer.

How vulnerable is your boy when he's taking a stroll in your yard? Not at all. While the upper respiratory bugs are airborne, they only pass over a distance of a few feet. They die quickly and don't persist in the environment. None of these organisms are present in stool or urine in enough numbers to be a risk in the soil. Mosquitoes are not a factor. But someday, outside the safety of your yard, this fellow may meet a virus that could hit him like a Mack truck. Make sure he has a crash helmet. Protection is good.

## Vaccinations for Puppies and Kittens
### What they really need and what's unnecessary.

### QUESTION:

My kids, my wife, and I decided that we want to have a pet, but can't agree on a dog or a cat—so we got both. We know they need shots, but I've called a few vet clinics and I'm getting different answers on how many shots they need. Can you advise us on what's best?

### DR. NICHOL:

Boy, am I glad to hear this question. It is painful for me to recall the number of these babies who have died of preventable diseases only because their owners assumed they were too young to vaccinate. The reasons for the different answers to your questions result from different types of vaccine as well as the dated information that's included with the vaccine itself.

Let's start with the kitties. The best vaccine is a combination against panleukopenia, feline viral rhinotracheitis, and calici virus (FVR-C-P). Ideally this protection is started at 6 to 9 weeks of age. The combination vaccine is given a total of three times with an interval of about three weeks between each booster. At the time of the last vaccine, the one rabies vaccine is given. Cats are boostered annually after that. Now for the confusing part. There are combinations that contain a few additional vaccines. Many folks, including some veterinarians, feel that when it comes to vaccines, the more the merrier. But there is skepticism among specialists in internal medicine and immunology. Many experts feel that if a young puppy or kitten does not have an exposure risk to some of these less common diseases, the extra vaccine may do more harm than good. This is because more vaccine or "antigenic load" given at the same time can overwhelm the immune system, thus reducing that youngster's response to the other, more important vaccines. On the other hand, if your kitten will be spending a lot of time outside with other neighborhood cats, protection against feline leukemia will be important. But, again, it is much better in the babies not to include the leukemia vaccine with the others, but instead to give it as a series of two injections after the regular series is finished. A blood test for the leukemia virus is useful first to make sure that your new kitten is not already infected. (This can happen to the litter of kittens while they are still in the uterus.)

For your new puppy: The biggest difference in vaccines is the parvo component of the distemper–parvo combination (DA2PPL). Many vaccines still in use contain low-titer parvo vaccine. But the newer high-titer vaccines are much better because they stimulate an immunity faster and with greater reliability. While the insert that is shipped with some vaccines recommends longer series, independent research has clearly shown that most puppies get a reliable protection with a series of three high-titer DA2PPL vaccinations starting at 6 to 9 weeks of age. Space the vaccines about three weeks apart.

What happens if you give more in a series "just to be safe"? Infectious disease specialists feel that by overloading the immune system this way, we may actually be setting up some puppies for immune-mediated disease later in life. They point out that vaccines are necessary for protection, but they can be harmful if overused.

Lastly, there are additional vaccines available for puppies. These include corona virus, Bordatella, and Lyme disease. Some puppies will need these, but most will not. Adding them in all together, however, can reduce the effectiveness of the distemper and parvo components that are most important. If additional vaccines like these are needed, it is best to give them separately at the end of the series. When we see the puppy for his or her last booster, we give the one rabies vaccine; then we repeat the vaccinations once yearly after that.

Can these vaccines fail? There is a rare puppy or kitten who fails to fully respond. But by far the most common cause of so-called vaccination failure occurs with vaccinations purchased by mail or from pet supply stores. Is it because it's bad vaccine, administered incorrectly, or stored improperly? Hard to say. But when it comes to the protection of an important family member, saving money on vaccinations could cost a life. Protect those new babies and keep them safe.

# PART 4

# Medical Care: The Best Pet Hospital and First Aid at Home

# How to Choose the Right Veterinarian

Aren't all veterinarians trained alike? If they give good service and have convenient hours, isn't that enough?

Sorry. All veterinarians are not created equal. Deep down inside, you already know that. In fact, if you're interested enough in the well-being of your pets to read this book, I'm sure you're going to be thinking about who you'd like to have for your veterinarian.

I could be glib in addressing this question. It would be simple to say, "Pick me." I am a good veterinarian. I've been at it a long time (I graduated from the College of Veterinary Medicine at Michigan State University in 1974). I take more than twice the required continuing education that my state requires for licensure. I'm conscientious and I communicate well. I have a great support staff, and everyone on that staff cares deeply about pets. I'm an advocate of thorough preventive, diagnostic, and treatment techniques. I am single-minded about giving the best health care to every pet. I don't know any other way.

Would I be perfect for you and your pets? Well, maybe. To be honest, there's more to this choice than just checking out my qualifications.

I'm a firm believer in excellent, healthy relationships. I also believe that if you want a specific type of service and you are willing to pay for it, you ought to get it. Toward this end, I will provide you with a list of qualifications and considerations that good veterinarians satisfy. Then I will help you evaluate the "short list."

Having said all that, I will not be so presumptuous as to assume that you want the same things in a veterinarian that I think are best. While you love your pets, you may not want to invest your hard-earned paycheck in procedures like advanced dental treatments, endoscopic biopsies, ultrasound, or electrocardiography—and that's okay with me. We live in a free market economy, and I believe that you have a legitimate choice. But here's what I would do if I were in your shoes, and trying to find the best doctor for a favorite pet: Break it down into a couple of simple components.

There are two steps. First, make sure your veterinarian-to-be meets a list of objective criteria that you can quickly and easily research. Second, spend some face-to-face contact time with the contestants who reach the finals. It's sort of like an interview with a few of the Miss America Finalists. Shucks, this is getting exciting.

So, whip out the Yellow Pages and flip to "V." Look for the following in the listings—or call the best prospects and ask a few questions. These are the topics worth covering:

1. *The AAHA logo.* If you're like most pet owners, you've never heard of this organization. It stands for American Animal Hospital Association. This is a lot more than a club. It is not mandatory for a veterinary hospital to join. While membership is open to all animal hospitals, only those adhering to stringent voluntary requirements and inspections are allowed to display the AAHA logo. It is expensive, but veterinarians who are serious about quality invest the money and energy to pass. These are the good guys. Only 15 percent of animal hospitals qualify.

2. *More than one doctor in the practice.* A practice with at least three doctors is best. Why? Because, as Confucius said, "None of us is as smart as all of us." The best doctors don't need to be asked to get a second opinion for their clients. At a good hospital anything that is not clearcut warrants a consultation. Buy one opinion, get two more for free.

3. *"Closed for lunch"?* What the heck does that mean? Closed for *lunch*? So if your pet gets hit by a car at 12:15, the people at the veterinary hospital need to finish their pie a la mode before they can come to the rescue? I don't think so. You need a veterinarian whenever your pet does.

4. *Extended hours.* A hospital that's open 24 hours is great, but few are. Many are open until 7 P.M. or later, as well as every day of the week. Very few pet health problems have to be treated immediately, but there will be times when you'll want to see the doctor sometime before the end of the day. Besides, the convenience of evening and weekend hours is, well, a convenience.

5. *"By appointment only"?* This is a red flag! What is this? We'll see your pet on our terms? Take a number? Get in line? If your pet is sick enough to need help, you want to be able to come in now. (A word of advice, though: When a problem crops up, and you need to take your pet in right away, better call ahead. Most hospitals don't have a clairvoyant on staff.)

6. *Services you want.* For instance, if the ad for the veterinarian lists spays, neuters, and vaccinations and that's about it, you won't be

happy. "Wellness only"-type clinics will refer anything else to a general practice. I recommend looking for a broad range of services such as cancer treatment, dental care, illness, and injury. Better yet: Look for an ad that lists behavior management, too. Try to find most of what you may need under one roof.

7. *Proximity to home.* This is by far the most common criterion used by folks searching for a new veterinarian. It makes sense in case of emergency, but don't rank convenience over quality.

Okay, have you found one or two that pass the above criteria and are located in the same hemisphere as your home? Now for the warm and fuzzy part: If you're going to entrust the health of your beloved pet to this stranger, you'll need to get beyond the stranger thing. The process of meeting and sizing up the doctor, the staff, and the facility will tell you volumes about how people- and pet-friendly they are. Here's what to do:

1. Call the clinic and tell the receptionist that you are looking for a veterinary hospital, and that you'd like to stop by to meet one of the doctors and take a tour of the facility. Ask when would be a good time. Let the receptionist know that you plan to bring your pet with you.

2. Show up a few minutes early and look around the reception room. Is it clean or does it stink? Presentation counts. Do the folks at the desk wear clean uniforms? Do they smile? Are they polite? Every one of these things translates directly into how attuned to detail the entire operation is. Those little things matter.

3. Observe the manner of the staff regarding your request. Do they act like it's the goofiest thing anyone has ever asked—to meet the folks and take a tour? If so, feign acute abdominal distress and exit gracefully.

4. Do they say hello to your pet? I hope they like pets and they're not afraid to show it.

5. So they're genuinely nice people, happy to have you there. They want you to feel comfortable. That's what you want, too. Ask a couple of questions. What happens to severely sick or injured pets? Is there a policy for quick handling of urgent cases? The providers of customer service will tell you much more than the doctor about the running of the hospital. That's because most doctors know how they want their support staff to behave, but not all of us know how to motivate peo-

ple to do it. Ask at the reception desk and you'll learn what truly does happen.

6. If you're waiting for a long time (more than 20 minutes), does anyone get back to you to explain the delay? Do they offer you a drink? (Not a cocktail, I mean something like water or soda.)

7. When the doctor invites you into the exam room, does he or she introduce him- or herself? Is the doctor rushed? A harried doctor makes more mistakes. A good organization has composed professionals.

8. Does the doctor say hello to your pet? Friendly is good.

9. Ask the doctor how he or she handles a case that is outside his or her area of expertise. Wait for the doctor to say that there is a specialist, in most cases, who will take referrals. If it's clear that this veterinarian knows his or her limitations, you have a winner. Nobody knows it all. There is just way too much to be known for anyone to specialize in everything.

10. Ask the good doctor if he or she has an area of special interest or skill. Each of us should have one or a few areas of medicine that really turn us on. If there is nothing in particular that gets this doctor's juices flowing, I would feel underserved.

11. The tour: Do they show you everything? How about the area where the cages and runs are? Are they spacious and clean, or does it look and smell more like the "back room"? At our place I tell my staff that our hospital ward is the most important room. If our greatest priority is the pets who are the sickest, then we had better give them the very best. If they're going to get well, they need to be in a clean and comfortable environment.

Now the tour is over and the staff seemed glad that you and your pet came. Do they seem like the kind of folks who would help you whenever you had a problem? How about if you called the third or fourth time about dispensed medication? Maybe you were so flustered that you were *still* confused about the directions on the bottle. Would the staff be caring and understanding? If the answers to most of the above is yes, then I think you just hit paydirt. Sign up.

## THE RISK OF A LOW-FEE DEAL

You might be tempted to look for a discount fee by visiting a "low-fee clinic." I strongly advise against it. High-volume, low-fee veterinary clinics move so fast and furiously that they sometimes miss important problems. You won't get what you don't pay for.

Going forward, it appears that there will be fewer of these clinics. Pet owners are becoming more savvy. They research their pets' diseases on the Internet. Heck, some even read books like this one. Veterinarians are increasingly aware of this trend, as well as their own liability.

Our job is to advocate for the pet's needs at the start of the problem. But as technology and medicine advance, so do the costs. Not only do we have increasing equipment needs, but we must also hire and retain skilled and committed staff. None of that comes cheap. A good veterinarian will diagnose first and treat second. We don't look for ways to save our client's money by "trying this or that first and if it doesn't work we'll work on getting a diagnosis." You want a doctor who will go after the cause of the problem right from the start.

# Emergency Home Care: Recognize the Signs— Do the Right Things First

## Contents

Abscesses  *397*
Appetite—Poor Appetite or No Appetite  *399*
Bleeding—Without Injury  *401*
Cold, Sluggish, Trembling, Shivering (Hypothermia)  *403*
Coma—Unconsciousness  *404*
Constipation—Straining to Pass Stool  *407*
Coughing or Difficult Breathing  *410*
Delivery of Puppies and Kittens—Problems  *411*
Drowning or Near Drowning  *413*
Eyes  *415*
Fainting and Weakness  *417*
Heat Stroke (Hyperthermia)  *419*
Injuries—Severe  *420*
Insect Bites and Stings  *423*
Lameness  *425*
Pain  *429*
Paralysis and Staggering  *430*
Penis—Discharges  *432*
Penis—Swollen/Engorged  *433*
Seizures (Convulsions, Fits)  *434*
Snake Bites  *437*
Swelling of the Abdomen or Bloating  *439*
Swelling of the Face, Legs, and Paws  *440*
Urination—Inability to Urinate  *442*
Vaginal Discharge  *444*
Vomiting and Diarrhea (Severe)  *445*
Weakness and Fainting  *447*

# Introduction

The purpose of this section is to neither entertain nor educate. It's to give you a quick reference when your pet's life or health is at stake.

The most common urgent health problems are listed by the symptoms. After all, you're likely to notice the symptoms first—even before you start to figure out what's wrong. I'll list the major causes and the signs first, then follow up with your most important priorities—that is, the sequence of actions you should take to rescue your dog or cat from either big or small troubles.

In providing this information, I realize that every loving pet owner is a highly emotional being—especially during times of crisis or perceived crisis. None of us can be truly detached and objective when our dog or cat is in trouble.

If we're lucky, the apparent emergency will turn out to be little more than our fears running wild. I understand this. Despite my intensive training as a doctor of veterinary medicine and my years of experience, I revert emotionally to an irrational state of emotional Jell-o if I think Raoul or Peter Rabbit is in trouble. For them I defer to one of my capable colleagues. Feelings are everything. Perception is reality.

One basic: **When in doubt, call the doctor and ask for advice.** If you don't have a veterinarian whom you would feel comfortable calling for help, I advise you to turn now to the section, How to Choose the Right Veterinarian on page 391. You want to have that relationship in place before you have an urgent need for it. Trying to find the right doctor when your dog or cat is in deep trouble—well, that's just the worst possible time.

There is no best possible time for emergencies.

# Abscesses

## Causes:

Penetrating wounds resulting from:

- Cat fights and dog bites.
- Stab-type wounds from sharp wire or other contaminated, pointed objects.

- Bacteria gets deposited deep beneath the skin at the time of injury:
    - —The wound at the surface of the skin is narrow and quickly seals and begins to heal.
    - —The body's defense system tries to eliminate the bacteria, but gets overwhelmed.
    - —Pus forms as white blood cells die in the immune system's failed attempts to resolve the infection.
    - —The skin over the original wound swells as the area beneath it accumulates pus.

## Signs:
- The resulting abscess will likely be warm and painful to the touch.
- Your pet may have a fever over 103 degrees F.
- If the abscess has been swelling for more than one day, your pet may become lethargic and fail to eat.
- Neglected abscesses may cause vomiting, dehydration, and death.
- Some pets may chew or claw an abscess open.
- Pus draining from an open wound may be the first noticeable sign.
- Your pet may feel better after drainage begins.
- If the abscess is not treated by a veterinarian soon, the dried pus that becomes stuck to the wound may seal it closed. This will allow the abscess to refill with pus. Your pet will then become ill all over again.

## Things to do:
- Take your pet's rectal temperature. Any temperature over 103 degrees F suggests an infection.
- Clean any drainage using a moist washcloth.
- Wear rubber gloves and wash your hands when finished.
- Take that pet to your veterinarian. All abscesses are potentially dangerous. If your pet is feeling well, waiting a few hours is OK. Waiting a day is not OK.

## Things NOT to do:

- Don't handle the abscess at all if you live in an area known to have cases of plague.
- Don't use hydrogen peroxide. While it will do a good job of breaking down the discharge, it can damage the tissue. It can also release oxygen into the blood. This can be fatal.
- Don't try to lance the abscess. While this can be valuable, it will also be necessary to lance it in a way that will allow continuous drainage—this must be done by a veterinarian. Some abscesses need to have a latex drain installed. The doctor will also irrigate the interior of the abscess to prevent reinfection.

## Follow-up:

- The doctor may need to sedate or anesthetize your pet to prevent struggling. Abscesses can be painful. Treatment can hurt even worse.
- Antibiotics will be needed by injection. This will be followed by oral medication for use at home.
- Pets who get frequent abscesses (for instance, cats who fight often) are at high risk of kidney failure because bacterial toxins repeatedly released into the blood.

# APPETITE—POOR APPETITE OR NO APPETITE

## Causes:

- Loss of appetite is an important but vague symptom that can be caused by nearly any problem including:

    —Stomach or intestinal upset.

    —Foreign material in the stomach or intestine. Pets who swallow toys and other junk do not always attempt to vomit.

    —Heart or lung disease.

    —Kidney or liver disease.

—Pain or injury.
—Diseases of the nervous system.
—Nearly anything.
- What are *not* causes of poor appetite:
  —Tired of the food.
  —A pet who is just trying to get your attention.
  —"Just not hungry."

## Signs:
- Suddenly no longer eating.
- Gradual appetite loss.
- Intermittently good, then poor, appetite.
- Additional symptoms sometimes seen with appetite loss:
  —Lethargy and weight loss.
  —Vomiting and/or diarrhea.
  —Excessive drinking/urinating.

## Things to do:
- If your pet seems fine in all other ways (poor appetite is the only problem), you can "wait and see" for 24 hours. If the appetite has not returned in one day, your pet may be truly ill. Take your pet to see the doctor.
- Observe your pet and your home and yard carefully for *any* other symptoms such as those listed above. Since poor appetite can be a part of nearly any health problem, look for anything out of the ordinary. Your pet will not answer his or her doctor's questions. Your veterinarian will rely heavily on you for information.
- If you have doubt about your decision to monitor your pet instead of getting a physical exam, call your veterinarian and ask.

## Things NOT to do:
- Don't try to offer your pet a variety of tasty pet food substitutes. You will want to know if your dog's or cat's appetite for pet food returns.

You may never learn whether the appetite loss is a real problem if your pet develops the habit of holding out for the yummy stuff. An apparently poor appetite may just be a sign that you are being trained by your pet. Dogs and cats are clever.

- Don't give aspirin or other medications. By "playing doctor" you might mask other important symptoms. Some medicines can worsen an upset stomach.

## Follow-up:

- If your pet starts eating again within one day, keep watching carefully. The problem may repeat. An appetite that comes and goes can be an important sign of a smoldering disease. If your pet refuses food again, get an exam.

- Depending on your pet's physical exam, your veterinarian may recommend a variety of lab tests. Encourage the doctor to be thorough. Whatever the problem, a complete diagnosis will be essential to treat that pet right.

# BLEEDING—WITHOUT INJURY

## Causes:

- Poisoning with D-Con or other rat and mouse poisons may cause bleeding from anywhere in the body.
- Congestive heart failure, lung diseases, and severe dental disease can cause bleeding from the mouth.
- Diseases of the normal blood-clotting mechanisms of the body. Some of these diseases are hereditary.
- Severe infections of the stomach and/or intestines, such as parvo virus in dogs, can cause blood in the vomit and/or in the diarrhea.
- Diseases of the prostate or bladder in the male can cause blood in the urine or bleeding from the penis.
- Disease of the uterus or vagina in the female can cause vaginal bleeding.
- Some cancers and chemotherapies.

- Daily aspirin use.
- Ehrlichiosis—a blood parasite carried by ticks.

## Signs:
- Bleeding from any normal body opening such as: mouth, nose, penis, vagina, rectum, ears, eyes
- Weakness, depression, sometimes vomiting
- Difficulty breathing
- Excessive bleeding from a wound; bruising

## Things to do:
- Take a bleeding pet to a veterinarian ASAP. Any external bleeding may represent only a fraction of the blood loss that may be occurring internally.
- Handle the pet gently. Excessive activity will increase bleeding.
- If a dog or cat is known to have eaten rodent poison or if your pet has been given aspirin or ibuprofen, induce vomiting even as much as 12 hours after ingestion. Do this only if the pet is fully alert and conscious. Pets in a state of depression or coma can vomit and then inhale the vomitus, causing suffocation.
- If the bleeding is spurting bright red blood, see the section on INJURIES—SEVERE.
- If there is vomiting and diarrhea with blood, see the section on VOMITING AND DIARRHEA—SEVERE.

## Things NOT to do:
- Don't induce more vomiting in a pet who has already vomited.
- Never give a cat *any* household medications.
- Don't give aspirin or ibuprofen to a bleeding pet. This will worsen the bleeding.
- Don't wait too long. Normally, bleeding lasts two or three minutes before normal blood clotting begins. If active bleeding lasts longer than this, you have a true emergency.

## Follow-up:

- If initial blood tests show significant blood loss, a transfusion may be necessary.
- If poisoning is suspected, the pet's stomach may need to be rinsed out. Activated charcoal will then be put into the stomach by tube.
- If the cause of the bleeding is not clear, a series of tests will be needed. Managing emergency needs are the first concern. Preventing further crises is the next priority.
- Cancers, urinary and prostate problems, or diseases of the uterus may require surgery.

# COLD, SLUGGISH, TREMBLING, SHIVERING (HYPOTHERMIA)

## Causes:

- Exposure to cold or wet weather.
- Leaving a pet unsheltered.
- Sick pets, infant puppies and kittens, and injured pets need more protection from heat loss—and are at increased risk.

## Signs:

- Rectal temperature below 99.0 degrees F
- Severe lethargy, inactivity; weak, slow pulse; slow rate of breathing
- Shivering in pets with temperatures of 90.0–99.0 degrees F; no shivering under 90.0 degrees F

## Things to do:

- Act quickly and decisively.
- Take the pet's temperature by rectal thermometer.

- If the temperature is 97.0–99.0 degrees F, increase the room temperature and cover with blankets. Provide drinking water.
- If the temperature is 90.0–97.0 degrees F, put hot-water bottles next to your pet, use a hair dryer set on low, cover with blankets, and get your pet to the doctor.
- If the temperature is less than 90.0 degrees F, get to the nearest veterinarian fast. Try to call on the way. Cover the pet and use hot-water bottles—but move quickly.

## Things NOT to do:
- Don't be conservative and wait.

## Follow-up:
- Take your pet to the veterinarian soon—even if he or she seems to get over it quickly. There may be an important physical reason why it happened in the first place.

# COMA—UNCONSCIOUSNESS

## Causes:
- Failure to breathe properly.
- Failure of the heart to pump blood normally. This includes cardiac arrest (a stopped heart).
- Head injury or other brain disease.
- Severe blood loss.
- Very low blood pressure, which can occur with shock. Severe injuries, such as being hit by a car, cause shock and coma.
- Low blood sugar:
    —Poorly managed diabetes
    —Puppies or kittens who have gone several hours without feeding.
- Drug overdoses, such as certain heart medications.

- Rare cases: cancers, some liver diseases, blood clots to the brain.
- Anything resulting in a lack of oxygen or inadequate amounts of blood sugar to the brain.

## Signs:

- A pet in a coma is alive but unconscious.
- The pet responds to neither sound, movement, nor light.
- There is no response to pain. (If you squeeze the toe of a pet who is in a coma, he or she won't respond.)
- The pet will not try to stand.
- The pet may or may not be breathing.
- There may or may not be a pulse or heartbeat.
- The pet's gums and tongue are:
  —Purple or purplish blue, which is an indication that the blood isn't getting enough oxygen. Getting the pet to breathe should help.
  —Pale or gray, indicating that there isn't enough blood reaching the brain. This will occur if the heart has stopped or if there is severe shock or blood loss.
  —Normal pink. Pink/red gums mean that breathing as well as blood and oxygen flow are good. Coma, in this case, may be due to a brain disease or brain injury.

## Things to do:

- Act immediately and decisively. This may be your pet's only chance.
- Straighten the neck to allow better air passage into the lungs.
- Handle the pet gently in cases of injury. Keep the pet flat on a board. If injury to the neck or back has occurred, rough handling could make problems worse.
- If your pet is diabetic, rub honey or Karo Syrup on the gums. (A young kitten or puppy in a coma may respond well to this treatment, too.) This will provide sugar to the bloodstream quickly. Pets who are comatose, due to low blood sugar, may improve in minutes.

- **CPR (Cardiopulmonary Resuscitation) Using Two People:**
    In cases of **no breathing** (gums are **purple/blue**):
    1. Open the mouth and remove any foreign material that may be blocking air movement.
    2. Lay the pet on his or her side.
    3. Hold the muzzle/mouth closed and put the entire nose of the pet in your mouth.
    4. Blow hard enough to cause the chest to expand. Blow at a rate of 80 to 120 times per minute. This means **1½ to 2 times per second**.
    5. Continue until the color of the gums returns to pink.

- If the pet's gums are still purple/blue in 90 seconds or in cases of **no breathing** with gums that are pale or gray, start chest compressions in addition to breathing.
    1. While the breather continues at the same rate of 1½ to 2 times per second, the other person places the heel of one hand on the side of the pet's chest. The correct spot for the hands is the place where the point of the elbow would be when the front leg is pulled up next to the chest. After finding that spot, move the front leg away. Place the heel of the other hand on top of the first hand so that you can push down using the heels of both hands together—that is, one hand on top of the other.
    2. The person doing chest compressions pushes hard on the chest using a quick thrust at a rate of 80 to 120 times per minute. That means pushing hard on the side of the chest at the same rate as the breather: **1½ to 2 times per second**.
    3. The breather blows into the nose as the chest compression person raises his or her hands between pushes. So it goes like this: **Push–breathe–push–breathe–push–breathe . . .**
    4. Continue until the color of the gums returns to pink.
    5. If the gums are still purple/blue or pale/gray after 10 minutes, stop and wait to see if the pet will breathe voluntarily.

- Failure to revive an arrested pet in 10 minutes indicates a failed attempt. This is a dead pet. In these cases, I am very sorry. You did your best. Try to accept that some lives were meant to go to their Maker.

## Things NOT to do:

- You shouldn't stop CPR to load the pet into the car for the trip to the emergency veterinarian. It's far better to do CPR at home right away than to wait for the doctor to do it when you arrive at the animal hospital. No pet can be revived unless CPR is started immediately after breathing stops.
- Don't be afraid of this process. Your efforts are the pet's only chance.

## Follow-up:

- In cases of successful life-saving efforts, the pet will need hospitalization for further treatment. There are many systems in the body that may have been damaged during the period of poor blood and oxygen delivery.
- The causes of the cardiac and pulmonary arrest will need to be completely understood to prevent a repeat occurrence.
- Other tests will be done when you arrive at the veterinary hospital. These tests include electrocardiogram, doppler blood pressure, and pulse oximetry (measurement of the oxygen levels in the red blood cells).
- Drugs and oxygen therapy may be needed to manage abnormal heart rhythms and fluid in the lungs.

# CONSTIPATION—STRAINING TO PASS STOOL

## Causes in Cats:

- A common problem in cats over age 10 years, constipation seems to be a part of aging for many.
- Can be seen with hair that a cat has swallowed.
- Occasionally seen with kidney failure.
- Sometimes seen with dehydration due to other causes.

## Causes in Dogs:

- Poultry and pork-chop bones that have been chewed and swallowed.
- Other foreign material that has been swallowed can cause constipation—such as multiple small slivers of bone from chewed beef bones. These will stick to fecal matter in the rectum and form rock-hard stools.
- Occasional constipation can be seen with low functioning adrenal glands (Addison's disease).
- An unneutered male dog can strain if he has an enlarged prostate gland.

Constipation never "just happens." It is never a normal occurrence in dogs. There is always a deeper cause.

## Signs:

- Frequent straining with *no* stool—or very hard stools—being passed.
- Severe, prolonged constipation will cause failure to eat and vomiting in some pets.
- Pets who have strained repeatedly may also develop rectal prolapse. This is a serious complication. A prolapsed rectum is an external protrusion of the interior of the rectum. It appears as a red swelling sticking out of the rectum.

## Things to do:

- Look carefully on the ground or around your home for any sign of fluid stool, indicating diarrhea rather than constipation. A pet who tries and fails to pass stool may not be truly constipated. If a dog or cat has had diarrhea, the inside wall of the rectum may be inflamed and swollen. The thickened rectum sends a nerve signal to the brain indicating an interior "mass." Thus, the pet thinks that the thickened, swollen rectal tissue is stool. He or she will strain, but pass nothing. If you don't find the diarrhea that started the problem, you will believe your pet to be constipated. But the treatment for diarrhea is quite different.

- If you are sure the pet is truly constipated, but is doing fine otherwise, you may try to correct the problem at home.
  - —Old-fashioned enema bags and bottles are fine. Use warm water only. No soap. Detergents irritate the wall of the rectum and colon, and cause inflammation and swelling. You can add some K-Y Jelly or other water-based lubricant.
  - —Smear the nozzle with Vaseline and slide it into the rectum. Release the water flow and run as much water into the rectum as you can. Continuing to run water into the rectum even as it leaks out around the nozzle is fine.
  - —Repeat these enemas every one or two hours until the pet passes normal or soft stool.
- Make an appointment to have your pet examined. There is always an important reason for constipation in pets. They are not subject to "occasional irregularity" like people.

## Things NOT to do:

- Don't use Fleet or other packaged, phosphate-containing enemas. They can be dangerous for small-breed dogs. *They are fatal for cats.*
- Don't gamble. If there is *any* question that your pet may have problems other than simple constipation, see your veterinarian.

## Follow-up:

- A thorough medical exam for constipation will include a rectal exam. This is only mildly uncomfortable. It is essential for understanding the condition of the stool and the rectum.
- Your veterinarian will want some investigative lab work and possibly X-rays of the abdomen.
- Follow the doctor's advice. Constipation alone rarely kills a pet, but it could be caused by something much more serious.

## COUGHING OR DIFFICULT BREATHING

### Causes:

- Partial or complete blockage of the airways (the windpipes in the throat, and lungs).
- Pneumonia, bronchitis, asthma.
- Some head injuries.
- Severe chest injury—possibly from being hit by a car. This can cause bleeding into the chest, free air in the chest, or abdominal organs in the chest due to a torn diaphragm (diaphragmatic hernia).
- "Sharp" injuries such as wounds that penetrate into the inside of the chest—gunshots, sharp objects, and bite wounds.
- Heart failure.
- Overheating in pushed-in-faced dog breeds (Bulldogs, Pugs, etc.) can lead to excessive panting, which may cause coughing and breathing difficulty. This can be rapidly fatal (See the section on HEAT STROKE).
- Sometimes minor infections.
- Severe allergic reactions.

### Signs:

- Rapid, noisy, forced breathing.
- Lying on the chest with the neck extended and elbows out.
- Weakness or exhaustion.
- Gums and tongue that are purple in color.
- Coughing, choking, or harsh fast breathing. If this goes on for more than three minutes, you may have an emergency situation.

### Things to do:

- Open the mouth, in good light, and look for foreign material such as a toy or a large piece of food. Remove the blockage with the fingers or a pair of needle-nosed pliers. Move quickly.

- If a dog or cat is having trouble with normal activities such as walking, eating, drinking, or panting, get your pet to the veterinarian immediately. Check the color of the gums and tongue. Call the animal hospital on your way, so that the doctor and assistants will be ready for your pet's arrival. Your pet may be facing imminent death.
- If someone nearby has an oxygen cylinder, hold the breathing tubes close to the pet's nose and mouth, and allow the pet to inhale the oxygen on the way to the animal hospital.
- Handle the pet gently and move him or her slowly to prevent pain. Pain can cause struggling, which may worsen the problem.

## Things NOT to do:
- Don't give any medications that have not been prescribed by your veterinarian to treat this problem. Avoid human over-the-counter medications such as cough syrups and cold remedies.
- Don't allow the pet to become excited. This will increase your pet's oxygen needs and worsen the problem.
- Don't apply pressure around the neck or chest. Your pet needs to breathe as easily as possible.

## Follow-up:
- There are any number of tests and procedures that could be necessary to fully understand respiratory disease. A less-than-complete diagnostic workup can result in "educated guesswork" in attempting to arrive at the correct treatment. Be sure you choose a competent, thorough veterinarian. For your part, don't economize. Respiratory problems are often high risk.

# DELIVERY OF PUPPIES AND KITTENS—PROBLEMS

## Causes:
- A mother's birth canal that is too small to allow passage of the babies.

- A birth canal that has been injured or compressed by previous injury to the bones of the pelvis, such as a badly healed fracture from a hit-by-car injury.
- Babies who are too big to pass through.
- A uterus that lacks the strength necessary to push the babies out.
- Problems are seen most often in small dogs (especially the "pushed-in-face" breeds like Pugs), large-breed dogs with huge litters, and in purebred Persian and Himalayan cats.
- Older or overweight mothers are at higher risk.

## Signs:

- Pregnant cats and dogs will have a normal drop in body temperature prior to the start of contractions. When her rectal temperature reaches approximately 99 degrees, you should expect the first baby within 12–24 hours. Longer than 24 hours means trouble.
- The mother pushes and strains for more than 30 minutes without delivering a baby.
- More than 2 hours between the arrival of one baby and the arrival of the next baby.
- Crying, intense pain, and constant licking of the vulva. A small amount of this is normal.
- More than 70 days from breeding without signs of delivery.

## Things to do:

- Allow the mother to remain relaxed and free of a noisy, crowded environment. Her normal sleeping area is best. People (especially children) hovering, causes stress.
- If a baby remains at the vulva for several minutes, grasp it and pull it gently with a clean, dry towel in your hand.
- After the baby is delivered, allow the mother 30 seconds to start to clean it. If she ignores it, rub the baby with a towel gently but vigorously. Rub the face and chest to stimulate breathing.

- If the above time limits are exceeded, call your veterinarian or emergency animal clinic to alert them that you are on your way. This is the time to turn the mother and litter over to the pros.

## Things NOT to do:
- Don't move the planned birthing area near the delivery date. This is stressful to the mother.
- Don't poke and prod. Allow Mother Nature to work. Eliminate commotion.
- Don't waste time. If you suspect trouble even within the above time guidelines, get help.

## Follow-up:
- The veterinarian may recommend injections of the hormone Oxytocin to help stimulate contractions of the uterus.
- Cesaerean section may be necessary. Don't resist this suggestion. It is usually quite safe.
- Most mothers will refuse food until the entire litter has been delivered. When she finally eats, she is probably done.
- A veterinarian should examine all mothers and their litters within 24 hours of delivery, even if all seems well. Retained babies or placentas are not rare. Problems with the breasts can occur as well.
- Feed an expectant mother a high-quality puppy growth diet from early pregnancy through the time of weaning. This will reduce the risk of eclampsia (convulsions due to calcium deficiency). Don't add milk.

# DROWNING OR NEAR DROWNING

## Causes:
- Immersion of the head under water causing the pet to lose consciousness.
- Lungs that are filled with water, which means oxygen can't be transferred to the blood. (Death from drowning is most often due to brain injury from lack of oxygen.)

- Low oxygen in the brain can also cause death due to abnormal heart rhythms.
- Some pets die from drowning with very little water in their lungs. This can happen if the pet has throat spasms that close down the larynx. A pet will lose consciousness and die if he or she continues trying to suck air through a throat that is closed.

## Signs:
- Coughing and spitting up water.
- Loss of consciousness.
- Vomiting.
- Seizures due to poor oxygen flow to the brain.
- A pet who is still conscious may continue to cough or choke. Even if the pet hasn't lost consciousness, he or she may get severe lung, brain, or heart damage.

## Things to do:
- Hold the pet's head in a downward position to allow water to drain from the lungs. This is especially important if the pet vomits.
- Straighten the neck and pull the tongue forward through the front teeth. This will help open the airway and allow for better breathing.
- Perform CPR. See the section on COMA—UNCONSCIOUSNESS.
- Take the pet to the nearest veterinarian immediately following CPR.
- Do these things as quickly and decisively as possible. Your efforts are the pet's only chance.

## Things NOT to do:
- Don't stop CPR to load the pet into the car for the trip to the emergency veterinarian. You are far better off doing CPR on-site than waiting for the doctor to do it when you arrive at the animal hospital. No pet can be revived unless CPR is started immediately after breathing stops.
- Don't assume that a pet who looks fine will stay fine. There may be a lag in the onset of serious near-drowning complications.

## Follow-up:

- Any pet who survives a near-drowning will need hospitalization for oxygen therapy, IV fluids, and treatment of possible brain injury.
- Long-term lung damage may be a permanent handicap.

# EYES

## Causes:

- Injuries, lacerations or wounds on the outer surface of the eye (the cornea).
- An eye that appears "popped-out" of the eye socket (proptosis). This occurs most commonly in the breeds that have pushed-in faces (brachycephalic breeds) such as Pugs, Pekinese, and Boston Terriers. Proptosis can also occur in cats and other dog breeds.
- Blunt trauma. This is an eye that has been hit by an object that did not cut the eye, but has bruised it badly. Severe damage to the interior of the eye can occur this way.
- Damage from caustic substances such as Mace, shampoos, or other fluids splashed on the eyes.
- Sudden blindness, often associated with glaucoma (excessive pressure inside an eye).
- Foreign material penetrating the eye or, more often, imbedded in the tissue surrounding the eye.

## Signs:

- Severe squinting of the eyelids. This means eye pain.
- A dog or cat who is reluctant to open the eye in bright light.
- Severe redness of the tissues surrounding the eye.
- Redness of the iris of the eye.
- Thick pus-like eye discharge.
- Wounds to the surface of the eye.

- Sudden clouding of the surface of eyes and redness of the surrounding tissue may indicate glaucoma, especially if the pet shows signs of pain or blindness.

## Things to do:

- Protect an injured eye with a lubricant. K-Y Jelly or another water-based lubricant is best, but you can also apply a petroleum jelly like Vaseline. Spread the lubricant generously right on the eyeball to prevent the eye tissues from drying.
- If eye damage has occurred because fluid was splashed on the eyes, rinse the eyes with water continuously for 30 minutes or until your pet's eyes can be examined by a veterinarian.
- Have all eye injuries examined, no matter how minor the injury appears to be. The sooner, the better.
- Sudden clouding of the eye—with or without pain—should be examined ASAP. Your pet may have glaucoma.
- A "popped out" (proptosed) eye needs medical attention on an emergency basis. Apply K-Y Jelly or Vaseline immediately.
- Foreign material lodged in the tissue next to the eye may be removed at home if the pet will hold very still. Use your fingertips only. Instruments like tweezers are risky as eye injury can occur if your pet makes a sudden move.
    - —Take that pet to your veterinarian after you remove the foreign material. While the eye may look much better, it is important for the doctor to check for damage to the cornea. The doctor will also look for more foreign material.
- Carefully clean away discharges because discharges are teeming with bacteria. Be careful not to apply pressure to the eye itself during cleaning. Clean the eye using cotton or a wash cloth moistened with tap water only. *Never use hydrogen peroxide.*

## Things NOT to do:

- Don't "wait and see" with eye injuries. Damage to the interior of the eyeball can be difficult to recognize at home. Serious eye injuries can only be successfully treated if the pet is examined quickly.

- Don't try to pull out foreign material if it's imbedded in the eye itself. The doctor will do this only after he or she has assessed damage to the interior of the eye. The penetrating foreign material may be sealing a leak. If you try to remove the object at home, you may cause serious complications.
- Don't let the pet rub an injured or diseased eye.
- Don't let other pets lick the problem eye. This can worsen the damage.
- Don't try to clean the discharge away from the eye if the pet struggles. Let the medical staff manage a frightened pet.

## Follow-up:
- Any eye injury can cause long-term glaucoma, dry eyes, internal eye infections or inflammations, and eyelid deformity. Take your pet to the doctor for an eye exam even if you manage to solve the problem at home.
- "Popped-out" (proptosed) eyes *must* be surgically managed ASAP. If you wait longer than 30 minutes, the eye may have to be surgically removed.
- If the corneal surface of the eye is injured, it may need to be stitched. Other wounds on the eye's surface will need topical treatments. Some pets will need oral medications as a follow-up.
- Some eye problems result from disease in another part of the body. Your veterinarian may recommend other testing.

# FAINTING AND WEAKNESS

## Causes:
- Heart failure
- Shock
- Severe pain
- Head injury
- Blood loss and other causes of anemia (low number of red blood cells)

- Infections of the brain and spinal cord
- Advanced internal disease, including:
  - —Diabetes mellitus
  - —Low blood sugar
  - —Infections of the pancreas or abdomen (peritonitis)
  - —Liver or other internal organ disease
  - —End-stage infections
- Poisoning (see also pages 195 and 345)

## Signs:

- Depending on the cause, some pets will be fine when resting, but become unable to walk without weakness or fainting.
- Many pets with this problem will be unable to rest without fainting.

## Things to do:

- Get that pet to the veterinarian immediately. Check the color of the gums and tongue. See the section on COMA—UNCONSCIOUSNESS (pages 404–407). Call the animal hospital on your way, so that the doctors and staff will be ready for your pet's arrival. Your pet may be facing imminent death.
- Provide drinking water.
- On the way to the animal hospital take the rectal temperature. If the temperature is above 103.5 degrees F or below 99.0 degrees F, treat according to the instructions in the sections on HEAT STROKE (HYPERTHERMIA) or COLD, SLUGGISH, TREMBLING, SHIVERING (HYPOTHERMIA).
- If someone nearby has an oxygen cylinder, hold the breathing tubes close to the pet's nose and mouth, and allow the pet to inhale on the way to the animal hospital.
- If you know your pet has diabetes, rub some honey or Karo Syrup on the gums to improve what may be low blood sugar.
- Apply firm pressure with a cloth bandage or an article of clothing to any bleeding wound.

- Handle the pet gently and slowly to prevent pain. If you aggravate the pain, the pet may struggle, which could make the problem worse.
- Act decisively. You don't have time to "wait and see."

## Things NOT to do:
- Don't allow the pet to become excited. This will increase his or her oxygen needs and worsen the problem.
- Don't allow any pressure around the neck or chest. The pet needs to breathe as easily as possible.
- Don't give your pet any medications.

## Follow-up:
- Be prepared for the doctor to recommend extensive diagnostics including ECG, X-rays, blood and urine testing, and doppler blood pressure.
- Hospitalization may be needed to stabilize your pet. Some pets need lifelong treatment following an episode of this kind.

# HEAT STROKE (HYPERTHERMIA)

## Causes:
- Humid conditions.
- Blockages of air flow into the pet's chest. In the case of breeds with pushed-in faces like Bulldogs and Pugs, blockages to normal air flow can result from that breed's anatomy. Some cancers can cause air flow blockages as well.
- Direct exposure to the sun.
- Excessive activity in hot humid weather.
- Poor ventilation, such as the inside of a vehicle with rolled-up windows.

## Signs:

- Rectal temperature above 105.0 degrees F
- Early hyperthermia: rapid panting, dry gums, fast heart rate
- Advanced hyperthermia: coma, gray gums, progressing to vomiting and diarrhea

## Things to do:

- Take the rectal temperature. If it's under 103.5 degrees F: Bathe the pet in ice water. If ice is unavailable, cover the pet with cold wet towels, replacing the towels often as they get warm. Offer water to drink.
- If the rectal temperature is over 103.5 degrees F: Get that pet to a veterinarian fast. Try to call on your way. Be careful offering water to drink, as the pet may not be able to swallow normally.

## Things NOT to do:

- Don't continue cooling the pet after the temperature drops below 103.5 degrees F.
- Don't give medications.
- Don't monkey around with ice water enemas. They may be useful, but giving enemas should be the doctor's call.

## Follow-up:

- Have the pet seen by a veterinarian even if things go great. The doctor will make sure there are no lasting effects.

# INJURIES—SEVERE

## Causes:

- Hit by a car
- Kicked by a horse

- Falls, such as from a moving vehicle
- Cats and small dogs mauled by big dogs
- Gun shots
- Arrows and other projectiles
- Physical abuse

## Signs:

- Struggling to inhale or exhale.
- Debris or foreign objects in the mouth or throat that could obstruct breathing.
- Gums that have a purple cast or color—meaning there is insufficient oxygen in the blood.
- Pale gums indicate poor blood circulation.
- A dull mental state; it's another sign of poor circulation.
- Arterial bleeding. Bright red spurting blood must be stopped fast using a *very* firm compression bandage made of cloth or bandage material.
- Sucking chest wounds, that is, when air moves in and out through a hole in the side of the chest.
- Inability to stand or walk due to broken bones, back injury, or nerve injury.
- Abdominal pain.
- Flaccid or rigid limbs. (This indicates serious nerve injury.)
- Pupils that fail to respond to bright light. (If the pupils don't change size or shape when you shine a bright light in your pet's eyes, it indicates a head injury—a very bad sign.)

## Things to do:

- Be cautious. Injured dogs and cats can lash out from fear and delirium. It's hard to help a pet if you're injured, too.
- Take any injured pet to an emergency veterinarian ASAP. The first hour after a serious injury is crucial to survival. A pet can appear to

be miraculously fine immediately after a trauma. But complications can develop quickly that could end that life. Never gamble or assume.

- Carefully open the mouth and clear away any foreign material.
- Bright red, spurting blood must be stopped fast using a *very* firm compression bandage made of cloth or bandage material.
- Seal a sucking chest wound fast using a bandage or cloth tied or taped snugly—not tight—around the chest. Apply ointment or Vaseline to the bandage to form a seal with the wound to prevent more air leakage. Do this quickly, while you're transporting your pet to the animal hospital.
- Handle fractured limbs and neurologic injury carefully. Use a board or sheet of plywood to keep the pet flat. If a pet with a fracture starts flailing around, the pain will intensify and there will be damage to the blood supply to the broken bones.
- Transport the injured pet with the head and neck extended (head pointed straight out) to provide an open airway for ease of breathing.
- Have someone call the emergency veterinarian so that the hospital is ready for your arrival.

## Things NOT to do:

- Never apply a tourniquet to a bleeding limb. Tourniquets usually do more harm than good.
- Don't use a muzzle on a dog who has any difficulty breathing. If a muzzle is used, it must be removed as soon as it is no longer essential. Breathing problems can start anytime.
- Don't panic. The phrase "Don't just stand there—do something" does not apply. Much better, in an emergency, is to stand there for a minute and do nothing but breathe. Think carefully—then act decisively.
- Don't "wait and see." Even a competent emergency veterinarian would not assess an injured pet at home and opt for observation only. Thorough lab work, X-rays, and repeated exams are necessary in the hospital to learn that a pet may actually have "dodged the bullet."

- Never remove a projectile. If an arrow, stick, metal rod, wire, or other object has stabbed into the body, *leave it!* If you remove an object that is still in place, you may unleash severe bleeding. Oftentimes an object that has penetrated an important blood vessel prevents leakage of blood as long as it remains. Allow the surgeon to remove the object when your pet is on the operating table.

## Follow-up:

- Allow no delays in getting the pet treated. Delays kill.
- Turn the pet's well-being over to the veterinary medical staff. Do not economize. Shortcuts have cost the lives of many pets who could have survived.
- Treatment options of internal injuries can be debatable even for an experienced emergency staff. You must trust the judgment of the professionals. Surgery may be recommended immediately or within one or two days of the injury.
- You may be given an uncertain prognosis for your pet's recovery. This can be emotionally difficult. Say a prayer and ride it out. Don't press the doctor for clear-cut answers early in the process. He or she may make the mistake of giving you an educated guess. These are meaningless, because anything can happen in the early stages of emergency treatment.
- Fractures seem to get the most attention from pet owners, but taking care of a fracture is rarely a life-saving priority. Protect the fractured limb during transport to the animal hospital, but allow the emergency staff to manage the higher priorities first.

# INSECT BITES AND STINGS

## Causes:

- Most commonly honeybees, wasps, hornets, yellow jackets, and fire ants. Here are the characteristics of each:
  —Honeybees leave their stinger and venom sac behind in the skin. This kills the bee.

- —Wasps and hornets do not leave their stinger in the victim. Thus, they can sting the pet repeatedly.
- —Fire ants: First they bite the skin with two powerful pinching jaws, then they sting. This causes a circular pattern on the skin with two central holes.
- More rarely, black-widow spiders cause a nonpainful bite that can progress to severe muscle cramping. Abdominal cramping can cause difficult breathing, muscle spasms, and anxiety—even seizures. Cats can be so sensitive to black-widow bites that they can become paralyzed.
- Brown-recluse spider bites are nonpainful, but develop pain and redness two to six hours later. A blister forms later, followed by a bull's-eye pattern on the skin.
- Scorpion stings cause pain immediately.

## Signs:

- Local redness, pain, and swelling.
- If a pet gets several stings, he or she can get a fever and become lethargic up to several days later. Watch for the following:
  - —Staggering
  - —Paralysis of the face
  - —Seizures
  - —Vomiting, possibly brown in color
  - —Red-brown urine
  - —Bloody stool
- Joint pain can follow brown-recluse spider bites.
- Scorpion stings can result in drooling, watering of the eyes, and dilated pupils. The worst case (unusual) is death from abnormal heart rhythms and respiratory arrest.

## Things to do:

- For bee stings, scrape the stinger out with a knife blade as soon as possible. A stinger can release venom for up to three minutes after the bee leaves it behind in the skin.

- If several stings have occurred, take the pet to the animal hospital right away as the pet could develop shock.
- If your pet has been attacked by fire ants, treatment is rarely required. Applying ice to the stings usually helps.
- For a minor sting of any kind, quickly applying an underarm antiperspirant helps reduce the swelling and pain.
- For bites by a black widow, brown recluse, spider, or scorpion, take the victim to the doctor quickly—just in case.

## Things NOT to do:
- Don't squeeze the skin around a bee sting. If any of the stinger is still in the skin, this will release more venom.

## Follow-up:
- For pets with multiple bee stings or black-widow spider bites, the veterinarian may recommend hospitalization. IV treatments may be necessary.
- Medical treatment may be the same as for SWELLING OF THE FACE, LEGS, AND PAWS.
- Black-widow bites may also need treatment with IV calcium gluconate.

# LAMENESS

## Causes:
- Injuries:
  —Hit by a car
  —Falls
  —Crushing by sliding doors, horse hooves, car tires, or other objects
  —Twists and sprains (Even if injuries are nonviolent, they may damage supportive structures inside joints.)

- Birth defects
    - —Bone and joint deformities that develop as a youngster grows. The best known is hip dysplasia, seen mostly in medium- to large-breed dogs, and dislocating kneecaps (luxating patellas) found often in smaller dog breeds. Any joint can be affected, however, in both dogs and cats.
- Diseases of the nervous system of an adult pet:
    - —Herniation of the discs in the backs of German Shepherds, Dachshunds, Lhasa Apsos, Shih Tzus, Welsh Corgis, Beagles, Cocker Spaniels, Pekingese, and occasionally Labrador Retrievers.
    - —Tumors of the spinal cord or of the nerves of the limbs.
    - —Nerve damage of the back or limbs (from being hit by a car or other injury.)
- Infections beneath the skin such as abscesses (See ABSCESSES.)
- Arthritic-joint degeneration:
    - —Age related
    - —Joint disease resulting from penetrating wounds
    - —Multiple-joint involvement such as rheumatoid arthritis
- Nutritional
    - —All-meat diets result in weak bones that fracture easily
- Cancer
    - —Usually in older, large-breed dogs
    - —Usually quite painful
    - —Cancers that spread from other sites, such as some breast and prostate cancers

## Signs:

- Severe pain in some cases. Other injuries can be pain-free. This does not make them less important.
- Signs of limping can vary, depending on the severity of the problem and its cause. The limp may be barely detectable in some pets—or it may be so pronounced that a pet won't put any weight at all on a leg.

- Some pets are lame on more than one leg. Shifting of weight to reduce pain can falsely implicate the wrong limb. Accurate diagnosis of some lamenesses can be challenging, even for specialists.

- Some kinds of lameness will improve over several days or weeks. Beware of this. Mother Nature will thicken supportive structures as the pet learns to shift the load-bearing to other legs. This will give the appearance of natural healing when, in fact, the affected joint is developing permanent degenerative arthritis.

## Things to do:

- If your pet has been hit by a car or endured other severe injury, follow the guidelines for INJURIES—SEVERE.

- For a nonlife-threatening lameness, do the following:

    —Raise the pet's lip in good light and evaluate the color of the gums. If pale, gray, or purple, the pet is in serious trouble and needs a doctor immediately. See the section on COMA—UNCONSCIOUSNESS.

    —Shine a bright light into the eyes. If both pupils do not constrict within two or three seconds, the pet may have had an undetected serious injury. This pet needs an exam ASAP.

    —Observe your pet to make sure he or she feels otherwise OK—that is, breathing normally, eating well, and staying bright and alert. Watch to be sure your pet can urinate and pass stool normally. If all of the above is OK and there is no sign of bleeding, swelling, bruising, or other injuries anywhere, you can take your time.

- Be gentle and slow. Pain may be severe and confined to a small, specific area. If you touch this place roughly, even the most gentle, loving pet can bite quickly.

- Handle each limb carefully and thoroughly, starting at the tip of the paw. Gently squeeze the muscles as you move up the limb. Bend and straighten each joint.

- A minor lameness can be observed at home for one to three days. *Any* pet who is still lame (even a little bit) after three days needs a thorough exam and possibly X-rays.

- Home remedies:
    - —Can be dangerous. *Aspirin, Ibuprofen, and Tylenol (acetaminophen) are never to be used on cats.*
    - —Tylenol can be used on some dogs. Others may get liver damage. Ibuprofen is dangerous for dogs. Best to avoid.
    - —Aspirin for dogs: You may give one tablet per 50 pounds of body weight every 8 to 12 hours for one to three days. If the dog is normal after one to three days, stop the aspirin. If the lameness returns, you must have that dog examined. *Never give aspirin to a vomiting dog.*
- Call your veterinarian and discuss the symptoms—even in apparently minor cases where the lameness seems to be improving nicely at home. The more medical information and advice you can get, the better.

## Things NOT to do:

- Don't try to apply a splint or cast. If your pet has a fracture or other serious injury, this can worsen the damage.
- Never transport a dog in pain unless that dog is muzzled. Be safe and careful. Remove the muzzle when possible to allow for panting—and never leave a muzzled dog unattended. Do not muzzle a dog who has difficulty breathing.
- Don't move a cat in pain unless the cat is wrapped in a thick towel. There are two reasons: (1) Cats feel more secure when they're snugly wrapped, and (2) a cat who's wrapped in a thick covering can neither bite nor claw.
- Reminder: *Never give a cat aspirin or Tylenol (acetaminophen).*
- *Never give aspirin to a vomiting dog. Avoid Ibuprofen.*

## Follow-up:

- If your pet has a lameness that at first improved with home care, but then reappeared, be sure to get a good exam. A problem like this may be setting the stage for a long-term, painful disability.

- Follow your veterinarian's advice on X-rays. Sedation or, better still, general anesthesia will allow the veterinary staff to position the affected limb carefully for a detailed and diagnostically accurate X-ray. Don't cut corners on expense. A missed or incorrect lameness diagnosis is often the result of poorly positioned X-rays taken without the benefit of sedation or anesthesia.
- Second opinions: If the doctor recommends surgery or other treatment that you are not pleased to hear, do not shoot the messenger. Instead, explain that you would feel better if the doctor could provide the consultation of one more knowledgeable expert outside of his or her animal hospital. Make it clear by your tone that you trust the doctor. You just want one more perspective. Good, confident doctors are glad to oblige and keep you happy. Do not damage the relationship.

# Pain

## Causes:

- Injury
- Joint or bone disease
- Abdominal disease
- Cancers

## Signs:

- Crying
- Sudden behavior change, moodiness, grumpy, attempts to bite when handled
- Violent thrashing
- Subdued behavior, especially in cats
- Hiding

## Things to do:

- Look for a clear cause.
- Don't overstress the pet.

- Look for injuries.
- Give aspirin to a dog only if:
  - There is no sign of bleeding.
  - There is no vomiting.
  - You have a dog over 12 weeks of age. The dose is one tablet per 50 pounds of body weight. Tablets can be split for smaller dogs.
- Handle the pet gently if back pain is suspected. Transport the dog or cat on a board or sheet of plywood to keep the back as straight and as flat as possible.

## Things NOT to do:
- Don't give aspirin to a cat—ever!
- Don't give ibuprofen, Tylenol, or any other human medication to a pet without a veterinarian's advice.

## Follow-up:
- If pain is the only noticeable problem, we must still find and treat the cause. Get an appointment to see the doctor ASAP.

# PARALYSIS AND STAGGERING

## Causes:
- Injuries such as falling or being hit by a car or taking a fall. (See the section on INJURIES—SEVERE.)
- Spinal cord damage from a herniated disc in Dachshunds, Lhasa Apsos, Shih Tzus, Welsh Corgis, Beagles, Cocker Spaniels, Pekingese, German Shepherds, and occasionally Labrador Retrievers.
- Cancers
- A slowly progressive spinal cord disease of German Shepherds called degenerative myelopathy
- Infections and other inflammation of the nervous system and middle or inner ear

- Antifreeze and other toxic agents
- Overdose of the drugs metronidazole (commonly prescribed for liver and intestinal disease) and Heartgard (monthly heartworm preventive)
- Geriatric vestibular syndrome (This problem occurs suddenly in cats and older dogs. It resolves by itself, but these pets must be examined by a doctor to rule out other, more serious causes.)
- Heart Disease

## Signs:
- A paralyzed pet is one who cannot stand on the rear limbs or on any limbs. This pet is fully conscious. The paralysis may be partial—that is, allowing some movement and feeling of the limbs.
- Complete paralysis occurs when the pet has neither pain sensation nor the ability to move the front or back limbs.
- Staggering (ataxia) lack of coordination of the limbs.
- Head tilt, walking in circles, head shaking, and rapid eye movements.

## Things to do:
- Strictly confine the pet until a thorough exam can be done by a veterinarian. Movement can cause further injury if your pet has spinal cord damage.
- Handle the pet gently. Transport the dog or cat on a board or sheet of plywood to keep the back as straight and as flat as possible.
- Get the pet to the veterinarian ASAP, especially if the pet is a dog breed prone to spinal cord damage from a herniated disc. (See above in "Causes.")
- Quickly scan the area where your pet may have spent time. Look for possible poisons like automotive antifreeze.

## Things NOT to do:
- Don't "wait-and-see." There are so many different possible causes for paralysis and staggering that you may be jeopardizing your pet's recovery by delaying treatment.

- Don't try home remedies. If your pet has been given a drug overdose or has drunk antifreeze, you may worsen the problem.
- Don't induce vomiting unless you're instructed to do so by your veterinarian. An uncoordinated pet who vomits can inhale some of the vomitus and suffocate.

## Follow-up

- Depending on the cause of the symptoms, the doctor may recommend X-rays, CT or MRI scans, surgery, or treatment for poisoning.
- In some cases, the doctor may recommend rest and confinement for your pet.

# PENIS—DISCHARGES

## Causes:

- Infections of the prostate (The prostate is a male gland that sits just behind the bladder. The tube that carries urine—the urethra, runs through the prostate.)
- Bladder infections, which also cause frequent straining to urinate.
- Urinary blockage—bladder stones or crystals that lodge in the urethra.
- Many dogs who have not been neutered have a persistent pus-like discharge from the penis. If it's only a small amount and your dog licks it only occasionally, it's really OK. If you neuter that boy, it will almost certainly stop completely.

## Signs:

- Stones, a gritty paste-like substance, pus, or blood from the penis
- Straining or difficulty urinating
- Persistent licking of the penis

## Things to do:

- If you find a stone or a gritty paste-like substance at the tip of your cat's or dog's penis, save it in a jar for your veterinarian to send for analysis.
- Get that pet treated fast. A male cat who strains often in the litter pan could be in serious trouble. These boys can die quickly from urinary blockage. Male dogs can also experience a complete blockage of urine flow that can kill.

## Things NOT to do:

- Don't try home remedies. There is nothing you can do at home that will make any positive difference.

## Follow-up:

- If your dog or cat has a discharge, but eats and feels well, it's OK to wait until the next available appointment before going to the doctor.
- A dog or cat who is eating poorly or has pain when handled may be a medical emergency. Don't break the speed limit, but get this fellow seen ASAP.
- Diagnostic work may include X-rays and urine tests. Surgery could be necessary.

# PENIS—SWOLLEN/ENGORGED

## Causes:

- Failure of normal blood return from an erect penis (This condition is called paraphimosis.)
- Paraphimosis is caused by the haired sheath of the penis getting caught behind the swelling of an erect penis. The sheath, or the hair on the sheath, can prevent the blood that has filled the erect penis from flowing normally.
- Without proper return of the blood from the penis, the tissue of the penis may die.

## Signs:

- If a dog's penis looks red, swollen, and enlarged for more than ten minutes, he may have paraphimosis.
- A normal erection is normal. It should not persist more than several minutes.

## Things to do:

- Lubricate the penis, especially the portion near its base. K-Y jelly or other water-based lubricant is best. If not available, use Vaseline.
- After the area is well lubricated, pull forward gently on the haired sheath that you will find behind the shaft of the swollen, erect penis.
- If the erect penis does not slip back inside the sheath, you will need the help of your veterinarian. Do not waste time. Call the animal hospital and get going.

## Things NOT to do:

- Don't "wait and see." Mother Nature will cause a normal erection to relax and return to the inside of the haired sheath within several minutes, even right after breeding.

## Follow-up:

- If you are successful at getting the erect penis into the sheath and the swelling resolves in a few minutes, your dog is probably fine. Keep a close eye on that guy for a few days to be sure that the problem does not repeat.

# SEIZURES (CONVULSIONS, FITS)

## Causes:

- Epilepsy
- Nursing mothers with low blood calcium (eclampsia)

- Low blood sugar; can occur in puppies and kittens who are fed only one or two times per day
- Head injury
- Brain tumor and infections
- Blood loss, which robs the brain of oxygen, sometimes causing seizures
- Shock; low blood pressure
- Heart disease
- Some cancers; kidney and liver diseases
- Poisoning by:
    —Insecticides including those in pet store flea-and-tick shampoos, dips, and sprays.
    —Lead, which can be swallowed from old paint, fishing sinkers, pipe joint compound, old lead toys, curtain weights, dust and paint flakes from bridges and water towers, artist's paints, lead shot, lead-glazed pottery, solder, linoleum, putty, gasoline, motor oil, tar paper and roofing materials, golf balls, batteries, some insulation, and some inks and dyes.
    —Automotive antifreeze.
    —Agricultural pesticides that can be absorbed through the skin or by being swallowed.
- Some birth defects

## Signs:

- Seizure activity is a sudden onset of uncontrolled jerking or flexing of the limbs or of the entire body.
- A resulting increased body temperature occurs in cases of frequent or continued seizures.
- Continued seizure activity can cause nerve death in the brain.
- A pet who has had one seizure is likely to have another.
- A seizure can cause a pet to be unresponsive to his or her owner's voice. Some pets are partially responsive.
- Partial seizures cause symptoms such as staring blindly, tail biting, snapping at imaginary flies. These are important, but are not emergencies.

## Things to do:

- If a seizure continues for more than ten minutes, your pet has a true emergency. Get your pet to the doctor ASAP.
- On the way to the doctor's, try to calm the pet (don't struggle) while the seizure activity quiets down.
- In cases of continued or frequent seizures, take the pet's rectal temperature. If greater than 105 degrees F, follow instructions in the section on HEAT STROKE (HYPERTHERMIA).
- For pets with continual seizures, keep the neck extended to allow free passage of air into the throat and lungs.
- During a seizure, move objects so that the pet does not knock things over and cause injury.
- Be observant. If the pet's mouth is open, note the color of the gums and tongue in a good light. Time the length of the active portion of the seizure as well as the recovery period. The seizure is not completely over until the pet is standing.
- When the pet has relaxed enough to allow safe handling of the mouth, rub honey or Karo Syrup on the gums. This will provide sugar to the bloodstream quickly. A pet who's had a seizure due to low blood sugar will improve in several minutes. This step is especially important if your pet has diabetes or if that pet is a youngster.
- When a nursing mother dog has a seizure, it's usually the result of low calcium. Take the rectal temperature and cool the pet as directed in HEAT STROKE (HYPERTHERMIA). Take this dog to your veterinarian ASAP for intravenous calcium.
- Head injuries can cause seizures either immediately or within several months after the injury. If your pet has had a head injury, go to the veterinarian immediately.
- Quickly scan the area where your pet may have spent time. Look for possible poisons like automotive antifreeze or insect or rodent bait.
- If your pet faints, it's an emergency. If your pet doesn't recover consciousness in three minutes, it's a high-priority emergency.

## Things NOT to do:

- Never reach into a seizuring pet's mouth. These pets have out-of-control brain activity. You can easily get bitten. Pets can't swallow their tongues, so there's no need to reach into the mouth.

## Follow-up:

- All pets with occasional seizures need a thorough diagnostic workup, including blood and urine tests.
- Seizures that, in the doctor's estimation, are not typical of epilepsy may require further investigation. This may include a spinal tap, CT scanning, or MRI.
- If heart disease is suspected, an electrocardiogram and X-rays will be needed.
- Poisoning suspects will need specific testing and treatment.
- Prevent low calcium in nursing mother dogs by feeding your mother dog a high-quality puppy diet from early pregnancy through weaning.

# SNAKE BITES

## Causes:

Poisonous snakes belong to three groups in the U.S.:

- Colubrids—minor importance
- Elapids
    - Poisonous brightly colored coral snakes: *"Red on Yellow—Kill a Fellow"*
    - Nonpoisonous King Snakes: *"Red on Black—Venom Lack"*
- Pit vipers, which include water moccasins, copperheads, and rattlesnakes—all are poisonous!
    - Copperheads and most rattlesnakes usually produce minimal symptoms in pets.
    - Mojave rattlesnakes can cause respiratory arrest and rapid death.

## Signs:

Snake bites can be hard to diagnose. Look for the following:

- Fang marks
- Swelling and pain that appear within one hour after the pet is bitten
- Redness and bruising
- Sometimes vomiting, difficulty breathing, rapid heart rate, rapid eye movements, and fever

## Things to do:

- Take the snake-bitten pet to the nearest animal hospital ASAP. Try to call on the way.
- If you're unsure whether the pet was snake bitten, measure the swollen area often. Rapid, increased swelling means a likely snake bite.

## Things NOT to do:

- Don't get bitten as you rescue the injured pet.
- Don't bother with tourniquets or try methods of sucking out the venom. Those measures just delay getting the pet to the doctor—and they don't really help.

## Follow-up:

- Quick IV treatment for shock and possible complications like bleeding disorders.
- Urine and blood tests to assess kidney function and normal blood clotting.
- Antivenin antidote therapy is occasionally administered, but it's seldom necessary, and the cost is high. This therapy can also be risky because the antivenin may produce serum sickness and allergic reactions.

# Swelling of the Abdomen or Bloating

## Causes:

- Swelling and twisting of the stomach. Called gastric dilatation-volvulus (GDV), this problem is seen in medium- to large-breed, deep-chested dogs. It is a true emergency if you see a swelling in the portion of the dog that is midway between the shoulders and the hips.
- Cancers—common in dogs over age 8.
- Injuries that cause severe internal bleeding or rupture of the bladder, such as being hit by a car or getting mauled by a large dog.
- Fluid accumulation caused by heart and/or liver failure.
- Severe infections of the uterus.
- Poisoning with anticoagulants like rat or mouse bait. Internal bleeding can result.
- Pregnancy. If your dog or cat is unspayed, has a swollen abdomen, and eats and feels normal, you don't have to believe in her virtue. Your sweet young girl doesn't mean to mislead you about her private life; she just feels that it's none of your business. If in doubt, have her examined.

## Signs:

- Swelling of the belly behind the ribs.
- If severe enough, the pet may also have some difficulty breathing because of pressure on the diaphragm.
- Pets with moderately to severely swollen abdomens may have a poor appetite and lethargy. Vomiting may also occur.
- Sudden onset of abdominal swelling (GDV) in a medium- to large-breed dog may cause attempts to belch or retch.

## Things to do:

- Even if the pet is walking, eating, and breathing normally, see the veterinarian soon. If there are problems with these basic functions, take that pet to the animal hospital right away. It's an emergency.

- Medium to large dogs with sudden onset of swelling of the abdomen must go to the animal hospital as a true emergency as they may have GDV. The prognosis for GDV is good only if surgery is done within a few hours after the onset of swelling.

## Things NOT to do:
- Don't try home remedies like antigas or antiacid medications.
- Don't squeeze the pet's abdomen. This could cause bleeding, rupture of organs, or difficulty breathing.

## Follow-up:
- Swollen, twisted stomachs and uterine infections are curable by surgery if treated early.
- Cancers are usually best treated first by surgery, followed by chemotherapy. This diagnosis will require some in-depth testing.
- Severe abdominal injuries may require surgery. This will be the doctor's judgment call.
- If the abdomen is swollen by fluid because of organ failure, the condition isn't curable. But it may be manageable with medications.
- For more on poisoning, see the information on pages 195 and 345.

# SWELLING OF THE FACE, LEGS, AND PAWS

## Causes:
- Allergic reactions to insect stings.
- Injuries such as severe bruising and fractured bones (See the section on INJURIES—SEVERE.)
- Infected wounds including pus-filled abscesses (See the section on ABSCESSES.)
- Snake bites (See the section on SNAKE BITES.)

## Signs:

- Sudden onset of swelling of the entire face.
- Leg and paw swelling also occurs in some cases of allergic reactions to insect stings.
- May be accompanied by vomiting and diarrhea. Severe allergic reactions can also progress to difficulty breathing. This is called anaphylaxis and, if it occurs, is likely to be seen within a few minutes after a pet has been stung.

## Things to Do:

- A quick visit to the doctor is in order anytime a general swelling of the face or other large body part occurs. Most swellings of this type resolve without treatment. But for the unusual case that worsens, medical treatment may be necessary to save a pet's life.
- Handle the pet gently and slowly. Prevent excitement.
- *If your pet has a known risk of anaphylaxis*, you can administer an injection of epinephrine under the telephone supervision of a veterinarian. Advance preparedness and practice before the event is ideal. Kits are available for human use that include an injection of epinephrine. The proper dose is 0.01 to 0.02 milligram per pound of body weight injected subcutaneously (under the skin). To avoid fiddling with the math when minutes count, have it well planned if your pet has had a prior close encounter with anaphylaxis.

## Things NOT to do:

- Don't allow the pet to become excited or active. If breathing difficulty ensues, exertion could be risky.

## Follow-up:

- Don't wait and see if facial or limb swelling causes advanced symptoms. Once an allergic reaction progresses to anaphylaxis, you may run out of time.

- If epinephrine has been given and the pet looks good, go to the animal hospital quickly anyway. Additional treatment may still be important.
- The doctor may want to give injectable antihistamines, corticosteroids, or IV fluids. Also, your pet may need to be hospitalized to monitor for delayed reactions.

# URINATION—INABILITY TO URINATE

## Causes:

- Urinary blockage, that is, bladder stones or crystals that lodge in the urethra. Most often seen in male cats and male dogs.
- Bladder infections and inflammations. These will also cause frequent straining to urinate.
- In Dalmatians, bladder stones composed of ammonium urate are a common problem. All Dalmatians must be watched closely for straining or difficulty urinating.
- Cancer.
- Diseases of the urethra and prostate are seen in dogs who have not been neutered.
- Nerve injuries, most likely due to trauma such as being hit by a car.
- Birth defects.

## Signs:

- Attempts to squat or hike the leg to urinate for prolonged periods with little or no urine flow
- Stone, gritty, paste-like substance, pus, or blood from the penis
- Straining or difficulty urinating
- Persistent licking of the penis
- Crying in pain, poor appetite, vomiting, and lethargy
- Coma and death if not treated in time

- Sometimes, excessive drinking with a prior history of excessive urinating

## Things to do:

- If there is any doubt about a pet's ability to pass urine, treat it as an emergency. If you "wait and see," your pet could die quickly.
- A pet who is eating poorly or who has pain when handled may be a medical emergency. Get this fellow seen ASAP.
- If you find a stone or a gritty, paste-like substance at the tip of your cat's or dog's penis, save it in a jar for your veterinarian. The veterinarian may want to send it in for analysis.
- A male cat who strains often in the litter pan could be in serious trouble. This boy can die quickly from urinary blockage. Get him treated fast.

## Things NOT to do:

- Don't try home remedies. There is nothing you can do at home that will make any positive difference.

## Follow-up:

- Diagnostic work may include X-rays, and urine and blood tests. Surgery could be necessary.
- Pets with dehydration, electrolyte imbalance, or rupture of the bladder will need emergency supportive care including IV fluids and hospitalization. Abnormal heart rhythms may also occur. These pets need intensive treatment and may not survive.
- If your pet can't urinate, the back-up of urine can quickly cause kidney damage. To save your pet's life, emergency anesthesia for urinary catheterization and/or surgery of the penis or urethra may be essential.
- Long-term diet changes will be needed for pets with bladder stones or urethral stones.
- Antibiotics for infection.
- Neutering for prostate disease. The prostate itself may also need surgery.

## Vaginal Discharge

### Causes:
- Infections of the vagina or uterus
- Urinary infections (less common)
- Occasionally foreign material, such as a piece of plant material lodged in the vagina

### Signs:
- Pus-like discharge seen at the vulva (the female genitals)
- Persistent licking of the vulva
- Spotting of pus or blood where the female dog has laid down
- Sometimes poor appetite, lethargy, and excessive drinking and urination
- Sometimes abdominal pain

### Things to do:
- Provide plenty of drinking water.
- Hurry to the veterinarian if that girl is feeling sick.
- If she feels normal but has a pus-like vaginal discharge, have her examined within the day. Sooner is better.

### Things NOT to do:
- Don't "wait and see." Left untreated, your pet could get a severe infection of the bladder or uterus that may lead to organ disease or death.

### Follow-up:
- Follow the doctor's instructions. Medications or surgery may be recommended. There is no "do-it-yourself" on this type of problem.
- Blood and urine tests may be important. An infected uterus may necessitate spaying (ovariohysterectomy).

# Vomiting and Diarrhea (Severe)

## Causes:

- Dietary indiscretion (garbage gut)
- Blockages of the stomach or intestine with foreign objects, or from twists of the stomach or intestine
- Cancers, nervous system disorders, hormone imbalances
- Diseases of the pancreas, liver, kidneys, uterus
- Infections caused by parvo virus and/or bacteria
- Inflammatory disease
- Parasites (worms and other parasites)
- Stress
- Over-the-counter household medications such as aspirin, Tylenol, and ibuprofen

## Signs:

- Repeated throwing up and/or passing soft or fluid stool. Blood in the vomit or stool is a very serious sign usually indicating significant inflammation or damage from aspirin or other medications.
- Frequent attempts to vomit and/or straining to pass stool. If your pet is passing nothing, look carefully to find stool (sometimes just fluid) or vomitus. In severe cases of vomiting and diarrhea, the pet can eventually "run out" of stuff to vomit or pass rectally. Thus, it may look as though the pet is trying to vomit or defecate without success when in fact the symptoms are continuing despite a lack of matter to be passed.
- Dehydration and shock, which can cause death.
  - —Rub your finger along the gums. Dry, sticky gums usually mean significant dehydration.
  - —Pick up a handful of skin over the neck or shoulders and let it go. If the skin takes longer than one second to snap back to its normal position, the pet is probably dehydrated.
  - —Shock is a problem if the gums are pale pink or gray in color.

- General weakness often associated with electrolyte imbalance.
- Little or no appetite.

## Things to do:

- If a dog is trying *unsuccessfully* to vomit, see the section on SWELLING OF THE ABDOMEN OR BLOATING.
- If you're unsure whether the problem can be treated at home, call your veterinarian for answers.
- Provide water.
- Take your pet to the veterinarian if repeated vomiting and/or diarrhea continues for longer than one or two hours. If a pet vomits every time he or she drinks, provide water in small amounts often.
- Wash your hands thoroughly after handling your pet. Some organisms can be infectious to humans.

## Things NOT to do:

- Don't give your pet home remedies like Pepto Bismol, Kaopectate, or Imodium for repeated, severe symptoms. While these treatments can be useful for minor cases, they could damage the health of severely sick pets. Your veterinarian can advise you.
- Don't give your pet any food until you're instructed to do so by your veterinarian.

## Follow-up:

- Severe vomiting and diarrhea will require hospitalization for IV fluid and electrolyte replacement.
- Diagnostic tests will include blood, urine, and stool tests, as well as X-rays to find the underlying causes.
- Endoscopy may be needed to retrieve foreign material or to take diagnostic biopsy samples.
- If infectious causes are considered, wash down surfaces using a Chlorox: water mixture in a dilution of 1 part Chlorox to 30 parts water.

# Weakness and Fainting

## Causes:
- Heart failure
- Shock
- Severe pain
- Head injury
- Blood loss and other causes of anemia (low number of red blood cells)
- Infections of the brain and spinal cord
- Advanced internal disease, including:
  - Diabetes mellitus
  - Low blood sugar
  - Infections of the pancreas or abdomen (peritonitis)
  - Liver or other internal organ disease
- Advanced infections
- Poisoning

## Signs:
- Depending on the cause, some pets will be fine when resting, but become unable to walk without showing weakness or fainting.
- Many pets with this symptom will be unable to rest without fainting.
- Gray or pale gums are signs of shock or blood loss. Purple gums indicate low oxygen in the blood. Any abnormal color is a sign of a true emergency.

## Things to do:
- Handle the pet gently and slowly to prevent pain. Pain can cause struggling which may worsen the problem.
- Get that pet to the veterinarian immediately. Call the animal hospital on your way so that the doctor will be ready for your pet's arrival. Your pet may be facing imminent death.

- Provide drinking water.
- On the way to the animal hospital, take the rectal temperature. If the temperature is above 103.5 degrees F or below 99.0 degrees F, treat according to the instructions in the sections on HEAT STROKE (HYPERTHERMIA) or COLD, SLUGGISH, TREMBLING, SHIVERING (HYPOTHERMIA).
- Supplemental oxygen may be helpful in cases of pale, gray, or purple gums. If someone nearby has an oxygen cylinder, hold the breathing tubes close to the pet's nose and mouth, and allow the pet to inhale on the way to the animal hospital.
- If you know that your pet has diabetes, rub some honey or Karo Syrup on the gums to improve what may be low blood sugar.
- Apply firm pressure with a cloth bandage or an article of clothing to any bleeding wound.

## Things NOT to do:
- Don't allow the pet to become excited. This will increase his or her oxygen needs and worsen the problem.
- Avoid applying any kind of pressure around the neck or chest. The pet needs to breathe as easily as possible.
- Don't give your pet any medications.
- Don't delay. Immediate treatment is essential.

## Follow-up:
- Be prepared for the doctor to recommend extensive diagnostic testing including ECG, X-rays, blood and urine testing, and doppler blood pressure measurements.
- Hospitalization may be needed to stabilize your pet. He or she could need lifelong treatment, so you may have to learn how to administer medications or therapy at home.

# Index

# Index

## A

Abdomen, swollen, 231–32
    first aid for, 439–40
Abortion, in dogs, 80–82
Abscesses, 397–98
Absence anxiety, 100–101, 114–16
Addison's disease, 237–39
Adenocarcinomas, 283–84
Adoption:
    age for kittens, 19
    age for puppies, 7–8
    selecting a cat, 17–22
    selecting a dog, 12–16
Adrenal glands, 237–39
Advantage, for fleas, 354
Age of adoption:
    cats, 19
    dogs, 7–8
Age of neutering/spaying, 82, 83, 85
Ages, in dog/cat years, 49
Aggression:
    and neutering, 74, 75
    arctic breeds, 62–63
    between dogs, 73–76
    between household cats, 271–72
    in mother cat, 274–75
    in puppies, 61–64
    in rottweilers, 63–64
    severe, 67
    toward other pets, 76–77
    toward strangers, 65–67
Aging, *see also* Older dogs; Older cats
Aging, in dogs, 56–57
AIDS, 39
    in cats, 366–67

Air travel, for cats, 370–71
Allergies, 106–07
    itchy skin, 203–04
    scratching, 217–18
    to cats, 287
American Animal Hospital Association (AAHA), 392
Amputation:
    as cancer treatment, 283–84
    of cat's tail, 357
    of injured limb, 323
    of tail, 221
Anal glands, 233, 234, 359–60
Anemia, from fleas, 362
Anesthesia
    for dental work, 164–65
    older dogs, 57
    safety of, 324–25
Anger, *see also* Aggression
    in dogs, 61–64
Antianxiety medication, for cat, 337–38, 342, 379
Antibarking collar, 45–47
Anticonvulsants, 199–200
Antifreeze poisoning, 346–47, 358
Antioxidants, and back problems, 154–55
Appetite, loss of:
    in cats, 36–37
    in dogs, 130–31
    first aid for, 399–401
Arthritis, 58, 144–47
Aspirin, toxicity to cats, 359
Asthma, 106–07
    from dog hair, 82
    in cats, 310

**451**

Attachment to humans:
  kittens, 17–19
  puppies, 7–8
Attention-getting behaviors:
  in cats, 335–36
  in dogs, 64–65
Auricular hematoma, 293

# B

Baby teeth, dogs, 166
Bad breath, dogs, 167–68
Barking:
  compulsive, 45–46
  in car, 47–48
  in greeting, 45
  surgery, 46–47
Bathing, itchy dog, 203–04
Bedding, 85–87
Bee stings, 210–13
  first aid for, 423–25
Behavior modification:
  and diet, 119–22, 131
  cats, 32–33
  dogs, 31
  for biting cats, 270–71
  for jumping, 241–42
  house-training, 250–55
  litter box habits, 377–79
  poison-proofing, 197
Behavior problems:
  *see also* Aggression; Biting; Barking
  in arctic breeds, 62–63
  attention-seeking behavior, 64–65
  cats, 37
  destructive chewing, 99–100, 102, 103
  dogs, 24–25
  hitting a dog, 30–31
  jumping, 183

  neglected, 25
  stealing food, 184–85
  urination and defecation, 248–55
Behavior
  of den animals, 23–24
  of pack dogs, 62–63
Behavioral changes, in older cat, 339–40
Bells, on cat's collar, 265–66
Benign tumors, 92, 93
Binge and gorge instinct, 60–61
Birth, first aid for delivery, 411–13
Bitch, defined, 78
Biting:
  in cats, 270–71
  of children, 70–72
  controlling behavior, 64–65
  due to illness, 69–70
  food protection behavior, 60–61
  in puppies, 61
  strangers, 65–67
Black claws, 58–59
Black widow spider, 424
Blackheads, 213–14
Bladder problems:
  infection, 79, 246
  loss of control, 255–57
  stones, 247
Bleeding tumors, 91–92
Bleeding, first aid for, 401–03
Bloating, 231–32
  first aid for, 439–40
Blood clots, 310, 322
Blood disorders:
  anemia, 234–35
  clots, 310, 322
  parasites, 213
Boarding pets, 51–53
Body temperature, 53–54, 403–04, 419–20

Bone cancer, 93–94
Bone chips, 230
Bone deformities, 159–60
Boosters, for vaccination, 262, 386–88
Boredom:
    in cats, 313–14
    destructive dog, 102
Bott flies, 353
Brain tumors:
    in cats, 351–52
    in dogs, 69–70
Breast cancer:
    in cats, 285
    in unspayed dogs, 80
Breathing difficulty:
    *see also* Respiratory problems
    first aid for, 410
Breeding:
    dogs, 78–79, 80
    cats and kittens, 276–77
    overbreeding, 83
Breeds:
    arctic, 62–63
    cat, 22
    characteristics of, 8–10
    dog, 8–10
    inbreeding, 39–40
    and life expectancy, 49
    single-purpose, 8–9
    size of, 9–10
Brown-recluse spider bites, 424
Brushing, 50
Buspar, 337–38, 342, 379, 381

## C

Calling:
    cats, 34
    puppy, 14

Cancer:
    amputation, 284
    in cats, 35–36
    in dogs, 89–95
    treatment for cat, 281–84, 285, 286
    and vaccinations, 280
Candy, *see* Chocolate
Canine cognitive disorder, 255–56
Canned pet food, 50
Car sickness, 240
    in cats, 370
Car travel, dogs, 47–48
Cardiomyopathy, 309–10, 322
Cardiopulmonary Resuscitation, 406
Cat fights, first aid for, 397–99
Cat food, 302–03
Cat litter, ingested, 313–14
Cat-human diseases, 287–88
    parasites, 320
Catnip garden, 343–44
Cats, leaving home, 330–31
Causes of death, dogs, 25, 89–95
Chemotherapy
    *see also* Cancer; Tumors
    for cats, 284
    for dogs, 95
Cherry eye, 111
Chest injury, first aid for, 410–11
Chewing
    *see also* Biting
    bones, 229–30
    cats, 289
    nonfood items, 290–91
    of paws, 206
    puppies, 99–100
    rawhide chews, 129
Cheyletiella, 220
Children:
    and biting dogs, 70–72
    and pet ownership, 176–77
    and pet selection, 11, 20

Chocolate, 195–96
Chocolate, for dogs, 124–25
Circling, 351–52
Citronella antibark collar, 45–47
Classes, for puppies, 242–43
Clawing furniture, 289–90
Claws:
   see also Declawing; Dewclaws
   alternative Soft Paws, 308
   black, 58–59
   removing, 57–58, 308
Climate, and dog breed, 9
Clothes dryers, and cats, 349–50
Clumping fur, 355–56
Clumping litter, 313
Cold exposure, 403–04
Collars:
   on puppies, 219
   to stop barking, 45–47
   training, 244–45
Coma, first aid for, 404–07
Comedones, 213–14
Constipation:
   in cats, 317–19
   causes in cats, 319
   first aid for cats, 407
   first aid for dogs, 408
Consultation, in veterinary practice, 392
Contagious diseases, 53, 106
Convulsions, 236–37
   see also Seizures
   first aid for, 434–37
   in dogs, 197
Coprophagy, 185–87
Corrective methods, for barking, 45–48
Cost of pet ownership, 49–51
Coughing:
   cats, 34–35, 310
   dogs, 26
   first aid for, 410

Counterconditioning, 73
CPR, 406
Crating, 65
   fearful dogs, 115–16, 117
Cross-breed litters, 80–82
Crystal buildup in urethra, 373–75

## D

Daily care of dogs, 54
Dangerous animals, 65–73
Dangers to pets, 349–50
   see also Poisoning
D-con, danger to pets, 348
Death:
   effect on dogs, 177–78
   effect on other pets, 178
   in family of cats, 329–30
   of newborn cats, 367–68
Declawing, 289–90
   cats, 308
   as last resort, 292
   postoperative pain, 292
Defecation:
   indoor, 64–65, 248–49
   outside litter box, 377–78
Degenerative myelopathy, 153–54, 255
Delivery, first aid for, 411–13
Den-animal behavior, 23–24
Dental cleaning, dogs, 164–65
Derm-Caps, 218
Destructive behaviors:
   and boredom, 102
   cats, 289
   puppies, 99–100
   when left alone, 100–102
Dewclaws, 57–58
Diabetes, in cats, 360–61
Diapers, ingesting, 229

Diarrhea:
    in dogs, 27
    first aid for, 445–46
    in kittens, 314–15
    simple, 227
    unresponsive, 225–26
Diet:
    changes in cat's, 302–03
    corn in, 127
    and cost, 50–51
    eating stool, 185–87
    and flatulence in dogs, 223–25
    food allergies, 203–05
    food supplements, 123–24
    for kittens with diarrhea, 314
    human food for dogs, 119–22
    loss of appetite in cats, 304
    milk for cats, 302
    and price, 127, 129–30, 133–34
    toxic foods for dogs, 122
    variety for cats, 36–37
    vegetables, 123
Digging:
    adult dogs, 104
    puppies, 105
Discharge:
    from ears, 109–10
    from eyes, 112, 298–99, 301
    from penis, 432–33
    vaginal, 444; see also Vaginal discharge
Discipline:
    see also Behavior modification
    for dogs, 30–31
    shock collars, 47
Diseases, dog-human, 106–08
Distemper, 316–17
    disinfecting, 317
    in dogs, 261
    vaccination for kittens, 315

Docking, 159
Dog food, 119–22, 127, 129–30, 133–34
    see also Diet
    designer, 133–34
Dog whistles, 265
Doghouses, 191–94
Dominance exercises, 60
Dominance order, 12–13, 62
    and biting, 67–68
    in cats, 329–30
    and children, 70–72
    and mounting behavior, 181–82
    and new puppies, 173–75
    in pack, 74
Dominance:
    in Rottweilers, 63–64
    testing for, 15
Dragging rear end, 359–60
Dramamine, 240
    for cats, 370
    for dogs, 48
Dreams, 179–80
Droncit, for tapeworm, 312
Drowning, first aid for, 413–15
Dry skin, 207
Dryers, and cats, 349–50
Drywall, dogs eating, 196

# E

Ear infections, 294–95
    in dogs, 109–10
Ear mites, 294–95
Earflap, swelling, 293
Ears:
    problems in cats, 293–97
    sores on, 297

Eating habits:
    of cats, 36–37, 40–41
    eating stool, 185–87
    food protection, 60–61
    inappropriate items, 30
    loss of appetite in dogs, 27, 29–30
Efa Tabs, 218
Elderly dogs, *see* Older dogs
Electric shock collars, 47
Electronic fence, 189–90
Elimination:
    *see also* Diarrhea; Urination
    inappropriate places, 23–24, 37
ELISA test, 78–79
Enema:
    for kitten, 318
    technique for adult cat, 318–19
Epilepsy:
    *see also* Seizures
    in cats, 273
    in dogs, 199–201
    first aid for, 434–37
Equilizer odor eliminator, 378–79, 380
Estrus cycle, 79
Euthanasia, 17
    cats, 37
    dogs, 25
    for destructive dogs, 101
    reasons for, 70
Excessive drinking, in older cat, 365
Excessive sleeping, 362
Exercise:
    hiking, 198
    for small dogs, 190–91
Expenses, 49–51
    of veterinary care, 359
Exposure, first aid for, 403–404, 419–20
Extra claw, *see* Dewclaws
Eye problems, 111–12

Eyes:
    discharge from cat's, 298–99, 301
    discharge from dog's, 216–17
    first aid for injuries, 415–17
    popped-out, 415–17
    third eyelid, 299–300

# F

Fainting, 236–37, 417–19
    first aid for, 447–48
False pregnancy, 83–84
Fanbelt injuries to cats, 350
Fatigue, cats, 362
Fatty liver disease, 315
Feathers-on-a-stick toy, 268, 270, 271, 275
Feeding tube, 97–98
Feeding:
    *see also* Diet
    dog food only, 119–22
    toxic foods for dogs, 122
Feline AIDS, 366–67
Feline distemper, 316–17
Feline heartworm, 288
Feline hepatic lipidosis, 315
Feline hyperesthesia, 272–73
Feline leukemia, 281, 299–300, 301, 387
Femoral head and neck ostectomy (FHO), 152–53
Fences, 189–90
Fibrosarcoma, 280
Fighting dogs, 73–76
    cats and dogs, 334–35
Finicky eaters, 302–04
FIP, feline infectious peritonitis, 368–69
First aid, 396–448
    *See page 396 for list of illnesses and injuries.*
Fish bones, 128

Flatulence, 223–25
Fleas, 354
   and anemia, 362
   infestation, 236–37
   and tapeworms, 279
Flies, 194
Fly larva, under skin, 353
Food allergies, 203–205
Food protection behavior, 60–61, 341
Food supplements, 50–51
   potassium for cats, 364
Food:
   see also Cat food; Diet; Dog food; Feeding;
   for cats, 36–37, 40–41
   for dogs, 119–22, 127, 129–30, 133–34
Foot pads, cracked, 215–16
For-Bid, 186
Foxtail awns, in ears, 294–95, 295–97
Frightened dog, 72–73, 114–16
   leash training, 117–18
   thunderstorms, 116–17
Frightened puppy, 113–14
Frontline:
   for fleas, 354
   for ticks, 212, 213
Fur:
   falling out, 355–56
   grooming a cat, 307–08

## G

Garage door openers, 349
Garbage, eating, 228–29
Gas, 223–25
Gastric dilation-volvulus (GDV), 231–32
Geriatric gestibular syndrome, 202

Giardia, 225–26
Glucosamine, for dogs, 144
Glycoflex, 144, 147
Grass awns, see Foxtails
Grief:
   see also Death
   loss of pet, 178
Grooming:
   bathing, 135
   cat's fur, 356
   clipping nails, 58–59
   costs of, 50–51
   of undercoat, 82
Guinea pigs, and vitamins, 51

## H

Hair loss, 216–17
Hairless breeds, 107
Hantavirus, 287–88
Haverhill Mouser, 343
Head halters, 64, 66, 68, 244–45
Head shaking, 295–97
Head tilt, in cats, 295–97
Hearing, cats and dogs, 265
Heart disease, cats, 309–10
Heart failure, 139
Heart murmur, 138
Heartworms, 107–08
   in cats, 322
   and human risk, 288
   prevention, 136
   symptoms and treatment, 137
Heat stroke, 419–20
Heat, see Estrus cycle
   and meowing, 333–34
   cats reproductive cycle, 277
Hemangiosarcoma, 94–95
Hemolytic anemia, 234–35

Hernias, 96–97
Hiding, 34
Hiking, with dog, 198
Hips:
    dislocated, 161–62
    pain in, 150–53
    surgery on, 150–53
Hissing at other cats, 336–37
Hitting a dog, 30–31
    during training, 245
Hookworms, 320
Hormones:
    Addison's disease, 237–39
    for cat aggression, 272–73
    thyroid, 216–17
Hot spots, 205–206
House training, 23–24, 250–55
Houseflies, 194
Houseplants, and cats, 343–44
Hunting, 342–43
Hybrid vigor, 39–40
Hydrogen peroxide, and wound care, 355
Hyperactivity, 100–101
    in puppies, 241–44
Hyperthermia, 419–20
Hyperthyroidism, in cats, 273, 333, 340
Hypoallergenic breeds, 106–07, 287
Hypoallergenic diet, 218
    for cats, 273
Hypokalemia, 364
Hypothermia, first aid for, 403–04
Hypothyroidism, 216–17

Incision, post-surgical care, 206–207
Indoor cats, spaying, 278
Infections:
    in cat's ear, 293–94
    of the pancreas, 226–27
    of the ear, 110
Infectious disease, cats, 316–17
Infestation, fleas, 354
Inguinal hernia, 96–97
Injections, for ear mites, 294–95
Injuries:
    first aid for, 420–23
    from fights, 355
    and amputation, 323
Insect bites, 210–13
    first aid for, 423–25
Insulin injections, 360–61
Interviewing veterinarians, 393–94
Intestinal problems:
    blockage, 313–14
    diarrhea, 225–26
    flatulence, 223–25
    giardia, 225–26
    parasites, 320–21
    parvo, 222–23
    strangulated intestine, 97
    virus, 222–23
Invisible fencing, 189–90
Ipecac, 196
Itching, 203–06
    dogs' paws, 206
    hot spots, 205–06

# I

Ibuprofen, and cats, 359
Immunity from disease, 385–86
In heat, *See* Reproduction;
    Estrus cycle; Heat

# J

Jaundice, 239
Joint disease, 148–49
Joint pain, in dogs, 144–47
Joint replacement, 151

Jumping, 183, 241–42
Junk food, for cats, 36–37, 40–41

# K

Kennel cough, 53, 142–43
Kennels, 51–53
Kidney failure, 120, 132
   in cats, 365
Kidney problems, 39
Kidney transplants, 366, 375–76
Kittens:
   age to adopt, 19
   constipation, 317–18
   diarrhea, 314–15
   differences from dogs, 17–18
   early death, 367–68
   eye and nose discharge, 298–99
   first aid for delivery, 411–13
   introducing to household, 271–72
   introducing to other cats, 336–37
   litters with different fathers, 276–77
   needing enema, 317–18
   orphaned, 19
   playfulness, 21–22
   posture test, 20–21
   selection process, 19–22
   socialization of, 18–19
   temperaments, 19–20
   vaccinations for, 386–88
Knee ligament rupture, 155–56
Kneecaps, 156–57

# L

Lameness, 145–48
   first aid for, 425–29
   shifting, 160–61
Larval infection, under cat's skin, 353

Leaking urine, 255–57, 258–59
Leaving home, cats, 327–28
Leukemia, feline, 281, 387
Licking, 180
   in older cat, 339–40
Life expectancies, 49
Lipomas, 93
Litter box:
   imperfect aim, 379–80
   refusal to use, 377–79
   training older cat, 382
Litter Maid, 380
Litter:
   observations of, 12–13
   runt of, 20
   separation from, 7–8, 18–19
Liver damage, 125
Liver disease, 239–40
   in cats, 41
   in overweight cat, 315
Long hair breeds, dogs, 214–15
Loss of appetite, 29–30
   cats, 36–37, 304
   dogs, 27, 130–31
   first aid, 399–401
Loss of consciousness, *See* Coma; Fainting
Lost pets, 54–56
   cats that leave home, 327–28
Low-fee veterinary clinics, 395
Lumps, 28, 35–36
   *see also* Skin masses
Lung disease, 35
Luxating patella, 157
Lyme disease, 213

# M

Malignancy, 27, 28, 35–36, 89–93
   tumors in cats, 281–84

Mange, 207–08
Manx cats, and tail problems, 328–29
Marking, by dogs, 249–50
Mast cell tumors, 90–91
Masticatory muscle myositis, 171–72
Meat, in excess, 120, 132
Medical histories, cats, 39–40
Megace, 272–73
Meningioma, 351–52
Meowing, 333–34, 335–36
Microchips, 54–56
   and lost pets, 266–67
Milk bones, 168–69
Milk for cats, 302
Mites, 220
   in cats' ears, 294–95
Motion sickness, 240
Motives for pet ownership, 3–4
Mounting behavior, 181–82
Mouth problems, 163–65, 166–67
   bad breath in dogs, 167–68
   bad teeth in cats, 324
   dental disease in dogs, 166–67
   masticatory muscle myositis, 171–72
   serious mouth disease, 170–72
Moving, effect on cats, 337–38, 341–42
Multiple-cat household, 331–32
Myelopathy, 153–54

# N

National Dog Registry, 55–56
Nausea, 27, 240
   *see also* Vomiting
   car sickness, 47–48
   cats, 37–39, 311
Navel, 51
Near-drowning, first aid for, 413–15
Needle aspirate, 90, 91, 281–82

Nerve problems, in Manx cats, 328–29
Nervous dog, 72–73
Neutering:
   aggressive dogs, 75
   male dog, 85
   older dogs, 56–57
New pets in household, 173–76, 271–72
   companion for older cat, 339
   multiple cats, 331–32, 339
Nighttime urination, 187–88
Nipples, dogs, 88
Noises, 179
Nose surgery, 309
Nose:
   change in pigment, 209–10
   cracking/bleeding, 208–09
Nyla bones, 100

# O

Obesity, 29, 39, 41
   in cats, 305–06
Odor eliminators, 378–79, 380
Older cats:
   and constipation, 319
   diet, 303–04
   excessive drinking, 365
   odd behavior and, 333, 339–40
Older dogs, 56
   and anesthesia, 57
   arthritis, 144–47
   and cancer, 89–95
   cognitive dysfunction, 181
   geriatric gestibular syndrome, 202
   urinary problems, 255–56
Orphaned kittens, 19
Orthopedic Foundation for Animals (OFA), 152

Ostectomy, 152–53
Osteochondritis Dissecans (OCD), 148–49
Osteosarcoma, 93–94
Otoscope, 109
Outdoor cats:
  risks to, 330–31, 346–47
  in small apartment, 337–38
Outright odor eliminator, 378–79, 380
Overeating, and boredom, 305
Overweight:
  *see also* Obesity; Weight management
  and liver disease, 315
Ovulation, testing for, 78–79
Owner-pet relationship, reasons for, 3–4
Owners, types of, 4

# P

P.E.G. tube, 98, 315
Pacing, 181
Pack hierarchy, 65, 74
  *see also* Dominance order
Pain:
  after surgery, 235–36, 362–63
  and Duragesic patch, 292
  during urination, 246
  first aid for, 429–30
  signs of, 363
Pancreatitis, 226–27
Panosteitis, 161
Paper training, 253–55
Paralysis, first aid for, 430–32
Parasites, 314–15
  *see also* Heartworms; Tapeworms
  hookworms, 320
  intestinal, 320–21
Parvo, 222–23, 260
  related to distemper, 317

Paws:
  cracked, 215–16
  itchy, 206
  swelling of, 440–42
Penis:
  bleeding from, 79
  discharge, first aid for, 432–33
  swollen, first aid for, 433–34
Perfect pets, 5
Peritonitis, 316
  feline, 368–69
Personality:
  *see also* Temperament
  in kittens, 17–18
  in puppies, 10–11, 13
Pet food:
  canned, 50
  expense, 50–51, 129–30, 133–34
Pet ownership:
  and children, 176–77
  cost of veterinary care, 359
  expense of, 49–51
  gift of, 326
  ID chips and tattoos, 266–67
  justifying, 3–4
  rules for cats, 32–41
  rules for dogs, 23–31
  types of pet owners, 4
Pet sitters, 51–53
Pets as gifts, 326
Pig ears, 128, 168–69
Plaster, eating, 196
Plastic, chewing on, 291
Playfulness, in kittens, 21–22
Poisoning, 195–96
  antifreeze, 346–47
  first aid for, 401–03
  rat poison, 347–48
  snake bites, 198, 437–38
  Tylenol and cats, 345–46

Porcupine quills, 189
Post-nasal drip, 139–40
Post-operative pain, 362–63
Potassium deficiency, 364
Pregnancy:
    see also Breeding
    badly timed, 80–82
    cats, 279
    false pregnancy, 83–84
    terminating, 81
    test for, 84
Problem behaviors:
    attention-getting, 64–65
    cats, 37
    dogs, 24–25
    neglected, 25
Progesterone, 78, 84
Prostate problems, 56–57, 79
Protection, 66
Punishment, shock collars, 47
Pupils, different size, 300–301
Puppies:
    age to adopt, 7–8
    attachment to humans, 7–8
    biting, 61
    broken tail, 158
    care of newborns, 85–86
    and collars, 219
    controlling wild behavior, 241–43
    and destructive chewing, 99–100, 103
    digging, 105
    and epilepsy, 200–201
    fearful, 113
    first aid for delivery, 411–13
    introducing to cats, 175–76
    introducing to household pets, 173–74
    and mounting behavior, 182
    and puppy food, 149
    selection process, 7–16
    surgery on, 96–97
    training not to jump, 241–43
    vaccinations for, 86, 386–88
    with heart murmur, 138
Purring, in kittens, 21
Pyometra, 87–88

## R

Rawhide chews, 129, 168–69
Rear-end irritation, 233
Rear-end itch, 359–60
Reproduction, 78–85
    cats and kittens, 276–79
Reproductive cycle, of cats, 333–34
Respiratory diseases, in cats, 298–99
Respiratory problems, 141–43
    cats, 34–35, 310
    dogs, 26–27
    in Persian cats, 309
Rheumatoid arthritis, 149
RIA test, 79
Roaming, 327
Rocks, ingesting, 228
Rodent poison, 347–48
Rottweilers, aggressive behaviors, 63–64
Routine, daily, 54
Runt of litter, 20

## S

Safety tips, 349–50
Scat Mat, 290, 379
Scratching, 217–18
    see also Allergies; Food allergies; Itching

of cats' ears, 294–97
  year-round, 204–05
Screwtail, 158
Second opinions, 286
Seizures, 28, 139–40
  in cats, 351–52
  in dogs, 197
  epileptic dog, 199–201
  first aid for, 434–37
  from eclampsia, 86
  in puppies, 200–201
Selection process, 5–6
  and children, 11, 20
  dog breeds, 8–10
  kittens, 17–22
  materials, 12
Self-mutilation in cats, 19, 357
Separation anxiety, 101, 114–16
Septic peritonitis, 227, 228
Shedding, 214–15
  prevention of, 82
Shelter, for outdoor pets, 191–93
Shivering, first aid for, 403–04
Shock collars, 47
Shy dogs, 118
Sickness in cats, 358–59
Single cats, 267–68
Sizes, of dog breeds, 9–10
Skin cancer, cats, 297
Skin disease, scratching, 217–18
Skin lesions, 205–206
Skin lump, medications for, 281–82
Skin masses, 90–91, 93
  abscesses, 397–99
  on cat's abdomen, 285
  cats, 35–36, 281–84
  dogs, 27, 28
Skin pigments, cats, 297
Skin problems, 203–08

*see also* Allergies; Itching; Skin Masses; Wound care
  change in pigment, 209–10
  dry skin, 207
  hot spots, 205–06
  mange, 207–08, 220
Skunk smell, 307
Smells, from urination, 378–79
Smoking, 124–25
  effect on dogs, 26–27
Snake bites, 198
  first aid for, 437–38
Sneezing, 140–41
Snorting, 139–40
Social behavior, cats, 267–69, 271–72
Socialization:
  of cats, 40
  of kittens, 18–19, 20
  of puppies, 7–8, 14
Soft Paws, 308
Spaying, 82, 87–88
  cats, 333–34
  indoor cats, 278
Spinal cord disease, 153–54
Spinal disease, 255–56
Spleen, cancer of, 94–95
Squamous-cell carcinoma, 297
Staggering, 351
  first aid for, 430–32
Staring down a dog, 114
Stealing food, 184–85
Stiffness, in cat's legs, 364
Stings, 210–13
  first aid for, 423–25
Stomach bloating, 230–32
  first aid for, 439–40
Stomach problems, cats, 311
Stool, eating, 185–87
Strangulated intestine, 97

Straw bedding, 85–87
Stray cats, 330–31
Stress, in cats, 298–99, 300
Striking a cat, 40
Striking a dog, 30–31
Striking biting puppies, 61
String, as cat toy, 316
Stroke symptoms, in dogs, 202
Strongid, for parasites, 321
Strychnine poisoning, 197
Submissive dogs, 13
Surgery:
    to aid breathing, 309
    amputation of injured limb, 323
    and anesthesia, 324–25
    for bladder stones, 247
    for brain tumor, 351–52
    to correct barking, 46–47
    to correct noisy breathing, 141
    declawing, 290, 292
    on dewclaws, 57–58
    dogs' hips, 150–53
    eye, 111
    for hernia, 96–97
    for intestinal blockage, 313–14
    on knees, 157
    minimizing risks, 278
    of mouth and throat, 97–98
    for peritonitis, 227
    on puppies, 159
    postoperative pain, 235–36
    vitamins for recovery, 51
    wound care, 206–207
Swellings:
    *see also* Abscesses
    cat, 35–36
    dog, 27
    in ear, 293
    of stomach, 231–32
Swollen belly, first aid for, 439–40
Swollen face, legs or paws, first aid for, 440–42
Symptoms of sickness, in cats, 358–66

## T

Table scraps, for dogs, 121–22
Tail:
    broken, 158
    chasing, 234
    docking, 159
Tapeworms:
    in cats, 279
    and fleas, 312
Tattoos, 54–56
    for lost pets, 266–67
Taurine, in cat's diet, 132
Temperament:
    of cats, 17, 19–20
    of dog breeds, 8
    testing kittens, 19–20
    testing puppies', 10–11
Temperature, body, 53–54
Testicular cancer, 56–57
Testing, kittens, 19–22
Testing, puppies, 14–16
Thermometers, 54
Third eyelid, 299–300
Thromboembolism, 309–10
Thunderstorms, 116–17
Thyroid disease, 216–17
Thyroid problems, 124
    in cats, 333
Ticks, 211–13
Tobacco smoke
    effect on dogs, 26–27
    secondhand smoke, 124–25
Toenails, *see* Claws

Tooth care:
   *see also* Mouth problems
   cats, 324, 325
   dogs, 164–65, 169–71
Tooth pain, 163–64
Tooth problems, cats, 340–41
Toxic foods, for dogs, 122
Toxics, to cats, 345–48
Toys:
   for cats, 268, 270, 271
   use to socialize cats, 336–37
   training with, 99–100, 103
Training:
   halters and collars, 244–45
   and hitting, 30–31
   and mistreatment of pets, 245
   puppies, 241–45
Tranquilizers, for cats, 371
Transplants, of cats' kidneys, 375–76
Treats, for cat, 303
Trembling, first aid for, 403–04
Trimming claws, 58–59
Triple pelvic osteotomy (TPO), 150–51
Tumors, 90–93
   *see also* Cancer; Skin masses
   benign, 92
   in hindquarters, 92–93
Tylenol poisoning, 345–46, 359

## U

Umbilical hernia, 96
Unconsciousness, first aid for, 404–07
Unspayed cat, 382–83
Urinary diseases, diagnosing, 246–47, 372–75
   urinary tract infections, 372–73
Urination:

Urination, and pack dominance order, 257–58
Urination, cats, 34
Urination, excessive, 238–39
Urination, first aid for blockage, 442–43
   from excitement, 256–57
   frequent, 372–73
   housebound dogs, 23–24
   inability to urinate, 373–75
   inside the house, 249–50
   in kids' sandbox, 383–84
   killing grass, 190
   nighttime leaking, 258–59
   nighttime, 187–88
   older dogs, 255–56
   outside litter box, 378–80
   unacceptable, 37, 64–65, 378–83
Urine smell on breath, 365
Uterine infections, 87–88

## V

Vaccinations:
   at home, 260
   distemper, 261, 262, 317
   feline leukemia, 281, 387
   feline peritonitis, 368–69
   for indoor cats, 385–86
   for kennel cough, 142–43
   for kennels, 52–53
   for puppies and kittens, 386–88
   reaction to, 262
   and sarcomas in cats, 280
Vaccines, for parvo, 222–23
Vaginal discharge, 87–88
   first aid for, 444
   in dogs, 334–35
Vegetables, in dog's diet, 123

Vestibular disease, 351
Vestigial claws, see Dewclaws
Veterinarians:
    choosing, 391–94
    low-fee clinic, 395
    services provided, 392–93
Veterinary hospitals, touring, 393–94
Vicious dogs, see Aggression; Behavior problems
Viral infections, 106
Viruses:
    AIDS in cats, 366–67
    distemper, 317
    feline peritonitis, 368–69
    hantavirus, 287–88
    intestinal, 222–23
    leukemia, 281
    respiratory disease in cats, 298–99
    and vaccines, 385–86
Vitamins, 50–51
Vomiting, 226–27
    cats, 37–39, 311
    distemper, 316–17
    dogs, 27
    first aid for, 445–46
    inducing, 196
    overweight cat, 315
    poisons, 346–47

## W

Water, and exercise, 191
Weakness, 417–19
    first aid for, 447–48
Weight loss, cats, 39
Weight management:
    see also Obesity
    and arthritis, 145
    cats, 36, 39, 41, 305–06
    resuming normal diet, 126–27
    thyroid problems, 124
Wet nose, in cats, 359
Wild cats, 327–28
Wound care, 206–07
Wounds, from cat fights, 354–55

## Y

Yarn, as cat toy, 316
Yellow gums, 239–40

# About the Author

Jeff Nichol, D.V.M., born in Detroit, Michigan, has been practicing full-time companion pet medicine and surgery since graduation from the College of Veterinary Medicine at Michigan State University in 1974. Dr. Nichol is a member of the American Veterinary Medical Association, the New Mexico Veterinary Medical Association, and has served as president of the Albuquerque Veterinary Association.

Dr. Nichol began practice in Albuquerque, New Mexico and in 1976 moved to Sacramento, California to practice and take additional training in cardiology. In 1978 he purchased the Adobe Animal Medical Center in Albuquerque and remains its hospital director. Adobe enjoys a four-year certification from the American Animal Hospital Association and is now a member hospital of National PetCare Centers.

The questions and answers that comprise a major portion of this book have been a popular weekly feature of the *Albuquerque Journal* since 1996. Dr. Nichol lives a charmed life in Albuquerque with his wife, Carolyn, and sons, Jake and Frank, along with family pets Peter Rabbit and Raoul.